LAURENCE BINYON

Laurence Binyon
Poet, Scholar of
East and West

JOHN HATCHER

CLARENDON PRESS · OXFORD
1995

Oxford University Press, Walton Street. Oxford OX2 6DP
Oxford New York
Athens Auckland Bangkok Bombay
Calcutta Cape Town Dar es Salaam Delhi
Florence Hong Kong Istanbul Karachi
Kuala Lumpur Madras Madrid Melbourne
Mexico City Nairobi Paris Singapore
Taipei Tokyo Toronto
and associated companies in
Berlin Ibadan

Oxford is a trade mark of Oxford University Press

Published in the United States
by Oxford University Press Inc., New York

British Library Cataloguing in Publication Data
Data available

Library of Congress Cataloging in Publication Data
Hatcher, John Trevor, 1951–
Laurence Binyon : poet, scholar of East and West / John Hatcher.
Includes bibliographical references.
1. Binyon, Laurence, 1869–1943. 2. Poets, English—20th century—
Biography. 3. Art, Asian—Appreciation—Great Britain—
History—20th century. 4. British Museum—Officials and employees—
Biography. 5. Museum curators—Great Britain—Biography. 6. Art
historians—Great Britain—Biography. 7. Orientalists—Great
Britain—Biography. 8. Translators—Great Britain—Biography.
9. East and West. I. Title.
PR6003.I75Z68 1995
821'.912—dc20
[B] 95–1324
ISBN 0–19–812296–9

1 3 5 7 9 10 8 6 4 2

Typeset by Best-set Typesetter Ltd., Hong Kong
Printed in Great Britain
on acid-free paper by
Biddles Ltd.,
Guildford & King's Lynn

Preface

LAURENCE BINYON'S reputation lies literally in pieces—not shredded or submerged like that of many of his contemporaries in the awkward 'transitional' period between the Victorians and the modernists, but in discrete, relatively intact pieces, tesserae of a mosaic that has lost its shape because the world of letters has lost its cohesion. The erosion of his reputation has progressed alongside the academic specialization against which he fought a stubborn rearguard action. Poet, dramatist, art historian, museum curator, editor, critic, biographer, lecturer, and essayist, he was, in the most comprehensive sense, a man of letters. The exhaustive four-volume *A Literary History of England*, for example, awards him a sympathetic paragraph among the early twentieth-century poets, beside his close friends Walter de la Mare, Thomas Sturge Moore, Gordon Bottomley, Lascelles Abercrombie, and John Masefield, but unlike them he reappears twenty-four pages later, where Binyon, Roger Fry, and Clive Bell are declared the three 'most notable art critics of the period'.[1]

As a poet, Binyon is most often remembered today for one poem, one of the most famous in the language, his 1914 war elegy 'For the Fallen'. Recited annually at Remembrance Day services for the dead of two world wars, carved on thousands of tombstones and war memorials, its central stanza is so familiar as to be virtually anonymous, wholly absorbed into the ritual substructure of British cultural life:

> They shall grow not old, as we that are left grow old:
> Age shall not weary them, nor the years condemn.
> At the going down of the sun and in the morning
> We will remember them.

Eighty years on, these ritual cadences continue to fulfil a need. On 5 June 1994, at the climax of the drumhead service on Southsea common to commemorate the fiftieth anniversary of the fateful eve

---

[1] *A Literary History of England*, ed. Albert C. Baugh, 4 vols. (1948; London, 1967), iv. 1573–4, 1602.

of D-Day, in the presence of the Queen, President Clinton, as-
sembled heads of state, and D-Day veterans, the Archbishop of
Canterbury pledged continued remembrance for the war dead and
sealed it by intoning slowly, like a prayer, 'At the going down of the
sun and in the morning | We will remember them'. Carried live
worldwide by CNN, ABC, and BBC satellite news, they became
some of the first lines of poetry ever broadcast across the electronic
global village.

Binyon himself, however, rightly thought 'For the Fallen' by no
means his best poem. His career spanned six decades which saw
revolutionary changes in English poetry, and, although he was
perhaps never an avant-garde poet, his lifetime's work in poetry
reflected these changes, from his impressionist London poems of
the 1890s to the spare, luminous meditations of his old age during
World War Two. During the 1920s, many of his diehard contemporaries saw in the humanist poet of *The Sirens* (1924–5) and *The
Idols* (1929) a champion holding out against Eliot and the
Wastelanders, but although he stood on the far side of the gulf
between the late Victorian/Edwardian and modernist generations,
the situation was more complex than oversimplifying literary histories suggest. During the 1930s his work, especially his *terza rima*
translation of Dante's *Divina Commedia*, came to be appreciated
by both Pound and Eliot. He persevered, never stopped experimenting, and his last poems were his best.

As an art scholar, Binyon's main contributions were in the fields
of Oriental art and British art. During his forty-year career at the
British Museum, he built a world reputation as a pioneer scholar
and interpreter of Eastern art, one of the first to challenge the
West's myopic assumption that it held a monopoly on beauty and
truth. His writings were important not only for their sensitivity to
the arts of Asia themselves but also for his insistence that the
philosophies that lay behind them had something to say to the
twentieth-century West. As well as introducing British readers to a
new world of aesthetic and spiritual experience, books like *The
Flight of the Dragon* (1911) influenced avant-garde writers like
Pound and Wyndham Lewis and helped fuel the intellectual fer-
ment of these heady days just prior to the First World War. At the
Museum, often against ingrained Eurocentrism, he built up the
Oriental art collections, laying the foundations for the modern
Departments of Oriental Antiquities and Japanese Antiquities.

He was equally influential in the field of British art. Modern appreciation of the great tradition of British watercolours owes a debt to his pioneering studies, and he contributed much valuable work on Blake, Palmer, Calvert, and the English visionary school. As an art critic, he promoted the work of young British artists such as Augustus John, while his writings on both Asian art and the nineteenth-century British watercolour and visionary traditions subtly influenced modern British art, including Neo-Romantic painting in the 1920s.

It is something of an accident that Binyon's story was not told decades ago. Many of Binyon's friends and contemporaries, Yeats for example, anticipated or even preempted their biographers by leading creatively choreographed, self-edited lives. Binyon did not. He was, by nature and philosophical inclination, remarkably unegoistic. When approached by publishers with a view to writing his autobiography, he courteously declined. After his death in 1943, his widow turned down one would-be biographer on the eminently reasonable grounds that he was one of the very few people Binyon had ever disliked. Instead she preserved his correspondence, manuscripts, and other papers with a view to writing a memoir which, as the years slipped by, never got written. In the meantime Binyon's reputation, like that of virtually all his contemporaries except Yeats, was eclipsed by that of the Eliot–Pound modernist generation. For decades now countless books and articles have sieved ever-finer minutiae from the lives and works of Yeats, Pound, Eliot, and Bloomsbury figures, while Binyon's generation has languished amid stereotypes of the Yellow Nineties and the overstuffed Edwardians. This is a pity, as the period is a fascinating one. Studies are now gradually starting to appear, however, and we are beginning, tentatively, to chart the continuities between late-Victorian and modernist culture, and the ways in which transitional figures such as Binyon helped prepare the ground for modernist breakthroughs.

This lack of critical attention has been compounded in Binyon's case by the fact that his work spans so many and such diverse fields. Academic professionalization and specialization have teased his world apart. His name is known to specialists in disciplines which rarely if ever overlap. Few literary scholars are interested in Asian art, and vice versa. Perhaps the author of 'For the Fallen' deserves a full-length book solely on the strength of his poetry, but his real place and stature in British cultural history can only emerge through an interdisciplinary study giving equal weight to the various aspects of his long career and the continuities between them. By rediscovering Binyon the scholar of Japanese prints as well as the poet, the lover of Chinese ink landscapes as well as the dramatist, the Taoist sage as well as the art critic, and the subtle interplay between these roles, this study reveals a man very much of his time and yet whose writings, especially on Oriental art, are in some ways more contemporary and relevant than those of the great modernists. By reassembling the exploded components of his remarkably diverse career, it seeks to restore Binyon to the place he deserves in our cultural history, as one of the most benign and quietly influential voices of the early twentieth century.

J.H.

Acknowledgements

NUMEROUS PEOPLE have contributed to this book in equally numerous ways. Binyon's letters are widely scattered in libraries across Britain and the United States and I must record my gratitude to the librarians and archivists of the following institutions for their generous assistance and for permission to quote from unpublished letters and manuscripts: the Bodleian Library and Ashmolean Museum, Oxford; the British Library, London University Library, India Office Library, Imperial War Museum, and St Paul's School, London; the Brotherton Collection, Leeds University Library; the National Library of Wales, Aberystwyth; Glasgow University Library; the Library of Trinity College Dublin; the libraries of King's College and Trinity College Cambridge; the Houghton Library and Pusey Library at Harvard University; the Boston Public Library; the Department of Manuscripts and the Department of Rare Books, Huntington Library, San Marino, California; the Harry Ransom Humanities Research Center, the University of Texas at Austin; the Yale Collection of American Literature, Beinecke Rare Book and Manuscript Library, Yale University; the New York Public Library; George Eastman House, New York; the University of Chicago Library; and the Freer Gallery of Art/Arthur M. Sackler Gallery Archives at the Smithsonian Institution, Washington, DC. For permission to quote from Binyon letters in their possession, I would also like to thank John Bagenal and Yashiro Wakaba.

Binyon's letters and manuscripts are quoted by permission of Mrs Nicolete Gray and the Society of Authors on behalf of the Laurence Binyon Estate. For permission to quote from other unpublished letters and manuscripts I am indebted to Mrs Valerie Eliot (T. S. Eliot), Michael Yeats, A. P. Watt, and Oxford University Press (W. B. Yeats), Riette Sturge-Moore and Léonie Sturge-Moore (Thomas Sturge Moore, Charles Ricketts), Giles de la Mare (Walter de la Mare), the Society of Authors on behalf of the John Masefield Estate, Lord Bridges (Robert Bridges), Frederick Whitridge (Matthew Arnold), Yashiro Wakaba (Yashiro Yukio),

Jennifer Gosse (Edmund Gosse), Rhys Bell (Idris Bell), George Trevelyan (G. E. Trevelyan), Richard Gordon Lancelyn Green (Gordon Bottomley), George T. Sassoon (Siegfried Sassoon), the Estate of Charles Freer, David Higham Associates (Augustus John), the Gordon Craig Estate, and the Controller of Her Majesty's Stationary Office. Ezra Pound materials are quoted by permission of Faber & Faber Limited and New Directions Publishing Corporation. I have attempted to track down the copyright holders of all unpublished materials used in this book, and apologize in the few cases where I have been unable to do so.

I would like to thank the curatorial staff at the Freer Gallery of Art in Washington, DC, especially Thomas Lawton and Martin Amt, and the Gallery's Archivist, Colleen Hennessey. In Japan, I am grateful to Hayashi Sae of the Yokohama Museum of Art, Sato Yoko of the English Literary Society of Japan, Shigeno Keijun of Homyoin, Miidera temple, Otsu, Robert Coghlan of the British Embassy, Tokyo, the curatorial staff at the Tokyo National Museum, the Nezu Institute of Fine Arts, Tokyo, and the Yamato Bunka-kan, Nara, and my colleagues at Fukuoka University, one of whom, Professor Ueno Terutaka, has recently completed a Japanese translation of Binyon's *Landscape in English Art and Poetry*. In Britain I would like to thank Roma Woodnutt of the Society of Authors, Stanley Hunter, Nicholas Hardwick, Lady Waterhouse, R. A. Close, Mrs Mary Burn, Mrs Catherine Martineau, Mrs Belinda Norman-Butler, and Mr and Mrs R. V. Hay-Drummond for their hospitality at Westridge Farm House, where Binyon retired and wrote his finest poetry.

I owe a special debt of gratitude to two institutions with which Binyon was intimately concerned. At his old college, Trinity College Oxford, I would like to thank Assistant Archivist Clare Hopkins for unearthing photographs, letters, and other documents, Matthew Steggle for additional assistance, and Fellow Archivist Dr Bryan Ward-Perkins and the Fellows of Trinity College for permission to use these materials. At the British Museum, Binyon's home for forty years, I would like to thank the Archivist, Janet Wallace, for initiating me into the arcane mysteries of the Museum's Central Archives, and the Trustees for permission to quote from unpublished archival materials. I am grateful to Anthony Griffiths, Keeper of the Department of Prints and Drawings, Dr

Jessica Rawson, Keeper of the Department of Oriental Antiquities, and Lawrence Smith, Keeper of the Department of Japanese Antiquities, and their staff, especially Dr Ann Farrer and Dr Tim Clark, for their co-operation and help in numerous ways. I would also like to thank two ex-members of the Department of Prints and Drawings: Reginald Williams, for helping me map out Binyon's kingdom with the aid of old photographs, and the late Dudley Snelgrove, who warmly remembered Binyon taking him under his wing when he entered the Print Room as a 15-year-old Boy Attendant in 1920.

This study began as a doctoral dissertation at Oxford University, and I am happy to acknowledge what I owe to my tutors at Christ Church, Peter Conrad, Christopher Butler, and Richard Hamer, and to my supervisor, Dr Michael Weaver, whose wide-ranging, cross-cultural sympathies in art and literature made him the ideal supervisor for this highly interdisciplinary project. I also benefited from help and encouragement from John Fuller, Dr John Kelly, Professor A. Walton Litz, Omar Pound, and Dr David Peters Corbett. My grateful thanks go to Paul Harvey, Vi Hughes, and Jill Haas for their helpful comments after reading earlier versions of the manuscript, and to my expert editors at Oxford University Press.

Some debts cannot be repaid, only acknowledged, and this is the kind I owe to Laurence Binyon's family, in particular to his last surviving daughter, Nicolete Gray, who is, like her father, a distinguished scholar–artist. In the months it took me to work my way through Binyon's papers preserved in her house in Oxfordshire, Mrs Gray set them in an enriching context with memories spanning seven decades. In her I had a precious living link with the poet whose letters and manuscripts I was studying upstairs, and I am grateful to her for her generous hospitality, both there and more recently in Chelsea. I had the privilege and pleasure of meeting her husband, Basil Gray, several times before his death in 1989, and benefited greatly from discussing Binyon, the British Museum, Asian art, and much else with him. In various ways I have been helped by all of Binyon's grandchildren: Edmund, Marius, and Sophy Gray, Cecilia Wolff-Metternich, Jonathan and Andrew Higgens, and Harriet Proudfoot. I am particularly indebted to Edmund Gray and Harriet Proudfoot, who provided information and materials essential to my research. They could not have been kinder, more helpful, or more encouraging.

Finally, my wife, Yasuko, whom I met while living in Kyoto in the early 1980s, when I first became interested in Binyon's writings on Asian art. Our love and comradeship and this study have grown together, and without her it would never have been completed.

Contents

List of Illustrations

4. *Rabbits and Autumn Grasses*, detail from 6-fold screen, Rimpa School, eighteenth century, Department of Japanese Antiquities, British Museum.

5. Sesshū, *Haboku Landscape*, hanging scroll, dated 1495, Tokyo National Museum.

Page 159 Handbill for 'Art & Thought in East & West' lecture series, March 1909, Houghton Library, Harvard University.

Permissions

Black and white plates: nos. 1, 3, 5, 10–14 reproduced courtesy of Mrs Nicolete Gray; no. 2 courtesy of the Archive, Trinity College, Oxford; nos. 4, 7 courtesy of the Trustees of the British Museum; no. 6 courtesy of the Bodleian Library, Oxford; no. 8 courtesy of the Freer Gallery of Art, Smithsonian Institution, Washington, DC; no. 9 courtesy of Mrs Harriet Proudfoot.

Colour plates: no. 1 reproduced courtesy of Mrs Nicolete Gray; nos. 2–4 courtesy of the Trustees of the British Museum; no. 5 courtesy of Tokyo National Museum.

Figure on p. 159 reproduced courtesy of the Houghton Library, Harvard University.

I would like to thank the Great Britain Sasakawa Foundation for a grant towards reproduction costs.

Abbreviations

1. Abbreviations in the Text

All works by Laurence Binyon unless otherwise stated. Full publication details are given in the bibliography.

BC	*The Art of Botticelli* (1913)
BL	*The Burning of the Leaves and Other Poems* (1944)
CP	*Collected Poems of Laurence Binyon* (2 vols., 1931)
FD	*The Flight of the Dragon* (1911)
FDF	*For Dauntless France* (1918)
G	Manmohan Ghose, *Collected Poems*, i (1970)
JCP	*Japanese Colour Prints* (rev. edn. 1960)
LA	*Landscape in English Art and Poetry* (1930)
MG	Introductory memoir. *Songs of Love and Death*. By Manmohan Ghose (1926)
NS	*The North Star and Other Poems* (1941)
PFE	*Painting in the Far East* (1934 ed.)
PI	'Post-Impressionists', *SR* 12 Nov. 1910: 609–10
SMAA	*The Spirit of Man in Asian Art* (1935)
WF	*Western Flanders* (1899)

2. Abbreviations in Notes

ALi	Autograph letter initialled
ALs	Autograph letter signed
AMS	Autograph manuscript
BL	Dept. of Manuscripts, British Library
BL–HRC	Binyon Letters, Harry Ransom Research Center, Texas
BM	Central Archives, British Museum.
BM	*Burlington Magazine*
BMQ	*British Museum Quarterly*
BRBM	Beinecke Rare Book and Manuscript Library, Yale
CMB	Cicely Margaret Binyon
EG–BC	Edmund Gosse Papers, Brotherton Coll., Leeds University Library
HRC	Harry Ransom Research Center, Austin, Texas
LB	Laurence Binyon
NS	*New Statesman*
R&S–BL	Ricketts & Shannon Papers, British Library
SR	*Saturday Review*

TMs	Typed manuscript signed
TLs	Typed letter signed
TSMP–LU	Thomas Sturge Moore Papers, University of London Library
WRP–HH	Sir William Rothenstein Papers, Houghton Library, Harvard

A Note on Romanization of Japanese and Chinese Words

JAPANESE WORDS are spelled according to the Hepburn system of romanization, with macrons indicating long vowels, for example Kōrin, except in place names like Tokyo, where they are omitted. Words such as *ukiyo-e* and *chanoyu*, which take various forms in English-language publications, appear in the forms given in *Japan: An Illustrated Encyclopedia* (Tokyo, 1993). Chinese words are romanized according to the Wade-Giles system used by Binyon, but *pinyin* romanizations are given in parentheses in the index, and, in some cases, in the text. Japanese and Chinese personal names appear in their traditional forms, with surname followed by given name, except in the case of Yoshio Markino and Yone Noguchi, and in the footnotes, where the names of authors of works written in English are given as published.

1   *Early Years*

When in 1940 the 71-year-old Laurence Binyon asked of T. S. Eliot, 'Do you realize that nearly half my life belongs to Victoria's days?', he was not only speaking of chronology. Binyon's career spanned the 1890s, the Edwardian period, the Great War, and the troubled interwar years, but, like his friend W. B. Yeats, who was born three years earlier and died four years earlier, many of his core values and attitudes remained late Victorian.

Robert Laurence Binyon was born in the historic city of Lancaster on St Laurence's Day, 10 August 1869, the second of five sons of Frederick Binyon, an Anglican clergyman, and his wife Mary. On both sides the family's historic roots were in Wales. The name Binyon derives from the Welsh *Ap Einion*, a fact Binyon privately recalled in moments when he despaired of stolid Anglo–Saxon pragmatism. On his mother's side he was related to the vast Lloyd clan and through them descended from the early Welsh kings and patriarchs. No royalist, he took little interest in this, although, as a poet with a lifelong passion for Arthurian legend, he was aware that some Lloyds wishfully traced their ancestry back to Arthur. The Lloyds' family seat had been Doloban Hall, built in the fourteenth century by Celynin ap Rhiryd in the valley of the river Vruwy, 8 miles north of Welshpool in Merioneth. The name Lloyd ('grey-haired') was taken by his great-great-grandson, whose son established the enterprise that grew into the powerful Birmingham-based iron smelting, processing, and distribution dynasty, and later evolved into the commercial banking giant that still bears the Lloyd name. The family were also involved in canal-building and later in the development of the railway system. Binyon's maternal grandfather, who built the Oxford to Cambridge railway line and the Roundhouse engine shed near Euston Station, was a man in the same mould. On both sides Binyon was descended from old Quaker families. His paternal grandfather, who had married into the famous Manchester calico house of Hoyle, came from a line of

Northern Quaker businessmen, but broke with the Friends following the traumatic Beaconite separation in the Manchester Meeting
in the 1830s.[1]

Little of this Victorian enterprise, affluence, and religious conflict
impinged on Binyon's immediate family. Shortly after graduating
from Trinity College Cambridge, in 1860, Frederick Binyon had
served as a volunteer curate at St Peter's, Blackburn, working
without a stipend during the 'cotton famine' of the 1860s when the
American Civil War cut off the supply of Southern cotton. A man
of strong social conscience, he was one of the first to organize
sewing and other classes in an attempt to relieve the poverty of the
unemployed mill workers. In 1866 he was appointed vicar of
Burton-in-Lonsdale, north-east of Lancaster, at the western edge of
the West Riding of Yorkshire. The parish was newly formed and a
new church and vicarage still under construction, so when he
married Mary Dockray in the same year, she continued living in
Lancaster, where Laurence and his older brother Jack were born at
1 High Street.

The young family moved to Burton in 1870. Although still
largely an agricultural community, the parish also contained a
thriving pottery industry utilizing good quality local clay. Smoke
belching from the kilns of the Waterside and Townend Potteries
gave the village the local name 'Black Burton'. According to his
wife, Binyon 'always felt himself a north countryman'.[2] His allegiance was primarily to the landscape, the austere beauty of the
Yorkshire Dales, to Wordsworth's Lake District to the north and
Brontë country to the south-east, wild, literature-saturated landscapes. His earliest memories were of the Vale of Lune and especially of Ingleboro as seen from the Burton vicarage, which
instilled in him a lifelong love of mountains. He later voiced his
'craving for the hills' to a fellow poet living near his childhood
home: 'It is odd how persistent that is, when they are mixed with
one's earliest recollections. I always liked that Psalm which says "I

[1] For details of Binyon's family background, and a concise overview of LB's
career, see David Steel, introduction, *Laurence Binyon and Lancaster: An Exhibi-
tion Held at Lancaster Museum 28th April–26th May 1979* (Lancaster, 1979), 3–7.
See also John Beckett and Andrew Gardiner, *Merlewood Grange-over-Sands and the
Lancashire Cotton Industry* (Grange-over-Sands, 1987), 7. For the Lloyds, see E. V.
Lucas, *Charles Lamb and the Lloyds* (London, 1898).

[2] CMB, memoir of LB, AMS, incomplete 2pp., n.d., n.pag. Unless otherwise
stated, all manuscript materials cited are in the Binyon Archive (see Bibliography).

lifted my eyes unto the hills".... I envy you your daily vision of Ingleboro.'[3] This same hill inspired his late poem 'Inheritance':

> To a bare blue hill
> Wings an old thought roaming,
> At a random touch
> Of memory homing.
>
> .   .   .   .
>
> Beautiful, dark,
> And solitary,
> The first of England
> That spoke to me.
>
> (*NS* 37–9)

He was, however, destined to forgo this Wordsworthian childhood for a more Coleridgean childhood in London. The Burton parish of 700 inhabitants was a poor one, yielding an income of only £85, which, rather than providing a living, proved a drain on the family's resources. What remained of Frederick's inheritance was needed to educate his five sons, eked out by scholarships. Partly because of this and partly because Mary Binyon, a town woman, disliked the loneliness of Burton, the family stayed here only four years before moving south to Chelmsford in 1874, when Binyon was 5 years old. A second move brought the family to London, where Frederick served successively at St Mary's in Bryanston Square, St Paul's in Hammersmith, and St Andrew's in Fulham, followed by moves to Gloucestershire in 1888 and Devon in 1892. This somewhat nomadic existence ended when the family moved back up north on Frederick's retirement.

Binyon's education was less disrupted than it might have been. From 1877 to 1880 he and Jack attended King Edward's Grammar School in Chelmsford, first as day pupils, then as boarders when the family moved to London. He was not a precocious student, but gradually over these three years worked his way up from fourteenth in the class to fourth. In 1880 the brothers joined the family in London. Binyon spent two terms at the Godolphin School in Hammersmith, the 'cheap school' where Yeats, 15 years old to Binyon's 11, was an unhappy fellow pupil.[4] In May 1881, along with fifty-six other candidates, he sat the rigorous two-day Founda-

---

[3] ALs to Gordon Bottomley, 5 Feb. 1918 [CMB transcript].
[4] See Yeats, *Autobiographies* (London, 1955), 32–42.

tion Scholarship examinations at St Paul's and won one of the eight scholarships on offer. J. W. Shephard, his future housemaster, reported: 'For a boy of his age his Latin was particularly good; and he was far ahead of the other candidates below the age of 12.'[5]

Entering St Paul's in September 1881, he felt privileged to live through the school's last three years on its ancient site in the Cathedral Churchyard, steeped in memories of Dean Colet, Richard Mulcaster, Samuel Pepys, and its most famous student, Milton. It was here that Binyon's romance with London began. When in 1884 the school moved to new neo-Gothic red-brick buildings amid spacious grounds in Hammersmith, the school magazine, the *Pauline*, celebrated the escape from the inner-city 'incubus of noise, and fog, and cramped space' to the 'light, and air, and freedom' of suburbia.[6] Binyon, however, 'perversely lamented' the move:

for what amplitude of play-fields could make up for those solitary rambles about the by-ways of Cheapside, the towers and spires, the shipping in the Thames, the crowds and animation, the sense of history, of being in the centre of things, the deep-toned bells of the Cathedral sounding down the smoky air, the little seclusions of peace in the church-yard, the glory of the spaciousness beneath the dome? These had been my dreamy haunts. We had been transferred to Hammersmith and prose.

(MG 8)

The urban poet of *London Visions* of the 1890s was born here, in the foggy inner city mythologized by Dickens and Whistler.

In a poem written for the school's fourth centenary in 1909, he would celebrate the Renaissance humanism of its founder, John Colet:

> When the long-clouded spirit of Europe drew
> Life from Greek springs, frost could no longer bind,
> And old truth shone like fresh dawn on the blind,
> Our Founder sowed his pregnant seed: he knew
> No crabbed rule but rather chose a clue
> That should emband us of our historied kind
> Comrades, and keep in us a morning mind,
> Since to the wise Learning is always New.

(CPi.187)

---

[5] ALs to Snowden, 5 May 1881.
[6] Editorial, *Pauline*, 2 (Oct. 1884), 263.

By 1881, however, St Paul's was in the throes of an overhaul that laid greater stress on 'crabbed rule' than 'morning mind'. The High Master, Frederick Walker, had taken on the languishing school in 1876 and was busy masterminding an academic renaissance and expansion that would see it regain all its former prestige.[7] The 12-year-old Binyon knew the authoritarian Walker from firsthand experience as a 'formidable personality famous for his prescience in judging a boy's future capabilities' (MG 9), for as a Foundation scholar with high Latin scores he was automatically enlisted in the crack corps dedicated to winning Oxbridge scholarships. This entailed what a later student, Leonard Woolf, described as an 'extraordinarily intensive system of teaching Latin and Greek',[8] which excluded virtually any other subject except English history and poetry. When, half a century later, Ezra Pound lamented 'Binyon's sad youth, poisoned in the cradle by the abominable dogbiscuit of Milton's rhetoric',[9] he could hardly have known how true this was, for memorizing great swathes of Milton for recitation in class was indeed a feature of the syllabus. Milton apart, Binyon found it a grind for which he had little natural aptitude. Walker's early term reports bear terse comments like 'Is making progress. His extreme slowness stands in his way.' His growing love of classical literature, however, gradually transformed toil into pleasure, and by July 1887 Walker was suggesting that he 'ought to aim at the highest things'. His final report a year later concluded: 'I feel confident that with reasonable care & effort he has a brilliant career ahead of him. He carries with him to the University my respect & regard.'[10]

While this did indeed pave the way to an Oxford scholarship, it left him little time to form close friendships. He seems to have been regarded as a reserved, rather enigmatic figure. His contemporary Cyril Bailey, later a Fellow of Balliol, remembered:

He was himself naturally a scholar and he knew more than most boys of the inner meaning of the classics. But he was always an independent

---

[7] See Michael F. J. McDonnell, *A History of St Paul's School* (London, 1909), 426–53

[8] Leonard Woolf, *Sowing: An Autobiography of the Years 1880–1904* (London, 1967), 74.

[9] 'Hell', rev. of *Dante's Inferno*, by LB, *Criterion*, 13 (Apr. 1934), 382.

[10] St Paul's School reports for Sept.–Dec. 1881, Jan.–July 1887, Jan.–July 1888.

person, far more mature than most of us and a little aloof from the general
school life. . . .

As a boy he had already that magnificent head, covered with its dark
hair, a lock falling over his forehead, and the serious look, which at times
broke into an almost convulsive ripple of laughter. I think most of his
contemporaries regarded him with some awe and he did not make many
close friends. . . . But we all felt that there was that in him which no one
else had, even if it was not till later that we knew that it was the eye of the
artist and the mind of the poet.[11]

He was able to relate best with his schoolfellows through
the ritualized combat of debate, and in 1887 was elected librarian
of the Union Society, the preserve of the seniors. The society
gave him a forum for his radical political views. In February
1888 he supported a motion in favour of socialism. 'Binyon
called himself a meliorist,' reported the *Pauline*, 'believing that
human nature could change, and that man could be educated to
the level of Socialism.'[12] In the same month he promoted
radical ideas in the French Debating Society, of which he was
assistant secretary. On 9 February he seconded the motion 'Que la
conscription est nuisible', spicing his argument with 'an anecdote
which the Society considered wild and improbable'. On 23
February he proposed the motion 'Que la monarchie est une
institution peu civilisée et doit être abolie en Angleterre'. The
Pauline observed: 'Binyon delivered an ingenious and somewhat
impassioned speech, traced the origin, progress, decline and fall of
the monarchical principle, and implored the Society not to be
deluded by superstition.' The motion was carried 7–6 as 'the high
spirits of the Society led them to revise the constitution of the
country'.[13]

Despite a punishing academic schedule, Binyon was increasingly
absorbed in his twin passions, writing poetry and drawing. His
surviving notebooks are full of draft poems interspersed with careful pencil portraits of family members and friends. He kept his
'secret ambition' from his schoolfellows, but Bailey recalls that they
'had a suspicion that he was a poet and called him "the Bard"'.
Chosen partly for alliterating with 'Binyon'—the four sonnets he
published in the *Pauline* in 1886–7 were signed with a modest 'B'—

---

[11] TMs memoir of LB, 1p., 3 Apr. 1945.
[12] A.L., 'Union', *Pauline*, 6 (Mar. 1888), 637.
[13] 'French Debating Society', *Pauline*, 6 (May 1888), 664.

the nickname hinted also at the enigmatic presence and vatic silences that would characterize the adult poet.

If Binyon shielded his creative work from an unsympathetic academic environment, this was equally true of the family to whom he returned each evening in nearby Edith Road. His mother numbered among her ancestors Charles Lloyd, poet friend of Lamb and Coleridge, and was very distantly related to Wordsworth, but the young Binyon found his family dourly oblivious to literature and art. Years later school and family coalesced for him into a composite image of Victorian philistinism: 'My home was indifferent to the arts, my school fellows also, so far as I knew them' (MG 9). 'It has always been a grief to me that I have so little in common, as far as interests go, with my family,' he wrote. 'I love all beautiful things, & they care so little for them. And my father's pet hobby was mathematics, at which I am painfully stupid.'[14] It is perhaps indicative that though he was christened Robert after his maternal grandfather, he chose early on to use only his middle name, Laurence, after the saint on whose day he was born.

Fortunately he had a second family to hand at 10 Edith Road in the remarkable household of his mother's sister, Agatha Sophia Phillips. Open-minded, passionately interested in literature and art, Sophia was the profoundest influence on his early life. She epitomized everything his own oppressively masculine family lacked. 'She was a wonderful woman,' he wrote later, 'gifted in every way but most in her womanliness & sympathy. I owe enormously much to her.'[15] In the warm, creative atmosphere she nurtured in her Hammersmith home she treated him as one of her own children, coaxing him out of his natural reserve, sharing his joys and fears, reading poetry with him and encouraging his own verse. As he matured, more in her home than in his own, he became in turn Sophia's closest friend. 'I knew *you* understood me (the only person who did),' she wrote when he left for Oxford, 'and I felt as if the sun had gone out of the sky when I saw you go.'[16] Sophia gave Binyon his ideal of womanhood, but she also came to symbolize for him life's potential creativity crushed by the obtuse materialist world, taking visible shape in her clergyman husband, whom the young Binyon detested, oedipally no doubt, but also with reason given the role imposed on women in middle-class Victorian fam-

[14] ALs to CMB, postmarked 18 May 1903.
[15] ALs to CMB [19 May 1903].   [16] ALs, n.d. [1891?].

ilies. Heartbroken at her early death in 1892, he wrote in his elegy
'In Carissimam Memoriam: A.S.P.':

> Too much hadst thou of pain, and fret, and care;
> Yet surely thou wast meant for joy

(CPi.3)

Among Sophia's children Binyon was closest to Stephen Phillips,
five years older and himself an aspiring poet whose *Orestes and
Other Poems* was published privately in 1884. They shared a
strong facial resemblance, the same square jaw and small, tight
mouth, but in other ways Binyon could hardly have been more
different from his robust, extrovert cousin, who in 1885 became an
actor in the company of another cousin, the great Shakespearean
actor-manager Frank Benson, in whose troupe he exploited his
good looks and talent for mimicry in a series of minor roles over the
next ten years. The two poets were good friends, criticizing and
encouraging each other's verse. While quite different from his own,
Binyon found Phillips's flamboyant verse more congenial than the
tired Tennysonianism dutifully admired by his St Paul's teachers.

Binyon made only one deep friendship at St Paul's, but it is
difficult to imagine a more decisive one for a man who would
devote much of his life to studying Asian art and philosophy. In
1884 a young Indian boy named Manmohan Ghose joined the
school. He came from a famous Bengali family whose patriarchs
included Rajanarayan Ghose, one of the leaders of the Bengali
Renaissance and a prominent nationalist. Manmohan's father,
however, was a confirmed Anglophile, who, having studied in the
'mother country' himself, in 1878 brought his sons to England
to be educated. Having lived in England since he was 9 years
old, Manmohan was destined to suffer the subtle fractures of
double exile. He was, he wrote Binyon years later, 'four-fifths an
Englishman, if not entirely one'.[17]

As yet unconscious of the complex ironies of colonialism, the 15-
year-old Binyon saw this exotic newcomer as 'an unaccountable
apparition from an unknown hemisphere', who opened his eyes to
a world beyond grey, smoggy Victorian London: 'The legendary
East seemed suddenly to have projected a fragment of itself into our

---

[17] Letter to LB, March 1889, in Manmohan Ghose, *Collected Poems*, i, ed. Lotika
Ghose, 4 vols. (Calcutta, 1970–5), 196. Ghose's 1886–90 letters to LB are published
in this volume, pp. 111–251 (hereafter G), but later Ghose letters in the Binyon
Archive remain unpublished.

little world of everyday things and humdrum studies, disturbing it with colour, mystery, romance' (MG 7). At a level deeper than this boyish exoticism, however, the young Binyon responded positively to what we would now call the Other, setting a precedent for his later contacts with Asia.

The two boys met in the Seventh Form *Aeneid* reading class. What attracted Binyon was that, on being introduced to the class, Ghose broke the ice by wittily quoting *Othello* 'in a voice low and thrilled that seemed itself to glow': 'No doubt I should not have been moved as I was had not the new-comer spoken the rich lines in a voice that betrayed the capacity to be intoxicated by poetry: and of such capacity I had found no trace in my class-mates. I felt immediate sympathy' (MG 7).

When Binyon discovered that Ghose was also writing verse, the tyro poets became constant companions, taking long country walks 'discussing everything in heaven and earth, after the manner of youth, but especially poetry and the poets' (MG 9). They shared a passion for Greek and Elizabethan lyric verse and Romantic poetry, while in contemporary poetry they admired Arnold and Whitman, sympathized with Swinburne's atheism and republicanism, detested Tennyson, and diverged only over Binyon's 'ardent worship of Browning' (MG 9).

'The capacity to be intoxicated by poetry' meant much more than just reading or even writing poems, however. It implied a whole way of being and responding to life that both boys felt they had to struggle to preserve in the inimical environment of public school and lonely families. Binyon drew Ghose into his own second family, the Phillipses. Ghose's description of the family reveals clearly why Sophia and her children meant so much to Binyon:

All that beautiful family have a wonderful fascination for me. Your aunt I adore. She is more like our own Indian women than the cold marmoreal creatures, who are called by that name in this country; full of warmth and sweetness to others . . . and fascinatingly intellectual, besides. . . . How altogether un-English they are!

(G246–7)

Ghose too was in desperate need of this human warmth. The companionship he found with Binyon and the Phillipses filled a void in his life, for, as he confessed to Binyon, his mother had succumbed to insanity and his father was kind but stern and often absent, leaving him with a deep craving for affection, something he felt Binyon could understand (G162–3). His domestic situation was difficult. He lived in lodgings with his younger brothers Aravinda and Binoy Bhushan, eking out a precarious existence on increasingly irregular remittances from their father in Bengal.

Manmohan was not the only promising Ghose. Three years younger, Aravinda was already a talented classicist at St Paul's, but no one could have foretold the future awaiting this apparently Anglicized agnostic intellectual, who, after a brilliant Cambridge degree and spectacular career as a nationalist revolutionary, would undergo a spiritual transformation and emerge as Sri Aurobindo, one of the greatest Indian spiritual philosophers, whose ashram in Pondicherry would draw disciples from all over the world. When in 1889 the 17-year-old Aravinda showed him one of his Greek translations, Binyon urged him to write original verse, advice that set him on a path that would lead to a lifetime's worth of difficult but profound English poetry.[18]

Manmohan Ghose left St Paul's in July 1887 after winning an open scholarship to Christ Church Oxford, while Binyon remained and entered the Upper Eighth, but their friendship remained close. Ghose pinned a Binyon self-portrait above his desk in his rooms in Peckwater Quad and wrote 'To Robert Laurence Binyon', urging his friend to write the healing, humanist poetry he felt was in him:

> Then mayst thou heal men's hearts to hope, t'endure,
> As thou has heal'd mine!—This I wish to thee,
> Who canst so draw the whole love of a friend.

> (G126)

'You are the only company to me,' he wrote from Christ Church, 'and I can commune with you alone. I triumph in the thought of this' (G165). He wrote frequently, everything from detailed critiques of Binyon poems to invectives against Oxford moneylenders. By turns whimsical, profound, self-dramatizing, this splendid series of letters continued on and off until 1905. Binyon's letters, preserved by Ghose and later deposited in the University of Calcutta Library, have unfortunately been lost, but it is possible to glean the gist of them from Ghose's and they provide our clearest insight into Binyon's life during these formative years.

Crucially for both men, they chart Ghose's awakening consciousness of his Indian heritage in both nationalist and religious terms

---

[18] See A. B. Purani, *Sri Aurobindo in England* (Pondicherry, India, 1956), 21.

and thus Binyon's education in a new, non-Anglocentric, indeed non-European way of seeing. Slowly growing disillusioned with the Raj, Ghose's father sent his sons cuttings from Indian newspapers, and Ghose passed on to Binyon stories of unreported cholera epidemics, the Salt Tax, torture, and other iniquities. 'I would write volumes to convert you,' he wrote in 1887. 'I would never take such trouble with any one else. I would only meet with the same cold and weary unbelief which every one meets, who tries the same task' (G143). Ghose's own response to all this was more equivocal than that of his radical brothers. After writing a political poem entitled 'The Necessity of Republicanism', he abjured political activism and set himself instead to becoming a poet, which for him, trapped as he was in a complex web of loyalties, meant staying in England. India was, he wrote Binyon, 'that land I love so much, but which it would be fatal for my feet to tread—fatal I mean to any faint genius that may be in me—fatal to my friendship with you—and fatal to my doing any good to my own country' (G138).

Ghose was at first equally equivocal about Indian philosophy and religion, but he introduced Binyon to ideas that would concern him all his life, their impact deepened by the fact that they coincided with a decisive turning-point in his own spiritual life. From at least his sixteenth year Binyon had found himself increasingly at odds with his father's Anglicanism. In February 1888 he wrote to Ghose confessing that he had radical doubts about Christian dogma, especially the immortality of the soul.[19] This was no modish adolescent gesture, for, as a clergyman's son, he knew that it would mean even greater alienation from his family. 'What a terrible misfortune to feel that you must take a path which will lead you away from all who are most dear to you,' Ghose responded (G173).

One would give much to unearth the February or March 1888 letter in which Binyon described the home-made 'theory' he had concocted to replace his lost Christian faith, but from Ghose's replies it appears to have been a humanist, quasi-Platonic philosophy in which God is impersonalized as the 'sum of all good'. He challenged Ghose to 'a battle about the immortality of the soul' to clarify and enrich their respective philosophies, and Ghose accepted (G166). A year earlier Ghose had been astonished to learn that his father had turned Buddhist. 'He believes', he wrote Binyon, 'that all

---

[19] See Ghose, 165–6.

the forces of nature and human souls will merge into God, which seems to me a very strange theory. This is the doctrine of Nirvana' (G112). This inspired Manmohan himself to delve into Indian philosophy as a means of breaking through a painful impasse in his personal life, to recreate himself as 'a self-centred collected soul' who aspired 'to be an ascetic and think to eternity' (G164–5). Six months later on 2 September 1888, just before Binyon joined him at Oxford, he returned to the fray armed with the Upanishads. His letter deserves quoting at length, as it was perhaps the most important Binyon ever received. He begins by taking issue with Binyon's conception of the divine as the sum of all good:

My conviction (and it is a very deep one) is that God is 'the sum of all existence'. We have both departed from the popular anthropomorphic idea of God; but after that we seem to have parted and gone widely different roads. There is no conviction I hold so passionately as this one, no truth is so dear to me; and I would fain try and convince you that this is more likely to be true than what you believe. Will you let me try? I think, what dissuaded me from accepting your belief was this thought. What after all is that which we call good? Are not good and evil terms merely relative to us alone. Mankind calls a thing good, because it makes *them* glad and a thing bad which gives *them* pain: and this is true both bodily and spiritually. . . . But is God to be so limited to the spheres of the human soul (if by *the sum of all good* you mean *spiritual good* as no doubt you do) or to humanity (if you include all that man finds good for himself). Surely God must be an infinite being in whom we are all contained, rather than the limited being you suppose who is, so to speak, contained in humanity alone. For what is good to humanity may be evil to other parts of what people miscall the creation. Miscall—because I hold that the creation is nothing else but God. We and all the forms of life we see are but passing phases of God, the fluctuations of this eternal life. Man undoubtedly is the most perfect phase, and expresses the deity most. By right of our spirits, which most express the essence of the deity, we are imperishable. And it is very natural to suppose that the soul when it has starved out the rebel powers, that array it by its incessant growth will escape into unfettered liberty. No, I certainly cannot agree with your belief. I am, it is true, naturally pagan-minded. But I know and can appreciate Christian ideas; and after some experience of that I have gone back to my native bent. I reverence the word God, and it is too beautiful and expresses too much to die out of the world—But to me Nature is a word more sacred than God. The definition I gave is not mine. It was the conviction of the old Hindu philosophers—it was Spinoza's—it was Goethe's—and it surprises me that so clear-minded a man as Matthew Arnold should have thought otherwise.

I shall always be ready to maintain a truth I feel so deeply—that God is nothing working at the back of Nature like an absolute monarch, as Christians suppose. It is my rooted conviction that God is in Nature and Nature in God.

(G191–2)

Succeeding chapters will show how such ideas helped shape Binyon's life's work as poet and art historian.

SCHOOLBOY VERSE

The poetry Binyon wrote at St Paul's falls into two distinct categories that would remain a lifelong feature of his work. On the one hand we have the poems he wrote for the school's Milton Prize, composed on a given subject and designed to be read aloud at the Apposition Festival, necessarily a rhetorical, public poetry. On the other hand there are his lyric meditations, intensely personal disquisitions on self and world.

Binyon won the Milton Prize two years running, with *Niobe* in 1887 and *Joan of Arc* in 1888, as well as the Thruston Prize for Latin Hexameters with 'Columbus' in 1888. When he recited *Niobe* to the audience of pupils, teachers, parents, and dignitaries at Apposition on 20 July 1887, High Master Walker declared 'that he did not remember such good verse from a schoolboy since the days of Clough'.[20] Ghose heard his friend had 'made quite a sensation' (G118), while Cyril Bailey vividly remembered it as the moment when 'we realized how far he was above the run of schoolboy poets'.[21]

Many of Binyon's St Paul's poems are contained in a notebook comprising mostly fair copies of forty-eight poems written between August 1885 and January 1888, along with translations from Lamartine, Beaumarchais, and Lucretius.[22] It is laid out like a published book, with contents page, and divided into sections. They show the young poet experimenting with various lyric and narrative forms and rhyme and metrical schemes, mimicking different voices in quest of his own. They also show him striving for self-

[20] E.V.F., 'The Apposition', *Pauline*, 5 (Oct. 1887), 543.
[21] Bailey, n.pag.
[22] 'Robert Laurence Binyon / Poems: Aug. 1885–Dec. 1886', AMS notebook, 'Xmas 1884', n.pag.

critical integrity: the wholly conventional sonnet 'To the Cuckoo' is struck out as 'insincere'. Seven of these poems, all sonnets, were published before Binyon left St Paul's. 'The Wanderer's Return' appeared in the April 1886 issue of *Macmillan's Magazine* alongside Hardy's serialized *The Woodlanders*; 'Desiderium' in the November 1887 *Academy*; 'A Dead Emperor', 'Sleep and Spring', 'A Greek Death' and 'Ophelia' in the *Pauline* in December 1886 and March 1887. The most remarkable accolade came from William Sharp, who printed 'The Past, Asleep' in his notes to the second edition of his popular anthology *Sonnets of this Century* (1887), remarking that for an effort by a 16-year-old it displayed 'marked maturity of conception'.[23] These and the unpublished sonnets display a fascination with the intricacies of form, playing variations on the Petrarchan, Miltonic, and Shakespearean forms in search of structures tailored to chosen themes and tones of voice.

Biographically, the most interesting poem in the notebook is one impatiently struck through for cancellation, the long 'Di aut umbrae' (October 1885), in which brief pencilled notes gloss key passages. The poem obeys the archetypal pattern of Romantic quest romance. The protagonist wanders 'thro' a dim and desolate land' of 'lifeless rocks' and 'broken sea' which is a projection of his own angst (glossed 'Doubt'). His philosophical Christianity breaks down ('Failing Philosophy') and he sees death as the only means of breaking into the Absolute. The Greek gods are momentarily revived as giant statues but in their sterile marble perfection they cannot answer his pleas. In despair he sees that he is entirely alone, both God and gods evaporated ('Atheism'). He falls asleep gazing at the east and dreams of 'Paradise', only it is not the supermundane spiritual paradise he had yearned for but the 'self-same shore' of his wandering, now irradiated by dawnlight:

> I woke; and lo! all that I dreamed was true:
> For far on the dusk ocean, beam by beam,
>   Broke the soft light thro' dew.
>
> .   .   .   .
>
> I bowed me down unto the happy earth
>   I bowed me down to the warm earth I trod,—
> I & my soul, before that heavenly birth,
>   And knew it was of God.

[23] *Sonnets of this Century, Edited and Arranged with a Critical Introduction on the Sonnet*, rev. edn. (London, 1887), 278.

The quest romance pattern is fulfilled by return to a world reinvested with meaning, seen aright by a mind cleansed of egoism, fully found because so fully lost. Keats's great analogy, 'The Imagination may be compared to Adam's dream—he awoke and found it truth',[24] underpins this final stanza, just as Shelley's *Alastor* fathered the narrative itself. The poem may be little more than an anthology of Romantic topoi, but it was obviously therapeutic, enabling the 16-year-old poet to explore the erosion of his faith while staving it off by attributing the redeemed landscape to 'God', ambiguous as that word was becoming for him by October 1885.

The problems of belief recur constantly in a probing of death and immortality. In 'Parting at Midnight' in March 1886 he can still claim 'Earth hath no pillow but the hope of heaven, | And in that hope I live, & pray for this,' but the sestet of 'Sleep and Spring', written the same month, denies immortality altogether. In 'At the Tomb' in October, 'God' is struck from the line 'O God, is heaven so near to hell?' and replaced by 'Christ', the Hebraic father ousted by the suffering human son. All this prefigures the anguished letters to Ghose in 1888.

The search for transcendence in non-Christian terms leads inevitably to nature. Here too we find a pastiche of Romantic attitudes, some of which survive into his mature poetry, some not. While many of the poems are Keatsian in imagery and theme, nature here is Shelleyan, non-biological, mountains, stars, sea, and sky, all minerals and blue air. The notebook's holy places are hills and mountains. It is easy to dismiss these as the usual papier mâché props, but they were real presences in Binyon's life. 'On the Heights' was written at Curbar in the Peak District in August:

> the tranquil scene,
> The blue, soft distance, the hill-side's rough green,
> And over all the wind-washed perfect sky.
>
> Pure rains and peace have made an altar here,
> Where fitly might we worship and be calm.

Space, the infinite in nature, calls forth an answering infinite in man. In 'Aspiration' (August 1885), the twilight dissolves the world into a seamless flow in which the human mind can shed its individuality and participate, only for the emerging moon to disrupt the poet's reverie:

[24] To Benjamin Bailey, 22 Nov. 1817, letter 31, *Letters of John Keats*, ed. Maurice Buxton Forman, 4th. edn. (London, 1952), 67.

O mystical and virgin silver light
Why has thou parted thus our earth from heaven?
Why has thou shone so soon upon our sight,
Revealed our littleness, and given
Bounds to our infinite?

In Chapter 8 we shall see how Binyon would find these ideas in a more profound form in Chinese painting, where space does indeed become a medium of meditative transcendence.

One of the highlights of Binyon's boyhood was coming across Robert Browning purchasing a ticket at a London railway station. He recalled the incident over half a century later:

As he was then my most idolized poet, it was for me a thrilling moment. He was rather short but sturdy and erect. What immediately attracted attention was the strong contrast between his dark brown complexion and his snow-white hair and beard. His eyes looked out of his face with alertness, as if nothing escaped them. In the whole carriage of the man there was an impressive consciousness of power.[25]

The curious thing is that Browning, the object of his 'ardent worship' during these years, is one of the few voices missing from these ventriloquistic schoolboy poems. Binyon's career might have taken a quite different course, perhaps even towards Poundian modernism, had he mimicked Browning instead of a quite different contemporary poet, whose elegiac voice would haunt his poetry for decades: Matthew Arnold. Neither Binyon nor Ghose met or even saw Arnold, but it was as if 'Matthew' or 'Matt', as they called him, was an invisible member of their family. Praising some lines from one of Binyon's poems, Aunt Sophia wrote to him: 'I *know* Matthew would have liked them too.'[26] It is no coincidence that it was to Arnold that Binyon sent one of his poems in September 1887. The master replied:

You are full young, I will not say to write, but to publish poetry; you should set yourself some large task of study, such as to read Homer right through, Iliad and Odyssey, in the Greek. But there is certainly much that is of promise, much to please, in the lines which you have sent me. Remember that the point is everything, and that effect depends on keeping this in mind and sacrificing superfluities to it.[27]

---

[25] 'The Brownings and Emily Brontë', AMS, Athens lecture series, 1939, n.pag.
[26] ALs to LB, 18 Sept. [1890].   [27] ALs, 8 Sept. 1887.

When Arnold died ten months later, Binyon and Ghose grieved as if they had lost a father. Binyon worked it off by writing an essay which sought to retrieve Arnold the poet from Arnold the ossified Great Victorian savant. Published in George Bentley's *Temple Bar* magazine in September 1888, 'Matthew Arnold's Poetry' is moving precisely because it refuses to be an elegy, treating Arnold as a contemporary whose work is there to be mined by young poets like himself.[28]

By the time the essay appeared, launching his lifelong career as an essayist, Binyon was preparing to leave behind his family and school and enter a far more congenial environment. Arnold's letter had concluded, 'I envy you going up to Oxford,' for, entirely appropriately, when Binyon left St Paul's in July 1888 with his hard-earned scholarship he followed Ghose to Arnold's dreaming, golden city.

[28] *Temple Bar*, 84 (Sept. 1888), 106–11.

2   Oxford and London

The Trinity College Binyon entered at the age of 19 in October 1888 was small enough for members of all four years to fit comfortably in the college photograph taken annually in Garden Quad. In these photographs he looks very young and, in his own self-deprecating word, 'dreamy', but his boater tilts at a jaunty angle, wryly mocking his shyness. He stands at the extreme right of the back row, as if ready to step out of the frame, but this too is deceptive, for at Trinity he found the congenial environment lacking both in his own home and at St Paul's. The college quickly became for him a microcosm of the Oxford he would remain close to all his life, a near-ideal world of youth, freedom, and grace.

Trinity in the 1880s was an intimate, friendly college. It had its cliques but they were less divisive than in some colleges, and freshmen were swiftly absorbed into communal life. A custom which allowed fourth-year men living out of college to order their lunch to be sent up to any room they chose encouraged friendships between younger and older students. The college was administered with a light touch by the Dean, Charles Cannan, and the new President, Dr Henry Woods. The university was still overwhelmingly male, but things were slowly changing. Woods was the first married President of Trinity, and he and his wife Margaret lived up on Boar's Hill, Matthew Arnold country, in the first house on the ridge that would later grow dense with the houses of dons and literati. A poet and novelist herself, Margaret Woods had read Binyon's Arnold essay in *Temple Bar* and took a special interest in his poetry, inviting him to Boar's Hill on several occasions, and introducing him to literary friends. Had a brilliant young Irish scholar from Magdalene College not failed his examination for a classics fellowship at Trinity nine years earlier, Binyon might have had Oscar Wilde as his tutor.[1]

---

[1] See Richard Ellmann, *Oscar Wilde* (New York, 1988), 105.

Like Ghose, he read Greats, the most prestigious of the Honour schools, a four-year course comprising five terms of classical literature followed by seven of ancient history and philosophy. Whereas Ghose complained of being 'made to work so awfully hard by these rapacious Dons, just because I am a scholar' (G151), he wore his scholar's gown lightly and felt an enormous sense of liberation. The years of enforced cramming at St Paul's paid off as he found he had already covered the Classical Moderations syllabus, sailed blithely through his first two years, and gained a First in Mods in March 1890. This gave precious time for poetry and especially for friendship, as he now set about building up the extended family of friends that would be a marked feature of his life. Years later his daughter Nicolete asked him what he did at Oxford and was told, 'I am afraid that I was very sociable.'[2] His family left London for Gloucestershire in 1888 and, although he spent part of the vacations with them, they had less and less contact. He spent time in Wales, hiking in Snowdonia in August 1890, and in Cornwall, his favourite part of England. Despite delicate health, prey to flu and other minor ailments, he was keen on exercise, regularly taking long walks in the country around Oxford and rowing on the Thames, a passion that would last well beyond his Oxford years.

His Trinity friends included F. W. Hall, Mike Furse, Hugh Thursfield, F. D. Mackinnon, Arthur Hirtzel, W. J. Roxburgh, Henry Plumptre, Frederick Lowndes, Hugh Legge, and Arthur Cripps, men destined for a wide variety of careers: Hall became President of St John's, Furse Bishop of St Albans, Mackinnon Lord Justice, Hirtzel Under-Secretary of State for India, and Cripps a poet–missionary in Mashonaland. Robert Routh, his closest friend at Trinity, left this sketch of Binyon as an undergraduate:

The free and friendly life of Trinity was an immediate joy to him—he soon had a wide circle of acquaintances & established close friendships with some . . . he was a scholar & therefore one of a small, marked company; he was quickly known as a poet, & poets were rare & his own personal qualities lent him a natural distinction. He was completely free from any masculine coarseness, was of an almost austere morality, gentle in manner, sensitive & swift in sympathy. Somewhat grave in facial expression, he brightened into gaiety when interested; his approach was friendly, his talk unusually well-informed & salted with a pleasant humour. He walked

---

[2] Nicolete Gray, 'Friends of My Father, Laurence Binyon', *Private Library*, 3rd ser. 8/2 (1985), 81.

lightly, with short, quick steps, dressed usually in grey & affected self-coloured ties, deep green, terra cotta, crushed strawberry, which became him well & a little set him apart. He was always neat. He numbered scholars, athletes & plain men among his many friends.[3]

Another close friend was James Smith, a homesick Scot who roomed on the same landing for three years. Both classicists, they shared a passion for poetry that would shape both their careers. After serving as Chief Inspector of Schools for Scotland, Smith would go on to become Professor of English Literature at Edinburgh University and a lifelong champion of Binyon's poetry. Smith vividly recalled 'his austerity, gentleness & gravity, his deep thrilling voice', his ties and his simply but tastefully furnished rooms, where pride of place went to a print of Botticelli's *Primavera*.[4] Binyon was certainly no full-blown aesthete of the type satirized in Gilbert and Sullivan's *Patience* seven years earlier, but, as the Botticelli and those pastel ties suggest, he was a citizen of Pater's Oxford of the late 1880s, the consummate aesthetic environment, perfectly blending nature and art. Routh recalled:

He would rejoice in the curve of the High, as we walked on a glorious June morning to lectures in the Examination Schools. He would constantly take the short cut through the Old Divinity School, that he might see the tree against the sky, through the tracery of the window, or, he would drag us into Wadham that, from the vantage point of the great copperbeech, we might properly rejoice in the beauty of the garden facade.[5]

Smith remembered Binyon's 'deep, thrilling voice', echoed by Routh in a typical recollection: 'One memory must remain with all who heard him, that of his deep voice charged with restrained emotion, as in the dim loveliness of the candle-lit chapel he read: ' "O my son Absalom, my son Absalom; would God I had died for thee, O Absalom, my son, my son." '[6]

Binyon's St Paul's nickname, 'the Bard', stuck. He founded a small Trinity society called the Fruit Club, which met on Sunday mornings, while the faithful were in the college chapel, to eat fruit, drink milk, and read poetry, a diet which looks back to the honey-dew-fed, milk-drinking poet in 'Kubla Khan' rather than forward to Gandhi. Within weeks of his arrival, his first poem appeared in

---

[3] 'R.L.B.', memoir of LB, AMS, n.d. [1945], 4 pp., p. 1.
[4] J. C. Smith to CMB, ALs, 18 July 1944, 9 Feb. 1945.
[5] 'R.L.B.', 3.   [6] Ibid.

the November 1888 *Oxford Magazine*, 'The Garden of Criticism', an accomplished parody of Swinburne's 'The Garden of Proserpine'. Binyon omitted it from his *Collected Poems*—a pity since it displays a comic brio missing in his published canon yet characteristic, in certain moods and ambiences, of the man himself. This was no mere undergraduate *jeu d'esprit*, however, but a parodic continuation of his Arnold essay in *Temple Bar* two months earlier, in which he argued that Arnold's austere poetry was lost on a public taste blunted by Victorian word-music:

Tennyson has accustomed us to such elaborate richness and sumptuousness that any less ornate writer strikes us as homely after his luxury of language; Browning has imbued his readers with his passion for originality, too often, in his own case, degenerating into oddness; Swinburne has infected many of us with the delirious mannerisms of his fascinating music. What wonder then if the adorers of these gorgeous idols found little to delight them in the pale beauty, bathed in moonlight air, of Matthew Arnold's muse of marble?[7]

Or, as he puts it in 'The Garden of Criticism':

> From too much love of Browning,
>   From Tennyson she rose,
> And sense in music drowning,
>   In sound she seeks repose.
> Yet joys sometimes to know it,
>   And is not slow to show it,
> That even the heavenliest poet
>   Sinks somewhere safe to prose.
>
> Then rhyme shall rule o'er reason,
>   And Swinburne over Time,
> And panting poets seize on
>   Each continent and clime;
> Aching alliteration,
>   Impotent indignation,
> Eternal iteration,
>   Wrapt in eternal rhyme.[8]

Binyon's reputation as the most promising poet of his generation at Oxford was cemented by two signal achievements in his second year. In May 1890 he arranged for Basil Blackwell in Broad Street

[7] 'Matthew Arnold's Poetry', 107.
[8] 'The Garden of Criticism (with Humble Apologies to "The Garden of Proserpine")', *Oxford Magazine*, 21 Nov. 1888, 107.

to publish *Primavera*, a small book of poems by Ghose, Phillips, Cripps, and himself, named after the Botticelli print in his rooms at Trinity. Praised by Oscar Wilde, who archly suggested 'undergraduates might read it with advantage during lecture-hours',[9] the slim volume was an immediate success, swiftly running into a second edition. Within days, as if timed to boost sales as well as his own celebrity, Binyon won the prestigious Newdigate Prize for Poetry with his poem *Persephone*. He was elated, not least because he was emulating Arnold, who had also won his school's poetry prize and then the Newdigate. 'It was the only time I ever saw him excited,' Smith recalled. 'The excitement did not show in his manner or speech, but in two red spots on his cheeks, a thing I never saw in him either before or after.'[10] He had his excitement well under control when he recited *Persephone* under the painted sky of Wren's Sheldonian Theatre on 25 June, an Encaenia Day dubbed by the press 'Stanley's year' because the African explorer appeared to receive his honorary degree.[11]

As well as friendships, Binyon found at Oxford the intellectual stimulation lacking at St Paul's. He was a keen member of the Gryphon Club, a Trinity debating society comprising twenty students and dons who met in members' rooms on a rota basis. The Club's minute book reveals that, as at St Paul's, Binyon belonged to the Society's rather beleaguered radical wing. In January 1891 he was one of only three who spoke for the motion 'That it is the opinion of this House that the principle of nationality is pernicious'. The motion was lost, as was that Binyon himself had proposed two months earlier, 'That this House considers that the state of art in England is far from satisfactory'.[12] One of the members who spoke for Binyon's motion was George Calderon. In Gryphon Club photographs Binyon, only a year younger, looks a naïve teenager beside the lounging Calderon, who wears his gown and waxed moustache with all the panache of his Spanish ancestry. Binyon was probably rather in awe of the swashbuckling scholar–athlete described by one contemporary as the 'most popular man in the college',[13] but in the midst of an adventurous life as lawyer,

[9] *Pall Mall Gazette*, 24 May 1890, 3.   [10] ALs to CMB, 18 July 1904.
[11] See 'The Encaenia at Oxford', *The Times*, 26 June 1890, 8.
[12] Entries for 25 Jan. 1891 and 9 Nov. 1890, Debating Society Minute Book, AMS, Trinity College Archives, n.pag.
[13] Qtd. Percy Lubbock, *George Calderon: A Sketch from Memory* (London, 1921), 39.

traveller, folklorist, political activist, and dramatist Calderon would later join him at the British Museum and become a close friend. After his death in action at Gallipoli in 1915 his body was never found, and it was to this pristine, semi-mythic Oxford that Binyon restored his 'friend dear and dead':

> By Oxford towers and streams
> Who shone among us all
> In body and in brain so bold?
> ('In Memory of George Calderon', CPi.253)

FITZROY

Socially, emotionally, and intellectually, Binyon's life was centred in Oxford, but this did not mean that he lost touch with London, quite the reverse. Friendships formed at Oxford fed into a wider network of friendships which drew him into the fringes of the London avant-garde two years before he returned permanently to the capital in 1892.

Within weeks of arriving in Oxford he met another young poet, Lionel Johnson. Two years older yet looking like an ethereal child, Johnson was an enigmatic presence at Oxford, a brilliant scholar, bookish and aloof, yet already prey to the insomniac drinking that would see him dead within fourteen years. Binyon described him as 'curiously small and neat. . . . [H]is nervous mouth, the pallor of his face, the intent eyes, as of one who never slept, the air of dominating intellect and learning combined with the extreme youthfulness of his person, made a singular impression' (MG 11). The young poets took an interest in each other's work. They shared an admiration for Arnold and Whitman and a deep love of Cornwall, Johnson dedicating his 1892 lyric 'Cadgwith' to Binyon. Both had found their parents' Anglicanism sterile and both had had some contact with Eastern philosophy. Johnson had flirted with a theosophized form of Buddhism at Westminster School before deciding he was 'too essentially Western to appreciate Buddhism',[14] whereas Binyon was perhaps more fortunate in having Ghose rather than Madame Blavatsky as mediator. While Johnson was

---

[14] Ian Fletcher, Introduction, *The Complete Poems of Lionel Johnson* (London, 1953) p. xx.

now on the road to the Catholicism he would convert to in 1891,
he kept an open mind.

In Johnson's New College rooms towards the end of his first term
he met a group of men who would be his bridge between Oxford
and literary and artistic London. Arthur Galton, a 36-year-old
senior student at New College, was an essayist, occasional poet,
and author of a book on contemporary British poetry. An austere,
ambitious man, he was a veteran of the Victorian religious wars,
but was now swimming against the tide of the 1880s and 1890s.
Raised an Anglican, he had converted to Roman Catholicism at
Cambridge in 1875, trained for the priesthood, then turned violently anti-Catholic. Going in the opposite direction from friends
like Johnson, he would later take Anglican Orders. When Binyon
met him at Oxford he was still working his way through this
spiritual crisis, deep in 'the work of reconstruction' through a study
of the classics inspired by Matthew Arnold, whose writings had
saved him 'from leaving the papal Church a dulled and blank
materialist, thoroughly and violently anti-Christian'.[15] So steeped in
Arnold that Pound later nicknamed him 'Mat-Mat', Galton had
corresponded with his revered master since 1887 and was bereft at
his sudden death. He was delighted to befriend Binyon, whose
Temple Bar essay was, he wrote, 'the only essay which I liked of all
the innumerable reviews which I tried to read'.[16] In December 1888
he visited Arnold's widow and reported: 'You'll be glad to know
that Mrs Arnold was pleased & comforted by your essay.'[17]

Through Johnson Binyon also met Herbert Horne, one of the
most remarkable of the multitalented all-rounders inspired by
William Morris. Aged 23, poet, essayist, architect, designer,
typographer, art collector, and art historian, he was in many re-
spects the epitome of the complexly inwoven London world Binyon
would enter after Oxford. He looked suitably *fin de siècle*, as
Binyon later recalled: 'He was then of remarkable appearance, with
jet black hair, one wisp of which fell over a finely shaped forehead,

[15] *Rome and Romanizing: Some Experiences and a Warning* (London, 1900), 39,
38. See also Verna Coleman, *The Last Exquisite: A Portrait of Frederic Manning*
(Melbourne, 1990), 19.
[16] ALs to LB, 3 Dec. [1888]. For 'Mat-Mat' see Pound, *Ezra Pound and Dorothy
Shakespear: Their Letters 1909–1914*, ed. Omar Pound and A. Walton Litz (London, 1984), 344.
[17] ALs to LB, Dec. 1888.

dark eyes & a complexion of extreme pallor heightened by the full red of sensuous lips.'[18]

Through Horne Binyon met two equally remarkable Londoners of the older generation, Arthur Mackmurdo and Selwyn Image. As well as being an innovative architect, Mackmurdo was also one of the pioneers of modern design, anticipating Art Nouveau motifs in book and furniture design, writer, editor, Arts and Crafts theorist and polemicist.[19] Equally versatile if less gifted, Image was a stained-glass artist, designer, essayist, and poet, and future Master of the Art Workers' Guild and Slade Professor at Oxford. A warm, avuncular man who emerges from autobiographies of the period as one of the best-loved men in London, he helped and encouraged the young poet. He created a distinctive woodcut design of interwoven leaves and flowers for the cover and title page of *Primavera*, which was cut by William Morris's associate Emery Walker. Binyon admired everything from 'the wisdom and sweetness of his nature' to his 'beautiful penmanship'. 'There was', he recalled years later, 'choiceness and a sense of beauty in all he wrote, said, and produced.'[20] As this suggests, what drew Binyon to these artist–craftsmen and became the core of his own aesthetic was their holistic approach to art, which they conceived not as a retreat from the banality of quotidian life but as permeating and transforming its every aspect, from handwriting and typography to architecture and city planning.

In 1882 Mackmurdo had founded the first of the Arts and Crafts guilds, the Century Guild, an association of artists and craftsmen dedicated to dismantling class-bound Victorian barriers between fine and applied arts, restoring the crafts 'to their rightful place beside painting and sculpture', and making art 'a thing of our century, and of the people'.[21] Image and Horne were founder

---

[18] 'Italy & Italian Art', AMS lecture, n.d. [*c*.1935], n.pag. For Horne's career, see Ian Fletcher, *Rediscovering Herbert Horne: Poet, Architect, Typographer, Art Historian* (Greensboro, GA, 1990).

[19] See Nikolaus Pevsner, 'Arthur H. Mackmurdo: A Pioneer Designer', *Studies in Art, Architecture and Design*, 2 vols. (London, 1968), ii. 132–40.

[20] LB, 'Selwyn Image', *DNB* (1922–30), 445.

[21] Publisher's note, *Century Guild Hobby Horse*, 2/6 (April 1887), n.pag. For a contemporary view, see Aymer Vallance, 'Mr. Arthur H. Mackmurdo and the Century Guild', *Studio*, Apr. 1899, 183–92; on the guilds, see Gillian Naylor, *The Arts and Crafts Movement: A Study of its Sources, Ideals and Influence on Design Theory* (London, 1971), 115–20.

members, and it was they who invited Binyon to his first Guild meeting at its abode at 28 Southampton Street in spring 1899. Horne was editor of the *Century Guild Hobby Horse*, founded by Mackmurdo in 1884 as a forum for Century Guild ideas. Printed on handmade rag paper with an Image cover, the *Hobby Horse* was conceived as a 'total art' production, the first and most complete of its kind in England, described by one scholar as 'perhaps the most handsome magazine of its kind ever published'.[22] It was widely influential, both on later periodicals and private presses, inspiring Morris's Kelmscott Press, founded in 1890, and as a major channel for avant-garde aesthetic and literary ideas. Galton had regularly contributed poems and essays since 1886, Johnson since 1888. On the evidence of his Arnold essay, Galton urged Binyon to contribute prose as well as poetry, and his first essay appeared in April 1890, 'On Certain Confusions of Modern Life, Especially in Literature', a paper he had read to the Gryphon Club, including an attack on 'specialism' which chimed with *Hobby Horse* eclecticism.[23] His poems appeared fairly regularly from then on, alongside the work of such diverse poets as Johnson, Dowson, Horne, Symonds, 'Michael Field', and Wilfrid Scawen Blunt. Browsing through the magazine's heavy pages is the best way to get the flavour of the late Pre-Raphaelite Arts and Crafts milieu into which Binyon found himself drawn. It is no coincidence that, apart from its near silence on Eastern art, the *Hobby Horse* championed many of the art forms, movements, and artists which would figure largely in Binyon's critical writing.

In October 1889 Mackmurdo purchased for himself and his Century Guild collaborators a large Adam-period house at 20 Fitzroy Street in London's radical, down-at-heel Latin Quarter just west of Tottenham Court Road. A typical Fitzrovia rabbit warren of a house, the ground floor housed a Guild workshop, while the upper floors provided either studios or accommodation for Horne, Galton, Image, Johnson, and the artist T. Hope McLachlan. One of the first to move in after leaving Oxford was Galton, who wrote to Binyon in January 1890 inviting him to stay in the spare room and

[22] Peter Frost, 'The Century Guild Hobby Horse and its Founders', *Book Collector*, 27 (1978), 56. See also Carl Beckson, *London in the 1890s: A Cultural History* (New York, 1992), 237–41. For Horne's editorship, see Fletcher, *Herbert Horne* 59–90.

[23] *Hobby Horse*, NS, 18 (Apr. 1890), 58–68.

share their vegetarian food. Binyon took up the offer on several occasions over the next two years, sometimes using Galton's rooms when he was away, and so found himself in one of the most exciting environments in London. Known variously as Whiteladies, Hobby Horse House, the Fitzroy Settlement or simply Fitzroy, this protean household was one of the great bohemian centres of the 1890s, described by Victor Plarr, who later took over Galton's quarters, as a 'sacred house, about which a volume might be written', the epicentre of 'a movement, an influence, a glory'.[24] Several visits coincided with the 'Hobby Horse Evenings', whose participants comprised a Who's Who of the London avant-garde, ranging from artists such as Walter Crane, Walter Sickert, Frank Brangwyn, Roger Fry, and William Rothenstein to writers such as Shaw, Dowson, Arthur Symons, John Gray, Richard Le Gallienne, and Ernest Rhys.[25] Among many others, it was here that Binyon first met, on the same evening, Wilde and Yeats. Wilde held forth on the incursions of women and predicted that they would soon be wearing beards. Forty years later Binyon recalled:

Wilde's talk was better than his writing. He talked and the rest of us listened. But I was attracted more by a young man who said little, and seemed mostly lost in a dream. He was tall and slim, with a pale face and black hair. This was William Butler Yeats, who was then unknown, but who had just published his first book of poems.[26]

From 1890 onwards, then, Binyon lived an amphibious life as Oxford undergraduate and fringe member of Fitzrovian Bohemia. These London friendships enriched his sense of continuity with Oxford's High Victorian past. Galton had corresponded with Arnold, Mackmurdo and Image were disciples of Ruskin, and all admired Trinity's most famous alumnus, Cardinal Newman, who died in 1890 during Binyon's second year. Another legendary Oxford figure was still very much alive. The year Binyon arrived at Oxford, 1888, the third edition of Walter Pater's book *The Renaissance*, one of the key texts of the *fin de siècle*, appeared with a slightly modified version of its controversial Conclusion restored. Binyon admired this and Pater's philosophical novel *Marius the*

[24] *Ernest Dowson 1888–1897: Reminiscences, Unpublished Letters and Marginalia* (London, 1914), 67–8.

[25] Plarr, 68; Fletcher, *Johnson*, 140–1.

[26] 'English Poetry & Drama of To-Day and To-Morrow', *Studies in English Literature* (Tokyo), 10 (Jan. 1930), 1–2.

Epicurean (1885). Johnson and Horne were convinced Paterians, while Galton's letters to Binyon suggest the mingled admiration and unease Pater inspired in a man steeped in Arnold. Pater was a fascinating disease, energizing in homeopathic doses but potentially lethal, Arnold the antidote to be kept close at hand:

I suppose the taste for Pater is really a fascination & a disease we catch from the morbid atmosphere round us. I do not think it will do me any hurt; & it will not harm you, as long as you maintain the simple & healthy instincts which you reveal in your Arnold essay. But I can understand Pater doing harm to certain natures. At the same time, Pater is inward, he has a keen sense for spiritual things; & that is not common in this reign of the mammon of unrighteousness.[27]

Binyon was able to test myth against reality when Pater invited him to dine with him 'quite quietly' in his austere panelled rooms at Brasenose on 24 March 1892.[28] He later recalled feeling 'very much honoured by being asked by such a man when I was a boy.... I think I dined with him twice, & he talked delightfully to me & the one other man there. He also gave me a little box of incense our talk having chanced on old-fashioned scents, gums & spices.'[29] Unusually for a man of the mauve decade, Binyon disliked incense, but that little box remained one of his few treasured possessions, along with subtler gifts of influence.

May 1890 saw another crucial meeting when Margaret Woods invited Binyon to dinner at Boar's Hill to meet a man in a quite different mould, the poet Robert Bridges. Aged 45 and as yet not well known, Bridges had a personal intensity, leonine physical presence, and encyclopaedic knowledge of poetry that impressed him deeply. When Bridges and his wife invited him to stay over-night in their eighteenth-century manor-house at Yattendon, in preparation he read Bridges's *Shorter Poems*, which had just come out, but was more impressed by his highly technical tract *Milton's Prosody*, and in an exchange of letters their friendship bloomed out of a shared interest in metrics and prosodic experimentation.

It was probably this that prompted Bridges on Binyon's first visit to Yattendon several weeks later to introduce him, albeit posthumously, to a greater poet than either of them, his friend Gerard Manley Hopkins, who had died the year before. That evening

[27] ALs, 9 Jan. 1889.   [28] Pater, visiting card, n.d. [Mar. 1892].
[29] ALs to CMB, postmarked 23 May 1903.

Bridges read aloud from Hopkins's manuscripts, which were in his care and would remain unpublished until 1918. 'Among the poems I then heard were one or two of the "tragic" sonnets, which greatly impressed me,' Binyon recalled in 1939. 'Manifestly this unknown poet who had never published was a poet of extraordinary originality, utterly unlike any other.'[30] Bridges explained how Hopkins 'had invented a new prosody for English verse', measured by stresses rather than syllables. This caught Binyon's imagination, as 'it seemed to promise scope for fresh effects and for admitting a fresh kind of matter into verse'.[31] Within weeks he was sending Bridges tentative experiments in natural stress and receiving highly technical replies. From Binyon's point of view, it is hard to imagine anything more valuable than the craftsman–apprentice correspondence that now ensued. Binyon took Bridges as his model of a dedicated, fiercely independent poet, while Bridges had high hopes for his young protégé, who was blessed with 'good feeling, a true mind and a wonderful visual memory'.[32]

PRIMAVERA

In this welter of new friendships, Binyon did not lose touch with either Stephen Phillips or Ghose. He occasionally saw Phillips in London and when Benson's company performed at Oxford. He and Ghose continued to discuss poetry and planned to write an Indian 'tale' together, and of course the three friends collaborated, along with Arthur Cripps, in the publication of *Primavera* in Trinity term 1890. With its brown paper wrappers and delicate Image design, *Primavera* is, as Wilde remarked, 'charmingly "got up"'. Its forty-one pages contain sixteen poems almost equally shared between the four poets. 'One of the tiniest modest booklets that ever adventured into a world of critics,' as the *Athenaeum* described it in a generous review,[33] the shilling volume was received with surprising kindness by that carnivorous world. Even the *Cambridge Review* laid aside

---

[30] 'Gerard Hopkins and His Influence', *University of Toronto Quarterly*, 8 (Jan. 1939), 264.

[31] 'Hopkins', 264.

[32] Qtd. Catherine Phillips, *Robert Bridges: A Biography* (Oxford, 1992), 170.

[33] *Athenaeum*, 21 June 1890, 796.

intervarsity rivalry to conclude, 'Oxford may very well be proud of them.'[34]

The fact that the publication of *Primavera* and the announcement of Binyon's poem *Persephone* winning the Newdigate prize came within days of each other in early May was fortuitous but apt. *Persephone* and Binyon's lyrics in *Primavera* both express in different ways Binyon's continuing allegiance to Matthew Arnold. In his *Temple Bar* essay, Binyon had celebrated Arnold's 'Greek . . . sense of form', the equilibrium he achieved between the competing claims of subject matter and self-expression, architectonic form and local texture.[35] Behind this lay Arnold's preface to his 1853 *Poems* and its call for a self-effacing, classically-inspired poetry which eschews mannerist imagery and 'occasional bursts of fine writing' for 'total impression'.[36] Within its modest ambit *Persephone* fulfils these criteria, telling its story swiftly and succinctly, building momentum by playing off open against closed heroic couplets, through its emphasis on verbs, often strategically postponed to line-ends in order to garner the double emphasis of rhyme and iambic stress, and by emulating Arnold's notoriously bland adjectives, which Binyon saw as agents in the service of 'truth and directness' in contrast to Tennysonian 'magic of manufacture' word-painting.

Binyon's poems in *Primavera* bring similar concerns to bear on the lyric. Through careful selection the four quite different poets sought to submerge their poetic identities in an ensemble performance with shared vocabulary and images in a lyric equivalent of the self-effacement Arnold prescribed for narrative poetry. The ideal striven for is the impersonal, transparent singing voice of the Elizabethan lyricists Binyon and Ghose admired. Here is Binyon's 'Testamentum Amoris', praised by Wilde for catching 'the sweet echoes that sleep in the sonnets of Shakespeare':

> I cannot raise my eyelids up from sleep,
> But I am visited with thoughts of you;
> Slumber has no refreshment half so deep
> As the sweet morn, that wakes my heart anew.

---

[34] *Cambridge Review* (Supplement), 29 May 1890, p. lxxxviii.
[35] 'Matthew Arnold's Poetry', 108.
[36] *The Complete Prose Works of Matthew Arnold*, ed. R. H. Super, 11 vols. (Ann Arbor, 1960–77), i. 7–8.

I cannot put away life's trivial care,
But you straightway steal on me with delight;
My purest moments are your mirror fair;
My deepest thought finds you the truth most bright.

You are the lovely regent of my mind,
The constant sky to my unresting sea;
Yet, since 'tis you that rule me, I but find
A finer freedom in such tyranny.

Were the world's anxious kingdoms governed so,
Lost were their wrongs, and vanished half their woe.
(*CP*i.5)

Even the residual self of this purely conventional 'I' has evaporated
from Binyon's paean 'O Summer Sun!':

O summer sun, O moving trees!
O cheerful human noise, O busy glittering street!
What hour shall Fate in all the future find,
Or what delights, ever to equal these:
Only to taste the warmth, the light, the wind,
Only to be alive, and feel that life is sweet?
(*CP*i.11)

The early poem 'Psyche', written at St Paul's, begins with the
same lyric weightlessness.[37] The poet and art historian John
Addington Symonds, writing to Galton from Venice, praised
Binyon as 'very remarkable indeed' and remarked about this
'interesting poem': 'I don't seem to catch the note of a woman in it
though. It has the tone of having been written about a friend or an
abstraction.'[38] There was perhaps a touch of wishful thinking here
from a man who three months later would send Binyon his photograph, request one in return, and later send him his homosexual
rhapsody *In the Key of Blue*. He was surely right about the 'abstraction', however, for the girl is the poet–lover's muse, the real
subject of *Primavera*. Phillips's poem 'No Muse will I invoke; for
she is fled' begins as a typical piece of Victorian Hellenism, a lament
for the muse exiled from the Greek landscape she used to inspirit,
but modulates into something closer to the spirit of the late 1880s,
covertly celebrating this wan, indoor *fin de siècle* muse too anaemic

---

[37] *Primavera* (Oxford, 1890), 23.
[38] 13 May 1890, *The Letters of John Addington Symonds*, ed. Herbert M.
Schueller and Robert L. Peters, 3 vols. (Detroit, 1969), iii. 461.

to inspire anything but nostalgic dreams: 'Oh, let her dream; still lovely is her sigh: | Oh, rouse her not, or she shall surely die.'[39] 'Psyche' is Binyon's antiphonal reply, affirming that the muse 'can still conceive' and equating her redemptive power with the soul's capacity for self-transcendence.

The lyric simplicity of these poems was much admired at Fitzroy. In the *Hobby Horse* Image diagnosed in *Primavera* 'a healthy and scholarly reaction' against the 'overwrought and oppressive sensuousness' of Swinburnian verse.[40] Johnson agreed:

The most immediate and evident distinction of these poems is their simplicity. . . . But the authors of *Primavera* do not deal with very simple things: their subjects are very grave and high; Youth, and Love, and Love's loss, and Death, and Nature. . . . In this little book these matters are presented with a singular dignity: and further, with a singular sincerity. . . . But they are far from being pleasant moralists merely: their verse is full of life, of colour, and of natural magic.[41]

The copy of *Primavera* Binyon gave Johnson, now in the Huntington Library in California, is a fascinating document in its own right. Johnson copied into it five poems by Dowson, including early versions of 'Nuns of the Perpetual Adoration', 'Amor umbratilis', and 'Non sum qualis eram bonae sub regno Cynarae', which were published in the *Hobby Horse* months later. The flyleaf carries an unpublished poem by Johnson addressed to Binyon and Ghose. It opens with the question with which Binyon's Arnold essay begins, whether the blunted taste of late Victorian England can still appreciate uncontorted verse:

> Now is there any love at all
> In all England left, for simple song?
> Let all such lovers hear your call:
> You have a strain, shall charm them long.

Johnson sees their poems as a return to an earlier period of lyric grace, when 'In ancient England . . . | Minstrels sang beneath a rising sun', in contrast to 'our poor England, wild with noise'. The poem ends with a five-stanza benediction on the two poets, who, unlike Johnson, were fortunate enough to have two more years at Oxford, 'Arnold's dearest home'.

---

[39] *Primavera*, 4. [40] *Century Guild Hobby Horse* 5/19 (July 1890), 119.
[41] *Church Reformer* 9/8 (Aug. 1890), 185.

And fair befall you both! And may
Your friendship hold all grace in store:
Friends in one art; and, day by day,
True sons of Arnold's, more and more.[42]

'Frost at Midnight', *Endymion*, and 'Ode to the West Wind' all haunt Binyon's most ambitious poem in the volume, 'Youth', but Galton recognized the mood uniting its shifting ventriloquistic voices: 'I cannot praise "Youth" more, than by saying it has got closer to Matthew Arnold's way than anything else in the volume; indeed I doubt whether Matthew Arnold himself could improve the greater part of it.'[43] In reality, rather than the beneficent influence Johnson and Galton suggest, Arnold haunts the poem rather than inspirits it, undermining its youthful *joie de vivre* in the guise of the prematurely aged authorial voice. In the *Academy* Symonds noted that 'Youth' 'dwells less on the rapture of youth than on its sadness', adding in a letter to Binyon that he had been 'struck with the gravity, the seeking (as it were) after the virtues of maturity, in what were avowedly young poems'.[44]

Ghose, Arnold's other 'true son', was equally afflicted, but within months of *Primavera*'s appearance he repudiated their poetic father and urged Binyon to do the same:

Do you aspire to be another 'Matthew', or why do I see in you these fits of puritanical gloom? But your name is not Matthew. . . . Your name is Laurence, a beautiful pagan name . . . and you should be pagan and nothing else; like Stephen, that adorable and wonderful being, and like my own poor self. (G243)

During his second year at Christ Church Ghose had encountered problems with his studies and spent an increasing amount of time in London. By March 1890 debts and dwindling remittances from his father had convinced him that he should leave Oxford and find a post in the Civil Service or the British Museum in order to secure his position in England. Despite Binyon's attempts at dissuasion and Christ Church's offer to increase his scholarship by £25, he failed to return to Oxford for Trinity term. Used to monopolizing Binyon's friendship at St Paul's, he had had difficulty coming to

---

[42] Book 42040, Rare Books Department, Huntington Library, San Marino, California.
[43] ALs, 9 May 1890.
[44] *Academy*, 9 Aug. 1890, 104; ALs to LB, 21 Aug. 1890.

terms with the 'change' that had come over him at Oxford, with his passion for 'athletic and other pursuits' (G195). 'You are quite right, I think, to plunge into society at Oxford, if you take pleasure in it,' he wrote from London in March 1899. 'Of course, being as you are so prodigally blest with friends, you cannot imagine my isolation' (G199–200).

This isolation ended dramatically when Binyon introduced him to Fitzroy. At the Hobby Horse evenings he met many literary figures, including the poet Ernest Dowson, who admired 'the beautiful lotus-eyed Ghose'.[45] After the publication of *Primavera* he enjoyed a brief celebrity in literary London as, in Dowson's words, 'Ghose the Primavera poet: a divinely mad person!'[46] He was later on the fringes of the Rhymers Club, which met at Fitzroy before moving to the Cheshire Cheese in Fleet Street, and his name appeared on the provisional list of contributors to *The Book of the Rhymers Club* in June 1891.[47] The most important friendship enjoined at Fitzroy, however, was with Oscar Wilde, whom he probably first met in Binyon's company. Wilde singled Ghose out for special praise in his review of *Primavera* in the *Pall Mall Gazette*, written at a time when he had given up regular reviewing to complete *Dorian Gray*, published in the July issue of *Lippincott's Monthly Magazine*. During the summer Wilde loomed large in Ghose's letters to Binyon. On 28 August he wrote defensively:

> You mustn't say anything bad of Oscar. Oscar has taken an immense liking to me; and now I know him well I love him very much. He is a wonderful and charming being. You are inclined to think him superficial, I know. You should know him as I do. . . . Oscar is . . . one of the most wonderful personalities of our age. (G238)

His letters increasingly lapsed into Wildean pastiche: 'I look upon life from an entirely artistic point of view. Badness is a colour as distinct as goodness. Both types should be preserved and encouraged. . . . And now, will you be a dear boy and tolerate my wickedness, as I tolerate your goodness?' (G242)

One of the symptoms of this was a changed attitude to the 'Hobby Horse people', who, from his new *l'art pour l'art* perspec-

---

[45] Letter to Arthur Moore, 16–17 Sept. 1890, letter 118, *Letters of Ernest Dowson*, ed. Desmond Flower and Henry Maas (London, 1967), 167.

[46] Letter to Charles Sayle, c.25 Nov. 1890, letter 128, *Letters*, 177.

[47] See Dowson's letter to Victor Plarr, c.9 June 1891, letter 152, *Letters*, 202–3.

tive, dwindled into 'useful people, but very *small* people' overburdened with social theories of art (G238). 'I have certainly changed,' he wrote to Binyon.

A great revulsion of feeling has taken place in me. I feel the absolute impotence of theorizing eternally about art and life—in short of the craze of our worthy friends of the 'Hobby Horse'. . . . Let me have *life*, the expression of my own personality and passions; and *thought*, too, but thought, springing from these, not a thing apart from them. I feel the danger there is of becoming a mere abstract thing like our friend Johnson . . . without a touch of that unique and glorious thing, 'Personality'. But what am I saying? Danger? Alas, the danger is just the other way; I am brimming with youth and passion, sweet and dangerous things; how sweet and dangerous those only know who yield themselves wholly to their crimson fascination! (G248)

He chose Wilde and Phillips, the charismatic 'pagan' actor, as exemplars of 'Personality' to set against the ethereal, haunted Johnson and, implicitly, Binyon himself (G243). 'I confess', he wrote on 13 July, 'I should like to see you descend sometimes from the calm heights which you inhabit, and write something inspired with more passion and *ordinary human nature*!' (G230). A month later he remarked 'how strangely calm and undemonstrative' Binyon was: 'I am sometimes inclined to look upon you as a kind of Ariel, a beautiful spirit indeed, but hardly human; without that "relish of passion", that frailty which is "the touch of nature making the whole world kin"' (G233–4). On 3 September, in his new Wildean dialect:

You are a dear boy, but too good, far too good for this world of ours. . . . Perfection, my dear Laurence, is a dangerous virtue. . . . That is the only fault I find in your character and in your poems; you are too perfect, too reasonable, too sinless, and on that account in danger of being a little cold. (G239)

Ghose thought Binyon too serene, too ascetic and chaste to understand his 'wild adorations'. The man who once admired Binyon's 'seraphic air' and prayed 'for calm, for a self-centred collected soul', 'to be an ascetic and think to eternity', now decried these qualities in Binyon. On 4 August he attacked the almost Buddhist sense of detachment expressed in one of Binyon's draft poems:

there is a beautiful sweetness and tenderness in all you write. But why do you wish so much to come to such a state of self-content, as to be able

> To exact no joy from any hour
> Nor love from any friend.

An unenviable state surely. For how much of love can you feel without
longing? Not much, I think. At least it is only a few rare and beautiful
souls, who are rich enough in themselves to afford to give without asking
to receive back again; and these are never poets. (G233)

Ghose had a real point. Admirable as these traits may be in a saint,
they present special problems for a poet, as Binyon would spend a
lifetime discovering. Hence Ghose's marvellously *fin de siècle*,
Paterian/Wildean advice, exhorting Binyon to live up to his 'beautiful pagan name' and 'be pagan and nothing else'. They should
slough off Arnold, he argued, in favour of a return to their 'old
admiration' for the highly developed, self-expressive poetic personalities of Byron, Shelley, and Keats. 'Be true to your real self', he
urged (G248). Good counsel, but the question facing Binyon, like
Ghose himself, was that which eventually confronts all young
poets: what exactly was his true self?

3   A BM Era

After his first in Moderations in 1890, Binyon's tutors at Trinity were disappointed that he took only a second in Greats in his final term, but he left Oxford in June 1892 with what few firsts have time to garner, a total Oxford education. Shortly after going down he wrote to Margaret Woods: 'It is terrible leaving Oxford: though at the same time one feels such a life can't go on forever. . . . My Oxford life certainly causes me no regrets, not even for my second (but please don't tell the President that). I could hardly have enjoyed it more: & I have made friendships that I prize.'[1]

Ghose had aroused in him a desire to go to India and, lacking any financial resources, he briefly flirted with the idea of the Indian Civil Service, but wisely, given his natural distaste for imperialism, he decided instead to apply for a vacancy in the Department of Prints and Drawings at the British Museum. Despite poor salaries, competition for posts in the Museum was intense. His references came from Woods and R. W. Raper of Trinity, and Robert Bridges. Raper called Binyon 'a born poet & artist', adding donnishly: 'if I were appointing to a post of this kind I sh^d as soon think of rejecting Pallas Athene, if she presented herself in a recognizable shape, as of not taking a man of Mr. Binyon's gifts.'[2] (Raper was over-sanguine about Athene's chances: women were not employed as anything other than charwomen, housemaids, and 'Ladies Attendants' until the manpower shortages of the First World War.) Bridges stressed Binyon's 'real enthusiasm and natural turn for art': 'I have been served several portrait heads by him, which, besides the knack of catching a likeness, show a feeling for drawing and modelling, which—if he sh^d never make any other use of it—seem

---

[1] ALs to Margaret Woods, 8 Sept. 1892, MS Eng. lett. d. 183, fos. 21–2, Bodleian Library, Oxford.
[2] Testimonial, 8 Oct. 1892, Binyon Application Papers, Central Archives, British Museum (hereafter BM).

to warrant that he w^d have a trustworthy discrimination of the work of others, and become a skilful judge.'[3]

Binyon had met both Sidney Colvin, the immensely cultured Keeper of Prints and Drawings, and his assistant Lionel Cust, probably through Image or Horne, both Print Room habitués. Friends treated his appointment as a formality. Symonds wrote in December saying Colvin and Cust were looking forward to him joining them in the Print Room, the 'pleasantest department of that huge place'.[4] There was a problem, however. With its important collection of German woodcuts, the Department required good German, a language he had not studied. In July Bridges had blithely assured him it could be mastered in three months and offered to coach him.[5] In November, accompanied by Routh, he went to Dresden to study the language and familiarize himself with German prints in the Dresden Museum. Despite this, in the competitive Civil Service examinations which ran for four days from 21 to 24 February he was narrowly pipped into second place by the superior German of a man he had known at Oxford, Campbell Dodgson, a close friend of Johnson's at Westminster and New College. He consoled himself by travelling throughout the spring and early summer in Holland, Spain, and Italy, and returned in June to find himself nominated for a post in the Museum's Department of Printed Books. This time he came top in the examination and began work on 9 September as a Second Class Assistant at a annual salary of £120.

And so what Ezra Pound was to dub a 'British Museum era' began for Binyon not among the watercolours and etchings of the Print Room but in and around the Reading Room, the great circular chamber under Sydney Smirke's blue, white, and gold dome.[6] Opened in 1857, it had already become the stuff of myth, less a library than a state of mind. Ernest Rhys, a Fitzroy regular who had co-authored a review of *Primavera* with Horne, found it 'the most extraordinary club in the world, where one met poets and lunatics, beggars and literary bigwigs'.[7] The 1893 vintage ranged from Samuel Butler and Shaw to Yeats and the Russian anarchist Prince

[3] Testimonial, 10 Oct. 1892, BM.

[4] ALs, 30 Dec. 1892, MS Symonds Letters, Harry Ransom Humanities Research Centre, Austin, Texas (hereafter HRC).

[5] ALs, 31 July 1892.   [6] Pound, *The Cantos* (London, 1975), 80/506.

[7] *Wales England Wed: An Autobiography* (London, 1940), 194.

Kropotkin.[8] The great Victorian icon was changing. Binyon's arrival coincided with the installation of incandescent lamps above
every desk, shelving space had recently been trebled by the introduction of sliding presses, and the transition from the old handwrit-
ten catalogue to the new print catalogue was well under way.[9]
It was only eighteen years since the Reading Room's infamously
fetid atmosphere had been alleviated by moving the steam pipes
from the outside of the windows to the inside, but to some the
improvement was marginal. Rhys complained to Binyon about the
'queer fusty odour that seemed to come partly from the old calf
bindings of the books on the reference shelves, partly from the
human cloth-bindings of the habitués of the room, some of whom,
poor things, could not afford hot baths.' 'Ah well,' came Binyon's
riposte, 'you see it is eighteenth-century air, it has never been
moved since then.'[10]

Far from suffering from the endemic snobbishness of senior
staff that had afflicted Edmund Gosse in the Department two
decades earlier, Binyon found his colleagues genial and the work
untaxing:

The first day that I entered in my official duties I was told to take charge
of one of the special reading rooms in the absence of the regular
superintendent. I did not even know what the room contained, but I
was to be the final arbiter & authority & was to answer all
questions. . . . My only instructions were: Be firm, polite & conceal your
ignorance.[11]

His main duty was cataloguing additions to the Library's three
million books. In November he wrote to Bridges:

The Museum on these dark days is gloomy enough. Yet I am fairly happy,
& don't overwork myself. . . . In the intervals between conversation with
one's colleagues, taking exercise, (it's nearly a quarter of a mile from my
place to the Catalogue), and playing with the black cat, it is possible to
catalogue from 20 to 30 books a day. This allows for reading those that are
of interest.

[8] P. R. Harris, *The Reading Room* (London, 1979), 24–5.
[9] See Edward Miller, *That Noble Cabinet: A History of the British Museum*
(London, 1973), 273–4; Harris, 23.
[10] *Everyman Remembers* (London, 1931), 83.
[11] 'Prize-giving Speech at St Paul's', AMS, n.d., n.pag. For Gosse, see Ann
Thwaite, *Edmund Gosse: A Literary Landscape 1849–1928* (London, 1984), 63–4.

And the following May:

Today we've been inventing statistics about the Library, in order to instruct visitors: e.g. that if all the pages of all the books were sewn together into one vast page, it would cover the whole of Asia, & no small portion of Russia as well: & if printed upon with type of a proportionate size, would be legible in Mars.[12]

Much as Binyon loved books, however, he loved pictures more, and his sights remained set on the Department of Prints and Drawings. His chance came less than two years later when Cust left to take up the Directorship of the National Portrait Gallery. Colvin recommended Binyon as 'an Assistant specially qualified for the work of the Print Room',[13] and he was transferred to the Department as a Second Class Assistant in April 1895. With its staff of eleven, the Department was housed in the White Wing (the aptly Whistlerian name derived from a bequest by William White), in the south-east corner of the Museum, overlooking Montague Street.

It is hardly surprising that Colvin wanted Binyon on his staff, for the young poet epitomized the breadth of culture Colvin had striven to create in the Print Room since his appointment in 1883 after a distinguished career as Slade Professor at Cambridge and Director of the Fitzwilliam Museum. He had raised the status of the Department within the Museum and laid the foundation for its scholarly reputation by introducing a new breed of university-trained scholars, of whom Binyon was the third after Cust and Dodgson.[14] No narrow specialist, Colvin had 'brought a new atmosphere into the Print Room', according to Binyon, who described him as 'one of the most accomplished, liberal, and learned of those who have made the history of art their study'.[15] Biographer of Keats and friend and editor of Robert Louis Stevenson, who had died the year before in Samoa, he was as much a literary figure as an art scholar, a friend of many of the great Victorians, including Ruskin, Browning, George Eliot, Rossetti and Burne-Jones, and claimed a living link

[12] ALs, 15 Nov. [1893], Dep. Bridges, 106, fos. 96–7; ALs 22 May 1894, Dep. Bridges, 106, fos. 102–3, Bodleian.

[13] Minutes of Trustees' Standing Committee, xlvii (CE3/47), p. 19659, BM.

[14] See Anthony Griffiths and Reginald Williams, *The Department of Prints and Drawings in the British Museum: User's Guide* (London, 1987), 25.

[15] Qtd. E. V. Lucas, *The Colvins and their Friends* (London, 1928), 181, from an appraisal of Colvin's career by LB (181–4); LB, 'Mr. Sidney Colvin', William Rothenstein, *English Portraits: a Series of Lithographs* (London, 1898–99), Part IV, n.pag.

back to the Romantics by having met Edward Trelawny and 'shaken the hand which plucked Shelley's heart out of the ashes'.[16] His house in the east wing of the Museum was one of the literary centres of late Victorian and Edwardian London, and it was memories of this hospitable house and of the Museum itself—'the many-pillared and the well-beloved'—that Stevenson celebrated in Apemama, nostalgic for an earlier British Museum era.[17]

For a young poet–scholar like Binyon it is hard to imagine a more sympathetic chief, a more congenial environment, or more agreeable work. His first work of art scholarship, *Dutch Etchers of the Seventeenth Century* (1895), appeared barely six months after he joined the Department. Colvin had set about supervising a complete critical revision of the Department's magnificent collections of drawings, watercolours, etchings, and prints to make them more accessible to students, and envisaged a comprehensive series of well-written, critically acute catalogues. He saw Binyon playing a vital role in this, as well as in writing guides for non-specialist visitors to Print Room exhibitions. His first task was the revision of Cust's index of the French artists represented in the collections, but his first major contribution was the four-volume *Catalogue of Drawings by British Artists and Artists of Foreign Origin Working in Great Britain, Preserved in the Department of Prints and Drawings in the British Museum*, a massive task that was not completed until 1905. The first volume, published in 1898, was the first catalogue produced by a member of the Department. In an internal memorandum to the Director, E. Maunde Thompson, Colvin later described the completed catalogue as 'a model of its kind, carried out with a remarkable combination of research, rapidity and literary finish'.[18]

This important catalogue, which, Denys Sutton has written, 'laid the foundation for the study of British drawings',[19] was a labour of love. Throughout his long career Binyon would champion the cause of British art, not out of jingoistic Little Englandism but in the belief that only a people who understood their own native traditions could fully understand those of others. His special interests were Blake, both as poet and artist, and the visionary artists in-

[16] *Memories and Notes of Persons and Places* (London, 1921), 251.
[17] 'To S.C.', *Collected Poems*, ed. Janet Adam Smith (London, 1950), 271.
[18] 3 July 1909, Original Papers CE4/208 (1909), n.pag., BM.
[19] 'Conversing With Paradise', editorial, *Apollo*, Aug. 1980, 57.

spired by him, especially Edward Calvert and Samuel Palmer; and the great eighteenth- and nineteenth-century watercolour tradition from Alexander Cozens through Francis Towne and J. R. Cozens to Thomas Girtin, J. M. W. Turner, John Sell Cotman, and beyond. During the years he spent compiling the catalogue he produced pioneering studies of Cotman, Crome, and Girtin, beginning with *Crome and Cotman* in April 1897, while his books and essays on Blake began with a facsimile edition of his wood engravings in 1902. He and Colvin did not always share the same priorities when it came to acquisitions, but through persuasion he set about strengthening the British art collection, aiming at 'getting together a full representation of the drawings of the English artists who really count'.[20] It was his persistence that led to the purchase in 1902 of the Reeve collection of drawings from the Norwich school, one of the Department's treasures. Meanwhile, he encouraged the work of contemporary British artists through acquisitions and his own writings.

Binyon could hardly have found a more congenial environment than the Print Room, for here, even more than in the poet-haunted Reading Room, his professional and private worlds dovetailed. It was his social rendezvous as well as his place of work. Horne often brought in his latest finds, Old Master drawings he had picked up for a song. 'Horne has come with a Rembrandt drawing,' he informed a friend in 1896. 'A vividerla!'[21] The Department's visitors' books comprise a roll call of the richly diverse London world Binyon had known since 1890 via Fitzroy. They show that during his first two years Print Room regulars included Horne, Image, Yeats, Charles Holmes, William Strang, William Rothenstein, Charles Ricketts, Charles Shannon, W. R. Lethaby, Althea Gyles, and Augustus and Gwen John. The list of artists, poets, novelists, scholars, and critics continues on through Bridges, Bernard Berenson, Lionel Johnson, Thomas Sturge Moore, Henry Newbolt, Stephen Phillips, Arthur Morrison, Gordon Craig, William Archer, C. R. Ashbee, D. S. MacColl, Esther Pissarro, Sidney Cockerell, and the French symbolist painter Odilon Redon.[22]

[20] Qtd. Lucas, 183–4.   [21] ALs to Olivier Georges Destrée, 5 Sept. 1896.
[22] Visitors Books, xi–xii (1895–1897), Archives of the Department of Prints and Drawings, British Museum.

The Print Room still drew collectors and professional dealers, but a high percentage of the visitors were either rising artists of Binyon's generation or young art students from the Slade School in nearby Gower Street, dispatched by Henry Tonks to study Renaissance drawings. The most brilliant among the latter when Binyon joined the Department was the 17-year-old Augustus John, whom he was one of the first to champion. As poet, art critic, amateur artist, and personal friend, Binyon was closer to artists than previous curators had been. 'Exciting morning at the British where I overhauled with Binyon the major part of a collection of old drawings,' Ricketts noted in his 1905 diary.[23] Contrasting him with the patrician Colvin, Rothenstein remarked that he 'was one of the few scholars who consulted us artists—rare modesty, which I have seldom met with in the expert'.[24]

The Museum was the centre of Binyon's rich social life in other ways too. His closest Museum friends were two men he met during his spell in the Library, Richard Streatfeild and Barclay Squire, who was in charge of the Music Room. The trio went on rowing expeditions on the Thames and occasionally travelled abroad together, including a hiking trip in the Dolomites in 1897. The ebullient Streatfeild, music critic for the *Daily Graphic*, was a particularly close friend. He introduced Binyon to the delights of that key 1890s subculture, the music hall and ballet. While Streatfeild was hopelessly in love with the Empire's première dancer Adeline Genée, Binyon admired that 'wonderful artist', the 'divinely vulgar' Marie Lloyd.[25] Binyon's worlds again overlapped when they bumped into fellow aficionados Image and Horne at the Empire or Alhambra, and convivial evenings were spent at the Crown in Charing Cross Road, a favourite Hobby Horse/Rhymers Club haunt.

If at night the Museum men merged anonymously with their raffish peers in the nocturnal demimonde mythologized by Arthur Symons and Walter Sickert, at lunch-time they formed a distinct, well-known group which held court every day at the

[23] 23 Nov. 1905, MS. 58103, Ricketts and Shannon Papers, British Library (hereafter R&S–BL).

[24] *Men and Memories: Recollections of William Rothenstein*, 3 vols. (London, 1931–9), i. 200.

[25] ALs to CMB, 29 July [1903]; postmarked 30 July 1903.

Vienna Café, where museum officials, literati, and exiles plotting arcane Reading Room revolutions could drink what Rhys reckoned was the best coffee in London.[26] The Austrian, as Binyon and other regulars called it, occupied the first floor above the Anglo–Austrian Confectionery Co. at 24–28 New Oxford Street, near the Museum. Although out of economic necessity a light meal usually consisting of shared half-portions, lunch here was, Binyon told Bridges, 'the most important event in Museum existence'.[27] The most vivid contemporary description is by Henry Newbolt, whom Binyon introduced to

'the Anglo-Austrians'—a set of men who were all either members of the Museum Staff or engaged like myself in daily work there. We met for lunch at the Vienna Café in New Oxford Street, lived mainly on excellent Viennese dishes and talked faster and more irresponsibly than any group of equal numbers in my memory: by the noise we made, the congestion at our table, the confusion in which we gave a dozen orders at once to Joseph, our Italian waiter, and the recklessness with which we shared portions with one another in shares impossible to disentangle, an onlooker might have taken us for a Bohemian society of students from some romantic foreign capital. Barclay Squire alone upheld our reputation for respectability, and there were times when he was the only one who was actually looking and speaking like a conventional Englishman.[28]

The core of the Anglo–Austrians comprised Squire, Streatfeild, Binyon, and several Museum colleagues. Regulars included Rhys, Oswald Sickert, and Walter Crum, while Samuel Butler, Edward Garnett, Yeats, Ricketts, Roger Fry, Robert Trevelyan, Image, Rothenstein, Calderon, John Masefield, Maurice Hewlett, Baron Corvo, and Lawrence Weaver all called in often. Binyon delighted in the group's vibrant eclecticism and 'Homeric laughter'.[29] Wyndham Lewis, who met Binyon while studying in the Print Room as a Slade student from 1899 to 1901, fondly remembered his lunches with the Anglo–Austrians, the 'entertaining group of people' who monopolized two tables along the south wall of the large triangular room under the mirrored ceiling, 'which reflected all your actions as if in a lake suspended above your head, surface

[26] *Wales England Wed*, 194.
[27] ALs, 15 Nov. [1893], Dep. Bridges, 106, fos. 96–7, Bodleian.
[28] *My World As in My Time: Memoirs of Sir Henry Newbolt 1862–1932* (London, 1932), 209–10.
[29] ALs to CMB, 23 Sept. [1903].

downwards'. 'It was in fact a club, in the sense that the café is the club of the Frenchman. It was a good club: and it was the only club of that sort in London.'[30]

LITTLE LONDON

From the vantage point of his eightieth birthday celebrations in 1938, the composer and musician Arnold Dolmetsch looked back on the 1890s milieu which had nourished his music:

> A sort of informal club had come to exist in London, containing all the poets and creative geniuses then alive; William Morris, Selwyn Image, Herbert Horne, Arthur Symons, W. Yates [*sic*], Swinburne, Sturge Moore, Laurence Binyon and others were my friends. I spent much time in their company. Their ideas filled my mind, and I became capable of illustrating their words with sympathetic music, or rather of crystallizing the latent music enshrined in them.[31]

So used have we become to lurid caricatures of the Yellow Nineties that Dolmetsch's list, where forgotten names cohabit with the canonized (and misspelt) great, comes as something of a surprise. Yet it is true to the character of this awkward transitional period between the Victorians and the modernists. The energy of the 1890s was communal, synergistic, epitomized by its ephemeral little magazines, households like Fitzroy, and collaborative art-works like Dolmetsch's 'Green' harpsichord decorated by Horne, Image, and Helen Combe, which Binyon saw at the Arts and Crafts Exhibition in October 1896. This is why autobiographies of the period and classics like Holbrook Jackson's *The Eighteen Nineties* (1913) are freighted with lists, which detail an age not of lonely, Promethean Victorian eminences like Ruskin and Carlyle but mul-tifaceted men and women, variously if not deeply talented, working within a supportive social and artistic-literary context.

Binyon first met Dolmetsch at his recitals in the music room at Fitzroy during 1891–2. In Fitzroy Binyon had the ideal gateway into what Ricketts called 'Little London', that intimate, clubbish, almost familial network of fluid cross-fertilizing groups which gave

[30] *Blasting and Bombardiering* (London, 1937), 279, 281–2.
[31] Qtd. Mabel Dolmetsch, *Personal Recollections of Arnold Dolmetsch* (London, 1957), 163.

late Victorian culture its characteristic tone and texture. Although
Fitzroy would continue as an institution until the Great War, by the
time he arrived at the Museum in 1893 the original bohemian
colony was breaking up. Horne had moved to King's Bench Walk
and would soon take up part-time residence in Florence, while
Galton had sailed for Australia as private secretary to his uncle, Sir
Robert Duff, Governor of New South Wales. Mackmurdo and
Johnson still lived in the house, but Johnson was slipping deeper
into alcoholism and was evicted by Mackmurdo in September
1895.[32] The *Hobby Horse* had run into financial difficulties and
folded in 1894.

The enduring legacy Fitzroy bequeathed Binyon was an unashamed eclecticism which set the agenda for his own career. At
Trinity he had told the Gryphon Club: 'It is a useful, and a profitable thing to be a specialist; but we may remember that there is a
sort of degradation about it; it tends to sink the man in the machine, and it takes him away from the centre to run in a groove.'[33]
The paradigm he had in mind was the man Dolmetsch put at
the head of his list, William Morris. Shortly after Morris died in
October 1896, Horne wrote: 'One quality of greatness William
Morris certainly possessed in a very high degree: both in his mind
and life he was, above all things, many-sided, a man of various
interests.'[34] With Morris's death, the Arts and Crafts movement lost
much of its messianic fervour and political edge, but his holistic
vision of life and art inspired creators like Walter Crane, Voysey,
Mackmurdo, C. R. Ashbee, Image, and Horne himself.

'I *should* have liked to be a painter, but I have no gift,' Binyon
told the artist Henry Tonks in 1932. 'It must be so jolly to have
one's hands active as well as one's brain.'[35] This yen for an art form
requiring more 'manual effort' than poetry reflected the Arts and
Crafts attitudes that permeated Fitzroy. From boyhood he had been
almost equally keen on drawing and poetry, his early notebooks
freely mingling verse and pen-and-pencil studies. Portraits of many
of his friends survive among his papers, and Ghose's daughter
chose a Binyon pencil portrait of her father for the frontispiece of

---

[32] Fletcher, *Johnson*, p. xxix.   [33] 'On Certain Confusions', 60.
[34] 'William Morris', First Illustrated Supplement, *Saturday Review*, Christmas
1896, 1.
[35] ALs to Henry Tonks, 29 Sept. 1932, MS Binyon Letters, HRC (hereafter BL–
HRC).

his *Collected Poems*. Bridges was right about his 'knack of catching a likeness', but these delicately modelled drawings lack psychological penetration and true vitality of line, and he was right to keep it as his hobby.

His interest in media with a stronger handicraft element seems to have been stimulated by his first contacts with the Century Guild in 1889. Shortly afterwards he asked Image about wax painting, an old Italian technique using modelling wax and oil paints, and before leaving Oxford he had taken up wood engraving, probably under Image's tutelage.[36] In 1896 he studied wood engraving with the Scottish artist William Strang, a powerful draughtsman who made several fine portraits of Binyon in various media. The following year he designed and cut a frontispiece for his book *The Supper* and supplied an original woodcut frontispiece for a new edition of George Darley's *Nepenthe*, a vigorously crude design called 'The Phoenix'. His engraving of Strang's design 'The Dryad' was used for the frontispiece of his 1901 *Odes*, and in 1905 he designed and engraved a woodcut frontispiece for his volume *Dream-Come-True*, produced by the Pissarros' Eragny Press. This made him one of the natural spokesmen for the artist engraver movement, as in his 1904 catalogue preface for the first exhibition of the Society of Twelve, whose members included Ricketts, Shannon, Rothenstein, Augustus John, Gordon Craig, and Sturge Moore. Also during 1904 he edited the short-lived quarterly *Artist Engraver* as a showcase for contemporary etchings, engravings, woodcuts and lithographs, which enabled him to commission artists as diverse as Strang, Shannon, and William Nicholson.

In this Binyon was a man of his age. In the intersecting circles within which he moved, it is often impossible to segregate creators into poets, artists, designers, critics or any other watertight compartments. He admired the combination of poet and artist in Thomas Sturge Moore, brother of the Cambridge philosopher G. E. Moore. 'I like Binyon very much,' Moore wrote to his parents soon after meeting him in 1898, 'he is very gentle and not at all I think a humbug, which is very rare.'[37] They became constant companions, poring over drawings in the Print Room, visiting galleries and exhibitions, dining together. Binyon introduced Moore to

---

[36] Image to LB, ALs, 7 Sept. 1889.
[37] Qtd. Sylvia Legge, *Affectionate Cousins: T. Sturge Moore and Maria Appia* (Oxford, 1980), 134.

Yeats, initiating their lifelong friendship and poet–designer colla-
boration.[38] Forty years later in his poem 'The Three Poets: A
Reminiscence', Wilfrid Gibson recalled meeting the trio in a
Holborn tea shop at the turn of the century:

> Binyon,
> Grave-eyed and gentle; Yeats, with lank dark hair
> And dark eyes flashing like the moonlit waters
> On some lone Irish lough; and Sturge Moore, faun-like,
> With a long straggly beard of russet brown:
> And I remember how I sat enthralled,
> A raw lad listening to those poets talking—
> Those poets in their thirties and the prime
> Of their creative energy, discussing
> Tolstoy's heretical 'What is Art?'—Yeats, pouring
> A stream of scintillating eloquence
> In his broad-vowelled brogue; and Sturge Moore, piping
> Keen commentary; while, for the most part, Binyon
> Sat silent, pondering like some Indian god
> Rapt in calm introspective meditation.[39]

Binyon's wide circle of friends was weighted in favour of artists,
partly through professional involvement but also because he preferred their company, finding them less preening than many
littérateurs during the 1890s, when 'people had the strange delu-
sion that we were in a kind of mental autumn. It was the fashion to
be tired, to be languid, to be rather ashamed of believing in anything, or to be fond of nature, or to have any passions or convictions. People talked a great deal about art. But it was rather like the
talk of invalids who are preoccupied about their health.'[40] He
preferred the company of those creating art rather than talking
about Art.

One of his earliest artist friends was Charles Ricketts, painter,
engraver, book illustrator and designer, writer, connoisseur, collector, pioneering stage designer, Wilde-class raconteur, and the most
diversely talented man of his generation. Binyon first saw his work
when Symonds sent him a copy of his *In the Key of Blue*, one of
Ricketts's early masterpieces of Art Nouveau book design. He

---

[38] See Sturge Moore, 'Yeats', *English*, 2/11 (1939), 273.
[39] *Solway Ford and Other Poems*, ed. Charles Williams (London, 1945), 73–4.
[40] 'English Poetry & Drama of To-Day and To-Morrow', *Studies in English Literature* (Tokyo), 10 (Jan. 1930), 1–2.

probably met him through Horne and Image soon after coming down from Oxford, while Ricketts and his lifelong partner, the painter and lithographer Charles Shannon, still lived at Whistler's old house, the Vale in Chelsea. He knew Ricketts's and Shannon's early work through their occasional periodical the *Dial* and the short-lived *Pageant*, edited by Shannon. He did not contribute to either magazine, nor was his enthusiasm for them unalloyed. A strong counter-influence to the more archly Aesthetic and Decadent elements in his London milieu came from Bridges, who once told him he had 'no sympathy with "aestheticism" "high art" etc.'[41] Nevertheless, Binyon became one of Ricketts's most loyal champions and was one of the few early friends the mercurial Ricketts remained close to all his life.[42]

Another lifelong friendship initiated in the mid-1890s was with the artist William Rothenstein, whose three-volume autobiography is one of the indispensable texts of this gregarious generation. They were introduced by the painter Charles Furse at John Singer Sargent's Chelsea studio in 1896. As Rothenstein remembered it, 'Furse flung at us, "Binyon! Rothenstein! don't you know one another? Two decadents!"' Rothenstein found it 'amusing to think of the scholarly Binyon being classed as a decadent'.[43] 'In Binyon I found a life-long friend,' he wrote in his autobiography, 'one who was quick to perceive and to welcome unusual talent in others, who rejoiced in what was new and vital in literature and painting, and yet loved, and retained, a fine taste for scholarship and lofty language.'[44] He drew several portraits of Binyon, including one for *Liber Juniorum*, a portfolio of lithographic portraits of Binyon, Beardsley, Yeats, Max Beerbohm, Phillips, and Laurence Houseman, Rothenstein's choice among the rising stars of 1899.

According to Rothenstein, together with Ricketts, Shannon, Beerbohm, Charles Conder, and other artists and writers they 'met constantly' for dinner at the Vale, now leased by Llewellyn Hacon, Rothenstein's patron and backer of Ricketts's and Shannon's Vale Press. On such occasions, as in the Holborn tea shop of Gibson's poem, Binyon 'Sat silent . . . | Rapt in calm introspective meditation.' In an era of great talk, of Whistler and Wilde, Ricketts and Berenson, Binyon was a sympathetic listener, silent unless he

[41] Bridges to LB, ALs, 22 Dec. 1890.
[42] See J. G. P. Delaney, *Charles Ricketts: A Biography* (Oxford, 1990), 54–5, 312.
[43] *Men and Memories*, i. 172.   [44] Ibid. 200.

had something that would genuinely add to the conversation. Rothenstein at first wondered whether his silence meant disapproval until he 'found it was not so, that behind a shy and diffident manner was a rich, humorous and most human nature'.[45] After dining at the 'Palace of the Heavenly Twins' (Wilde's name for Ricketts and Shannon), Binyon wrote: 'There is no need to talk when Ricketts & Rothenstein are on the go. You could not find two such wonderful talkers in London I think.'[46] Not only did he enjoy listening but, equally disabling to raconteurship, his thoughts ran deep: 'The other day at Ricketts' we were talking, & Ricketts had said he thought a great grief lasted just three days. I knew what he meant, & I said Yes if you feel it deeply, but if you don't feel it it lasts all your life.'[47] Binyon entirely lacked the instincts of the performer, the ability and desire, common to many 1890s figures, to play the self in a series of cameo roles, self-dramatizing what Ghose in his Wildean phase had called 'that unique and glorious thing, "Personality"'. Meeting Yeats and Binyon in the 1920s, Wallace Nichols was struck by the fact that while Binyon 'had that rare thing, a presence', it was quite unlike that of Yeats, who 'had a presence like an actor'.[48]

The more extrovert side of Binyon's character revealed itself among his own intimate crowd at the Vienna and other rendezvous. Since joining the Museum in 1893 he had lived in the quiet, run-down streets behind Westminster Abbey, first in a 'sequestered garret' in 25 Great College Street and later in Barton Street and Cowley Street.[49] One of his closest friends also lived in this area, the young painter Charles Holmes, his wood-engraving partner and, from 1896, office manager of Ricketts's and Shannon's Vale Press. Holmes, Binyon, and other friends ate together most evenings in convivial restaurants. As at the Vienna, tables became informal clubs, loose constellations based on personal friendship and breadth of interest that cut across more partisan groupings. Holmes remembered that their 'little company' of struggling writers, artists, and journalists often ate at Kirk's ham-and-beef shop in the Haymarket, where the food was monotonous but where 'for 1s.2d., or sometimes 1s.4d., the pangs of hunger could be

---

[45] *Men and Memories*, i. 200.   [46] ALs to CMB, 30 Oct. [1903].
[47] ALs to CMB, 7 Sept. [1903].
[48] Derek Parker, 'Poet of the Theatre', *Guardian*, 3 Aug. 1966, 7.
[49] ALs to Bridges, 2 Mar. 1894, Dep. Bridges, 106, fos. 98–9, Bodleian.

alleviated'.[50] Around 1897 Binyon discovered Roche's, a newly opened restaurant at 16 Old Compton Street in the heart of Soho. Here, when funds allowed, they could dine handsomely for eighteen pence, hors-d'oeuvres, soup, fish or eggs, entrée or joint, sweet or cheese all in, with jugs of water on the tables so patrons were not obliged to send out for beer or wine. Looked after by Roche and his cheerful wife, they commandeered the long table as a *stammtisch*, which rapidly established itself as an informal club to which, Holmes recalled, 'admission could be gained only by personal introduction, or by discreet waiting "on approval" below the salt'. Streatfeild and Binyon were again core members of this club, which included among others Edgar Jepson, Lawrence Weaver, Sturge Moore, George Calderon, the Strangs, William Morris's daughter May, and later Wyndham Lewis, while Whistler and other celebrities made experimental visits.[51] Other, nameless habitués included such surreal figures as the 'Profile' man, who was invisible full face, and the 'Cobra man', a Japanese-speaking judo expert and ex-bullfighter who, according to Binyon's wry letters, once imported Japanese wrestlers but now cured people 'by searchlights'.[52] Binyon ate at Roche's most evenings, rounding off his meal with a few games of billiards, a game he played with skill and passion.

These clubs catered for exchange not only of ideas but also of much-needed work. 'That table at Roche's', Holmes reported, 'was an ideal place over which to swop experiences, and pick up any little job that might be vacant, or be invented by Binyon, who had always a wonderful eye for the needs of a friend'.[53] Binyon was renowned for his generosity in helping friends and struggling young artists and writers. Among them was John Masefield, a 22-year-old ex-sailor turned bank clerk he befriended at one of Yeats's Monday evenings at Woburn Buildings in February 1901.[54] Masefield moved to Barton Street to be near Binyon, who helped him find more congenial work, including his first paid literary job, writing

[50] *Self and Partners (Mostly Self): Being the Reminiscences of C. J. Holmes* (London, 1936), 183.

[51] *Self and Partners*, 188–9.

[52] LB to CMB, ALs, 7 Sept. [1903] and 14 Sept. [1903]. For more details see Nicolete Gray, 82.

[53] *Self and Partners*, 189.

[54] See Constance Babington Smith, *John Masefield: A Life* (Oxford, 1978), 64–8; Rothenstein, *Men and Memories*, i. 373.

the notes for an edition of Keats Binyon was preparing for Methuen. In 1902 he introduced Masefield to Constance Crommelin, who became his wife within a year.

Another young man who became a Roche's regular was Binyon's cousin Arthur Ransome, who described in *Bohemia in London* his first visit, when an artist friend melodramatically announced: 'This is Bohemia'.[55] At 17 he had moved to London to become a publisher's assistant before embarking on his adventurous life as traveller and author of great children's books. 'Binyon had been extremely kind to the dumb young animal I was,' he recalled later, including giving him his first lesson in billiards at the Westminster Hotel. In awe of his poet cousin, he regularly made a detour past his Westminster lodgings 'to see the light in his window and to think of him in there at work'.[56]

Had he climbed the stairs, however, he would have seen that not all the midnight oil was burnt in the service of the muse. Holmes remembered 'his bed, and all else in his room, being almost buried under review books'.[57] This moonlighting helped Binyon chisel out his niche in literary London, but it was also a necessity for a man who, unlike Museum colleagues like Campbell Dodgson, had no private income. He lived frugally enough in London but needed money to fund his passion for travel. In a lecture on Italian art delivered in the 1930s he looked back on his efforts to get to Florence:

In those days Museum salaries in the junior ranks approached but did not exceed the earnings of a rather unsuccessful organ-grinder. Indeed, Mr Gladstone had pronounced that our work was so agreeable that we ought not to be paid at all. However, the Museum salary, which was all I had, would not allow of a journey to Italy. So I had to write a little book, and with the proceeds travelled to Florence, & for some years in order to get to Italy in the spring I had to write a book in the winter.[58]

In 1893 he had travelled extensively in Spain and visited Venice, a typical romantic English traveller in the south, experiencing 'to the full that spell which Italy lays on our Northern minds'. In 1894 and 1895 he visited Portugal, in spring 1897 he was in Venice with Streatfeild, in the autumn in Dresden, and in October 1898 visiting

[55] (London, 1907), 111.
[56] *The Autobiography of Arthur Ransome*, ed. Rupert Hart-Davis (London, 1976), 72–3.
[57] *Self and Partners*, 153.   [58] 'Italy & Italian Art', AMS, n.pag.

Horne in Florence. Like many another late Victorian, he combined his passion for Italy with a love of Flanders, both for its atmospheric medieval towns and for the Belgian Literary Movement. He knew and admired Emil Verhaeren, and one of his closest friends of the pre-war period was the poet and art historian Olivier Georges Destrée. They met at Fitzroy in 1895 and thereafter maintained a lively correspondence about poetry and art, punctuated by frequent meetings in London and Bruges, Binyon often slipping across the Channel for two-day stays. 'No, I have not killed anybody, but shall get 10£ for my Ode,' he wrote explaining a sudden visit to his equally impecunious friend in 1897.[59] In July 1898 Binyon travelled in Belgium with Strang, researching *Western Flanders* (1899), an impressive collection of prose meditations accompanied by Strang etchings.

Another trip to Flanders was made in the company of William Pye, whom he later called 'the most sympathetic man I have ever known'.[60] After meeting Pye in the Print Room in 1895, he had been virtually adopted into the family. The Pyes and their talented daughters Sybil and Edith filled the vacuum left by Sophia Phillips's death in 1892, and their home in Lee and later in Limpsfield, Surrey became his frequent weekend home, a pastoral retreat where he joined them in musical evenings, poetry games, and amateur dramatics.

EDITORIAL COMBAT

Small, idiosyncratic publishing houses lay at the heart of avant-garde culture in 1890s London. Binyon entered this world in 1893 when publication of the *Hobby Horse* was taken over by the Vigo Street publishers John Lane and Elkin Mathews, who published the Rhymers Club anthologies, the *Yellow Book*, and some of the most beautiful books of the 1890s. A 'west-end Mecca of poets, young and old',[61] the Bodley Head was little London further miniaturized. Almost all Binyon's present and future friends were involved as poets, designers or, like Horne, Image, and Binyon himself, both. Ricketts produced a string of masterly Art Nouveau book designs under its imprint.

[59] Postcard, 5 Oct. 1897.   [60] ALs to CMB, 27 Mar. [1904].
[61] Rhys, *Wales England Wed*, 152.

Binyon's initial contact was Lane, who with his reader Richard Le Gallienne largely controlled the publishing side of the business. Lane accepted his first book, *Lyric Poems*, at a propitious time. 'It is hard to get things to do for the papers, when you have no name at all,' Binyon wrote to him in September 1893. 'And a book is something solid to refer to: especially if published by you.'[62] *Lyric Poems* appeared in February 1894. A modest blue book with Image cover ornament and title page, it comprises forty-nine poems written at St Paul's and Oxford between 1887 and 1893. *Niobe* and all four *Primavera* poems are here, and the volume shares their strengths and weaknesses. There are more pellucid love lyrics and meditative Arnoldian pieces. Norman Gale in the *Academy* found it 'somewhat of a disappointment' after *Primavera*, but *The Times* reviewer praised its spontaneity and 'felicitous command of metre and diction' and Arthur Symons admired the Arnoldian poems of 'abstract meditation', especially 'Youth', which he thought 'full of poetic thought and reflection'.[63] Despite its generally favourable reception, however, sales lagged far behind Binyon's bestselling Bodley Head stablemates Richard Le Gallienne and Norman Gale, the targets of 'Two Magnificent Minor Poets', a lighthearted squib Binyon sent Bridges in March 1894:

> Rejoice, the Critic shouts, & the advent hail
> Of a great Galleon with this glorious Gale.
> Eager we watch O'er seas by no means rough
> Comes a small pinnace with a gentle puff.[64]

When the Lane–Mathews partnership broke up acrimoniously in September 1894, Binyon, along with Johnson and most of the Rhymers, elected to stay with Elkin Mathews, whom he preferred to the wily, entrepreneurial Lane.[65] With the great Victorian poets either dead or dying, sales of poetry reached a low point during the 1890s, a trend Binyon now tried in a modest way to reverse. Early in 1895 he proposed to Mathews a scheme for 'The Shilling Series',

[62] ALs, 28 Sept. [1893], BL–HRC.

[63] *Academy*, 24 Mar. 1894, 247; *The Times*, 16 Feb. 1894, 3; Symons, *Athenaeum*, 12 May 1894, 608.

[64] ALs, 2 March 1894, Dep. Bridges, 106, fos. 98–9, Bodleian.

[65] For the break-up of the Lane–Mathews partnership, see James G. Nelson, *The Early Nineties: A View From the Bodley Head* (Cambridge, Mass., 1971), 266–79.

a series of slim volumes of original verse, distinctive and attractive yet priced at one shilling rather than the usual five or six, aimed at the untapped market of 'young people with little pocket-money' who were, he argued, the nation's true lovers of poetry.[66] Simple as it sounds, this was a radical innovation in an era tending towards coterie exclusivity, codified by Le Gallienne in his 1893 *Limited Editions*: 'Let us, if need be, make our editions smaller and smaller, our prices increasingly prohibitive.'[67] Mathews tended to agree with Le Gallienne, and Binyon had to work hard to convince the incorrigibly cautious publisher, recalling years later in a letter to Henry Newbolt: 'It was I who forced the Shilling Garland down Elkin's throat: he was all against cheap poetry.'[68] Mathews succumbed, however, and was glad he did, as the series, modestly renamed 'Elkin Mathews' Shilling Garland', brought him acclaim.

In his twin aims of disseminating poetry among a wider, younger audience and publishing the work of little known contemporary poets, Binyon gained a fair measure of success with the ten slim volumes published between December 1895 and December 1898, now recognized as being among 'the significant publishing ventures in poetry in England during the eighteen nineties'.[69] He took charge of all aspects of the design and production process. In their delicate pastel wrappers with Selwyn Image motif and lettering, they are a testament to 1890s book design at its most modest, free from preciosity. He quickly discovered that handling human beings was trickier than choosing paper and typefaces, and his editorship of the series was marked by tactful but firm resistance to pressure from several sources. Privately admitting to Newbolt that 'Mathews is such an ass that he never makes the most of a book',[70] he quietly foiled the publisher's attempts to use the series as a catch-all for sub-standard poetry. More complex, fraught with master-disciple loyalties, was the involvement of Robert Bridges. Bridges's promise to contribute a new book, *Ode for the Bicentenary Commemoration of Henry Purcell*, was the bait Binyon used to lure

[66] Qtd. James G. Nelson, 'Elkin Mathews' Shilling Garland Series', *Papers of the Bibliographical Society of America*, 78 (1984), 18. This detailed account of the Shilling Garland appears in modified form in Nelson's *Elkin Mathews, Publisher to Yeats, Joyce, Pound* (Madison, Wisc., 1989), 31–55.

[67] *Limited Editions: A Prose Fancy* (London, 1893), 12.

[68] ALs, 10 Oct. 1932.   [69] Nelson, 'Shilling Garland', 17.

[70] ALs to Henry Newbolt, 13 Mar. 1897.

Mathews into agreeing to the series, but neither his gratitude for this nor his loyalty to his mentor extended to allowing the older poet's strong personality to dominate the series. 'I have no wish to appear as a kind of satellite to Bridges, much as I like & admire him: & if we two ran a series together, it would perhaps give that impression,' he confided to Mathews in July 1895, suggesting Bridges 'start a parallel series of his own'.[71] The second series never materialized and Bridges contented himself with influencing Binyon's choice of poets.

The series was launched in December 1895 with Binyon's *First Book of London Visions*, which sold well and went into a second printing. Next to appear, in April 1896, was *Christ in Hades and Other Poems* (No. 3) by Stephen Phillips. Binyon had long championed his cousin's work, having arranged for the publication of *Eremus* in 1894, and he now pulled out the stops to promote *Christ in Hades*. Calling on 'logrolling' skills learnt at Fitzroy, he enlisted Colvin's influential support and himself hailed Phillips in the *Saturday Review* as 'a new and powerful individuality, standing quite alone among our younger poets', launching Phillips on a career destined to trace perhaps the most spectacular rise and fall of any poet–dramatist in English literary history.[72]

Bridges's *Purcell Ode* (No. 2) followed a week later, Margaret Woods's *Aëromancy and Other Poems* (No. 4) in July, Richard Watson Dixon's *Songs and Odes* (No. 5) in October, Binyon's own *The Praise of Life* (No. 6) in December, and *Fancy's Guerdon* (No. 7) by Anados (Mary E. Coleridge) in April 1897, but the crowning success of the series, at least in financial terms, came in October 1897 with the overnight sensation of *Admirals All* (No. 8) by Binyon's Vienna Café crony Henry Newbolt. Binyon's prophecy that the ballads 'would make a very successful little book' was amply fulfilled when it went through four editions in a fortnight and eventually sold 25,000 copies, setting Newbolt on the path to

[71] ALs, 26 July [1895], BL–HRC; Nelson, *Mathews*, 33–4. For Bridges's references to the series, see *Selected Letters of Robert Bridges*, ed. D. E. Stanford, 2 vols. (Cambridge, Mass., 1984), i. 293, 300–2, 304, 328.

[72] *Saturday Review*, 20 June 1896, 629. For Phillips, see Peter Frost, 'The Rise and Fall of Stephen Phillips', *English Literature in Transition 1880–1920*, 25/4 (1982), 225–31.

a lucrative literary career and a knighthood.[73] The series also enabled Binyon to help Manmohan Ghose, who, unable to establish a literary or professional career in England, had reluctantly returned to India in 1894. His *Love-Songs and Elegies* appeared as Garland No. 9 in April 1898.

In the same month he published 'as an experiment',[74] an annual anthology of new poetry, *The Garland of New Poetry by Various Writers*, this time designing the entire book, including the cover, a flower trellis pattern on pale blue boards. This nearly brought his relationship with Mathews to a stormy end when the publisher, banking on the young poet's well-known indifference to money, tried to delay payment of Binyon's three guineas for designing the book, the only fee he had requested in three years of editing. Mathews had miscalculated: Binyon needed the money for travelling, the only thing worth getting angry over. 'You will get the editing of this volume, which has meant a good deal of time & trouble to me, for nothing,' he stormed; 'you have had all my work for the Garland for nothing, besides all the credit.'[75] More susceptible to displays of anger than loyalty, Mathews acquiesced, and continued to publish many of Binyon's books until his death in 1921.

In December 1898 Binyon neatly rounded off the series with the second volume of his *London Visions* and wound it up to concentrate on his own poetry. He was increasingly involved with another small publishing house, the Unicorn Press in Paternoster Square, owned by another mercurial 1890s figure, Ernest Oldmeadow, non-conformist minister turned journalist, music critic, comic novelist, and publisher, who would later metamorphose into a successful Soho wine merchant, convert to Roman Catholicism and become a pugnacious editor of the *Tablet*.[76] Binyon first became involved with the firm when Oldmeadow founded the *Dome* in 1897, the year which saw the demise of the *Yellow Book*, the *Dial*, and the *Pageant*. While Oldmeadow exaggerated in claiming for it 'a world-wide reputation as an organ of literary and artistic

---

[73] ALs to Newbolt, 13 Mar. 1897. See Newbolt, *My World*, 196; Nelson, *Mathews*, 47–51.

[74] ALs to Bridges, 8 Jan. 1898, Dep. Bridges, 106, fos. 108–9, Bodleian.

[75] ALs, 7 Sept. 1898, BL–HRC. See also Nelson, *Mathews*, 52–3.

[76] See Paul West, 'The Dome: An Aesthetic Periodical of the 1890s', *Book Collector* 6/2 (Summer 1957), 161.

opinion',[77] the *Dome* was one of the most accomplished of the arts-oriented literary magazines of the late 1890s. Far more than the arch-Aesthetic *Dial*, say, the slim volumes of the *Dome*, which ran from March 1897 to July 1900, epitomized Binyon's most congenial milieu at the turn of the century and beyond: wide-ranging, non-partisan, mildly avant-garde, symbolist but emphatically post-Decadent. Another point in its favour, a leitmotif in almost all Binyon's involvements at this time, was that at a shilling it was accessible to a wider audience than its more sumptuous predecessors and divested itself of the self-conscious marginality and coterie aura of the archetypal 1890s periodical. Binyon regularly contributed both art criticism and poems, most of which were collected in *Odes* (1901), also under the Unicorn imprint. Other regulars included Yeats with several major poems and essays, Symons, Sturge Moore, Holmes, Strang, Laurence Houseman, and Gordon Craig, while Fry, Dolmetsch, Elgar, Delius, and others also appeared. Binyon's lifelong friendship with another contributor, the poet Gordon Bottomley, began when Bottomley visited him in the Print Room to see some Calverts.

According to Holmes, Binyon 'was a welcome adjutant' to Oldmeadow when he joined the Press early in 1898.[78] As at Vico Street, he used his position to promote new talent and conjure up work for hard-up friends such as Holmes, Destrée, and Strang, who painted the firm's signboard when it moved to Cecil Court, St Martin's Lane in 1898. He joined after persuading Oldmeadow to publish the Artist's Library, an innovative series of art monographs which carried the Garland's criteria into art history: attractive, inexpensive and, as he stressed to one contributor, 'for students & not for collectors'.[79] His aim was a series introducing lesser-known artists through imaginative, accessible text, and collotype and process block illustrations as fine as the woefully tight budget would permit.

With a mere £25 to offer his authors, he began by calling on his friends, both established writers and young men out to make a name for themselves. The first of these was his neighbour and wood-engraving partner Charles Holmes. Helping Holmes earn

---

[77] Publisher's note in *Chord*, 1 (1899), n.pag.　　[78] *Self and Partners*, 187.
[79] ALs to D. S. MacColl, 16 Nov. 1898, MacColl B163, Glasgow University Library.

enough for dinners at Roche's in 1897, he had suggested that he write on the Japanese artist Hiroshige for the *Dome*, and he now put into effect his declared editorial aim of making 'the series as universal as possible' by choosing a non-European artist for the inaugural volume, commissioning Holmes to write on Hokusai.[80] *Hokusai* came out in early 1899, and Holmes followed it up with *Constable*, Artist's Library No. 5, in 1901, the first steps in a career that would bring him the editorship of the *Burlington Magazine* and ultimately the directorship of the National Gallery.

The second in the series was *Bellini* (1899) by the painter Roger Fry, whom Binyon first met at Fitzroy. A pioneering study of the Venetian artist, this was Fry's first book and helped launch his career as the most influential aesthetician of his generation. Binyon and Fry were never close friends, indeed clashed swords from time to time, but they had much in common. Both came from Quaker stock and shared an ancestral austerity and uncompromising honesty. Both were first-class lecturers and writers and both were critics *malgré lui*. Both scholar–artists, Fry's love went into his painting, Binyon's into his poetry.

Another friend Binyon turned to was Herbert Horne, who was already living part time in Florence when he accepted Binyon's invitation to write for the series in March 1898. Binyon had mooted Della Robbia or Pisanello as possible subjects, but Horne settled on one of his latest 'discoveries', Piero della Francesca.[81] In October he visited Horne in Florence, and with Horne's sister and other friends they made a 'Piero pilgrimage' to Umbria which Binyon still remembered vividly forty years later:

It was before the days of motors, & our conveyance was one of those light carriages with a roof like a four-poster bed & canvas screens to protect the open sides in wet weather. The lean horse, before it started, looked already as if it could go no farther; but it proved a wonderful stayer. When we stopped in a village the villagers came round & gave it bread, & a bottle of wine was poured down its throat by Raffaello, our youthful driver, and after this refreshment it went quite fast. . . . It poured with rain when we started & the rain lasted for a day & a half, after which we had warm cloudless days with cold nights; perfect autumn weather. We were bound for Arezzo; but though Piero was our special aim, we did not neglect things

---

[80] 'The Dome Advertiser', *Dome*, NS, 1 (Oct. 1898), p. v. See Holmes, *Self and Partners*, 186–7.

[81] ALs, 17 March 1898.

by the way, & sometimes went out of our way (oxen were harnessed to the carriage to pull us up steep hill sides) to see some Della Robbia or other work of note in a remoter village. It brought it home to me, travelling in this way, how far Italy surpasses all other countries in things of beauty. Buildings, sculpture, paintings that in another country would be rare and notable are there common as wild fruit, & found in out of the way little towns or places no tourist gets to visit. In no land it seems to me except perhaps China & Japan, has the artist produced in such happiness or so naturally, the general community sharing in his aims & sympathizing with his pursuit, not in a state of exile or defiance.[82]

By November Horne was deep in his researches into Piero, rummaging in archives, honing the skills that would, after years of patient research, yield his classic *Sandro Botticelli* in 1908.

Unfortunately, however, the book on Piero della Francesca never materialized, the first in a series of mishaps of the kind endemic to shoestring publishers. Another of Binyon's contributors, D. S. MacColl, champion of Impressionism and the best of the 1890s New Critics, chose to write on Alfred Stevens, but although the book was advertised and by November 1898 the collotypes and process blocks were under preparation, he fell ill and the book was never completed. By October 1899, when Rothenstein came down with jaundice, Binyon was beginning to wonder if the series was a 'pestilence' hospitalizing its would-be contributors.[83] Rothenstein had agreed to write on Goya, an artist Binyon greatly admired, but the book was delayed by an unrelated dispute between Rothenstein and Oldmeadow, and only Binyon's deft diplomacy got the book finally through the press in 1900.

Such rows were routine at the Unicorn. Binyon thought Oldmeadow a fool and told him so on many occasions, but he felt that, despite making flamboyant promises he could not keep, he had his authors' interests at heart. 'The only man who might possibly sell a book for you better than Oldmeadow is Lane,' he told one poet, '& I think you will find a little experience of his ways will go a long way.'[84] Having joined the Press he was determined to 'improve its ways', but this was an impossible task, as his cousin

---

[82] 'Italy & Italian Art', AMS, n.pag.

[83] LB to Rothenstein, ALs, 2 Oct. 1899, BMS Eng. 1148 (126), fo. 15, Sir William Rothenstein Papers, Houghton Library, Harvard University (hereafter WRP–HH).

[84] ALs to Sturge Moore, n.d. [1900], box 18/122, Thomas Sturge Moore Papers, University of London Library (hereafter TSMP–LU).

Arthur Ransome discovered when he joined the firm in 1902 and witnessed the way it 'lived under an almost continuous threat of disaster' under Oldmeadow's quixotic management.[85] As a result, much of Binyon's time was spent mediating between his feckless employer and a string of irate authors. That he emerged from all this with his friendships not only intact but strengthened speaks for a rare maturity and lack of egotism. He needed all his patience and peacemaking skills in promoting the career of the temperamental, combative Sturge Moore. Moore was not exaggerating when he told Robert Trevelyan Binyon had taken him under his wing,[86] for in addition to arranging for the Unicorn Press to publish his first volume of poetry Binyon commissioned him to write on Altdorfer for the Artist's Library and accompanied him on a research trip to Berlin and Dresden in May 1899. Despite rows and delays, by a mixture of tact, tenderness, and bullying he managed to steer both *The Vinedresser* (1899) and *Altdorfer* (1900) through the press, launching Moore's twin career as poet and art critic.[87]

Among the Artist's Library books advertised as in preparation in September 1900 were Yeats on Calvert, Image on Rowlandson, Dodgson on Cranach, and Cornelis Hofestede de Groot on de Hooch. Fry had agreed to write on Piero di Cosimo and Moore on Rodin, while Binyon had his eye on Beerbohm for Daumier. None were published. Binyon gradually withdrew, and in 1903 the series folded for lack of funds.

Chaotic and short-lived as it was, the Artist's Library revealed important facets of Binyon's attitude to art. His 1896 essay 'The Popularization of Art' stressed the role of museums, galleries, and photography in bringing art to a wider audience.[88] Art was for everyone, not to be fenced off in academic enclosures. As secretary of the Art for Schools Association, he worked to get art reproductions into schools. The Artist's Library was similarly devised to help broaden the base of art appreciation rather than promote the hegemony of professional scholars and connoisseurs. To this end he sought a range of voices, including poets like Yeats, and especially

[85] LB, ALs to Sturge Moore, n.d. [1900?], box 28/122, TSMP–LU; Ransome, *Autobiography*, 75–7.

[86] See Legge, 136.

[87] For LB's championing of *The Vinedresser*, see Frederick L. Gwynn, *Sturge Moore and the Life of Art* (London, 1952), 30–1.

[88] *The Civilization of Our Day*, ed. James Samuelson (London, 1896), 320–9.

artists, whom he felt had insights unvouchsafed to critics. This policy cost him his most illustrious contributor, the American connoisseur Bernard Berenson, whom he had known for several years and visited in Fiesole.[89] By March 1898 when Binyon invited him to join the series, the controversial Berenson was widely recognized as the foremost authority on Italian art and it was quite a coup when he agreed to write on Giorgione, especially as he had turned down all previous series editors. In the end, however, Binyon gained not a famous contributor but an education in the internecine rivalries endemic among 1890s scholars and connoisseurs, for Berenson balked at having his name linked with certain critics and was unhappy about artist friends Binyon had commissioned, especially Rothenstein, whom he considered scarcely a scholar, and he eventually withdrew.[90]

Binyon was saddened but uncontrite. The title 'scholar' held less prestige for him than for Berenson. When he entered the Print Room in 1895 the scientific connoisseurship pioneered by Giovanni Morelli was making 'a great stir in the little world' in which he found himself, opening up a floodgate of gleefully iconoclastic reappraisals of Old Master attributions. For young scholars like Binyon and Fry coming of age in the 1890s, Morelli's scientific techniques of style analysis also meant a fundamental shift away from Pater's impressionistic, 'literary' art criticism. Binyon was profoundly influenced by this critical sea-change, but although he played what he called the fascinating 'parlour game of Attributions . . . with enthusiasm', it remained for him a game, peripheral to the real concerns of art.[91] It ran counter to his deepest responses to art as a spiritual discipline rather than a scientific, or even scholarly enterprise. At heart a Blakean anarchist who distrusted all systems, he quietly resisted attempts to corral art within the closed shops of academic discourse and fought a rearguard action against the growing tendency to codify and unionize art appreciation, marginalizing works of art as cryptic mazes to be deciphered only by licensed scholars and critics.

[89] See Ernest Samuels, *Bernard Berenson: The Making of a Connoisseur* (Cambridge, Mass., 1979), 265.

[90] Berenson to LB, ALs, 25 Nov. 1898.

[91] 'Italy & Italian Art', AMS, n.pag.

4   Images of the Floating World

'I have got so much from the East—it has opened a new world of beauty for me.'[1] By the time Binyon wrote this in 1903 he had already been immersed in Asian art for a decade. It was to be a lifelong love affair, beginning in the early 1890s and lasting until his death in 1943. These five decades were crucial not only in establishing the study of Asian art as a scholarly discipline in Europe and America but also in the wider, more necessary and urgent task of the West's reluctant deblinkering, the slow shedding of closed Eurocentric modes of perception and thought in preparation for a postcolonial world in which relations would be based, in theory at least, not on military-economic power but mutual tolerance, understanding, and respect. Together with a handful of other contemporary writers and scholars, Binyon played a seminal role in this difficult, ongoing process.

Even today, with integrated Asian studies programmes at undergraduate and graduate level, intensive language training, accurate translations, shelves of densely illustrated reference books, air travel, funded field study, access to collections in Beijing, Taipei, Tokyo, Kyoto, Delhi—even with all this the young Western scholar of Asian art faces daunting challenges. We must make an imaginative leap to conceive the situation in the 1890s, when Binyon entered the hugely complex world of Asian art armed with only an Oxford classics degree, though fortunately backed up by qualities a classical Oxford education did not always impart: aesthetic sensitivity, intuitive insight, a keen visual memory, an unprejudiced mind open to non-Western forms of art and thought, and the desire, ingenuity, and persistence needed to build a great public collection with meagre financial resources and against ingrained Eurocentrism. That and a healthy dose of blissful ignorance, without which he might never have embarked on his life's work.

The range of Binyon's professional engagement with Oriental art at the British Museum is unthinkable today when with each gener-

[1] ALs to CMB, 24 July [1903].

ation of scholars the field is subdivided into ever narrower specializations. It was just as well that he had followed William Morris in eschewing 'specialism', because at the Museum, in addition to his work as a leading authority on British art, he took on responsibility for every branch of Asian art. If this resulted inevitably in a measure of what we have learnt to denigrate as amateurism, it also laid the foundation for future professionalism and allowed an enviably holistic approach to Oriental art.

When Binyon joined the Museum in 1893 there was nothing resembling the Department of Oriental Antiquities as we know it today. Examples of Indian and Far Eastern art the Museum had haphazardly acquired were scattered among its departments. The Amaravati frieze, for example, one of the masterpieces of Indian sculpture, was incongruously housed in the Department of British and Medieval Antiquities, though here at least it was in the caring hands of one of the Museum's great Victorian Keepers, A. Wollaston Franks, himself a collector of Asian art.[2] It was Franks and his assistant Hercules Read who laid the foundation of the Department of Prints and Drawings' Far Eastern art collection in 1881 by recommending the purchase of the large if undistinguished collection of Japanese paintings formed in Tokyo during the 1870s by the Scottish surgeon William Anderson, the first European specialist on Japanese art. Colvin arrived two years later. A friend of the Rossettis, he shared his generation's enthusiasm for things Japanese, and the first exhibition he had mounted in the newly-opened White Wing in 1888 was an exhibition of paintings from the Anderson collection. Colvin did not add to the collection, however, and it was Binyon's arrival in 1895 and the dynamic partnership he established with Colvin which provided the impetus behind the sudden acceleration in the Department's Oriental acquisitions after 1900, which in eight years between 1902 and 1910 saw the Department garner a collection of Chinese and Japanese art as good as any public collection in Europe.

This chapter traces Binyon's lifelong engagement with Asian art back to its roots in his first encounter with Japanese art, especially *ukiyo-e* woodblock prints, in the early 1890s.

[2] See Soame Jenyns, 'The Franks Collection of Oriental Antiquities', *BMQ*, 18 (1953), 103–6.

JAPONISME

It would be difficult to overstate the importance of the role played by Japanese art in the birth and evolution of modern Western art. More perhaps than any other single factor, it created the conditions for modern art, from painting and graphic arts like printmaking, poster art, and book illustration to architecture, design, ceramics, photography, and film. Other non-European influences, including Persian, African, and Oceanic art, all played their part, but the crucial initial breakthrough came in Paris in the 1860s and 1870s when Manet, Whistler, Degas, Monet, and other painters, all in different ways seeking a way out of the cul-de-sac of nineteenth-century photographic illusionism, discovered a new visual language in Japanese woodblock prints. This Impressionist pioneer phase of Japonisme laid the groundwork for a second, more mature phase, as from the 1880s onwards Post-Impressionist, Art Nouveau, and Expressionist artists drew on the inspiration of Japanese art to achieve a total reconstruction of pictorial space that paved the way for modern art.[3]

Binyon's generation of European creators were in the thick of this multifaceted, decidedly international second phase of Japonisme. We can use 'generation' in a precise sense here. Binyon was born in 1869, a few months after the Meiji Restoration had set the seal on the emergence of modern Japan. Even if we arbitrarily restrict it to those born three years either side, we get a list of avant-garde artists which reveals how widespread and diverse Japanese influence was: in France, Bonnard (1867), Vuillard (1868), Matisse (1869), Denis (1870); in Britain, Ricketts (1866), Frank Brangwyn (1867), Charles Rennie Macintosh (1868), the Beggarstaff Brothers (1869, 1872), Beardsley (1872), Gordon Craig (1872); in Belgium, Gisbert Combaz (1869); in Holland, Jan Thorn Prikker (1868), Mondrian (1872); in Germany, Thomas Heine (1867), Emil Orlik (1870); in Vienna, Kolo Moser (1868); in Russia, Leon Bakst (1866); and in the United States, Frank Lloyd Wright (1867).

[3] The wealth of research in all aspects of Japonisme is documented in Gabriel Weisberg and Yvonne Weisberg, *Japonisme: An Annotated Bibliography* (New York, 1990). Two magisterial synoptic studies are Klaus Berger, *Japonisme in Western Painting from Whistler to Matisse*, trans. David Britt (Cambridge, 1992), and Siegfried Wichmann, *Japonisme: The Japanese Influence on Western Art since 1858*, trans. Mary Whittall, *et al.* (London, 1981).

Japonisme in Britain took a very different course from that in France. In the Great Exhibition at the Crystal Palace in 1851, the British East India Company had exhibited some Japanese items in its display of Oriental artefacts, but their identity, like that of Japan itself, was largely subsumed in an ill-understood and homogenized 'Orient'. With the prying open of Tokugawa Japan by American warships in 1853 and the Treaty of Edo between Britain and Japan in 1858, however, Japan became a nation and culture of immediate interest to the British public. At the second Great Exhibition in London in 1862, the Japanese Court was one of the most admired sections. Organized by Sir Rutherford Alcock, Britain's first Consul-General in Japan, it contained the largest display of Japanese arts and crafts so far seen in Europe, ranging from bronzes, ceramics, and lacquerware to woodblock prints and books.[4] This exhibition, reinforced by the arrival of Whistler, who settled in London the following year, inspired many artists to collect Japanese arts and crafts, spanning the gamut of the Victorian art world from Leighton, Poynter, and Alma-Tadema to Rossetti, Simeon Solomon, and Albert Moore. Despite Whistler's radical stylistic experiments, however, Japanese influence on British artists did not go much beyond the inclusion in their canvases of kimonos, ceramics, fans, screens, and other Japonist icons.[5] There was little to suggest any revolution in pictorial composition of the kind Japonisme was beginning to inspire in Paris. In Britain it was in the applied arts, in architecture, interior decor, furniture and textile design, ceramics, metalwork, book design and illustration, in the work of artist-designers like E. W. Godwin and Christopher Dresser, that the discovery of Japanese arts and crafts had an enormous impact in the last third of the nineteenth century, sparking a revolution in design that would spread from Britain throughout Europe and the United States.

By the time the schoolboy Binyon had moved to London in the mid-1870s, Japonisme in its various forms was steadily permeating

---

[4] See Ellen P. Conant, 'Refractions of the Rising Sun: Japan's Participation in International Exhibitions 1862–1910', *Japan and Britain: An Aesthetic Dialogue 1850–1930*, ed. Tomoko Sato and Toshio Watanabe (London, 1991), 79–80. On the role of the universal exhibitions in disseminating Japonisme, see Berger, 103–6.

[5] Many examples were displayed in the fine *Japan and Britain* exhibition at the Barbican Art Gallery, London, 1991–2. See Sato and Watanabe, 'The Aesthetic Dialogue Examined: Japan and Britain 1850–1930', *Japan and Britain: An Aesthetic Dialogue*, 19–25. For a richly detailed account of Japonisme in Victorian Britain, see Toshio Watanabe, *High Victorian Japonisme* (Bern, 1991).

British upper- and middle-class cultural life, although his austere family in their modest Hammersmith home were far removed from the ambience of Aestheticism, the 'House Beautiful' movement, or the fashionable Japanese goods on sale in Liberty's in Regent Street from 1875. In his visits to Fitzroy while still an Oxford undergraduate, however, he came into direct contact with a milieu saturated with Japonisme. The more frivolous aspects of the cult of Japan, which had reached its apogee in Gilbert and Sullivan's *The Mikado* (1885), were on the wane, although as an *aficionado* of the music hall and an admirer of Marie Lloyd he may have seen her perform her 1896 song 'The Geisha', with its jaunty chorus:

> Ev'ry little Jappie chappie's gone upon the Geisha—
> Trickiest little Geisha ever seen in Asia!
> I've made things hum a bit, you know, since I became a Geisha,
> Japanesey, free and easy Tea house girl![6]

Such cheerful racial stereotyping stood at the opposite end of the spectrum from the mature Japonisme of the circles within which Binyon moved in 1890s London. In 1892, the year he left Oxford for London, the Japan Society of London was founded with the aim of encouraging the serious 'study of the Japanese Language, Literature, History and Folk-Lore, of Japanese Art, Science and Industries, of the Social Life and Economic Condition of the Japanese People, past and present, and of all Japanese matters'.[7] Four months before Binyon joined the Museum in 1893, Charles Holme, an active member of the Japan Society who had travelled to Japan with Lasenby Liberty and the artist Alfred East in 1889–90, founded the *Studio*, the most widely influential art journal of its time, disseminating the Arts and Crafts movement and Art Nouveau throughout Europe, America, and as far as Japan. The pages of this journal, to which Binyon himself contributed, provide perhaps the richest insight into the milieu in which he first encountered Japanese art, not as Print Room specimens but as a living force in leading-edge British culture. It regularly carried articles on Japanese arts and crafts, and a rich vein of Japanese influence seams the work illustrated on its pages, from Voysey textiles to Beardsley drawings. The architecture, interior decor, furniture, and artwork

---

[6] See *Japan and Britain: An Aesthetic Dialogue*, 41.
[7] Qtd. Sir Hugh Cortazzi, 'The Japan Society: A Hundred-Year History', *Britain and Japan 1859–1991: Themes and Personalities*, ed. Cortazzi and Gordon Daniels (London, 1991), 2.

showcased in the *Studio* were fleshed out in the homes of some of Binyon's friends. In domestic environments such as these, Japanese art enjoyed a quite different relationship to the total design of the house than the exotic fans and samurai swords of cluttered Victorian interiors. Japan was no longer, as it had been for the Pre-Raphaelites and men such as William Burges, a charming fantasy as distant in space as the Middle Ages was in time. It was contemporary, emphatically post-Victorian.

Although from early on Binyon appreciated the brilliant decorative art of Ogata Kōrin and the Rimpa artists, his first encounter with Japanese art was via *ukiyo-e* woodblock colour prints. In Japan these prints were despised by connoisseurs as a vulgar, ephemeral folk-craft of the merchant quarters, more akin to fashion than genuine art. In Victorian Britain they were admired, alongside textiles and other craftworks, as remarkable specimens of design, but few joined Whistler in seeing them as genuine works of art to be evaluated on aesthetic criteria. This was the task undertaken by Binyon's generation. Many of his friends collected prints and albums, which were still comparatively cheap in the 1890s, and it is crucial to our understanding of Binyon's response to *ukiyo-e* that he first encountered it not in the context of museums and scholars, dealers and collectors, but among painters, graphic artists, and designers who, like the Impressionists before them, studied Japanese prints for ways of transforming their own art. Rothenstein first encountered *ukiyo-e* as an art student in Paris in the 1880s, where he met Bracquemond and other pioneers of Japonisme.[8] Binyon's Westminster neighbour and close friend Charles Holmes pored over Japanese prints in his eclectic programme of self-education, learning lessons reinforced practically as he and Binyon studied woodcutting under William Strang, to the extent that Binyon later detected Hokusai's influence in his friend's landscapes.[9] Binyon encouraged him to write on *ukiyo-e* for the *Dome* and, as we have seen, commissioned his 1899 book *Hokusai*.

In Binyon's milieu, however, as in Britain as a whole, the influence of *ukiyo-e* was much more pronounced on architects, designers, and illustrators than on painters. Mackmurdo had been exposed to Japanese art as a young architect through his friendship

    [8] *Men & Memories* i. 41.
    [9] Holmes, *Self and Partners*, 152; LB, *English Water-Colours*, 2nd edn. (London, 1944), 167.

with Norman Shaw and Whistler. The asymmetry and swirling, flame-like plant forms of his famous 1882–3 chair and woodcut title page for *Wren's City Churches* (1883), acknowledged as clairvoyant precursors of Art Nouveau, derived from Japanese designs and Blake's illustrated books,[10] both later Binyon's expert province. Image collected Japanese prints, as did several other friends in what he described as the 'delightful fellowship' of the Art-Workers' Guild, of which he was elected an Honorary Member in 1913.[11] The Guild's spiritual father, Walter Crane, had in the 1870s been one of the first English artists to learn from Japanese prints, whose impact is evident in his later 'toy-books'.[12] Crane's experiments seeded the more radical innovations made by the succeeding generation of English illustrators, as *ukiyo-e* helped inspire the development and perfection of the Art Nouveau book, the greatest achievement of Binyon's generation. Art Nouveau and Japonisme were virtually twinned during the 1890s, especially in the work of Aubrey Beardsley, who took up where Whistler's Peacock Room left off and learnt from *ukiyo-e* techniques of cropping, asymmetry, absence of modelling and cast shadows, flat geometric patterning, expressive line, and sense of space with which to minister to his highly unjapanese muse.[13] The impact of *ukiyo-e* and artists like Kōrin is evident in the book designs, illustrations, and stage designs of one of Binyon's closest friends, Beardsley's rival and successor as Wilde's illustrator, Charles Ricketts. When in 1889 Wilde first visited Ricketts and Shannon at the Vale, he complimented them on the Japanese prints adorning the walls.[14] Ricketts's diaries vividly record his appetite for things Japanese, littered with entries like 'Read books on Japan all day'. In 1901 he mused:

I think, at their best, that nothing quite touches a first-rate Jap print, excepting a good Greek Kylix or first-rate Tanagra: even the latter hardly

[10] See S. Tschudi Madsen, *Art Nouveau*, trans. R. I. Christopherson (London, 1967), 78.
[11] LB, 'The Art of Yoshijiro Urushibara', *Ten Woodcuts, Cut and Printed by Yoshijiro Urushibara after Designs by Frank Brangwyn, R.A.* (London, 1924), n.pag.
[12] See Crane, *The Decorative Illustration of Books Old and New* (London, 1896), 156–8.
[13] For Japonisme and Art Nouveau, see Robert Schmutzler, *Art Nouveau* (London, 1964), 74–5.
[14] See Delaney, 44.

compare; only the masterpieces of the greatest masters go beyond: picked Titians or Rembrandts, or world-famous frescoes.[15]

He and Shannon were expert collectors, and Binyon watched the growth of their fine print collection with special pleasure, knowing that it would eventually come to the Museum, as it did after Shannon's death in 1937.

Another artist friend whose work was indebted to *ukiyo-e*, as well as Indian and Persian art, was Edmund Dulac,[16] whose witty, affectionate Sharaku-style caricature is the best portrait of Binyon. With Ricketts he designed Itō Michio's costume for a dance recital in 1915, and designed the masks, costumes, and make-up for *At the Hawk's Well* and Yeats's other 'Noh' plays, published in *Four Plays for Dancers* (1921). Keeping it in the Japanist family, the cover was designed by Sturge Moore, who had admired Japanese prints since the late 1880s. Two of Hokusai's most famous prints, *Mt. Fuji in Storm* and *Under the Wave at Kanagawa*, took pride of place in the front room of his house in St James's Square.

From the first Binyon was engaged at a deeper level than was necessary for his curatorial duties. In addition to his experiments in woodcutting under the tutelage of Image and Strang, his work for the Unicorn Press and the *Artist Engraver* involved him practically in the technical details of woodblock printing. This, and the problems experienced by colour printers like Shannon and Lucien Pissarro, gave him a keen appreciation of the peerless craftsmanship of Japanese woodcutters and printers. Writing to Rothenstein to recommend the work of his young Tokyo-trained friend Urushibara Yoshijirō, he stressed that Japanese craftsmen achieved work 'on a level totally beyond anything possible by our Western processes'.[17] Binyon was also a spokesman for a new generation of original engravers, including Strang, Ricketts, Pissarro, Sturge Moore, Augustus John, and Gordon Craig, all in different ways influenced by *ukiyo-e*. Launching the *Artist Engraver* in 1904, he could claim: 'Probably never before have so many artists at once

[15] Diary entry, 4 Aug. 1901, MS 58099, R&S–BL; *Self-Portrait*, 43. For Ricketts's and Shannon's collection, see Joseph Darracott, *The World of Charles Ricketts* (London, 1980), 136–48.

[16] See Colin White, *Edmund Dulac* (London, 1976), 11–15.

[17] ALs to Rothenstein, 10 Sept. 1912, MS EUR. B. 213, fo. 14, India Office Library, London.

been occupied with original wood-engraving.'[18] One of his chief criteria was the Arts and Crafts maxim of truth to materials, the belief that the 'true artist . . . is guided by the materials themselves to perfect the felicities these lend their nature to, and no others'.[19] In original engraving, he wrote in the catalogue for the Society of Twelve exhibition of 1904, the design must be 'a conception thought out in terms of' the material.[20] This is precisely what he found in Japanese prints, most nakedly and powerfully perhaps in the early phases of *ukiyo-e*. Moronobu's woodcuts, for example, were, he wrote, 'the final expression of the artist's thought, designed in terms of the material' (*JCP* 27).

Unlike their Pre-Raphaelite forebears, the new breed of 'artist engravers' cut and printed their own designs. Japanese print artists such as Harunobu and Utamaro were not artist engravers in this sense, but in the bustling Edo *ukiyo-e* workshops the 'arts of the designer, woodcutter, and printer [were] combined with a felicity unknown elsewhere in all the world' (*JCP* 23), thus blurring the barriers between art, design, and craft, barriers which Binyon's Arts and Crafts friends were seeking to dismantle in Britain. The entire team, including the designer, were craftsmen and, because nothing was mechanized, all artists. Sadakichi Hartmann, writing in the same year as the *Artist Engraver*, referred to the *ukiyo-e* craftsmen as the 'artist engraver' and 'artist printer'.[21] While entirely different in character and aims from Essex House or Fitzroy, the great Edo publishing house of Tsutaya Juzaburō was a community of artists, craftsmen, poets, and novelists which achieved unself-consciously something of what the Arts and Crafts guilds were vainly seeking with such Victorian moral earnestness.

Japanese prints were politically attractive because they were seen as a genuine art of the people. Whereas the paradox at the heart of the Arts and Crafts movement was that its handmade products were affordable only by the rich, *ukiyo-e* woodcuts were genuine expressions of popular culture, 'a living art', as Crane put it, 'an art

---

[18] 'Note', *Artist Engraver*, 1 (Jan. 1904), 4.
[19] LB, 'Three Artists', *Catalogue of an Exhibition of Water-Colours, Pastels, and Paintings by Charles Conder, W. Rothenstein and C. H. Shannon* (London, 1904), 8.
[20] Preface, *The Society of Twelve: First Exhibition, 1904* (London, 1904), n.pag.
[21] *Japanese Art* (London, 1904), 114.

of the people, in which traditions and craftsmanship were unbroken'.[22] Moreover, they reflected the refined taste, design flair, and craftsmanship, the feeling for the integrity of natural materials, the marriage of function and form in the commonest household utensils that had come as a revelation to Dresser and other Western visitors. Whistler's disciple Mortimer Menpes enthused in Morrisian terms:

Art in Japan is living as art in Greece was living. It forms part and parcel of the very life of the people. . . . Art is in Europe cultivated in the houses of the few, . . . the privilege of a class rather than the rightful inheritance of the many. But it is not so in Japan, as it was not so in ancient Greece. In Japan the feeling for art is an essential condition of life. This is why I expect so much from the interest in Japan which is now awakening in England.[23]

To a generation nurtured on Ruskin and Morris such a vision held as great an appeal as the myth of a rational, Utopian 'Cathay' had held for eighteenth-century European savants.

Ukiyo-e prints not only illustrated this supremely aesthetic culture through their subject matter—the Yoshiwara teahouses, gardens, textiles, and utensils—but were themselves vivid examples of it. For Binyon and his friends, opposed to the alienating working conditions and shoddy mass-produced goods of industrial technology, there was an inherent beauty in the natural materials used in Japanese woodblock printing, from its cherrywood blocks and handmade mulberry paper to its vegetable and mineral colours. The fact that the Japanese used no machine press was for Binyon symbolic of its pre-industrial sense of the craftsman's unalienated sympathy with and intimate feel for his materials:

A sensitive fidelity of tone and line never loses the quality of life. No photographic reproduction, however skilful, could compete with these products of an artist's hand. Choice of paper, subtle mastery in printing—with no machine's intervention—contribute to this perfection.[24]

[22] *Decorative Illustration*, 160–1. See also LB, *JCP*, 24. Modern scholarship suggests that during the classic *nishiki-e* phase *ukiyo-e* prints were more expensive than the early woodcuts and were patronized by the wealthier Edo samurai and merchants. See Richard Lane, *Images from the Floating World: The Japanese Print* (Oxford, 1978), 99–100.

[23] *Japan: A Record in Colour by Mortimer Menpes, Transcribed by Dorothy Menpes* (London, 1901), 31–2.

[24] Preface, *Leaves from the Sketch Books of Frank Brangwyn Cut by Urushibara* (Leigh-on-Sea [1940?]), n.pag.

It was a fully human craft, involving the whole man. The Japanese printers were themselves artists, bringing the original design to life by brushing on the water-based colours in subtle gradations, sometimes spattered for dramatic semi-random effects, and achieving through varying degrees of pressure on the *baren* pad subtleties of touch unachievable by the mechanical press. Even in a batch numbering thousands, each impression was subtly different, hand crafted, not a facsimile but a work of art.

THE CREATION OF A CLASSIC COLLECTION

Before Binyon joined in 1895, the Department of Prints and Drawings held very few *ukiyo-e* woodcuts. Some of his earliest discoveries in the Museum collections were not in fact sheet prints but two of the rarest and finest *ukiyo-e* books, Utamaro's *Ehon Mushi Erabi* and Kitao Masayoshi's *Raikin Zui*, which had been in the Museum for decades, hidden away in the Library until Binyon transferred them to the Print Room in 1915.[25] *Ehon Mushi Erabi*, Utamaro's famous 'Insect Book', had come with the library of the great botanist Sir Joseph Banks. It is one of the world's most beautiful books. Binyon considered it 'incomparable', both in its designs and 'the inconceivable delicacy of the printing' surpassing 'everything of the kind ever done' (*JCP* 140, 94). In the way it is conceived as a total work of art, its marriage of text and image, its flowing curves and sense of space, it had already perfected everything friends like Ricketts (who owned a copy of Utamaro's equally fine 'Shell Book') were striving to achieve. To appreciate the impact such books had on the young Binyon you must study them close to, as he did, for the textures of their handmade paper, delicate patinas of powdered mica and metal dust, and subtle use of gauffrage create a rich dialogue between surface and depth that is lost in reproduction (colour pl. 3).

As far as sheet prints were concerned, however, the Department of Prints and Drawings held only a handful acquired in 1860 as

[25] See Lawrence Smith, 'History and Characteristics of the Ukiyo-e Collection in the British Museum', English Supplement, *Ukiyo-e Masterpieces in European Collections: British Museum*, ed. Muneshige Narazaki, 3 vols. (Tokyo, 1987–8), i. 1, and 'Japanese Illustrated Books in the British Museum', English Supplement, ibid. iii. 1.

specimens rather than works of art. The bareness of the cupboard is shown by the fact that the reproductions Holmes chose for *Hokusai* were drawn from the South Kensington Museum collection and those of Shannon, Moore, and Holmes himself; not one came from the British Museum, despite Binyon's having commissioned the book. It was on this virtually non-existent foundation that Binyon, with Colvin's approval and support, in little over a decade constructed the finest public collection in Europe.

The drive to construct a Museum collection came from both men, but its direction and taste were moulded by Binyon. Had Colvin started building the collection when he joined the Museum in 1885, its character would have been quite different. The vast majority of the prints imported to Europe immediately following the opening up of Japan, and therefore dominant in most mature collections, were nineteenth-century prints. For the pioneers of Japonisme in Paris and London, Hokusai was the archetypal Japanese artist. In the first serious Western survey of Japanese art, a paper read to the Asiatic Society of Japan in Yokohama in 1879, William Anderson called Hokusai 'the soul of Ukiyo-ye' and in a brief list of *ukiyo-e* artists named no artist earlier than Hokusai and Hiroshige.[26] Four years later in his pioneering *L'Art japonais*, the first analytical study of Japanese art, Louis Gonse quoted approvingly Duret's assertion that 'Hokousaï . . . est le plus grand artiste que le Japon ait produit.'[27] He did not mention Harunobu, allotted a single paragraph to Utamaro and lumped the eighteenth-century artists together as 'Les Précurseurs d'Hokousaï'. Watanabe Toshio has shown that Whistler probably had access to prints by Eishi during the 1860s,[28] but for most British artists and collectors the work of the earlier masters could be glimpsed only through the distorting lenses of tired reissues, forgeries, and the journeywork of shadowy pupils.

During the 1880s and 1890s, however, sophisticated Western interest in Japanese prints gradually shifted to the great eighteenth-century artists like Harunobu, Koryūsai, Shunshō, Kitao Masanobu, Kiyonaga, Shunman, Eishi, Chōki, Sharaku, and

[26] 'A History of Japanese Art', *Transactions of the Asiatic Society of Japan*, 7 (1879), 358.

[27] *L'Art japonais* (Paris, 1883), 290.

[28] 'Eishi Prints in Whistler's Studio? Eighteenth-century Japanese Prints in the West before 1870', *BM* 128 (Dec. 1986), 874–80.

Utamaro. A consensus emerged that this was the classic period of *ukiyo-e*, its heart the four decades between Harunobu's first full-colour *nishiki-e* 'brocade' print in 1765 and the death of Utamaro in 1806, its apogee the Tenmei period (1781–9) dominated by Kiyonaga and the early designs of Utamaro. Hokusai and Hiroshige came to be viewed, not as the culmination of *ukiyo-e*, but as beleaguered geniuses in an era of rapidly declining standards.[29] The fact that this 'degeneration' had been hastened by the introduction of European aniline dyes was not lost on Binyon and others imbued with Arts and Crafts ideals. The chemical prussian blue which replaced *airō*, the fugitive water-based blue used so movingly by Harunobu, symbolized for them the disastrous impact on traditional Japanese culture of what Binyon called 'the Western contagion' of industrialization, science, and materialism (*JCP* 160).

The profound shift in taste that separated Binyon's generation from Colvin's was highlighted in 1901 when 225 prints and eight albums from the collection built during the 1880s by Ernest Hart was offered for sale to the Museum by his widow. Colvin admired this collection, rich as it was in prints by later artists like Eizan, but Binyon had doubts and at his suggestion Ricketts was invited to go through the portfolios in August 1901, before the purchase was made. Ricketts confided in his journal:

Up to town, Colvin of the British wishing to consult me on the purchase of some Japanese prints for the museum; these turned out to be Earnest Heart rubbish [*sic*], flagrant reprints and tired old reissues of those side aspects of Jap art which all Englishmen seem to get hold of; Kuniyoshi, Shigemasa, obscure followers of Shunsho, one or two Shunkos, tons of late Toyokuni, Yezan and Kunisada. I fancy the British mind shies at the large lines of Kiyonaga, & Outamaros, and seems insensible to Harunobu & his imitators. Outamaro seems to be collected when he has become Outamaro 2, & Yeishi when he is indistinguishable from his pupils. In about 6 portfolios there was one tolerable Outamaro, dit[t]o Koriousai, 2 good Shunkos, a small set of actor heads put down to Shunsho, and one good bridge by Hokusai. I felt some embarrassment in explaining to Colvin, who was

[29] See Berger, 94, and Lawrence Smith, 'Ukiyo-e Prints in the British Museum', English Supplement, *Ukiyo-e Masterpieces in European Collections: British Museum*, ed. Narazaki, ii. 1. Berger notes that the European assimilation of the successive phases of *ukiyo-e* took place in reverse chronological order, starting with Hokusai, moving back through the classic period, and finally discovering the 'primitives' (129, 214–15).

obviously taken by Yezan, that these were rub[b]ish, that when they were not vile they were reissues.[30]

Kiyonaga's supremely elegant *bijin-ga* (pictures of beautiful women) epitomize the qualities Binyon's generation admired: strong, rhythmic design combined with exquisite tact and restraint in colouration, all emotion absorbed in their clean, swift lines. Binyon leads us into the heart of this classicism when he describes the feminine type created by Kiyonaga:

His superb feminine forms, calmly sweet in a stable world and breathing the unconscious air of perfect health, are drawn with no parade of power, but impress as by the sensation of actual presence, so wonderfully does the contour evoke the shape of the rounded limbs that it encloses. This discovery of a type at once winning and stately, a type founded on reality but imaginatively enhanced so as to be in truth an ideal creation, is one of Kiyonaga's great achievements.

It is an impersonal art, this; no violence of expression or of restless line disturbs the poise of these harmoniously moving or statue-like goddesses, or the adjusted folds of their garments.

(JCP 92)

As well as its dedication to the task of perfecting an ideal type of feminine beauty, a major factor behind the Binyon generation's enthusiasm for this phase of *ukiyo-e* was the nature of the world it exhaustively inventoried, the 'Floating World' of the Yoshiwara tea houses and brothels. Quite as much as Nō and kabuki, which enthralled Yeats, Ricketts, Dulac, Bottomley, Pound, Waley, and Binyon himself, the world of the Yoshiwara courtesans as depicted in *ukiyo-e* prints—the realities of Edo brothel life were another matter—was a complex, highly allusive form of theatre. Like Nō, it was a non-naturalistic theatre of masks and stylized gestures, silences, and implicit, ambiguous emotions, 'an impersonal art', as Binyon describes Kiyonaga's. The Green Houses were closed worlds of art with their own rituals, etiquette, and aesthetic codes, dedicated to the traditional aristocratic arts of music, dance, poetry, flower arrangement, and the tea ceremony, as well as to the equally formalized arts of love. As a world wholly devoted to beauty, an aesthetic laboratory, it called for an art as subtle, allusive, and stylized as itself. To a generation distilling the lessons of Aestheticism, Decadence, and Symbolism, and which had dis-

[30] Diary entry, 5 Aug. 1901, MS 58098, R&S–BL.

1. (*left*) Laurence Binyon, *c*. 1895.

2. (*below*) The Gryphon Club debating society, Trinity College, 1891. LB (*3rd from left in 3rd row*), Arthur Cripps (*to his left*); James Smith (*2nd from left in back row*); front row (*on grass*): Robert Routh (*2nd from left*), George Calderon (*far right*).

3. (*left*) Laurence Binyon, *c.* 1900.

4. (*below*) The old Print Room in the White Wing of the British Museum, 1914. LB sits closest to the camera, Campbell Dodgson (*l*) and Arthur Waley (*r*) at the centre table.

5. (*left*) Cicely Binyon,
c. 1904.

6. (*below*) Frontispiece,
Dream-Come-True, 1905
(see p. 136).

7. Kitagawa Utamaro, *The Awabi Fishers*, woodblock triptych, 36.5 x 23 cm each, *c.* 1798 (see p. 88).

8. *Landscape* (details), handscroll, fourteenth–fifteenth century, ink and colour on silk, 64.3 x 1299.1 cm. Once attributed to Ma Yüan, now thought to be a Ming dynasty work based on Hsia Kuei's handscroll 'A Pure and Remote View of Streams and Hills' in the National Palace Museum, Taipei (see p. 181).

9. (*above*) The 'twins Twinyon': Helen (*l*) and Margaret Binyon (*r*), *c*. 1911.

10. (*left*) Lily Brayton as Ildico in LB's *Attila*, 1909.

11. (*left*) LB and wounded French soldier at Red Cross Hôpital Militaire, Arc-en-Barrois, France, 1915.

12. (*below*) LB's youngest daughter Nicolete and Basil Gray on their wedding day, 20 July 1933.

13. (*left*) Laurence Binyon in Greece, 1940.

14. (*below*) Laurence and Cicely Binyon with their cocker spaniel Genji, named after the hero of *Tale of Genji*, in the loggia at Westridge Farm House, *c.* 1941.

covered Japanese theatre, wrote verse dramas, designed costumes, carved masks, and were obsessed by dance, *ukiyo-e* held an endless fascination.

Although Binyon's own personal aesthetic was more inclusive, this was the canon of taste he inherited and helped perfect, delivering in *Japanese Colour Prints* (1923) its definitive expression. He gave it even more lasting form by physically embodying it in the British Museum collection, both directly through acquisition and indirectly through his educative influence on collectors, both through personal friendship and his writings. As Lawrence Smith, the present Keeper of Japanese Antiquities, has said, he became in effect the Museum's 'greatest *ukiyo-e* collector'.[31]

The Museum collection had to start somewhere, and so despite Ricketts's reservations the Hart collection was purchased in 1902 for £250, providing a foundation for the flurry of acquisitions that was to follow. The real breakthrough came in 1906 with the purchase of Arthur Morrison's collection of over 1,000 prints, the largest acquisition of *ukiyo-e* prints ever made by the Museum. Morrison was the most interesting of all Binyon's collector friends. As a novelist his fictional beat, the East End backstreets of *Tales of Mean Streets* and *A Child of the Jago*, could hardly have been further removed from Ricketts's cloistered aestheticism, nor could his manner of collecting prints, which often entailed late-night visits to the docklands where they could be picked up cheaply from sailors and marine stores. He would often carry his trophies to his friend, the poet W. E. Henley, 'so agog with his discovery that the Henley household would be roused from their slumbers to rejoice with him, even though it was past midnight'.[32] Although below the collection's market value, Morrison's asking price of £4,500 was a considerable sum for a Department with no special funding for Oriental art purchases, and had to be partly funded by selling duplicate mezzotints. This collection was altogether richer and better balanced than Hart's, comprising representative examples from almost every major artist and period, from rare early prints to

---

[31] 'Ukiyo-e Prints in the British Museum', 1. Wholly lacking personal acquisitiveness, LB had no interest in collecting art on his own behalf, even had he had the money to do so. At the Museum he could enjoy the pleasures of the hunt, the daily contact with and care of great works of art as well as being able to share them with students and visitors, all without the—as he saw it—psychological burden of ownership.

[32] Kennedy Williamson, *W. E. Henley: A Memoir* (London, 1930), 144.

late Kunisadas. It was a collection moulded by refined 1890s taste, numerically dominated by its Hiroshiges and Hokusais but rich also in the work of the artists Ricketts singled out as being too subtle for the 'British mind': Harunobu, Koryūsai, Eishi, and Kiyonaga, including two of the latter's finest triptychs, *Asukayama at Cherry-Blossom Time* and *Women Visiting Enoshima*.[33]

The following year proved equally momentous. The Department's collection of prints by the so-called 'Primitives' was enriched by the gift of a rare album from Sir Ernest Satow, British Ambassador in Tokyo from 1895 to 1900, and by the élite collection of over 300 prints donated by Sir Hickman Bacon. The Bacon collection was also rich in classic *nishiki-e*, as was the 360-print collection purchased in the same year for £1,800 from Samuel Tuke, part of the large collection he had formed in Japan between 1889 and 1892. After the halcyon years of 1906–7, the rate of acquisitions slowed dramatically, especially after the escalation in prices heralded by the Happer sale in 1909. The crucial 'purchases were made', *The Times* reported later, 'in the nick of time.'[34] It was now mainly down to gifts from such public-spirited collectors as W. C. Alexander (who enabled the Department to complete its set of Hokusai's *Thirty Six Views of Mt. Fuji* in 1908), R. N. Shaw, George Salting, Sir Robert Leicester Harmsworth, and Oscar Raphael. As and when funds allowed, purchases of individual prints or small sets were made from collectors and dealers, including the 1909 purchase from Sir Ernest Satow of a magnificent set of rare kabuki actor prints by Sharaku, perhaps the Museum's greatest *ukiyo-e* treasure.

UKIYO-E AS LITERATURE

For most young Englishmen of Binyon's generation, *ukiyo-e* meant the world conjured up with a novelist's skill by Edmond de Goncourt in *Outamaro* (1891) and *Hokusai* (1896). In a *Dial* article on the de Goncourts in 1889, the poet John Gray remarked that they were a unique example 'of literary men influencing the

---

[33] *Ukiyoe: Images of Unknown Japan*, ed. Lawrence Smith (London, 1988), pls. 75 and 77. All the woodcuts reproduced in this book come from the Museum collection, most of them acquired by LB.

[34] 'Japanese Prints', rev. of LB's *Catalogue*, *TLS*, 3 May 1917, 209.

manner of seeing, not thinking, of contemporary painters'.[35] They were indeed the first but not the last Western literary figures to become involved with *ukiyo-e*, for they initiated a little-known but fascinating sub-tradition of scholarship involving poets and novelists as diverse as Binyon, Arthur Morrison, and the contemporary bestselling novelist and *ukiyo-e* collector/scholar James Michener.

Ukiyo-e's first great literary exponent in English was Ernest Fenollosa, the American philosopher, art historian, and Emersonian–Whitmanian poet who arrived in Japan in 1878 as Professor of Political Economy and Philosophy at Tokyo University and spent twelve years in the country before returning to the United States as curator of the Japanese Department of the Boston Museum of Fine Arts in 1890. With his passionate regard for traditional Japanese art, Fenollosa was at first hostile to *ukiyo-e*, but during the 1890s he changed his mind in view of the key role Japanese prints had played in 'revolutionizing the world's art'.[36] His full-dress account was *An Outline History of Ukiyo-Ye* (1901), but his masterpiece was perhaps *The Masters of Ukioye*, written for a major exhibition in New York in 1896. A pioneering survey of the phases of the *ukiyo-e* school, *Masters* is that unlikeliest of literary genres, an exhibition catalogue that contrives to be a work of literature. Rather than a closed text of art history intoning completed taxonomies in the past tense, it dramatizes the history of *ukiyo-e* as a narrative unfolding in the present tense of the visitor's slow perambulation through the galleries, guided by Fenollosa not in the disembodied, omniscient voice of the scholar but in the breathless accents of the storyteller. He presents the genesis of revolutionary artists such as Harunobu and Kiyonaga as sub-plots in a suspense story in which the spectator, spurred by question marks and cajoled by exclamation marks, is encouraged to participate by anticipation and analysis, both in the literary realm of the catalogue and the visual realm of the prints lining the gallery walls. The rise and fall of *ukiyo-e* is not regurgitated as dead history, but embodied in the ongoing drama between the prints, Fenollosa's 1896 text, and the real time of the visitor as he or she moves from one picture to the next.

[35] 'Les Goncourt', *Dial*, 1 (1889), 12.
[36] *An Outline History of Ukiyo-Ye* (Tokyo, 1901), 12. See Lawrence W. Chisolm, *Fenollosa: The Far East and American Culture* (New Haven, Conn., 1963), 147–8.

Masters of Ukioye is also literary in a less sophisticated sense as it slips periodically into a fifth gear of poetic prose. Here Fenollosa meditates on two prints designed by Harunobu shortly before his premature death in 1770:

There is something unearthly about the line themes, orchestrated in black and ghost-tints, which lifts one to the infinities of Beethoven's purest melodies. The dreamy clarinet-player seems to droop and melt away into regions of sublimity where no earthly ear shall follow his dying chords. Thus indeed we are glad at the last to have Harunobu pass, transfigured, from our vision.[37]

Here he is on Hokusai:

in his themes we miss some last perfection of fibre, some inner tempering, some unfathomable depth, something which, in literature, constitutes the very soul of poetry; something that tones the soul like a bird's note at morning, makes it innocent and fragrant like a wild flower, pure as a child, of diamond texture, concentrating the flashing lights that no merely mortal eye hath seen.[38]

Passages like these render much of Fenollosa's prose an extinct species of impressionistic, 'literary' art criticism. It is a paradox true to this richly paradoxical period that while he was developing an aesthetic which, disseminated by Arthur Wesley Dow and Ezra Pound, would help revolutionize twentieth-century painting and poetry, Fenollosa never weaned himself off this nineteenth-century prose and the Romantic vision in which it was rooted.

Binyon's own generation suffered recurring symptoms, understandably so in the case of the poet Yone Noguchi, who was one of Binyon's first Japanese friends. Soon after arriving in England from New York in November 1902, Noguchi had his volume of poems *From the Eastern Sea* privately printed and circulated among the London literati, including Binyon and Colvin at the Print Room. Binyon's cousin Arthur Ransome was the first man to buy a copy and the volume was published by the Unicorn Press in 1903. Binyon introduced him to Roche's, and by February 1903 he could write to his wife: 'I made many a nice young, lovely, kind friend among literary *genius* (attention!) W. B. Yeats, or Lawrence Binyon, Moore and Bridges. They are so good; they invite me almost everyday. They are jolly companions.' Anxious to reassure

---

[37] *The Masters of Ukiyo-Ye* (New York, 1896), 53.   [38] Ibid. 100.

her that he had not fallen among Wildean aesthetes, he added: 'Their hairs are not long, I tell you.'[39] The problem with the books Noguchi later published on *ukiyo-e* is that their mélange of Japanese and eclectic Western styles bespeaks a vision as hybrid as any *chinoiserie*. The prints themselves enter as occasions for poeticizing, embroidered with references to English poets. Here he is, for instance, on Harunobu's 'dreams of the fairy kingdom':

There is neither east nor west for this fairy world. . . . The seasons there are only one spring when, like Tennyson's Land of the Lotus-Eaters, the languid air that swoons, makes a hundred flowers raise their tired eyelids. . . . Oh, how glorious it is to go to the fairy world where a dream that is sweetened with summer light drops, like an apple waxing over-mellow in Tennyson's song, to be picked by a girl whose silvery feet beat a golden rhyme along a hidden flowery path. . . . Oh, see Harunobu's pictures of the fairy world in which a soft mood-string of poetry binds the heaven and earth.[40]

It is salutary to remind ourselves, however, that we are not dealing here with modern books laden with crisp colour reproductions. Books by Binyon and his contemporaries were literary texts in the quite literal sense that they were word-oriented, phalanxes of unrelieved print illustrated at rare intervals with often poor quality half-tone or collotype reproductions. Almost unavoidably, writing about *ukiyo-e* was a literary enterprise. The novel tactic employed by the American writer Arthur Davidson Ficke in *Chats on Japanese Prints* (1915) was to allow his poetic prose to periodically crystallize out into actual poems inspired by the prints under discussion. Here he illustrates a Kiyonaga print with what amounts to a definition of *ukiyo-e* classicism in iambic pentameter:

> Serene, dispassionate, with lordly gaze
> They move through this clear afternoon of gold,
> Equal to life and all its deeps may hold,
> Calm, spacious masters of the glimmering maze.[41]

The continuity between Binyon's critical writing and his poetry is subtler, a matter of vision rather than self-conscious literary writing. His prose is patterned by rhythm, image, and symbol but is not lapidary or self-regarding. Lucid and unmannered, it is the prose of a poet rather than a Poet. As with Fenollosa, the deep structures are literary, but the climaxes come not in Fenollosan bursts of poeticism but in prose that slows, turns meditatively inward and grows simpler, more transparent.

Binyon's early research on *ukiyo-e*, from the 1890s to the outbreak of the First World War, took him many times to Paris and other European cities and twice to the United States to study public and private collections, and involved close collaboration with European, American, and Japanese scholars. This research was embodied in his *Catalogue of Japanese and Chinese Woodcuts Preserved in the Sub-Department of Oriental Prints and Drawings in the British Museum* (1916), which was the first detailed descriptive catalogue of any public *ukiyo-e* collection. With authoritative sections on dating, states, impressions, reprints, forgeries, and pigments, it was hailed as 'by far the most important work on the subject yet produced in England, or probably anywhere else'.[42] In one sense it was implicitly a work of criticism: by excluding many later prints and all Meiji period prints, it wishfully pruned the Museum collection into a classical shape, enacting on paper what Binyon sought to do in reality through acquisitions and his influence on collectors.

It is, for a museum catalogue, an engaging volume, described by the poet Gordon Bottomley as 'the most delightful book in the world—companion of my days, overshadower of my nights, inexhaustible, kindling, fortifying, illuminating, enchanting and mind-compelling'.[43] However, its seventeen-page introduction and brief descriptions gave Binyon little scope to develop his ideas. He included chapters on *ukiyo-e* in *Painting in the Far East* (1908) and *Flight of the Dragon* (1911), but his ideas were not fully aired until *Japanese Colour Prints*, published in collaboration with Major J. J. O'Brien Sexton in 1923. The standard text in its field for decades, this classic handbook is still in print and, though superseded in detail, remains, in its balance of scholarship and personal response, its empathy, and breadth of vision, one of the most attractive introductions to *ukiyo-e*.

The division of labour between Binyon and Sexton is unstated but quickly becomes obvious to the reader. The chapters are

[42] 'Japanese Prints', *TLS*, 3 May 1917, 209.   [43] ALs to LB, 15 Jan. 1918.

divided chronologically, each chapter beginning with a historical and technical summary of the development of woodblock printing during the period, followed by brief biographies of its major artists. This is Sexton's contribution, erudite and painstaking, at home with historical documents and the results of his field work in Japan. A space then signals the emergence of a more personal voice which, while less urgent than the narrative voice in *Masters of Ukiyo-ye*, similarly implicates the reader in the unfolding drama of *ukiyo-e*. This voice, Binyon's, develops as both narrative and ongoing meditation, duetting with the impersonal scholar's voice, paring away history and biography in order to focus the reader's attention on the inner biography of the artworks themselves.

Few contemporary writers on art could match Binyon's ability to share the joys of seeing, the simple and complex pleasures of art. Here he is describing a Kiyonaga diptych, which is not reproduced and so must be evoked in words:

It is a composition simple in its symmetry. At the left is one standing woman immensely tall; at the right two girls standing close together. In the centre are four seated or kneeling figures, a youth and three girls, arranged in groups of two. It is an hour of peace and idleness; one of the seated girls touches her *samisen*, and the imagined notes of music seem to hold the group in happy stillness; only the gesture of the girl, crouching beside the youth and holding up a lacquer wine-cup as she turns her face to the woman behind her, lends a touch of animation. But of what value to the composition is that central space of air and prospect of seashore! What largeness and infinitude seem drawn in among those idle figures! Here is Kiyonaga's new gift to Ukiyo-ye; completeness, 'envelope'. The landscape is no mere adjunct, it is an integral part of the conception. There is no effort at realism, no colour in the sky; the evocation is made by the simplest means; but one smells the seaweed on the sands and the salt moist air of evening at low tide, one seems to hear faint voices from the distant groups of people near the little cluster of stranded fishing-boats.

(*JCP* 92–3)

There are literary deep structures here. The 'imagined notes of music' that 'seem to hold the group in happy stillness' echo Keats's 'Ode on a Grecian Urn', for example, but this adds resonance without rupturing the textual surface. The passage stresses, and itself seeks to embody, the suggestivity of the print, the way in which the scene, its smells and sounds, its silences and sense of space, and its emotional resonance, is completed in the mind of the spectator, art not as mimesis but a disciplined and disciplining meditation which inveigles the spectator into participation in the creative process.

Binyon's critical style ranges from romantic poetic insights—as when he remarks of a Hiroshige landscape that 'Hiroshige seems to feel the rain as the trees feel it, drinking it into their fibres with a kind of patient ecstasy' (*JCP* 152)—to passages where, drawing on a largely formalist vocabulary, he explores *ukiyo-e*'s organization of pictorial space, especially evident when Kiyonaga, Utamaro, Eishi, and Shunman spread their designs across the great diptychs and triptychs which were the glory of the collection Binyon was building at the Museum. Here he describes Utamaro's superb early diptych *Colours and Scents of Flowers of the Four Seasons* (colour pl. 2):

> The variation in repetition of the swinging lines make a beautiful rhythm running through it; and the strong upright of the post near the centre, repeating the less definite upright lines of the figures, enhances the delicacy of the girlish form sitting on the boat's prow and clinches the whole composition. Note the value, too, of the outline of the wide sun-hat worn by the girl who stands foremost on the landing-stage. And how charming is the invention of the girl's face peeping through the young man's diaphanous dress which she has caught in her hand for a veil; how beautifully drawn the movement of the foot of the girl in the centre! Here there is a subtlety, a complexity, made to look simple, natural and spontaneous, such as no other artist of Ukiyo-ye could rival.
>
> (*JCP* 88–9)

Most early Western scholars, unable to see beyond the criteria of Renaissance and post-Renaissance European art, dismissed such prints as either merely 'decorative' or hamfisted, as in F. V. Dickins's diagnosis of the 'fatal defect' of Japanese art as 'paltry drawing of human form and feature'.[44] The affront was perhaps less to their aesthetic sense than to Western models of psychology. They found such prints disconcertingly impersonal, insufficiently human to be real art. The figures lend themselves so pliantly, so acquiescently to the rhythmic design—the serenely expressionless faces of the four girls and two young men are virtually identical, androgynous, neutral as masks—that it seems they are mere vessels

---

[44] *Fugaku Hiyaku-Kei or a Hundred Views of Fuji (Fusiyama) by Hokusai*, 4 vols. (London, 1880), i. p. xix.

for an energy that flows through them. The real drama is not psychological but spatial, the relationships between the figures expressed, not as confrontations between the separate egos of European art, but by gestural interplay in an eloquently complex language of linear rhythm that includes the boat, the waves, even the calligraphy of title and signature. This is even clearer in the early *ukiyo-e* masters working before the introduction of full colour printing, when the calligraphic element was still dominant. In 'the exuberance of Kiyonobu's swinging lines and twirling loops and rolling curves', Binyon writes, we encounter 'a kind of drawing which communicates the sense of gesture and movement rather than of form' (*JCP* 39). In this world of verbs, a girl is a calligraphic ink-stroke playing at being a girl, and so is a bird or a chair, a single energy restlessly assuming diverse temporary incarnations. There is no such thing as still life. In this democracy of expressive line and flat colour, everything exists with equal reality on the flat picture plane, with humans accorded no privileged status. In Kiyomasu, Binyon remarks, 'human face and hands appear as part of the general gay pattern, on equal terms with the devices on the dresses, the subdivided areas of colour, and the black lines surrounding them' (*JCP* 39).

This bespeaks a kinship between humans and their environment more intimate than anything in European oil painting, whether it be the man-made environment of clothes, furniture, and rooms or what Binyon's generation still capitalized as 'Nature'. One of the features of Japanese culture which impressed all Western visitors was the way in which it nurtured intimate links between the natural and man-made worlds, and this is reflected in all forms of *ukiyo-e*, not only landscapes. Even in indoor scenes, Japanese architecture— open plan, built for summer from wood, paper, and other light, breathing materials—ensures that nature is rarely entirely shut out. Few prints, even the most intimate erotic scenes, fail to reveal through sliding door or window a glimpse of cherry blossom or maple, snow or gusts of rain, and in these rare cases kimonos, textiles, fans, screens, and ceramics are decorated with natural motifs which, like the landscape outside, change with the season. The season is a vital emotional ingredient, whereas it would be absurd to enquire the season in, say, Velazquez's *Las Meninas*, whose protagonists are cocooned in a wholly human environment, mirrored rather than windowed.

Whereas in traditional Western art the landscape is choreographed around its owners, ministering to the humans who are the emotional focus of the scene, in a *ukiyo-e* landscape like Shunman's triptych *The Six Crystal Rivers*,[45] for example, humans and landscape are intricately woven into a single dynamic pattern which never for a moment denies its status as art—flat decorative forms flush with the picture plane in a series of telephoto views rather than a single organizing perspective—and yet which captures, in a typically playful manner, what Binyon saw as one of the key themes of Japanese art: the continuity, the identity almost, of man and nature. The importance of this for Binyon will become clear when we consider his work on Chinese and Japanese ink landscapes in Chapter 8.

Japanese Colour Prints is an even-handed book. Binyon writes with great sensitivity about all phases of *ukiyo-e* except the later nineteenth-century prints, though even here he seeks out the positive, since as both man and scholar his natural mode was praise. He writes with special insight of early masters like Masanobu, of the great landscapes of Hokusai and Hiroshige, and of the classics of the golden age, especially Harunobu. Perhaps the heart of the book, however, is his discussion of Utamaro. One of the patron saints of Parisian Japonisme, Utamaro was denounced by both Anderson and Fenollosa as the key figure in the degeneration of *ukiyo-e* after 1800. They abhorred the willowy, attenuated figures of his middle period, dubbed by Fenollosa 'dolichocephalic, spindle-legged monstrosities'. Riddled with 'unhealthy aestheticism', his Utamaro is a proto-Huysmans or Beardsley, 'a thorough "degenerate" of the end of the last century'.[46] (This twinning of Utamaro and Beardsley is amusingly corroborated by Yeats's anecdote about standing before 'an incomparable Utamaro' in the tower of Edward Martyn's Tulira Castle and hearing his companion remark, 'I never could stand those Beardsleys.')[47] Although it applied less to the historical Utamaro than the dissolute novelistic hero he had become in de Goncourt's *Outamaro*, this decadent label clung to Utamaro and was an article of faith among many of Binyon's fellow scholars.

[45] Reproduced in *Ukiyoe: Images of Unknown Japan*, pl. 113. LB acquired the left-hand print for the Museum in 1910 and the other two in 1912.

[46] *Masters*, 88, 45. See also Anderson, *Japanese Wood Engravings* (London, 1895), 36.

[47] *Autobiographies*, 387.

Almost to a man they fell into the moralistic trap that unerringly carbon-dates their writing. Ficke had Utamaro and Kiyonaga in mind when he wrote: 'The decadent artist . . . pours his visions into figures of slender languor and relaxation that parallel his own weariness and satiety; but the artist of the prime draws large-limbed, wholesome, magnificently normal figures as the symbols of his magnificently normal mind.'[48]

Utamaro was not much better served by his admirers. In Noguchi's poem 'The Lady of Utamaru's Art', Utamaro's line is 'spiritualized into odour', frail 'As a gossamer, the handiwork of dream',[49] while in his 1897 *Dial* article 'Outamaro' Ricketts nervously conscripts him as an effete *fin-de-siècle* aesthete 'untroubled . . . by any emotion outside a world that lived very close to the flowers': 'His name conjures up the vision of cloud-like colours, and . . . upon a world remote yet actual . . . he has shed that grace as of faded things, the troubled hues of a fresco about to disappear, of a flower dying in the twilight.'[50]

This wan hothouse orchid is a different species from the Utamaro celebrated in *Japanese Colour Prints*, whose vision of life is the antithesis of decadence. Far from being a decadent, Binyon's Utamaro explores central human experience, a poet of human labour, capturing 'the sheer beauty of natural movements in people who are absorbed in what they are doing' (*JCP* 110). Print after print 'gives a sense of something significant to what is ostensibly a most ordinary household scene' and unveils the 'sense of mystery in simple things' (*JCP* 110, 92). Binyon mocks the idea that 'this "decadent" Utamaro' could have designed his profound late mother-and-child prints, so 'full of the tenderness of insight' (*JCP* 120). He reads in them the same subtle 'elemental' psychology that Utamaro brings to his famous prints depicting courtesans gazing at themselves in mirrors: 'It is this seizure of the aboriginal, the essential, the instinctive, in feminine humanity that distinguishes Utamaro among all the artists of the world' (*JCP* 110). Binyon's Utamaro is almost Lawrentian in his search for 'the aboriginal, the essential, the instinctive' in women, through which he discovers humanity's deepest kinship with non-human, elemental nature. The

---

[48] *Chats*, 221. Ficke is referring to Utamaro's later prints. In his early prints he is 'as wholesome as Kiyonaga' (261).

[49] *The Pilgrimage*, 2 vols. (Kamakura, Japan, 1909), i. 44.

[50] *Dial*, 5 (1897), 24.

comparison may seem strange, but Binyon sees in Utamaro what he sees in Blake, 'a sense of the primeval and elemental in man and nature'.[51]

This is the way Binyon sees *The Awabi Fishers*, for him 'supreme among all the triptychs of Utamaro,' which he acquired for the Museum through the National Arts Collections Fund for a hefty £150 in 1910 (pl. 7).[52] It is one of the rarest of *ukiyo-e* sets, but he sees it neither through connoisseurial nor curatorial eyes:

Not so perfect perhaps as Kiyonaga's finest prints, this is something greater than Kiyonaga ever made; for perfection implies a limitation. The group of nearly nude forms, with unbound hair, on the rocks, with infinite sea beyond them, yield a sense of latent and mysterious powers, as if they shared in the secrets of the deep waters which they are used to plunge in; the human body appears strange and wonderful, a symbol more significant than it had ever been hitherto in the art of Ukiyo-ye. The theme is taken from daily life; there is a woman buying shellfish in the right-hand sheet, though she seems an insignificant intrusion from the superficial world; but the theme is indefinitely deepened and broadened into an imaginative 'beyond', as, in the print, the sea-waves melt away into the unseen.

(*JCP* 121)

Utamaro has been admired and vilified for many qualities but Binyon is the only Western writer to have seen his work in quite these Romantic terms. The scholar and poet are almost indistinguishable here. As we shall see in Chapter 10, Binyon was working on a long visionary ode, *The Sirens*, while writing *Japanese Colour Prints*, and there was some degree of osmosis between the two texts. This is not to say that Binyon simply read this dimension into Utamaro's prints, but it does show how deeply ingrained was this mode of vision that he should have chosen to illustrate it most powerfully through urban and urbane, 'decadent' Utamaro.

It permeates too the conclusion of *Japanese Colour Prints*:

In the limited number of Kiyonaga's central masterpieces we do, indeed, find a bloom as of perfect ripeness, which does not come again. Yet . . . it is in Utamaro and in Hokusai that Ukiyo-ye finds its summits, the one

[51] Introduction, *William Blake: Being All his Woodcuts Photographically Reproduced in Facsimile* (London, 1902), n.pag.

[52] LB, 'Eastern Art', *Twenty-Five Years of the National Art-Collections Fund 1903–1928*, ed. D. S. MacColl (Glasgow, 1928), 29, 166.

supreme in figure-design, the other in landscape. And this not only because of their creative invention and a range far exceeding the other masters, but because in these two, even more than in Harunobu or Kiyonaga, there is a capacity to divine and to communicate the elemental powers in man and nature, and to rise at times into an imaginative world where life is more deeply felt and its mystery more deeply apprehended.

(*JCP* 161)

Binyon never fell prey to the pervasive European fallacy that *ukiyo-e* represented the apogee of Japanese, let alone Asian, art, but at its greatest he saw it as a profound and ultimately spiritual art. Moreover, something of special significance for Binyon the poet, it is that rarest form of spiritual art which intuits the workings of the spirit, not in misty Chinese landscapes or portraits of the Buddhist saints, but in everyday life, in the midst of menial work, breastfeeding babies, lovemaking, picnicking under the cherry trees. It captures those moments when ordinary human actions momentarily lose their opacity and become, if not transparent, at least translucent, porous to the light.

5 *London Visions*

WHISTLER'S LONDON

One of the most distinctive features of British poetry in the 1890s was its attitude to urban life in general and, very much in particular, to London, that voracious 'world city' then at the height of its power and prestige as capital of the British Empire. Since its heyday in the era of Swift, Pope, Gay, and Johnson, London poetry had fallen into decline, all but buried by a doctrinaire Romantic anti-urbanism. Wordsworth had confronted his terror of London in Book 9 of *The Prelude*, but the major High Victorian poets were struck dumb by the threatening, 'unpoetic' reality of the expanding metropolis.[1] During the 1880s and 1890s, however, inspired by a complex of influences ranging from French poetry and the Aesthetic cult of the artificial to contemporary avant-garde painting, British poets turned increasingly to the city as a subject for poetry in the same spirit as the painter Walter Sickert, who in 1889 declared himself and his fellow London Impressionists 'strong in the belief that for those of us who live in the most wonderful and complex city in the world, the most fruitful course of study lies in a persistent effort to render the magic and the poetry which they daily see around them'.[2]

This flowering of London poetry was remarkable for its variety and the broad spectrum of poets it embraced. It spanned the Decadent divide, finding voice through the ideologically opposed muses of Oscar Wilde and W. E. Henley, and emerged in forms as different as Arthur Symons's impressionistic nocturnes and the pastoral debates between city journalists in Davidson's *Fleet Street Eclogues*. Its significance was first diagnosed in 1892 by Symons in his review of Henley's *London Voluntaries*:

---

[1] See G. Robert Stange, 'The Frightened Poets', *The Victorian City: Images and Realities*, ed. H. J. Dyos and Michael Wolff (London, 1973), ii. 475–94.

[2] Qtd. Robert Emmons, *The Life and Opinions of Walter Richard Sickert* (London, 1941), 99.

Here, at last, is a poet who can so enlarge the limits of his verse as to take in London. And I think that might be the test of poetry which professes to be modern—its capacity for dealing with London, with what one sees or might see there, indoors and out.[3]

Binyon was in the thick of this renaissance of London verse. Returning to London from Oxford in 1892 had re-energized his poetry, given it new focus and direction. Eight months after joining the Museum he told Arthur Quiller-Couch he had 'written more during the last year than during all the four years' at Oxford.[4] 'Life seems to me crammed with materials,' he wrote to Margaret Woods,[5] and these were increasingly urban materials. He joined the club of London poets when 'The Little Dancers' appeared in the *Pall Mall Gazette* in April 1895 and was snapped up by Henley for his *London Garland* (1895), a handsome gift-book anthology of London poetry from Chaucer to the present. With living poets ranging from Symons and Davidson to Bridges, William Watson, and Austin Dobson, the anthology encapsulated London poetry's ecumenical variety, the one significant omission being Wilde, now in Reading Gaol after his sensational trial months earlier.

The publication of the *First Book of London Visions* in 1896 established Binyon's reputation as a promising young poet. Of their first meeting in 1896 the artist William Rothenstein recalled, 'His *London Visions* had just appeared: he was a true poet, I thought.'[6] One reviewer described the poems as

twelve genuine things cut out of the heart of London life, and some of them are poems of a big order. . . . the stuff of poetry is in him as it is in few of our pleasant verse-writers to-day; and I doubt if one of the London poets— I am not forgetting Mr. Henley—has put so much of actual London into his poetry.[7]

By the time his *Second Book of London Visions* appeared in 1899, the *Dome* could celebrate Binyon as one of the 'high priests' of the 'cult of London', with *London Visions* ranking high among its 'canonical scriptures'.[8]

[3] 'Mr. Henley's Poetry', *Fortnightly Review*, NS, 308 (Aug. 1892), 184.
[4] 24 Apr. 1894, letter III, F. G. Atkinson, 'Unpublished Letters of Laurence Binyon (1): The Years of Struggle', *Notes and Queries*, NS, 29 (Aug. 1982), 336.
[5] ALs, 4 Oct. 1892, MS. Eng. lett. d. 183, ff. 23–24, Bodleian.
[6] *Men & Memories: Recollections of William Rothenstein*, 3 vols. (London, 1931–9), i. 200.
[7] *Sketch*, 5 Feb. 1896, 53.   [8] *Dome*, 2/4 (Jan. 1899), 88–9.

It is particularly apt that Henley's *London Garland* anthology should have been lavishly illustrated by members of the Royal Society of Illustrators, ranging from Whistler and Beardsley to Phil May and Arthur Rackham, for this underlined the deep affinities between poetry and the pictorial arts that is so striking a feature of the period, with its endemic pictorial poems and literary paintings. Binyon was no exception. Contemporary critics spoke of *London Visions*' 'pictorial effect' and 'power of making us see pictures'.[9] There were clear links between Binyon's poetry and his work at the Print Room. He told Alfred Miles that his early London poems were influenced by Rembrandt's etchings and that he had tried to emulate Rembrandt's technique of giving 'unity to his treatment of crowds by strongly focussed light'.[10] Poems like 'The Fire' bear this out.

Whistler was another major influence on *London Visions*, as on all London poetry of the 1880s and 1890s. Bernard Muddiman remembered the 'wonderful spirit of camaraderie' among Binyon, Symons, Dowson, Crackanthorpe, and other 'younger men' of the 1890s and the synergistic 'energy' they gained 'from this meeting together in London'. He then tied this in with the crucial catalyst: 'Indeed, coming together by chance, as it were, in London, they not only discovered one another and the ineffable boon of comradeship, but they also rediscovered, through Whistler, London for art.'[11] Binyon's evocation of the London he 'perversely lamented' when St Paul's moved to Hammersmith in 1884—his 'solitary rambles about the by-ways of Cheapside, the towers and spires, the shipping in the Thames, . . . the deep-toned bells of the Cathedral sounding down the smoky air'—is Whistlerian in seeing London as intrinsically poetic in contrast to the 'prose' Hammersmith of school playing fields and creeping suburbia, and indeed these solitary rambles took him regularly into Whistler's sketching territory along the Thames.

Binyon's work on Japanese prints may also have subtly influenced his way of seeing and portraying London. Whereas classical Japanese painting was primarily landscape-oriented, its archetypal

---

[9] *Dome*, 2/4 (Jan. 1899), 89; *Bookman*, 9 (Mar. 1896), 189.

[10] ALs, n.d. [1905], Beinecke Rare Book and Manuscript Library, Yale University (hereafter BRBM). Miles used this in his 'Laurence Binyon', *Robert Bridges and Contemporary Poets*, vol. vii of his *The Poets and the Poetry of the Nineteenth Century* (London, 1906), 621–3.

[11] *The Men of the Nineties* (London, 1920), 7.

exponent a Zen monk in a mountain temple, *ukiyo-e* arose in the great cities of Edo (modern Tokyo) and Osaka, as the art form patronized by the emerging merchant class. During the decades of its flowering and maturity it was an urban art form, moulded by and moulding a distinctively city consciousness. In fact, the depiction of the city was one of the major meeting points of Japanese and European art. From the mid-eighteenth century onwards, *ukiyo-e* artists experimented with linear perspective and other European techniques to lend depth to interiors and later to create a convincing sense of space in their depictions of the city itself, its streets, rivers, and bridges.[12] In neat symbiosis, the French Impressionists encountered Japanese prints just as they began experimenting with modern Paris as a subject for painting, and found that series such as Hiroshige's *One Hundred Views of Edo* (1856–7) offered new ways of seeing and portraying urban life.

Thanks to Whistler, London was an early beneficiary of this enriching of the European urban vision. It is no coincidence that the American painter was both the high priest of Japonisme in England and the artist responsible for re-educating Londoners' perception of their own city. This was keenly appreciated in Binyon's circle. In 1899 his close friend Charles Holmes discussed the influence of Hiroshige in the context of Whistler's unveiling of London's hitherto elusive beauty:

> The romance of a great city is so generally tragic, so often merely sordid, that the finding in it of some tender, mysterious beauty has the aspect of deliberate fiction. The wonderful thing is, that the beauty should really be there; that the Thames can be as exquisite as Mr. Whistler has made it appear in paint.[13]

From the stark Courbetian realism of the Thames Set to the dematerialized, near-abstract Thames nocturnes of the late 1860s and early 1870s, Whistler's London pictures were engaged in a continuous dialogue with Japanese art.

So, directly or indirectly, was poetry influenced by them. The clearest case is Oscar Wilde, an assiduous student both of Whistler and Japonisme, in poems like 'Impression du Matin' and 'Sym-

---

[12] For Western influences on *ukiyo-e*, see Michael Sullivan, *The Meeting of Eastern and Western Art, from the Sixteenth Century to the Present Day* (London, 1973), 41–5.

[13] 'Nature and Landscape', *Dome*, NS 2/5 (Feb. 1899), 146.

phony in Yellow',[14] but the Symons of *Silhouettes* and *London Nights* was also indebted to Whistler, Monet, and Degas. His London poetry not only borrows Degas's subjects but finds verbal analogues for such formal devices as oblique angles, cropping, and concentration on vivid isolated details—Symons's myopic focus on parts of the body, especially eyes, for example—that Degas derived partly from *ukiyo-e*. While Ernest Fenollosa spoke of Edo as an 'Asiatic Paris', there are also apt analogies between the Edo depicted in *ukiyo-e* and the London of *London Nights*, both specialized subcultures within their respective cities. Both were considered 'decadent', not least because both view the city as a privileged arena for forms of art, from drama and dance to the courtesan's sexual repertoire. In its evocation of a fragile world of pleasure tinctured with sadness and in its sense of transience as both alluring and tragic, Symons's nocturnal urban world touches on some aspects of the *ukiyo* of *ukiyo-e*, originally a Buddhist term for the transient world of illusion but later adopted for the 'floating world' of urban fashions and pleasures, the tea-houses and kabuki theatres depicted in *ukiyo-e*.[15] Superficial as these analogies are, they run deeper than the blue-eyed Japanese girls of Alfred Noyes's 'A Japanese Love Song' and other *japonaiseries* rife in contemporary poetry.

Japanese influence in a more blatantly Whistlerian form emerged in the work of Henley, feisty leader of the anti-Decadents, whose enthusiasm for *ukiyo-e* found kitsch expression in his 'Ballade of a Toyokuni Colour Print'. Whistler allowed one of his Thames nocturnes to be reproduced to illustrate Henley's 'Nocturne' in *A London Garland*, entirely appropriately since the poem, usually entitled 'To James McNeill Whistler', evokes a composite Thamescape collaged from several nocturnes, complete with such Hiroshigean motifs as the 'old skeleton bridge', while the phrase 'this floating, transitory world' not only captures the mood of the nocturnes but is also a perfect if unwitting translation of *ukiyo* in its original Buddhist sense.[16]

Although Binyon wrote nothing as specifically Whistlerian as 'Nocturne', his influence permeates *London Visions*. The contemporary reviewer who described Binyon as 'an impressionist

[14] See Earl Miner, *The Japanese Tradition in British and American Literature*, 2nd edn. (Princeton, 1966), 83–7.
[15] For the layered meanings of *ukiyo*, see Lane, 11.
[16] *The Works of W. E. Henley*, 7 vols. (London, 1908), i. 216–17.

word-painter' whose poems are 'mainly harmonies in grey and other sad tones', had Whistler in mind, for, like the nocturnes, they draw on a restricted palette mainly of cool blues and greys.[17] What Japanese influence there is in Binyon's London poetry is mainly mediated through Whistler, but there are perhaps subtler ways in which his London verse relates to his work on Oriental art.

'PHILANTHROPIST WITH A CAMERA'

In an essay on the British Museum *ukiyo-e* collection, Lawrence Smith writes of early British collectors' passion for 'classic' eighteenth-century prints:

> They loved the melancholy of the floating world depicted by Harunobu, Kiyonaga, Utamaro and Eishi, and the elegant, well-mannered screen the artists drew protectively over its hidden harshnesses. . . . they ignored the stronger emotions and seamier side of life. They sought refuge in this apparently delicate, remote and idyllic world of art.[18]

This is what one would expect of the 1880s and 1890s, a Paterian retreat into a cloistered world of art as a refuge from sordid reality. The description fits many collectors and writers, but it is less true perhaps of Binyon and Morrison. It is a remarkable coincidence that the pioneers of Japonisme in France, Edmond and Jules de Goncourt, were pioneers of the *roman documentaire*, and that Morrison, the leading British Japanese art collector–scholar of the next generation, also started out as a writer of such starkly realistic stories of East End deprivation and violence as *Tales of Mean Streets* and *A Child of the Jago*. *A Child of the Jago* and Binyon's *First Book of London Visions* both appeared in 1896 and both, though in very different ways, tackle the 'seamier side of life'.

Binyon's was an insider's view of the city, not that of a Tennysonian bard down for the weekend or a commuter from garden suburbs like Bedford Park but that of a man who lived and worked amid the grime and splendour of the inner city. Already stretched beyond its limits, London was still attracting fresh batches of impoverished immigrants from depressed rural areas of

---

[17] *Publishers' Circular*, 18 Jan. 1896, 83.
[18] 'Ukiyo-e Prints in the British Museum', English Supplement, *Ukiyo-e Masterpieces in British Museum*, ed. Narazaki, ii. 1.

Britain and from abroad. In just twenty years between 1870 and 1890 the population had swelled from 3,215,000 to 4,211,000, and quadrupled between 1800 and 1900. The results of this over-crowding and desperate poverty were evident everywhere. Forty years later Binyon still remembered 'the great numbers of people, especially children, whom one saw daily in the streets dressed in rags'.[19]

London Visions is marked by compassion for the London poor, both the alienated working class enslaved to the machine, like the factory workers in 'The Bathers', and the homeless underclass who have fallen out of society altogether. Several poems focus on vagrants, including 'The Rag Picker', 'The Paralytic', 'The Convict', and 'To a Derelict'. It was these poems that worried Norman Gale in his 1896 *Academy* review, which congratulated Binyon for embarking on 'a laudable, and even a beautiful mission', but warned that he 'must be observant lest he deteriorate from the genuine bard to the philanthropist with a camera'.[20] With every detail of Victorian London under intense scrutiny by photographers, especially in this first decade of the hand camera, such analogies were common and invariably pejorative. Although the 'pictorial effect' reviewers saw in *London Visions* is perhaps closer to contemporary painters such as Thomas Kennington, Edward Wilkinson, and Ralph Hedley than to contemporary documentary photography, the analogy holds good on some points.[21] Like the photographs of documentarists such as John Thomson and Paul Martin, these poems examine and revoke the curious invisibility of the destitute, who for the hurrying populace have faded innocuously into the urban decor.[22] The dying tramp in 'To a Derelict' has receded beyond even the minimal notice of street cruelty: 'The very boys | That mocked thee, mock no more; they pass thee by' (*CP*ii.50). Binyon's portraits seek to trawl them back into the visible:

[19] ALs to Gilbert Murray, 17 June 1939, Gilbert Murray MS 87, fo. 23, Bodleian.

[20] *Academy*, 29 Feb. 1896, 175.

[21] For examples of these artists' London pictures, see Julian Treuherz, *Hard Times: Social Realism in Victorian Art* (London, 1987), 115–18.

[22] For Thomson's London photographs, see the chapter 'Street Life' in Mark Haworth-Booth (ed.), *The Golden Age of British Photography 1839–1900* (London, 1988), 142–51. For Paul Martin see Roy Flukinger, Larry Schaaf, and Standish Meacham, *Paul Martin: Victorian Photographer* (London, 1978). In the staged, tableau-like manner of poems such as 'The Statues', Binyon is closer to Thomson.

> In the April sun
> Shuffling, shapeless, bent,
> Cobweb-eyed, with stick
> Searching, one by one,
> Gutter-heaps, intent
> Wretched rags to pick.
> ('The Rag-Picker' *CP*ii.13)

The absence of subject noun or pronoun in this opening stanza, sealed by the impersonal infinitive 'to pick', mimics the way the crowd sees the rag-picker, if at all, as a bundle of sordid details which fail to coalesce into a fellow human being. The blindness is mutual. So long consigned to invisibility, the outcasts confer the same invisibility on the London life swirling around them.

If, as Gale suggested, these are 'verbal photographs', they are not snapshots but static meditations, still-lifes with the shutter held open long enough to render the background a blur. Poem after poem contrasts the outcasts' immobility with the swift, anonymous crowds. In this environment where individuality is subsumed in the momentum of the crowd, where life equals motion, the outcasts' immobility seals their withdrawal from the human tide. So too, amid 'the jostling roar of the street' (*CP*ii.38), does their muteness. The outcasts in *London Visions* are all silent. William B. Thesing complains that Binyon 'rarely tells the life stories of the city's outcast victims',[23] but this reflects Binyon's acknowledgement of the impossibility, for him at least, of divining any narrative cohesion in the modern metropolis. Whereas Henley in *London Types* sees his subjects with an evaluating journalistic eye ('Liza's a stupid, straight, hard-working girl'[24]), the younger London poets aspired to no such clairvoyance. The sestet of Symons's sonnet 'The Blind Beggar' in *Silhouettes* comprises a series of unanswerable questions: 'What thoughts are his?'[25] Binyon does not wander the London streets as a detached *flâneur* in search of unfortunates in romantically posed attitudes, 'is not the inhuman, impersonal artist merely' as a contemporary reviewer put it,[26] but he knows that he cannot enter the world of the urban poor. By stopping to observe

---

[23] *The London Muse: Victorian Poetic Responses to the City* (Athens, Ga., 1982), 167.
[24] *Works*, ii. 109.
[25] *The Collected Works of Arthur Symons*, 9 vols. (London, 1924), i. 122.
[26] *Bookman*, 9 (Mar. 1896), 189.

these vagrants, he drops out of the purposeful crowd, and when he interrogates the crowd in 'The Rag-Picker' he does so in parenthesis, typographically acknowledging his isolation:

> (O you passers-by,
> Moving swift and strong,
> Answer, what seek you?)
> (CPii.13)

It is, however, only temporary. He has meaningful work to go to in the morning and his Westminster lodgings to return to at night. However compassionate, like the documentarists with their camouflaged hand cameras, he is a 'loitering eye' inspecting them from the outside (CPii.51). Unlike the *poètes maudit*, he does not pretend to himself that he shares their marginality and alienation. And so rather than invent picturesque life histories for these tragic victims, Binyon places their silence at the centre of his poems and allows it to become admonitory, disturbing, at times visionary.

Only once is this silence broken, in *The Supper*, where a rich young philanthropist invites to dinner 'a chance company of guests from the street—a blind beggar, a sandwich-man, a tramp, two women, and a thief, all fallen in the world' (CPii.81). They describe their lives on the street, scraping a living, beset by exploiting landlords. Averill, the philosophical sandwich-man, was salvaged from 'John Averil', a 'socialist' poem Binyon worked on at St Paul's. Ghose's Christ Church friends had hated it, he told Binyon. 'What can you expect from people who shudder as tho' from instinct at the name of "socialist" and believe that it hoards all the foulest meanings in the language?' (CPii.181). Averill explains that the real supper of the title is the feast they have brought, 'the blood-red wine | . . . pressed | From the wrongs of the helpless' (CPii.98). The philanthropist is outraged at being accused of being a tourist of misery, probing their distress only to medicate his own sickness, and realizes that his wishful, theoretical love of his 'kind' shrivels before this neat dose of reality: 'This love is more than I can dare' (CPii.99).

Binyon shared the Victorians' disgust at the way the capitalist city reduced all relationships to the cash nexus, isolating alienated individuals within their own cocooning private interests. While his more gifted contemporaries retreated from commonality of experience into élitist Symbolist poetics and other cordoned-off realms of art, Binyon remained committed to the vision of the interdependence of all life that Ruskin and Morris had inherited from Romantic thought. Rather than snatching impressionistic vignettes from the urban flux—poetry as a branch of the hectic consumerism that fuels the city's *laissez-faire* economy—he saw the city poet's task as seeking a deep-lying unity beneath urban rootlessness and fragmentation. Unlike Morris, however, he did not see this in political terms, at least not in his poetry. Averill's attack in *The Supper* is not developed in later poems.

Thus although William Archer wrote of the poems' 'realism', the poet Lascelles Abercrombie was closer to the heart of *London Visions* when he wrote of Binyon turning 'London into poetry' by perceiving 'its multitudinous activities as symbols or gestures of the unaltering human soul'.[27] Binyon saw this unity not in political but visionary terms. The apocalyptic night-time cityscape in 'Red Night', for example, explores the city as an arena for new forms of human kinship and solidarity.

> through kindled street and shadowy square
> The faces pass, the uncounted faces crowd,—
> Rages, lamentings, joys, in masks of flesh concealed.
> (CPii.27)

The crammed catalogue of the urban dispossessed in stanza 4 mimics the way in which, by compressing people into such close proximity and by speeding up the rhythms of life so that life lives cheek by jowl with death—'The last peace dawns upon the newly dead, | And in hushed rooms is heard the wail of the newly born' (CPii.28)—the city undermines the most tenacious illusion of all, the bourgeois myth of individuality. For Binyon, life is not something parcelled out and owned, like condominiums, but a process in which we participate. Humans are temporary 'masks of flesh' clothing eternal energies, cells 'Of the one infinite wrought human heart', all

> out of one flesh wrought,
> None separate, none single!
> Hater and hated, seeker and sought,
> O restless, O innumerable shapes,

---

[27] Archer, *Poets of the Younger Generation* (London, 1902), 49; Abercrombie, 'Eight Voices', rev. of *London Visions* (1908), *Nation* (supplement), 14 Nov. 1908, 282.

> Kneaded by one all-urging thought
> That none diverts, that none escapes.
> (CPii.28)

Through individual men and women 'Lives the supreme | Reality, diviner than all dream,' which is 'in every deed | Defaced or freed, . . . Possessed a moment, and then . . . . clouded in our own selves and lost' (CPii.29). The divine Reality incarnated in us can be 'Defaced or freed', distorted or fully expressed, by the nature of our acts, and it can be expunged by total identification with our individual life, 'clouded in our own selves and lost'. The image developed in the opening stanza, which pans slowly up through the red clouds to reveal amid the 'Spaces of silence . . . | The still eye of a star' (CPii.26), implies the possibility of identifying with the eternal Self rather than our dualistic individual self.

We are fairly close here to ideas which Binyon first heard from Ghose in 1888: 'We and all the forms of life we see are but passing phases of God, the fluctuations of this eternal life.' Reincarnation is a motif here, as in 'The Statues', where 'a changing flesh arrays' the constantly reborn souls (CPii.5). Transcending the dualism of 'Hater and hated, seeker and sought' is the task Krishna sets Arjuna in the Bhagavad Gita, the reiterated theme of the Upanishads, and a key concept underlying the aesthetics explored in Binyon's *Painting in the Far East*, published within months of the collected *London Visions* in 1908.[28] The literary origins of his vision of the oneness of all life and the need to transcend individuality, however, are native and Romantic. Binyon's 'one infinite wrought human heart' is the 'universal heart' Wordsworth saw ruptured by 'the outward marks | Whereby society has parted man | From man'.[29]

In fact, Binyon's vagrants are distant cousins of another 'unmoving man', the blind London beggar who admonishes Wordsworth from another world in *The Prelude*,[30] and one of the implicit tasks he undertook in *London Visions* was to revamp the Romantic myth of the outcast to see if it would take the strain in late Victorian London. It would not. Binyon was no Baudelaire. His vagrants cannot bear all that visionary weight, and his attempts to prod them across the threshold of sublimity end either in the bathos of

---

[28] See e.g. Bhagavad Gita 2. 11–53 and the Katha Upanishad.

[29] *The Prelude*, x. 218–20, *Poetical Works*, ed. Thomas Hutchinson, rev. Ernest de Selincourt (Oxford, 1978), 581.

[30] 7. 635–49, *Poetical Works*, 545.

'The Paralytic' or the richer confusions of 'Red Night' and 'The Statues'. Binyon's failure is part of the wider failure of English Romantic poetry to come to terms with the city, graphically illustrated by comparing Binyon with a poet he admired, Walt Whitman. The comparison is unfair, but one Binyon invites by numerous verbal echoes. The title and opening stanzas of 'Songs of the World Unborn' are pure Whitman, while 'The Sleepers' takes its title from Whitman's poem. 'The Sleepers' is Binyon's attempt to enlist Whitman's cosmic 'I' persona as a way of surmounting the opacity of the city. The buildings become transparent and the poet invisible—'The doors are closed and fast: unseen, | With stealthy feet I glide between' (*CP*ii.20)—but he aspires to Whitman's universal empathy without his strength. Whitman's driving certitudes dissolve into questions because Binyon lacks the confidence in the imagination which enables Whitman's great poem to accomplish the task it sets itself, with its climactic vision of humanity flowing 'hand in hand over the whole earth'.[31] By comparison, Binyon's remains a statement of intentions, programme notes for a healing humanist poetry.

SOFT-FOCUS CITYSCAPES

In an era fascinated by interiors such as the music halls and claustrophobic bedrooms of Symons's poems and Sickert's canvases, Binyon's London remains stubbornly alfresco. His vagrants may be isolated to the point of solipsism, but Binyon himself was fascinated by the community of the streets, 'the crowds and animation' of his schoolboy memories. Walking through a Whitechapel market, he shares in the solidarity of the human community, 'this press | Of life unnumbered' (*CP*ii.59). Annie in *The Supper* describes the camaraderie of the pavements, where misery is shared and human energy pooled:

> I know not how, but down in the street
> 'Tis not so heavy a task to meet.
> A power beyond me bears me along,
> The faint with the eager, the weak with the strong.

[31] 'The Sleepers', 162, *Leaves of Grass: Comprehensive Reader's Edition*, ed. Harold W. Blodgett and Sculley Bradley, *Collected Writings of Walt Whitman* (New York, 1965), 432.

> 'Tis like an army with marching sound:
> I march, and my feet forget the ground.
>
> (CPii.88)

In 'As I Walked Through London', Binyon experiences the same healing loss of self in the communal anonymity of the streets:

> the streets alive and bright,
> With hundreds each way thronging, on their tide
> Received me, a drop in the stream, unmarked, unknown.
>
> (CPii.17)

No Arnoldian fear of the mob here, none of the terror of the individual's absorption by the masses such as we find in Clough and other Victorian poets, for it is on the streets that 'the one infinite wrought human heart' visibly reassembles.

In Binyon's London, as in Whitman's Manhattan, God's letters fall in the street. Epiphanies occur, not in music halls or bedrooms like Symons's, but out beneath the open sky, where—all 1890s interiors being analogues for the occluded art space and hermetic image—they cease to be the poet's exclusive property. Sometimes they take communal form, as with the crowd in 'The Fire', the factory workers in 'The Bathers', or the housewives in 'The Storm', where the sunlight breaks into the slums and

> the living wind with nearness breathes
> On weary faces of women of many cares;
> They stand at their doors and watch with a soothed spirit
> The marvellous West asleep in endless light.
>
> (CPii.17–18)

In 'Trafalgar Square', dawn finds the homeless huddled together for warmth below Nelson's Column in the heart of imperial London, a tragically common sight depicted in Dudley Hardy's 1888 painting *Sans Asile*.[32] Being 'unfed' vagrants rather than well-nourished Whistlerian aesthetes, they are 'by the growing radiance unconsoled'. One of them, a woman, bathes her hands and face in the fountain. Unlike the prosperous city itself, the water accepts and gives back her image softened by 'liquid mysteries | Of shadow': 'The water without stain refused her not: | In that deep vision she rejoined the pure' (CPii.53–4). This casual sacrament enables her to internalize the fountain's clarity:

[32] See Treuherz, 106.

in her spirit a still fountain springs
Deeper than hunger, faith crying for life,
That to her eyes an inward clearness brings,
And to her heart courage for any strife.
(*CP*ii.54)

Such moments are rare, fragile and woven into no transcendental theology, yet they give their recipients what Binyon's mentor Arnold prayed for in Kensington Gardens:

Calm soul of things! make it mine
To feel, amid the city's jar,
That there abides a peace of thine,
Man did not make, and cannot mar.[33]

Disasters, conversely, happen indoors, whether in the Whitechapel slums or moneyed interiors such as that in *The Supper*. The vagrant in 'Trafalgar Square' is only yards away from the National Gallery, directed by Binyon's friend Lionel Cust, but it is at the fountain that she gains the rapture more Berensonian minds get from art. In 'In the British Museum' another woman falls asleep among the Egyptian and Assyrian monuments and has a nightmare about the indifference of art. Given Binyon's position at the British Museum, complacently described by Sidney Colvin as 'an epitome of the civilization of the world',[34] the poem is a remarkable critique of the way 'high culture' remains peripheral, even inimical to the lives of the vast majority. Binyon was haunted by the idea of museums and art galleries surrounded by urban deprivation and squalor.

It is significant that the only *London Visions* poem dealing with the key 1890s topos of the dance, 'The Little Dancers', is set in the street rather than in the music hall. Here, as two ragged children dance to the music of a barrel organ in a dark alley, the transaction between humans and their environment is complete. The pathetic fallacies of the opening lines—the 'Lonely . . . sky dreams', 'the little street . . . retires, secluded and shy'—shift the sentimentality inherent in the scene onto the city itself, leaving the dancers' emotions unspoken, tacit:

Two children, all alone and no one by,
Holding their tattered frocks, thro' an airy maze

[33] 'Lines Written in Kensington Gardens', 37–40, *The Poems of Matthew Arnold*, ed. Kenneth Allott (London, 1965), 257.
[34] *Memories and Notes of Persons and Places* (London, 1921), 201.

Of motion lightly threaded with nimble feet
Dance sedately; face to face they gaze,
Their eyes shining, grave with a perfect pleasure.
(CPii.3)

This metrically subtle little poem accomplishes what Binyon would later praise in Utamaro, the unveiling of the 'sense of mystery in simple things' (*JCP* 92). The girls are not card-carrying symbols as are Symons's dancers, but they bear the same connotations of transcendence of self through dance. This raptness is missing from A. S. Hartrick's illustration of the poem in Henley's *London Garland* anthology, which shows two pretty girls dancing outside a pub, watched by a loafer (inevitably, a man).[35] Instead of gazing gravely face to face one looks out of the picture to the left, the other smiles at us, the (again implicitly male) viewer, precisely the reverse of Binyon's intention: his ragamuffins dance for no one's pleasure but their own.

Binyon's London, then, like the landscapes of *The Prelude*, is seeded with potential 'spots of time'. What these men, women, and children happen on is an 'inward clearness' earned through a momentary union with a reality greater than their human selves, precisely what Binyon himself seeks in lyrics like 'The Threshold'. What gives the poor strength to survive in appalling conditions gives the poet faith to go on writing Romantic poetry in the post-Romantic city. To do this Binyon adopts a tactic as old as Wordsworth's 'Westminster Bridge' sonnet, transforming the city into a landscape, here through the related activities of walking, climbing, and seeing. Whereas Henley, Symons, and Le Gallienne celebrate hansom cabs and omnibuses, the lyrics in *London Visions* are walking poems, often structured by the poet's perambulation through the city. 'The Threshold' begins 'I walked beside full-flooding Thames tonight' and unfolds as a meditation controlled by his westward progress along the river and the shifting values of evening light falling on its wharves, bridges, and steeples, so that the city becomes not only the object but also the geography of his meditation. As well as physically entangling him in the city streets, promoting him from spectator to participator, walking also gives the poet time to see, not the impressionistic blurs glimpsed from

[35] *A London Garland: Selected from Five Centuries of English Verse* (London, 1895), 192–3.

Symons's speeding cab in 'Nocturne' but concentrated, meditative seeing. The verb that constantly punctuates these poems is 'gaze', always implying a loss of self in the intensity of the act. Poem after poem in *London Visions* explores the pun implicit in that title, the ways in which ocular vision modulates into transcendental vision.

Anything treated as an object of meditation becomes a mandala, however flawed, and the only way to see a mandala the size of a city is to climb and look down on it from above. Many early cities were literally mandalas, laid out around temple and palace in accordance with the rules of sacred geometry, and every ascent to see a city from above is an attempt to disinter this submerged mandala, an atavistic yearning to see the city sacramentally. In 'The Golden Gallery at Saint Paul's', Binyon climbs the man-made holy mountain of the cathedral only to discover the impossibility of the task in the expanding Victorian metropolis, whose sheer size defeats the choreographing eye:

> Beneath me spreading hazed
> In distance large it lay, nor nothing broke
> Its mapped immensity.
>
> (*CP*ii.11)

Seen from this height, the city is 'mapped' by its random grids of streets, but refuses to resolve itself into a map, still less a mandala which can be used as a map of the self. However, having grown way beyond the limits of eyesight it has become the next best thing, a landscape open to the sky and intimate with the protean English weather, which transforms the clouds into mountains, 'uplifting in dazzling line | O'er valleys of ashy blue, their wrinkled snow' (*CP*ii.11). Such images recur in other poems, and their incremental effect is to evoke a London open on all sides to infinity. *London Visions* is free from rural nostalgia because, like Turner's diaphanous cities, Binyon's London is still intimate with nature, not the Georgian nature of blackbirds and hedgerows but the High Romantic nature of sky and clouds and weather. Whereas in Henley's *London Voluntaries* nature binds Londoners and their world together in shared sexuality, in *London Visions* the binding force is nature at its most ethereal, the space that surrounds and permeates both city and citizens, like 'the marvellous West asleep in endless light' watched by the worn-out women in 'The Storm'. This is why, although he delights in gaslight diffused by rain and mist, Binyon cannot wholly endorse his fellow 1890s poets' celebration of the artificial lights which transform London into a 'Great City of the Midnight Sun'.[36] While Symons's paean to artificial light as part of London's 'décor' ratifies Walter Benjamin's insight into the way the *flâneur* sees the streets as an interior,[37] Binyon resists this domestication of the city, the way city lights render the night sky opaque, curtaining the city off from starry space and turning it into a self-absorbed, claustrophobically human theatre.

The seasons in *London Visions* are geared not to the biological cycle but the meteorological sub-cycles of winter fogs, spring clarities, summer haze, and November mists. Like every book on Victorian London, *London Visions* is fog-bound. Few phenomena provide as sensitive an index of the shift in intellectual climate between the High Victorian age and the 1890s as the attitude to London's smog-laden atmosphere in general and its infamous pea-souper fogs in particular. Ruskin saw urban pollution in pre-Aesthetic terms, poisoning his beloved sky and blunting the moral impact of architecture, as in this famous passage from 'The Study of Architecture in Our Schools' (1865):

All lovely architecture was designed for cities in cloudless air. . . . But our cities, built in black air which, by its accumulated foulness, first renders all ornament invisible in distance, and then chokes its interstices with soot . . . for a city . . . such as this no architecture is possible.[38]

For Whistler, who painted his first Thames nocturnes shortly after this lecture, the detail-obliterating fogs were a benign addition to London's naturally Impressionist climate. Wilde's conceit in 'The Decay of Lying' that the Impressionists had altered the English climate and created London's 'wonderful brown fogs' is Whistlerian both in its humour and its ultimate seriousness as a claim for art's transforming powers.[39] For Monet it was London's prime asset: 'It is the fog that gives it its magnificent amplitude; its regular and massive blocks become grandiose in that mysterious mantle.'[40]

[36] Le Gallienne, 'A Ballad of London', *Robert Louis Stevenson, an Elegy and Other Poems* (London, 1895), 26.

[37] Symons, *Works*, 1, 97; Benjamin, *Charles Baudelaire: A Lyric Poet in the Era of High Capitalism*, trans. Harry Zohn (London, 1973), 54.

[38] *The Works of John Ruskin*, ed. E. T. Cook and Alexander Wedderburn, 39 vols. (London, 1903–12) xix. 24.

[39] *Intentions* (London, 1891), 40–1.

[40] Qtd. William C. Seitz, *Claude Monet* (London, 1960), 148.

Binyon's Japanese friends were acutely sensitive to this aestheticization of the London fog. Yone Noguchi's first letter after arriving in London in 1902 moaned 'I can't see anything yet on account of the famous Fog. Cold! Windy!' but in his auto-biography he recalled standing on Westminster bridge in December and falling in love with the fogbound city: 'It was only in those days of fogs when London pleased to be lost in the grey vastness of mystery that I could speculate on my poetical feeling.'[41] (Almost exactly a century earlier, Wordsworth had seen from the same bridge a city 'All bright and glittering in the smokeless air'.)[42] Yoshio Markino, who painted luminous watercolour fogscapes and encouraged Noguchi to make 'many poetries about London Mists', was such a connoisseur that he derided insipid Paris fogs and in Rome 'often exclaimed, "Only if Rome had London fogs!"'[43]

From Whistler Binyon learnt a genuinely urban vision, an affec-tion for the 'London atmosphere, our peculiar climate' and a connoisseurship of such subtle, unruskinian beauties as 'the weath-ering effect of Portland stone in the sooty air'.[44] In other moods, however, he could not see in these specialized aesthetic terms. Like his friend Alice Meynell in her essay 'The Climate of Smoke,' he acknowledged 'the climate of London to be more than half an artificial climate', a 'sky of our manufacture' dense with 'the refuse from a million fireplaces'.[45] In *The Flight of the Dragon* (1911), he contrasted the Edo lovingly detailed by the *ukiyo-e* artists, 'tricked out by no aerial disguises, but outlined clear and plain as in a sharp morning light', with squalid Victorian London, where artists were 'driven to discover in the charm and mystery of atmosphere a consolation for the squalor of mean and miserable streets' (*FD* 43). Binyon's ideal of a city open on all sides to infinity was realized in

---

[41] *Yone Noguchi: Collected English Letters*, ed. Ikuko Atsumi (Tokyo, 1975), 82; *The Story of Yone Noguchi: Told by Himself, Illustrated by Yoshio Markino* (London, 1914), 122–4.

[42] 'Composed Upon Westminster Bridge, September 3, 1802', *Poetical Works*, 214.

[43] *A Japanese Artist in London*, ed. Sammy I. Tsunematsu (1910; Brighton, 1991), 66, 190. See Tsunematsu's introduction, 'Yoshio Markino—the Painter of Fog'.

[44] 'Town-Planning, and the New Bridge', *SR*, 29 Oct. 1910, 543.

[45] *London Impressions: Etchings and Pictures in Photogravure by William Hyde and Essays by Alice Meynell* (London, 1898), 9. Hyde's dramatic cityscapes provide perhaps the closest pictorial analogue to Binyon's poems.

the semi-mythic Edo of Hiroshige's *One Hundred Views of Edo*, with its ringing prussian blue skies.

Unlike Whistler's canvases and Wilde's Thames poems, Binyon's London poems are not meditations on the city as a work of art. The difference is highlighted by Binyon's attitude to London fog. At times in his poems, as in Dickens or Conan Doyle's contemporaneous Sherlock Holmes stories, it carries a symbolic charge, suggesting the traumatized lives of its inhabitants, but it also temptingly cloaks them. In 'Fog', the streets are 'Magically awakened to a strange, brown night' which transforms London into a dreamlike city of sounds, aesthetically gratifying but delusory: when the winter sun breaks through, the 'baffled hive of helpless man' is 'laid bare' (*CP*ii.73). 'Deptford' begins by welcoming the fog's camouflaging of the squalid streets, but only to renounce it as a form of meterological dishonesty, shrouding what should not be hidden.

Curiously, however, whereas Binyon holds out against the convenient camouflaging of dockland slums by fog, the transformations performed by mist are seen as redemptive, not in aesthetic but visionary terms, in their questioning of the city's ontological status. In 'Songs of the World Unborn', the 'ample teeming street' swiftly deliquesces in the 'misty morn', as purely pictorial images— 'Vistas of railing and roof, | Dim-seen in the delicate shroud of the frosty air'—modulate into a meditation on the ultimate unreality of the city. The image of 'Time . . . Stealing with patient rivers the mountainous lands' (*CP*ii.79) sets the city in the wider context of a planet also slowly dissolving, adrift from its Newtonian moorings, motion masquerading as matter. By rendering the city diaphanous, the mist enables the poet to see into its fluid essence. In Wordsworthian terms, by subduing the barrage of phenomena, London's 'press | Of self-destroying, transitory things,' mist makes the eye quiet and enables the meditative watcher to 'see into the life of things'.[46]

This is equally true of the 'soft-blown drifts of glimmering rain' (*CP*ii.74) and the numinous light of dawn and dusk. As Binyon wrote concerning the twilight effects Whistler learnt from Hiroshige, 'The soft and veiling atmosphere of London especially lent itself to the beauty of these effects' (*LA* 277). In 'November',

---

[46] *Prelude*, 7, 769–70, *Poetical Works*, 547; 'Tintern Abbey', 47–9, *Poetical Works*, 164.

the moist autumn twilight casts a 'magical softness' over the evening streets and triggers a corresponding shift in the poet's consciousness:

> The softness estranges my sense: I see and I hear,
> But know 'tis a vision intangible, shapes that seem.
> All is unreal . . .
> Houses and sky, a dream, a dream!
>
> (*CP*ii.69)

In 'The Fire', another remarkable instance of Binyon seeing human solidarity where Victorian poets had seen only mob anarchy, a crowd gathered round a destructive city blaze watch in 'impassioned silence' and 'with secret strange desire' as the inferno unmasks the city as 'perishable, trembling, brief, I Even as themselves' (*CP*ii.48). They are vouchsafed a moment of 'rapt', visionary insight into the ephemeral nature of this floating, dreamlike world. Binyon too aligns himself not with the *ukiyo* of alluring urban surfaces but *ukiyo* in its original Buddhist sense, a recognition of the ephemeral, dreamlike nature of the world that habit alone convinces us is solid and enduring.

What all these qualities of light lend is depth. By dissolving its stony imperviousness, they make the city available as an object of meditation and an image of consciousness. During the years Binyon was writing *London Visions*, British pictorial photographers like Walter Benington, John H. Anderson and John Dudley Johnson used out-of-focus exposures, soft-focus lenses, and manipulation of printing materials to simulate Whistler's contour-softening 'veil' of mist for cityscapes as well as landscapes.[47] Binyon's poems have some affinities with the cityscapes of Alvin Langdon Coburn, who photographed Binyon in March 1913. Like all artists and writers who saw London in terms of light and atmosphere, Coburn and Binyon shared a common ancestor in Whistler, but they shared other interests too, for both were dedicated students of Japanese woodcuts and Zen landscape painting, which, as Mike Weaver has shown, helped structure Coburn's London photographs.[48] For both

---

[47] For the British photographers, see the chapter 'Atmospheric Influence' in Mike Weaver's *The Photographic Art: Pictorial Traditions in Britain and America* (London, 1986), 46–8, and Margaret Harker, *The Linked Ring: The Secession Movement in Photography in Britain, 1892–1910* (London, 1979).

[48] *Alvin Langdon Coburn: Symbolist Photographer 1882–1966* (New York, 1966), 11–18, 37, 51–4.

Binyon and Coburn seeing is a meditative, ultimately spiritual act, and it comes as no surprise that both were drawn to Taoism, whose spirit permeates Far Eastern art. Their cityscapes are ultimately mindscapes. By entering the depth of the landscape, the mind enters its own depth, a concept which finds definitive expression in the Taoist-Zen landscapes which Binyon first encountered during the years he worked on *London Visions* and which in *Painting in the Far East* (1908) he celebrated as one of the highest achievements of world art.

6 Adam's Dream

In 1899 Binyon told the critic James Douglas that he was abandoning urban themes because he found having to 'wrestle . . . with brute material' made his verse 'languid',[1] by which he meant that chaotic urban reality had dragged his poetry too far in the direction of free verse. This was a critical moment in his development as a poet, and one wonders what might have emerged had he persevered in his attempts to marry the quotidian and the visionary in his city poems. As Karl Beckson has said, the impressionistic images of London created by Wilde, Henley, Symons, Davidson, and Binyon 'prepared the way in the fin de siècle for the symbolic vision of the modern city's sterility and death, particularly Eliot's *The Waste Land*'.[2] Having acknowledged the city as the primary, inescapable fact of modern life in *London Visions*, he now stepped back, returning to more distant, anodyne mythologies.

In retrospect, this was a fateful decision, stranding Binyon in the 1890s, but it did not look that way at the turn of the century, when he was a fully paid-up member of the London avant-garde, such as it was. In the March 1901 number of the *Monthly Review* Richard Streatfeild celebrated Binyon and Stephen Phillips as 'apostles' of a vital post-*fin-de-siècle* 'new age of poetry',[3] and for a while it began to look that way even to less partisan critics. Though it does contain some London poems, his fifth volume, *Porphyrion and Other Poems* (1898), is driven by a hunger for the one thing London lacks, horizons. Binyon's own favourite poem in the volume, 'The Renewal', leaves the London streets for the westernmost edge of Europe, a Portuguese pine forest overlooking the Atlantic. He glossed this poem in a letter to Edward Dowden of Trinity College, Dublin, who had reviewed the book warmly in the *Saturday Review*:

---

[1] ALs, 11 May [1899], HM 42740, Huntington Library, San Marino, California.
[2] *London in the 1890s*, 268.
[3] 'Two Poets of the New Century', *Monthly Review*, 2 (Mar. 1901), 94.

My main idea is something like this: that life in itself (if only we could live it properly) is greater & more desirable than anything it contains. This is a truth which we possess only at certain fortunate moments: but it is only at these moments that we are competent to understand & pronounce on existence. At such times the problem of pain disappears, delight & pain being drunk up in the intensity of mere living—

> 'As colours perish into perfect light.'

And my thought is always that we should live by the light of these moments, & never pursuing joy or happiness for its own sake but *complete life* we shall find the discordant elements fuse on a plane above grief & above pleasure.[4]

Described by William Archer as 'a really noteworthy philosophical utterance',[5] the poem is a celebration of these moments of pure, unmediated being when the individual self merges with the seamless 'one infinity of life that flows' from its unknowable divine source 'into these unnumbered semblances | Of earth and air, mountains and beasts and trees' (CPi.40). The speaker sees human life as the journey back to 'that central home', the universal Self, which is not a place, a final destination, but a path, a direction of quest in life conceived as pilgrimage:

> The Road that is before us and behind,
> By which we travel from ourselves, in sleep
> Or waking, toward a self more vast and deep.
>
> (CPi.40)

It cannot be possessed in 'Some dreamed-of goal beyond life's eager sphere', only experienced, ceaselessly sought, lost, and rediscovered in this world, where 'at every hour the goal is here' (CPi.40).

This theme informs 'Porphyrion', a 1,500-line blank verse narrative based on W. E. H. Lecky's account of early Christian desert hermits in his *History of European Morals*, which briefly recounts Rufinus's tale of a young ascetic tricked by a beautiful woman into abandoning his monastic life to seek her in a vain quest which ends only with his death.[6] In Binyon's dechristianized Romantic redaction, the elusive girl becomes Porphyrion's visionary guide on his quest for ideal love, truth, and life. The typology has all the

---

[4] ALs, 7 May 1898, TCD MSS 3147–3154a, fo. 1088, Trinity College Library, Dublin.

[5] *Poets*, 49.

[6] *History of European Morals from Augustus to Charlemagne*, 2 vols. (London, 1869), ii. 127.

vagueness endemic to his quest romance models, *Alastor* and *Endymion*, and one sympathizes with the reviewer who found it 'quite bewilderingly vague'.[7] Binyon's telling Dowden the girl typifies this ideal of seeking '*complete* life' rather than happiness renders it only marginally less opaque. She teaches Porphyrion that his self-mortifying practices designed to sunder pure soul from 'the dungeon of this flesh' (CPii.107) can never lead to enlightenment, which can only be attained through experience. She vanishes and he leaves the desert to seek her. After discovering in Antioch that wealth and sex cannot assuage his 'ineffable deep longing', he journeys on, gets caught up in a war, and is murdered while helping some of its victims. In that 'one transfigured instant', he is united with his elusive lover in death. The ascetic who spurned quotidian life finally finds lost wholeness of being in service to humanity.

Manmohan Ghose, who thought 'Porphyrion' 'one of the most wonderful things ever written',[8] had sown the seeds of the poem ten years earlier in 1888 when he wrote to Binyon about the 'ancient Indian philosophers' who 'fled into the desert to live as eremites and ascetics, and ponder alone on the eternal and the true' (G165). In his studies of Oriental art, Binyon was coming across pictures and stories of Indian rishis, Taoist hermits, and Zen monks, to which he responded at a personal as well as scholarly level. Ghose had evoked the Indian rishis because he wished to emulate them, 'to be an ascetic and think to eternity': 'O that I could thus abstract myself wholly from the soulless taskwork and jarring commonplaces of modern life—to give myself up with unremitting devotion to thought and productive toil' (G165). He had not done so. On his return to India in 1894 he had taken a series of academic posts and married, continuing to write poetry in the interstices of a life crammed with onerous 'soulless taskwork' and family duties. Unlikely as it might have seemed to the 29-year-old Binyon, he would soon be in an identical position. In its amorphously visionary way, 'Porphyrion' dramatized something crucial to both men: the problem of reconciling a contemplative, essentially mystical vision of life with the need, both financial and moral, to live in the world.

These concerns resurfaced months later in a specifically Indian context in 'Asoka', which first appeared in the November 1900

[7] *Pall Mall Gazette*, 2 Aug. 1898, 4.   [8] ALs to LB, 9 Feb. 1898.

Monthly Review as 'The Indian Prince'. Binyon was much exercised by things Indian at this time. While he was sending Ghose art books and reproductions of Japanese and Chinese paintings, Ghose was educating him in Bengali poetry. A member of Rabindranath Tagore's Calcutta circle, he was translating 'The Philosopher's Stone', which the Bengali poet suggested he show Binyon. In summer 1899 Binyon was seeking an Indian subject for a poem showing that 'the true Sources of Power' are not political but spiritual. At Ghose's suggestion he turned to the great Indian emperor Asoka, who, after annexing the kingdom of Kalinga in a great battle in 261 BC, was so sickened by the slaughter that he converted to Buddhism. As Binyon epigrammatically put it years later in his biography of another great Indian emperor, Akbar: 'Caesar "came, saw, and conquered". Asoka conquered, and then saw.'[9] Administering his empire wisely and benevolently according to Buddhist law, Asoka was the type not of the withdrawn ascetic but the philosopher–king who reconciles the spiritual and secular worlds.

In Binyon's poem, Asoka wearily leaves his palace one night and climbs a ridge to gaze down on the moonlit Ganges. The 'wide ecstasy of stillness heals | His heart' and in this meditative state he prays to the nameless 'heart of power' to burn off his 'bonds . . . | Of time and chance and doom' and reabsorb him into its 'radiance'. The true sources of power lie not in us but in the 'divine desire' which is each creature's inborn longing to rejoin the totality of which we are living fragments. At the climax of the poem he experiences a finely poised state of individuality and wholeness:

> O my soul melts into immensity,
> And yet 'tis I, 'tis I!
>
> (CPi.85–6)

Ghose wrote to Binyon that this 'beautiful thought of being merged in infinity, yet keeping one's individuality' held 'a lesson which India, alas! in her passion for the infinite has been too slow to learn: hence all her mistakes'.[10]

During these years Binyon studied Buddhism in his efforts to comprehend Far Eastern art, and 'Asoka' shows him trying to assimilate what he has learnt in terms of his own High Romantic

---

[9] *Akbar* (London, 1932), 26.   [10] ALs, 27 June 1900.

heritage. It fulfils the same archetypal quest pattern as 'The Renewal', in which the poet leaves the city, experiences a similar
epiphany while gazing at the ocean, then returns re-empowered to
his life in London, just as Asoka returns to the palace to resume his
duties. The modern poet and the Indian emperor both know that
the 'sources of power' are discoverable only by dissolving the bonds
of self and rejoining the divine totality, but only temporarily, since
action, growth, and spiritual understanding are possible only in the
world of becoming, within its dialectics of desire and fear, love and
loss. Wisdom is won by living through these educative experiences
without mistaking them for ultimate reality. Asoka stands in direct
contrast to his Western counterpart, Alexander the Great, existen-
tial hungering incarnate, imprisoned in the realm of becoming,
whereas Asoka, having conquered his own more modest empire,
undertakes the more difficult task of inner conquest.

'Asoka' appeared in *Odes*, published by the Unicorn Press in
October 1900. This volume marked a change of direction from
both the visionary mode of *Porphyrion* and the urban impressionism of *London Visions*, returning to the world of *Persephone* with
a series of poems, some narrative-pictorial, some dramatic, on
mythological and heroic subjects. Behind this lay Arnold's 1853
preface with its call for a self-effacing, classically-inspired poetry,
but a more immediate influence was Sturge Moore, whose
Vinedresser Binyon was seeing through the press in 1899. They
went on a fortnight's 'poetry working holiday' in Cornwall that
summer, and in addition to their almost daily meetings their dialogue was maintained in letters full of frank analyses of each other's
poetry. Post-Romantic, at times proto-modernist, Moore disliked
everything woolly, vague, or diaphanously Shelleyan in Binyon's
verse, while Binyon balked at the clotted consonantal density of
some of Moore's lines. Even the images in their letters are paradig-
matic, Binyon's organicist tropes of flowering and flow versus
Moore's building metaphors, poems as fabricated, craftsman-made
objects. *Odes* shows Binyon veering towards Moore's mythopoeic
world as an antidote to his tendency to drift into verse spun out
of filmy skeins of abstraction. His choice of his own engraving
of Strang's woodcut design 'The Nymph' for its frontispiece
announced his role as craftsman shaping given materials.

The success of the volume was 'The Death of Tristram', a
three-part poem in which Isoult and the dying Tristram are briefly

reunited for an ecstatic *Liebestod*. More dramatic than either Arnold's 'Tristram and Iseult' (1852) or Swinburne's *Tristram of Lyonesse* (1882), praised by Wilfrid Gibson for raising its Arthurian subject 'above the ruck of Sham-Medievalism',[11] the poem creates a rhetorical world heightened and ritualistically remote and yet, in its better moments, passionately physical. 'Yeats thinks it the greatest modern poem far surpassing Mat Arnold and everybody else,' Moore wrote Robert Trevelyan. 'And his seems to be only an outspoken version of the ordinary verdict. It is certainly almost popular, far more so than anything else Binyon has done or I or Yeats.'[12] Yeats, ready to slough off the 1890s and the Celtic Twilight, saw it as a superb example of the new heroic poetry towards which he himself was striving. He wrote excitedly:

I have not read all your book yet but I have just finished 'Tristram' & must write you what I think. It seems to me a great poem among the greatest for many years. I cannot criticize it. One criticizes the imperfect but when the perfect comes one can but say 'How gladly I would have died such a death or lived such a life'. There is something in this poem & in Sturge Moores recent themes—though he lacks as yet the crowning perfection of a great style—that moves one with a strong personal emotion. It is as though a new thing, long prophesied, but never seen, had come at last. It is the beauty of the heroic life. It has come to you & him in visable substance, lyric or dramatic, to me only as something far off that I reach for on unsteady feet, an invisible essense, a flying star, a wandering wind. It is that beauty which Blake says 'changes least from youth to age' & one turns to it, as though it were the visable face of eternity appearing amid the 'voluptuous beauty', which he says is all the moderns know. Swinburne['s] 'Tristram' has the 'voluptuous beauty' in its heart & Matthew Arnold's has but stray beautiful passages & nothing in its heart. But in your poem is the whole shining substance & for generations & generations it will come to lovers not as literature, but as their own memories. There will never be a true lover, who shall read it without tears, I think. I do not know whether I can rightly judge, rightly measure it for it is to me like some religious voice, some ritual, heard in childhood & then heard again after many years among barbarous peoples—it is the voice, the ritual of heroical beauty.[13]

---

[11] ALs to LB, 13 Dec. 1900.

[12] ALs, n.d. [Feb. 1901], box 16/463 (i–ii), TSMP–LU.

[13] ALs, 'Saturday night' [?5 Jan. 1901], *Collected Letters of W. B. Yeats*, ed. John Kelly, 3 vols. to date (Oxford, 1986–), iii. 6–7. For the background, see Dr Kelly's introduction and illuminating notes.

In the December *Academy* he voted *Odes* his favourite book of the year alongside Sturge Moore's play *Aphrodite Against Artemis*. The next decade or so would prove that Yeats was the greater poet, but he retained his admiration for 'Tristram' and chose it to represent 'Binyon . . . at his best' in the *Oxford Book of Modern Verse*, writing to him in 1934: 'I want this one long great poem.'[14]

When Gibson met Yeats, Binyon, and Sturge Moore in the Holborn tea shop discussing Tolstoy they might just as easily have been planning the revival of poetic drama in England. Binyon had been fascinated by the theatre since being taken to see Henry Irving as a child, and in the *London Visions* poem 'Eleanora Duse as Magda' he had celebrated one of the muses of the symbolist 1890s in her greatest role. He had written his own first play, a pseudo-Jacobean blank verse tragedy called 'Raimondi', at St Paul's between 1887 and 1888, and ten years later was working on another verse drama when he met Moore. The problem in 1898 was not writing poetic dramas, of course, but getting them staged in a city where the commercial West End theatres were dominated by profitable social comedies and melodramas. When Binyon arranged for Moore to read his play *Mariamne* to Johnston Forbes-Robertson in 1898, the great Shakespearean actor encouraged their aspirations but warned that poetic drama could only be staged by a non-commercial, subsidized theatre. In an essay in the *Dome* the following March Binyon claimed that the English stage could not be revived 'till poetic drama flourishes again', which required both better verse dramas and a new kind of experimental theatre organized around actors trained in verse-speaking techniques and using simpler, non-realistic scenery, the antithesis of the epics, full of lavishly detailed stage pageantry, mounted by Herbert Beerbohm Tree.[15] (Aptly, the same issue carried a woodcut by Gordon Craig, whose staging of the Purcell Society's production of *Dido and Aeneas* and *The Masque of Love* in 1901 would revolutionize English stage design.)

The two young dramatists concocted a 'theatre scheme', with Moore turning to Harley Granville-Barker for advice on actors and

---

[14] Yeats to LB, TLs, n.d. [1934]; Yeats, *Oxford Book of Modern Verse* (Oxford, 1936), xvi; 'Favourite Books of 1901: Some Readers: Mr. W. B. Yeats', *Academy*, 7 Dec. 1901, 568. For LB's own favourite book of the year in this *Academy* poll, see p. 133 below.

[15] 'Mr Bridges' "Prometheus" and Poetic Drama', *Dome*, 2/6 (Mar. 1899), 203–4.

Binyon seeking to raise funds. In June 1899 Binyon introduced
Moore into the Pye household at Priest Hill. Pye and his artistic
daughters Sybil and Ethel took a keen interest in the theatre
scheme, which slowly took shape as the Literary Theatre Club, for
which Pye was to be business manager and Binyon what Sybil Pye
called the 'dining-out missionary'.[16] Yeats became involved, seeing
Moore and Binyon as collaborators in his plan to create a 'Theatre
of Beauty' in London, and Ricketts grew interested in January 1901
when Moore discussed with him the creation of 'new decorative,
almost symbolic' stage scenery for the proposed 'Theatre society for
Romantic Drama'.[17] Six months later on 30 July 1901 the Literary
Theatre Club was inaugurated with a copyright reading of Moore's
Aphrodite Against Artemis in the empty Dalston Theatre by
Binyon, Florence Farr, May Morris, and other friends. Ricketts's
diary gives a drolly Dickensian account:

We all met like conspirators at the Austrian Restaurant, chaperoned by L.
Binyon. The party consisted of a batch of mere boys, Miss May Morris
(rather patronizing us all), and a good-natured middle-aged actress, Miss
Farr, who has appeared in countless efforts to stage Ibsen, Shaw, etc.
Moore wore an old straw hat with a wavy brim, he handed us a twopenny
tube ticket; we looked like a school treat. The Dalston Theatre seemed
closed; whilst waiting outside, I spoke to Miss Farr about her part in Yeats'
Countess Cathleen, where she had taken a man's part: had she found this
trying? 'Yes, oh yes; you see, Yeats had insisted on my wearing mauve—
such a trying colour—a mauve tunic just below the knees, you know, and
over that a great common purple cloak. . . .' Inside the Dalston Theatre
there was a pandemonium of charwomen, cleaning the place. . . . Enter
Miss May Morris from left. 'Am I to come on now?' Then follows the
tragic speech in a soft, inaudible voice, answered inaudibly by Binyon,
punctuated by loud conversational noises from the charwomen: 'Arris, are
you there?'—with street noises and an occasional street child peeping
through the scenery door. When the play was over and the stage properly
strewn with corpses, the curtain man was nowhere to be found, though
corpse after corpse sat up and called 'Curtain!' Then Phaedra in a tart voice
said, 'Curtain, please!', and a scene shifter turned round and said, ''Oo
says so?' When told by Aphrodite, the only professional, what we wanted,
he said, 'You mean the Act drop, Miss?' I was charmed watching T. S.

[16] Ronald Schuchard, 'W. B. Yeats and the London Theatre Societies, 1901–
1904', *Review of English Studies*, NS, 29 (1978), 419.
[17] Ricketts, diary entry, 27 Jan. 1901, MS 58099, R&S–BL. See also Schuchard,
417–19.

Moore, who listened with a rapt face to the sound of his 'winged words,' impervious to the comedy of the whole adventure.[18]

The following January Moore issued 'A Plea for an Endowed Stage' in the *Monthly Review*, urging patrons to endow a London-based theatre and drama school 'to renovate, restore and ennoble a fallen stage'.[19] Meanwhile the Literary Theatre Club, comprised mainly of young women such as Sybil and Ethel Pye, Isabel Fry, Eleanor Calhoun, Gwendolyn Bishop, and Mona Wilson, met beneath the Hokusais in Moore's rooms to learn verse speaking and rehearse experimental verse dramas 'without scenery and with acting reduced to a few large and rhythmic gestures'.[20] Among the first of 'the simplest and most aesthetic plays' to be chosen was *Paris and Oenone*, a stylized one-act blank verse tragedy Binyon had written in 1901, with Sybil Pye as Oenone. The verse speaking taught here by Moore and Binyon included the chanting techniques developed by Yeats, Florence Farr, and Arnold Dolmetsch. When Yeats organized a private demonstration of this new art form for drama critics at Clifford's Inn in May 1902 Binyon and Moore helped him and Dolmetsch explain the theory of chanting, while Farr demonstrated on the psaltery.[21] While Yeats himself was tone deaf, Moore proudly told Trevelyan that Dolmetsch thought he and Binyon would prove good chanters since they could 'distinguish notes . . . and usually in reading keep the music intervals with correction'.[22] Thirty years later Binyon recalled these bardic affairs, so redolent of the period, with appropriate irony:

Certain poets were chosen to read to Mr. Dolmetsch, who recorded their performances on an instrument which, as no one quite knew what a 'psaltery' is, was christened a psaltery. The result was not as fortunate as anticipated. Each of us disapproved of everyone else's way of speaking. I remember that I was rather proud because Mr. Dolmetsch said I was the only one who observed 'true intervals,' but the compliment was not very helpful, as I did not know what true intervals were, nor do I now.[23]

Binyon took the more magical, ritualistic Golden Dawn aspects of these activities less seriously than did Yeats and Farr, but he

---

[18] *Self-Portrait*, 63–4.   [19] *Monthly Review*, 16 (Jan. 1902), 126.
[20] Moore, 'The Renovation of the Theatre', *Monthly Review*, 19 (Apr. 1902), 113.
[21] Schuchard, 425–6.   [22] ALs, n.d. [July 1902], box 16/480, TSMP–LU.
[23] 'The Artistry of Speech', *Good Speech*, 3/20 (July–Sept. 1933), 5.

shared, in less occult terms, their sacramental view of the stage. In a 1904 letter he wrote:

It seems to me so strange that people should not think joy serious. Moore & I agree with Yeats in this, that we want the theatre to return to something of its old spirit as a religious festival: a festival in which the nation sees its ideals represented. To go to church with one part of your mind & go to a theatre with quite another is what ought not to be: & yet with the theatre in its present degraded state, it is impossible that it shouldn't be so.[24]

For Binyon and Moore, as for their mentor Yeats, the attempt to create a viable alternative to naturalistic theatre was one front in a war on nineteenth-century scientific materialism, a spiritual as much as a dramaturgical crusade.

Binyon's ambition to become a successful dramatist was given added edge by the astonishing success of Stephen Phillips, who was busily proving that poetic drama did not have to be a coterie, fringe affair by rattling off three straight smash-hit verse dramas in the commercial theatre, *Herod* (1900), *Ulysses* (1902), and *Paolo and Francesca* (1902). The cousins' friendship had cooled and, although he helped Tree's designer Percy Anderson find ideas for costumes for *Herod* in the Print Room, Binyon liked neither Tree's typically opulent production nor the play, which he found 'very effective on the stage' but 'second-rate and bombastic'.[25]

Things looked promising in 1901 when he met the great Mrs Patrick Campbell. In November she had him read *Paris and Oenone* to her and told him she would like to perform it at a matinée if the chance arose, but what she really wanted was 'a three act romantic modern play'.[26] When Binyon hit on the idea of dramatizing the brief Guidescarpi episode in George Meredith's novel *Vittoria*, Colvin wrote to Meredith, who not only gave permission but remarked that he thought 'hopefully' of Binyon's poetry.[27] On the strength of a synopsis, Mrs Pat commissioned Binyon to write the play, a tragedy prose drama called *Clelia*, which survives in several unpublished versions with Binyon's watercolour sketches for set and costumes. 'Mrs Pat came to see me yesterday, &

---

[24] ALs to CMB, 27 Mar. [1904].
[25] ALs to Henry Davray, 9 Nov. [1900], BL–HRC.
[26] LB to Pye, ALi [Nov. 1901].
[27] 24 Nov. 1901, Letter 2032, *Letters of George Meredith*, ed. C. L. Clune, 3 vols. (Oxford, 1970), iii. 1407.

stayed a long time, & ate a great many strawberries & smoked a great many cigarettes—all of which I suppose were signs of grace on her part', Binyon reported in June 1903, 'but I'm nonetheless very doubtful if she will do my play.'[28] He was right. Undismayed, he continued experimenting, working among other projects on a detailed synopsis for *Tristram and Isoult*, a five-act drama which shows him striving to achieve the heightened ritualistic intensity Yeats had praised in 'Tristram'.

In June 1904 *Paris and Oenone* appeared in the *Fortnightly Review*, prompting Philip Carr, President of the Mermaid Society, to produce it in September in a triple bill at the Mermaid Theatre in Great Queen Street. Ricketts made designs for costumes, suggesting that the characters 'should look like figures by Gustave Moreau', with Paris in reds, Helen in golds, and Oenone in green.[29] The Mermaid Society went bankrupt during rehearsals, but the play was taken up by the popular and enterprising actress Gertrude Kingston, who played the title role in a special matinée at the Savoy Theatre on 8 March 1906 in a triple bill with E. F. Benson's *The Friend in the Garden* and Shaw's *How He Lied to Her Husband*.

The play was well received by the packed house and, called onto the stage, Binyon bobbed shyly through the curtains, making what Shannon described as 'the quickest entrance & exit combined' he had ever seen.[30] Robert Ross felt the play proved 'the possibility of a renaissance of poetic drama not necessarily Celtic', adding:

I believe the public will now be able to see (with the aid of a telescope) Mr. Binyon on the higher slopes of Parnassus where Keats and Marlowe are plaiting garlands for his head in the enamelled meadows, and where he is feeling a little nervous at the prospect of being introduced by Milton to Mr. Bernard Shaw.[31]

Binyon stressed that 'the play was written expressly for the stage', which 'was visualised in every line of it',[32] but this did not convince William Archer, the most influential of the New Drama critics, who admired Binyon as a promising poet but felt that in *Paris and Oenone* he had 'versified an incident rather than written

---

[28] ALs to CMB, 3 July [1903].   [29] Delaney, 198.
[30] ALs to Ricketts, 8 Mar. 1906, MS 58085, fo. 36, R&S–BL.
[31] 'The Drama', *Academy*, 17 Mar. 1906, 263.
[32] 'Notable New Play: Mr. Binyon on His Version of "Paris and Oenone"', *Daily Chronicle*, 8 Mar. 1906, 10.

a play'.[33] Moore blamed the verse speaking, telling Pye it 'quite defeated' the play. Binyon admitted that if he were directing the play he 'would try to bring about a certain rhythm of gesture as well as of speech'.[34] It provided further proof that an endowed theatre and acting school were essential if verse drama were to be successfully revived. Efforts to found a 'Theatre of Beauty' in London, however, had not born fruit. In March 1903 the Literary Theatre Club had given way to the Masquers Society, which folded eight months later as Yeats concentrated his efforts in Dublin. December 1905 saw the founding of the Literary Theatre Society by Moore, Binyon, Ricketts, Shannon, Pye, Farr, and Gwendolyn Bishop, which mounted performances of five plays between April 1906 and March 1907, including Wilde's *Salome*, before merging with the Stage Society.[35]

Binyon was achieving more success as a poet, especially with 'The Death of Adam', to which Newbolt allotted twenty pages of the February 1902 *Monthly Review*. The poem was an ambitious if misguided attempt at resuscitating the Miltonic sublime in a sonorous blank verse derived from Milton by way of Keats's *Hyperion* fragments, which Binyon was rereading for his 1903 edition of Keats. After the restlessly mobile world of 'Porphyrion', here was a world inhabited by massively grave, marmoreal figures who think, talk, and move in slow motion, aspiring to the grounded, poised stillness of sculpture. On their last night together Adam and Eve

> spoke not, stirred not, but together leaned,
> Grand in the marble gesture of a grief
> Becalmed forever in the certitude
> Of this last hour that over them stood still.
>
> (*CP*ii.164)

Pictorial influences at work here include Michelangelo, but a more immediate influence was G. F. Watts, whose Adam and Eve series Binyon particularly admired. Writing of these paintings in 1905, he described Adam, Eve, and Cain as 'the most primitive and all-embracing symbols of mankind'.[36]

---

[33] 'Savoy Theatre: New One-Act Plays', *Tribune*, 9 Mar. 1906, 9.
[34] Sturge Moore to Pye, ALs, n.d. [Mar. 1906], box 21/279, TSMP–LU; 'Notable New Play', 10.
[35] Schuchard, 445.
[36] 'Watts and National Art', *Independent Review*, 5 (Mar. 1905), 209.

Described by the *TLS* reviewer as 'a philosophical poem of rare depth and distinction',[37] it ambitiously reinvents the Genesis myth, exploring a fascinating situation, the only human being who has never been born preparing himself to be the first, save the murdered Abel, to die. The dying Adam recalls how in the first moments after his creation he saw a world seamlessly continuous with himself, but that as soon as he walked in Eden the illusion was shattered. Through this sudden rupture between subject and object poured all the loneliness, yearning, and desire that is his legacy to his children, no Fall but the inevitable result of being human, encoded in creation from the moment Adam was born from 'God's rapture'. He asks his sons to carry him to a mountain from which he can see the gates of Eden:

> he saw beyond
> Ranges of endless hills, and very far
> On the remote horizon high and clear
> Shone marvellous the gates of Paradise.
> There was his home, his lost home, there the paths
> His feet had trod in bliss and tears, the streams,
> The heavenly trees that had o'ershadowed him,
> Removed all into radiance, clear and strange.
>
> (CPii.165–6)

He makes them leave him to die alone. His last sight is not of Eden but of 'his departing sons, | Inheriting their endless fate'. Rather than regretting the 'burning deep unquenchable desire' that is their tragic legacy, he sees that it is the necessary condition of humanity, the lure that draws them home, like him, after the adventures of existence.

Published in October 1903, *The Death of Adam and Other Poems* was Binyon's most successful book to date, both critically and with the book-buying public. The *Outlook* named the title poem 'certainly the poem of the year'. Looking back on the poetic output of 1903, the *Academy* declared: 'Only one of the accepted poets can be said to have made a notable advance in his art; and that, of course, is Mr. Laurence Binyon, whose "Death of Adam" has struck the popular imagination.'[38] Particularly satisfying was the *Pilot*'s remark that 'Adam' was 'a triumphant vindication of

---

[37] 'Mr. Laurence Binyon's Poems', *TLS*, 30 Oct. 1903, 312.

[38] 'A Tale of Troy', *Outlook* (supplement), 14 Oct. 1905, p. iii; *Academy*, 9 Jan. 1904, 33.

Matthew Arnold's famous dictum that subjects of remote antiquity are still applicable for poetical treatment'.[39] Binyon's search for heroic subjects took him, like Arnold, to Persia for 'Bahram the Hunter' and Homeric Greece for his next important poem, *Penthesilea*, published as a separate volume by Constable in 1905. He told Moore that *Penthesilea*'s 'chief merit' was that 'the subject itself is relied on not the embroidery',[40] in line with Arnold's advice to the schoolboy Binyon seventeen years earlier: 'Remember that the point is everything, and that effect depends on keeping this in mind and sacrificing superfluities to it.'

This long blank verse narrative gave Binyon ample scope for the grand manner. Even Moore, Binyon's best friend but severest critic, told Robert Trevelyan that *Penthesilea* was his best poem to date, revealing 'a great deal more go and energy than he has put into anything yet'.[41] 'The poem gives me more delight than anything you have done,' wrote Masefield. 'I think you might do *anything*.'[42] Several critics read it topically as a mildly feminist text, W. L. Courtney calling Penthesilea 'the first heroine of the woman movement',[43] and it is true that several of Binyon's later plays focus on strong women pitched against patriarchal military-political power. The *Speaker* correctly read the poem's subtext in scenting 'the central idea of the whole poem' in Binyon's unhomeric description of Penthesilea's and Achilles's climatic battlefield confrontation as

> That strange encounter, not alone the shock
> Of chosen champions, but a storm of worlds
> Where the deep blood-tides, man and woman, met
>
> (*CP*ii.212)[44]

Written during his courtship and honeymoon, *Penthesilea* was, among other things, a love poem.

DREAM COME TRUE

Binyon got on well with the talented women in his circle, including the Pye sisters, May Morris, Eleanor Calhoun, Roger Fry's sister

---

[39] 'Mr. Binyon's New Poems', *Pilot*, 21 Nov. 1903, 504.
[40] ALs, n.d. [Mar. 1905], box 28/151, TSMP–LU.
[41] ALs, 19 Feb. 1905, box 16/237 i–ii, TSMP–LU.
[42] ALs, n.d. [1905].   [43] *Daily Telegraph*, 26 Apr. 1905, 13.
[44] 'Mr. Bridges and Mr. Binyon', *Speaker*, 22 July 1905, 399.

Isabel, Constance Crommelin, and future Blake biographer Mona Wilson. Several friends were actresses, others artists or writers,— both, in the case of the symbolist artist and poet Althea Gyles, fellow contributor to the *Dome*, designer of several of Yeats's early books, and, like Yeats, a member of the Golden Dawn. Binyon had known her since his earliest days in the Print Room, when she was a Slade School student, writing to Mrs Pye in 1896 about his friendship with 'a quite mad Irish girl' who had 'been disowned by her people for taking to art, & paints in a Bloomsbury garret'.[45] He arranged for a book of her poems to be published by Grant Richards, although, like much else in her scrupulously disordered life, this plan floundered, and helped her through several crises, including her eviction by a drunken landlady in 1903 while so badly ill that both she and Binyon thought she was dying of consumption (in fact, flouting Romantic etiquette, she lived until 1949).[46]

Binyon's first great love, however, was another Irish artist, Elinor Monsell, who was also studying at the Slade. She liked and admired him but was in love with the painter Charles Conder, to whom she got engaged in 1900. For months Binyon was heartbroken, giving up even Fry's lectures on Italian art to avoid meeting her. She sued for his continued friendship, however, and turned to him when Conder later left her. By April 1903 they shared an 'understanding friendship' and one of her woodcuts appeared beside his poem 'The Clue' in Laurence Houseman's and Somerset Maugham's annual *The Venture*. He shared his grief only with Ghose and Moore, who, suffering problems of the heart himself, seems to have given his friend little support at this time, for when he later proposed to Sybil Pye and was refused he felt shamed by Binyon's sympathy and help. 'I cannot say how much I feel I owe to you,' he wrote, 'the consciousness that you have borne all that I was bearing and were so sweet and gracious makes me always glad to be near you.'[47]

In his reply, however, Binyon could report 'I am not sure that I am not in love with someone else.'[48] In fact he was sure, and had been since the moment Cicely Margaret Pryor Powell walked

[45] ALs, 18 Aug. 1896.
[46] Information from letters to Richards in BL–HRC. See also Ian Fletcher, 'Poet and Designer: W. B. Yeats and Althea Gyles', *W. B. Yeats and his Contemporaries* (London, 1987), 166–96.
[47] ALs, n.d. [1903]. See also Legge, 167–8, 217–18.
[48] ALs, 21 Apr. 1903, 28/139, TSMP–LU.

through the Print Room door on 19 October 1901. He had 'felt his heart go out to worship his dream come true', a phrase which held for him a special, almost occult meaning.[49] That night at Roche's he rhapsodized about the 'vision' he had seen that afternoon, but at first he accepted it as just that, a Dantean visitation by a Beatrice beyond his reach. Whereas Monsell belonged to his own world, Cicely Powell came from the same city but a different planet. Partly educated in Paris, she had been brought up in a cultured, moneyed milieu, in a Harley Street townhouse and a country house with a Gertrude Jekyll garden. Her father, Henry Pryor Powell, was a partner in a merchant bank in Leadenhall Street. Binyon's letters to Ghose from Oxford had argued that love as commonly understood was permeated by the mercantile, investment/profit-seeking Victorian spirit. Now, a decade later, he came face to face with that world. Like almost all girls of her class, Cicely had been assiduously groomed for only one career, marriage. She had been presented at court and, under her mother's watchful eye, attended the balls and other social events which were, beneath their glamorous veneer, the anguished hunting grounds of the competitive marriage market. Binyon was not a good match. Looked at from one perspective, he was a rising young poet and scholar, from another a civil servant with an annual income of £250, no family money, and some dubiously bohemian friends.

He had one thing going for him, however. Cicely admired his poetry, and presented him with a copy of *Odes* she had bound herself. That she was still unmarried at 25 suggests that she resisted dwindling into a decorative Edwardian 'angel in the house'. She was beautiful. Moore later remarked that G. F. Watts, a family friend, had missed a great opportunity in not painting her. At certain moments, particularly in front of a camera, she was apt to look dreamily introspective in a Pre-Raphaelite way, but she was in fact far from the diaphanous, moonlit muse figures which occasionally drifted through Binyon's verse. A 'vision' she may have been, but Cicely Powell was also a highly corporeal, intelligent, and shrewd young woman.

She was interested in art as well as poetry. Her father was a man of taste and artistic sympathies, and her maternal grandfather was Eden Eddis, a highly successful Victorian society painter. Indeed, it

[49] ALs to CMB, 16 Sept. [1903].

is difficult to say which loomed the greater obstacle, the socio-economic gulf or that of Art, for the family naturally revered Eddis as a great artist, whereas for Binyon on the New English Art Club wing of the Edwardian art world he epitomized the despised Royal Academy establishment. Nevertheless, this was Binyon's passkey into the Powell household. Visits to examine prints led to invitations to dinner in London and later in the country. Eventually, on Sunday 17 May 1903, beneath an umbrella in a thunderstorm in the wood under Leith Hill in Surrey, he proposed and was accepted. The formality of her world can be measured by the fact that only from that evening did 'Mr Binyon' become 'Laurence' in her diary.

Unashamed of his less affluent but more egalitarian and creative world, he introduced her to his Vienna and Roche's cronies, to Yeats and Moore, and to his artist friends. 'I really believe you will like my world,' he wrote. 'Artists are the most natural people there are: & it is good to be with people who are doing things.'[50] A symbolic marriage of their worlds was achieved in *Astromart*, a delightful play for children written by Binyon with songs by Streatfeild which revealed qualities of wit and grace lacking in Binyon's published plays until his children's play *Sophro the Wise* in 1927. It was performed by the Powell family and their friends at Herbert Crescent on 18 January 1904, with Astromart, like Penthesilea a female knight in a male world, played by Cicely's younger sister Betty.

Outside the charmed circle of amateur dramatics, however, there were problems. By Powell standards Binyon was near destitute. The day after proposing he reported:

I talked with your father this morning. He spoke very kindly, but of course was rather shocked at the smallness of my income—it *is* shocking!—but I am going to see if I can't make some more. I get about 250£ from the Museum—after ten years, it is certainly meagre—but if I accepted more work I could add another 100£. I have found it more than enough for myself, & never wanted for anything, but I have very few wants. . . . I have refused a great deal of work the last year or two, partly because I didn't want any more money, & partly because I wanted to devote myself to poetry, which after you I love best in the world.[51]

Had Cicely's parents read this letter it would have forewarned them of a facet of their prospective son-in-law's character that the

---

[50] ALs, CMB, 29 May [1903].   [51] ALs, 18 May [1903].

socially ambitious Mrs Powell in particular would find even more distressing than his bank balance. Friends remarked on his almost Franciscan ideal of simplicity and non-possessiveness, Moore telling Sybil Pye he thought it 'one of the most beautiful traits of Binny's character that he is so exceptionally free' from bourgeois materialism. 'I often envy him this freedom; he has so *many*!'[52] Cicely herself was a little disconcerted to receive love letters admitting that he felt physically sick walking into a jeweller's, or avowing: 'I don't like having things that cost much: it is giving materials too much importance, & they are quite uppish & tyrannical enough in the world already. Every tangible & senseless possession should be as perishable as possible.'[53] Or again:

My lovely Love, let us try to feel these things, which are of Life, always near us. It comes to my mind to put down the things I love & the things I hate. I love

YOU
Life,
The sun,
Making things,
Trees & flowers,
Brave & cheerful people,
Children,

Oh, there are so many

things—they come tumbling over each other. And I hate

THE WORLD
& with it   Clothes,
Ceremonies,
Machinery,
Commentators,
Dignitaries,
High hats, etc, etc.

—all the things that imprison & entrench, & tie one to materials. I want to be fluid & above all FREE. . . .

I'm already tired of being sorry about my poverty, so won't be any more. The best people have always been poor, or nearly always. I want you to think with me that whatever we do makes that distinguished & correct, & *never, never* to do anything we don't want to do or be, because we imagine that other people imagine we ought to.[54]

[52] ALs, n.d. [Mar. 1903], box 21/5, TSMP–LU.
[53] ALs, 3 Aug. [1903].   [54] ALs, 27 May [1903].

Cicely advised him to eschew talk of the simple life in his crucial interview with her father, who was after all a banker. 'Do try & sound as if you thought money very important,' she implored.[55] Much as he might hint that the Frys had married on £300 a year, her parents insisted on £600, and, with no help to be looked for from his family, he set about trying to double his income. Edmund Gosse particularly sympathized, since he had been in the same position three decades earlier when he too had wanted to marry on an inadequate Museum salary. 'There is no one among les jeunes for whom I have a greater respect and liking than I have for Laurence Binyon,' he wrote to Robert Ross in November, promising his help.[56] Gosse had solved his own dilemma by moving to a well-paid post at the Board of Trade, but Binyon did not want to leave the Print Room, where he was in the process of building up the Department's Oriental collection. When his friend Arthur Strong died suddenly in January 1904 his post as Librarian of the House of Lords fell vacant, but Binyon was reluctant to apply for this prized sinecure, appalled at the prospect of being back among books after the visual delights of the Print Room, and was secretly relieved when the post went, somewhat ironically, to Gosse himself. Feeling life away from London would be 'exile', he turned down the directorship of the Liverpool Art Gallery. Instead he chose to supplement his Museum salary with a part-time post at Constable the publishers, who offered him a generous £200 a year as reader and adviser on art publications. Powell made the couple an allowance to make up the shortfall.

Money, however, was not the only or even the most serious obstacle. A tough-minded, passionate young woman, Cicely was a devout Christian, while Binyon made no secret of his dislike of institutionalized religion. Things came to a head two months after their engagement, when Cicely wrote confessing both her love—'I love you more than I can quite understand or control just now *far* more than I can tell you ever'—and the pain caused by the 'awful gulf' that suddenly opened up between them.[57] He replied:

Dear, I am hurting you I know but I must say what I really feel. . . . I am against the whole idea of a Church, & especially against its being thought a divine institution. Do you think Christ wished for a Church or would

[55] ALs, n.d. [Sept. 1903].
[56] ALs, 4 Nov. 1903. For Gosse, see Thwaite 158–9.
[57] ALs, n.d. [7 July 1903].

approve of it now? . . . It has grown into a great Power, with enormous property & exclusiveness, & instead of devotion to an ideal teaches that the only way is to believe a series of propositions woven together out of Greek & Indian philosophy & far later than the New Testament which itself is much later than Christ, to whose teaching it is absolute antithesis. I cannot hear the Athanasian creed without my blood boiling with anger. I think of all the millions the Church has killed & tortured just for being sincere, & I think of the life & love of Christ & how his spirit denounces utterly the spirit of that creed. To my mind the very existence of a church is the corruption of religion. Inevitably grows up the property-feeling which prompted your Vicar to say that Christianity alone had done good in the world, & the Church is always insisting on this. Yet you know it must be ignorance or dishonesty to say so, when one remembers the divine words of Buddha & his wonderful example—to say nothing of others. Surely if God is everywhere it is in goodness everywhere he is revealed. . . .

. . . [B]ut you must have noticed the same kind of tendency all through me to be against institutions & Governments. They stifle me. . . . And you know I believe that the faith which is the sap & essence of all religions lies in us too deep for speech, & the more one tries to express it in words the more dangerous it is because then the words get to have a value & authority for their own sake, which is not inherent in them.[58]

It is worth quoting liberally from these letters, for they give us unique and short-lived access to the inner life of a poet reticent enough to inspire the jingle 'Mr Binyon | Reserved his opinion',[59] and illuminate his poetry and other writings of this and later periods. As Cicely found his state of mind 'almost inconceivable', he tried to articulate his own philosophy, hesitantly and reluctantly, both because he felt that truth 'lies in us too deep for speech', and because he had no intention of imposing his ideas on anyone, let alone the woman he loved. He wrote:

To live in the continual sense of the infinite being of which we are troubled fractions; to wish more & more to live in that; to worship & choose the beauty & the truth, wherever found, that we feel to belong to what is eternal; to refer everything we do to that standard, & to refuse the second-best; to try to realize the best & fullest self that our powers make possible, being gentle & considerate to everyone, but to radiate & *live* in the deepest sense we can; yet to feel always that is not by ourselves we are strong but

[58] ALs, 8 July [1903].
[59] Qtd. in Newbolt, *Later Life and Letters of Sir Henry Newbolt*, ed. Margaret Newbolt (London, 1942), 98.

by the truth, goodness & justice in which we live—it is something like this I mean by serving God & loving man.[60]

You know how much the thought keeps with me that life is a whole, life is one. When I judge pictures or poems, I judge them according to the measure in which they reveal a consciousness of the ideal rhythm & order which belongs to what neither time can destroy not science analyse away: & I think people's lives should be the same. Sometimes I feel I can lose myself in that eternal life, & then the shocks & losses & defeats & anxieties of the world seem to crumble away. But it is weakness to make an opposition between the life of the spirit & the life of the world; the first ought to be like fire melting & fusing the outer life, as the body should be the perfect & well-fitting garment—no, more than that, the picture & language of the soul. And yet it is so hard. The world is so subtle & powerful, that one instinctively recoils, & then one wants to house the soul a part, safe, when really it ought to be flowering in everything we do. . . . If I have sometimes bored you with talk of 'simplicity', it is only because I feel so much the danger of being clouded up from the things which live & in which we have real life. I truly believe that 'the kingdom of heaven is within you' and also that it is difficult for a rich man to enter that kingdom—not impossible, but very difficult. I think that all life should be service & ritual: but, because I am not strong enough, revolt sometimes into hatred of all that seems to me inessential, yet which really should be captured to the cause of life & beauty.[61]

Many religions have made a war between body & soul, because the equilibrium between the two is so easily upset & danger is more from the body, to be engrossed in which is to live a life of illusion & unreality. But believing that life is good, I believe that the body is good, through which we play our parts. I think the senses should be cultivated no less than the understanding of the soul.

The love of man & wife is the central thing in life, & therefore good in itself. And joy is good because it is the necessary accompaniment of a life that is really life. And beauty which gives us joy unalloyed by any transitory interest, which absorbs us into a radiant life, where eternal values prevail (not the values conferred by use, rarity etc) beauty is a great good, indeed it is but one aspect of reality (the bloom of it) & that which makes joy real.

Instead of renouncing desire and fleeing the world like his own ascetic Porphyrion, the human task is to transcend the dualistic fragmentation of life by

regarding everything as part of the whole, as related to the essence of life, as a symbol, the outward sign of an inward grace. If we have beautiful

[60] ALs, 8 July [1903].   [61] ALs, 10 Jan. [1904].

things around us, they should be to us as signs & shadows of the eternal beauty. . . . The world should not be a cold & rugged fact, but transparent from the light of meaning shining through it, with little hints & soft suggestions even in the trivial things & furniture of existence, but in the deepest & freest feelings flaming full into our souls & absorbing them into the essential life itself.

If we are careful & scrupulous to keep our selves open, clean & naked (so to speak) to the sunlight of the Meaning, jealous of everything that tends to smother & veil us from it, then we have a sure test by which to judge of men's actions & thoughts & productions in every kind of art. That is why Imagination, which is sensitiveness to the real reality, not fancy-building in the air, is so rightly prized. Without it we are not free, we stay in one place, slaves of Time.[62]

There is a constant stress on transcending the limits of selfhood and attaining union with the 'whole self of life' through imagination and joy. Passages read like prose versions of 'The Renewal': 'joy expands & liberates it melts us out of our little selves into the life which streams through all the world, it makes us greater by annihilating "self" in us, & yet we feel infinitely more our real selves'.[63]

I am forever haunted by Michelangelo's thought—of Beauty in the marble block crying for his hand to release her. Surely life is like that block, & we have but to discover the beauty—it is there—& live in it & be immortal. *Eternal life* is what every man has always thirsted for: but it is not a postponed futurity, it is here & now, & has been without beginning, though it is only by glimpses & moments that we realize it. Life moves in rhythm; & if we could only join that rhythm & be lost in it, we are free, & time & space drop off. I think personality, which modern people so strive for & admire, is limitation & hindrance. Do you remember a line of mine

As colours perish into perfect light.

Once I had a tooth out & consoled myself during the operation by addressing myself to the sensation & trying to think what it really meant. And it seemed to me that pain was a kind of contraction, one felt all driven & squeezed together into sharp identity; but joy expands & melts, & in great joy one is lost altogether & become a part of the whole self of life. Love has told me this.[64]

With their stress on the inner light and unmediated spiritual experience, Binyon's formulations often sound curiously like the

[62] AMS, n.d. [sent to CMB *c.*6–8 Mar. 1904], n.pag.
[63] Ibid.   [64] ALs, 20 Aug. [1903].

Quakerism of his ancestors shorn of its Christian theology, especially when he says that 'the words & forms that other men through long generations have invented . . . seem to come between me & the light'.[65] The 'light' recurs constantly: 'The secret is to be sensitive to the light, to train oneself to receive it through every hint & whisper of beauty & of Truth. Our ordinary education is mostly but a veiling & a swathing in prejudice & limitation: & we have to recover our innocence.'[66] Philosophical influences range from Plato to George Santayana, whom he considered 'the finest of living critics' and whose *Interpretations of Poetry and Religion* he had voted his favourite book of 1901.[67] Closer to home there is the tradition of English mystical poetry, especially Traherne, and Romantic poetry and thought, notably Blake, on whose art and poetry he was working intensively during these years. The influence of Asian thought is felt perhaps in the striving 'To live in the continual sense of the infinite being of which we are troubled fractions' and the quest to reintegrate the individual self in the universal Self, but he had only recently discovered the philosophy closest to his heart, Taoism, in Lionel Giles's translation of the *Tao Tê Ching* and Okakura Kakuzo's *The Ideals of the East* (1903), which he reviewed enthusiastically in the *TLS* in March 1903. Characteristically, it appears in the letters not as doctrine but in pervasive images which are also Binyon's own natural poetic images, especially that of water and rivers, and of life as 'rhythm'.

These affirmations came ultimately not from books, however, but from his own experience, especially in 'elemental' places like mountains and sea. In letters from Cornwall—his favourite part of England because its 'bareness' 'leaves you free for the sky'—he told Cicely of moments of pure discarnation, 'unconscious of having a body', when the slow movement of clouds or the 'rhythmical soft stirrings' of wheatfields, seemed events within his own mind, the sunlight of a Cornish August and 'the sunlight of the Meaning' the same thing:

The light has been bathing me through & through . . . & melts out all the illusions of words & I understood how all the thoughts & systems &

---

[65] ALs, postmarked 22 May 1903.   [66] ALs, postmarked 10 Mar. 1904.
[67] ALs, 8 July [1903]; 'Favourite Books of 1901: Some Readers: Mr. Laurence Binyon', *Academy*, 7 Dec. 1901, 568.

beliefs of all the countless generations of men were shadows & transparent images of the one radiant truth of life.[68]

Since it was based on experience not dogma, it did not matter that, as he freely admitted, his faith seemed 'vague': 'I feel no need for final conclusions, I am quite content to wait & grow, so long as I can in spirit turn back & lose myself in what I feel to be the infinite life that sustains us all.'[69] This too is a Taoist attitude, eschewing doctrinal certitudes for non-verbal experiential openness.

This was no modish spiritual posturing. These were letters written under pressure, in full knowledge that they could easily destroy his hopes for happiness. At the climax of their trauma in July 1903, he wrote:

Dearest, dearest Cicely, if you *really in your soul* think it wrong to love me, if it will mean unhappiness to you,—give me up. I can't tell you what pain it is even to write the words: but you can guess. . . . I love you so much that for your sake I would try to live on without you—if only I knew you were happy.[70]

She replied by return: 'once for all I love you. My life is done as far as that is concerned. . . . Do you believe I would cut myself off from you to save my soul alone?'[71] The letter arrived while Binyon was examining a 'Rembrandt' sketch a hopeful owner had brought in for inspection. Passion overcame professionalism as he ushered him out with the assurance that 'the Rembrandt was ever so genuine' and sat down to read his letter in peace.[72]

They married on 12 April 1904 at St Andrew's, Wells Street, Marylebone, and spent their honeymoon in Italy, mostly in Florence, where they stayed in Horne's apartment overlooking the Arno near the Ponte Vecchio.[73] When they returned in May they lived above a post office at 8 Tite Street in Chelsea, a street steeped in Aesthetic and Japonist history, for here E. W. Godwin had built Whistler's White House and redesigned Wilde's famous House Beautiful at number 16, the centre of the firestorm which effectively aborted the Decadent nineties in 1895. All ghosts now, though the painter John Singer Sargent remained to be one of the Binyons' neighbours. Cicely worried Binyon would miss his gregarious

---

[68] ALs 4 Aug. [1903]; 5 Aug. [1903]; n.d. [c.7 Aug. 1903].
[69] ALs, postmarked 10 July 1903.   [70] ALs, 8 July [1903].
[71] ALs, n.d. [8 July 1903].   [72] ALs, postmarked 9 July 1903.
[73] For the wedding, see *Court Journal*, 30 Apr. 1904, 724–5.

Roche's dinners and especially billiards. 'When we have a house of our own', she promised, 'we will pull down all the partitions, & all your friends shall join & give you a billiard table, & we will cook in the area & sleep in the passage & you will be quite well & we will be happy!'[74] In fact, the old bachelor world was already breaking up. Moore, Robert Trevelyan, and Holmes had all recently married, Binyon having been Holmes's best man.

Among the Binyons' wedding gifts was a pair of Sotatsu paintings from Ricketts, who in May gave Cicely an exquisite jewelled pendant he had designed and had made at Guiliano's, a generous gesture since this sudden spate of marriages among his protégés had left him punchdrunk. 'Michael Field', the aunt–niece poet team Katherine Bradley and Edith Cooper, recorded in their 1903 diary a conversation about Moore's and Binyon's approaching marriages in which Ricketts declared that marriages should be forbidden by law, since 'as soon as a woman is concerned in a man's life it becomes unintelligent and trivial from the senseless marriage festivities onwards'.[75] Neither Binyon nor Moore would have agreed, not only because they were in love but because their life philosophies were based on love, sexual fulfilment, children, and the comradeship of marriage. In his copy of Binyon's *The Flight of the Dragon*, Moore marked this sentence on page 22: 'To have achieved a beautiful relation to another human being is to realise a part of perfection.'[76] When Binyon wrote to Cicely that 'The love of man & wife is the central thing in life,' he was not muttering sweet nothings. When her mother accused him of making 'a religion of love', he pleaded guilty:

I know what she means, but love is not merely love, is it? Any more than a flower is just a flower, & not the final beauty that ages have wrought for—a sign of powers that pervade the world & mean joy for us. In my view love should be like religion: & I would not have it put apart from life, like a pleasure or recreation, but would have it *in* life, giving grace to everything. I am sure, because I love you so much, I love everyone more, in a sense. Yet you are Love to me. Through you I seem joined to what lives & triumphs for ever.[77]

'I can't argue it, but feel that love in its depth joins one to the deep-down purposes of life, feeds one's own life from the centre,' he

[74] ALs to LB, n.d. [1904].
[75] Qtd. in Delaney 177. For Cicely's jewel see Delaney, 179.
[76] Stirling Library, University of London Library.   [77] ALs, 8 Dec. [1903].

writes in another letter. 'The best & most real part of us is unknown to ourselves, & flowers only when we love . . . or flow out
in poetry.'[78] This linking of love and poetry recurs again and again:
'I think being always with a great force like the sea teaches gentleness,' he writes in March 1904. 'I want to have elemental things
near in my life. Well, love & marriage are that, & so is poetry.'[79]
Both entail a willing relinquishment of self, the discipline of ecstasy
in its original sense of being rapt out of oneself in the presence of
the Other.

The transition from bachelorhood to full family life was made
at breakneck speed, for on 9 December 1904 Cicely gave birth
prematurely to twin daughters, Helen and Margaret. 'I feel the
babies are going to deepen life for us & that will make ~~my~~ our
poetry better,' their father wrote days later.[80] That struck-out 'my'
is typical, parenthood as a further loosening of the bonds of
selfhood.

Five months later he published the poems he had written during
their months of betrothal, honeymoon, first year of marriage, and
the birth of the twins in *Dream-Come-True*, a limited edition
designed and printed by his friends Lucien and Edith Pissarro at
their Eragny Press, using Lucien's own Brook type with woodcut
borders engraved by Edith and a simple but effective Binyon woodcut incorporated in the opening poem (pl. 6). Moore thought it
'in every way an exquisite little book'.[81] The marriage lyrics are
instinct with a sense of parenthood binding the couple into the
larger purposes of life, as they join a human continuum stretching
backwards through ancestors and forwards through their unborn
children:

> O my beloved, my Bride,
> Lo where we stand, for whom in love and pride
> Unnumbered generations wooed and died;
> Their prayers are on us and our heads they bless;
> And lo, the generations all to come
> Wait for us, praying dumb[82]

The lyrics are self-effacing, choric, the anonymous voice of love
poetry, as the *TLS* reviewer remarked: 'His poetry is like the little

---

[78] ALs, 8 Oct. [1903].   [79] ALs, 23 Mar. [1904].
[80] ALs, 22 Dec. [1904].   [81] *Academy*, 13 May 1905, 512.
[82] *Dream-Come-True* (London, 1905), 21.

woodcut of his own doing on the frontispiece—there is nothing to mark it for all time as distinctively his own, but it is sweet and radiant.'[83] Binyon's lifelong work as a love poet, including unpublished poems commemorating anniversaries and birthdays, comprises an impressive corpus of that rarest of genres, a poetry of marriage, of human happiness and fulfilment, unmarred by the complexity that would have made it more arresting as poetry but moving in its sincerity.

The depth and tenacity of these emotions was soon put to the test. Within months of the twins' birth Cicely's father died suddenly and it was revealed that the firm was wholly owned by his partners, leaving his family little but debts. 'I can't help wishing sometimes that you belonged to poor people, like mine,' Binyon had written a year earlier.[84] Now, at the worst possible time, he had his wish.

[83] 'Some Recent Verse', *TLS*, 25 Aug. 1905, 267.   [84] ALs, 2 Nov. [1903].

7 The Generation Gap

ART CRITICISM

When the twins were born prematurely in December 1904, Margaret, born fifteen minutes after Helen, was not expected to live and the doctor is said to have murmured 'Perhaps it's just as well, because they can't afford two.' This backdates the Binyons' financial problems by several months, but it does suggest the drama which followed Henry Powell's death. The £100 allowance ceased, and Binyon had to find more work to make up the shortfall. Cicely secretly took over much of his reading for Constable, especially novels, to free him for other potboiling work, until the job came to an end at Christmas 1906 because the firm needed someone more involved in administration. She then began editing anthologies, beginning with *Nineteenth Century Prose* for Methuen in 1907 and *The Mind of the Artist* for Chatto and Windus in 1909.

Binyon turned to art criticism, but by necessity not choice. 'Commentators' featured on the 'I hate' list he sent Cicely in 1903. He distrusted judgemental views of art and had no wish to set himself up as an arbiter of taste, although he did not lack the necessary combative instincts, as he had revealed two years earlier in a public row with D. S. MacColl, the foremost English champion of Impressionism. The row was sparked off by Binyon's critical review of MacColl's *Nineteenth Century Art* in the January 1904 *Quarterly Review*, which inspired a rejoinder from MacColl, an exchange of letters in the *Saturday Review*, and a flurry of private correspondence.[1] Egged on by artist friends delighted at seeing this 'professional shooter' shot, Binyon reminded MacColl: 'You, a famous attacker of other people's opinions, must know how difficult it is to go hard for the opinions & entirely avoid all appearance of going

---

[1] LB, 'Art of the Nineteenth Century', *Quarterly Review*, 199 (Jan. 1904), 80–99; MacColl, 'A Quarterly Reviewer', *SR*, 6 Feb. 1904, 166–7; LB, 'A Reply to Mr. MacColl (1)', *SR*, 13 Feb. 1904, 202–3, 'A Reply to Mr. MacColl (11)', *SR*, 20 Feb. 1904, 232–3; MacColl, Letter, *SR*, 20 Feb. 1904, 233.

for the man who expressed them.'[2] The *Morning Post* enjoyed the contretemps, since 'to the judicious mind it is always wholesome to watch one critic demolishing another'.[3] Roger Fry watched interestedly from the sidelines, informing Mary Berenson in Italy 'Here the moderns are also squabbling, MacColl and Binyon in the *Saturday Review*',[4] and it was over dinner at Fry's house in March 1904 that the warring critics made their peace.

When MacColl was appointed Director of the Tate Gallery in 1906, Binyon assumed his mantle as art critic of the declining but still influential *Saturday Review*, joining a talented team which included his friends Max Beerbohm on theatre and Arthur Symons on music. The first of his fortnightly reviews appeared in December 1906, just as the post at Constable folded. His Museum work kept him largely confined to London except for hectic trips to France and Germany to study Oriental art collections and so, apart from European art exhibited at the International Society and other shows, he addressed himself mainly to the British art scene. This was also partly by choice, for Binyon had been concerned about the state of contemporary British art since at least 1890, when he had argued at the Gryphon Club 'that the state of art in England is far from satisfactory'. His *bête noire* was, inevitably, the Royal Academy, with its pseudo-traditional, market-oriented art, genre 'saccharinities', and 'portraits of bored successful people by bored successful painters', the art wing of Victorian commercialism.[5] The artists he supported exhibited in small galleries and in the annual exhibitions of the New English Art Club, the International Society, Frank Rutter's Allied Artists' Association, and other independent societies.

Binyon's first love was landscape, but with rare exceptions like Wilson Steer he saw the great English tradition as temporarily moribund, largely given over to pretty 'picnic landscapes' devoid of the emotional and spiritual depths of Chinese and Japanese ink paintings or the British watercolour tradition. It was this spiritual dimension that he found lacking in Impressionist landscapes, which

    [2] LB to MacColl, ALs, n.d. [Jan. 1904], MacColl Papers B164; ALs, n.d. [Feb. 1904], B165, Glasgow Univ. Lib.
    [3] 'Quarterly Review', *Morning Post*, 16 Jan. 1904, 9.
    [4] 27 Feb. 1904, letter 135, *Letters of Roger Fry*, ed. Denys Sutton, 2 vols. (London, 1972), i. 220.
    [5] '"Max", and a Peep at the Academy', *SR*, 4 May 1907, 553; 'The Royal Academy', *SR*, 30 Apr. 1910, 554.

he saw as the inevitable dead-end of nineteenth-century realism. The domination of art by science that had started in Renaissance Florence had reduced painting to a matter of optics and the artist's dispassionate vision recording instantaneous sense impressions on the passive retina. In fact, Binyon was not against Impressionist art *per se*, which he accepted as a valuable enrichment of our visual vocabulary, but Impressionist theory as promulgated in England by Francis Bate, R. A. M. Stevenson, and MacColl, according to which the meaning of pictures and reality alike lies exclusively in their surfaces, garnered through sensitively attuned optic nerves, rather than in depths intuited by the imagination. In direct opposition to this positivism, Binyon took an idealist, symbolist stance. Landscape's business is not mimesis of the surfaces of nature or fleeting effects of sunlight, 'purveying correct information',[6] but meditation on, empathy with, and intuitive insight into the living energies behind appearances.

In her book *Roger Fry and the Beginnings of Formalist Art Criticism*, Jacqueline V. Falkenheim rightly names Binyon alongside Fry, MacColl, Stevenson, and Charles Holmes as the critics who 'created much of the method for what would become formalist art criticism'.[7] However, it is equally important that Binyon was one of the few progressive critics to champion imaginative, subject-oriented art, holding out against its apparently imminent demise through overwhelming avant-garde prejudice against 'literary' painting. He traced this narrowly formalist strain back to Whistler's misreading of Japanese art: 'Whistler imagined that the art of Japan was an abstract art. As a matter of fact it is more saturated with literary allusion and deals more in moral ideas than our own. . . . They had none of Whistler's prejudices; art was part of life to them, not something detached and unrelated.'[8] Binyon often contrasted Asian art's glorying in the 'perpetual challenge of traditional subject' with modern European art's willed amnesia, refusing, with exceptions like Manet, to enter a creative dialogue with the past and so cutting 'itself off from the nourishing life-currents that flow through the history and inherited thought of a race'.[9] Just as he strove to invest traditional mythic subjects with new meaning in 'Tristram', *The Death of Adam*, and *Penthesilea*,

---

[6] 'Art and Life', *SR*, 20 Aug. 1910, 230.   [7] (Ann Arbor, 1980) 56.
[8] 'Whistler', *SR*, 7 Nov. 1908, 572.
[9] 'Art and Legend', *SR*, 18 Jan. 1908, 75–6.

so he defended painters' use of subjects from literature, history, and mythology as a fund of shared images which have accrued resonance and symbolic power over the generations, the repository of the nation's, and ultimately mankind's, communal imagination (*PFE* 150). His books and lectures on Oriental art were an important counterweight to pure formalism, as Yeats found when reading *Painting in the Far East* in 1909.[10]

For all its limitations, Binyon felt that Pre-Raphaelite art remained a 'deeper and more affluent source of inspiration' for British art than Impressionism, although he was far from advocating academic 'nerveless echoes of the Pre-Raphaelites'.[11] The basis for a viable tradition of Romantic British art had been laid by Blake, Palmer, Calvert, Rossetti, Burne-Jones, and G. F. Watts, while French influence should come not from Monet but 'that master of great spaces', Puvis de Chavannes, whose linear rhythm and simplified, flattened forms owed much to Japanese influence.[12] The contemporary British artists Binyon admired were those he judged to have 'the most capability for creative design', but who tended to produce their best work not in oils but in craftsmanly media like engraving and lithography.[13] His championing of Ricketts, for example, seems less misguidedly insular if we take into account, as Binyon certainly did, the totality of his work from book illustration to stage design, in which he emerges as a creator of European stature.

Binyon's hopes for the future of British art rested on successive generations of talented Slade School students, many of whom sought his advice in the Print Room. In this golden age of the Slade, the most lavishly gifted was Augustus John, whom he had long considered, as he wrote Cicely after his 1903 Carfax show, 'the most gifted of the young generation'.[14] Binyon was John's most perceptive and sympathetic interpreter during these pre-war years when he looked set to revolutionize British art. It is hard to imagine a greater contrast than the flamboyant bohemian and the diffident scholar, but in one respect at least they were well matched: the individualistic John owed allegiance to no school, just as Binyon

[10] See *Autobiographies*, 489–90, 547–8.
[11] 'Reflections on Two Great Movements', *SR*, 9 May 1908, 590; 'Some Autumn Shows', *SR*, 24 Oct. 1908, 511.
[12] 'The International Society', *SR*, 2 Feb. 1907, 137.
[13] 'Mr. Strang and Others', *SR*, 23 Oct. 1909, 497.   [14] ALs, 13 Mar. [1903].

abhorred all 'isms' and doctrinaire theories. Binyon's reviews of John exhibitions read like enlightened reviews of Post-Impressionism. When, for example, he writes in May 1909 that John 'feels the danger of his own skill; and he is determined not to acquiesce in the appearance of things, but to break it up resolve it into its elements, and remould it new', he could be talking about Cézanne, Gauguin, or even Picasso, whose studio John had visited in 1907, seeing several Blue Period paintings and probably the seminal *Les Demoiselles d'Avignon*.[15]

With his expressive line and gift for rhythmical composition, John was the one British artist capable of creating the great decorative figure compositions both he and Binyon admired in Puvis de Chavannes. Binyon felt that John's talents, like Puvis's, demanded large-scale public commissions and when plans for the mural decoration of the Palace of Westminster came under discussion in 1907 he urged that John be given a commission.[16] Public art was a lifelong interest of Binyon's, from his enthusiasm for Puvis to his later interest in the Mexican muralist Diego Rivera. He applauded efforts like William Rothenstein's 1910 project to have Leeds art students decorate the city's buildings and urged other cities to follow suit: 'That, above all, is what is wanted now; to have faith in youth and give it strenuous tasks, instead of calling in commercial abilities or tired successful men.'[17] Far from advocating a tame municipal art preachily imparting establishment values, Binyon hoped such commissions would nurture a blossoming of progressive art and sculpture. When in June 1908 Jacob Epstein's statues decorating the British Medical Association building in the Strand were attacked as immoral by the press and the National Vigilance Society, John turned to Binyon for influential support: 'Penniless & inarticulate, he is helpless. Believing him to be perhaps the only *European* artist I venture to call your attention to his work which else you might not hear of except perhaps through the medium of a police report.'[18] Binyon wrote to *The Times* praising the statues' 'remarkable original power', 'far removed from the enfeebled conventions too characteristic of British sculpture in

[15] 'The New English Art Club', *SR*, 29 May 1909, 684. For John and Picasso, see Michael Holroyd, *Augustus John: A Biography*, 2 vols. (London, 1974–5), i. 273–4.

[16] 'Old and New English Art', *SR*, 23 Nov. 1907, 631.

[17] 'Arts and Crafts; and the Twelve', *SR*, 22 Jan. 1910, 105.

[18] ALs to LB, 18 June 1908.

the past', and wrote to the BMA urging them to resist philistine pressure.[19]

Haunted by a sense of art's irrelevance for the vast majority when 'life for so much of our population has been so joylessly dehumanised by modern industrial conditions',[20] Binyon consistently attacked the Art for Art's sake doctrine not only in its *passé* Whistlerian form but also its subtler avatars in an era when criticism was proclaiming the autonomy of art from all but purely formal concerns. He championed public art against two trends he deplored: art dwindling into a bourgeois commodity, 'the affair of collectors and museums', on the one hand and on the other degenerating into a battlefield where avant-garde sects fought bitterly for supremacy, legitimized by élitist critics who 'assert that art is only for the few who can intimately understand and enjoy it', who 'divide the world into the initiated and "outsiders"', and 'make all art an exclusive mystery'.[21] His ideal was art taken out of the drawing rooms and museums and restored to its rightful place in civic life, the expression of the culture of an entire people, celebrating communal identity at the local and national levels:

Painting has become divorced from the other arts; no longer part of a great language expressing the whole spirit of a people, it has become a private thing, a personal expression corresponding to the personal taste and temperament of private patrons; and in these latest years an attempt has been made to separate it more and more from life.

But the signs of healthful reaction from painters' pedantry are everywhere at hand. . . . We begin to think that a public art may again be possible; we begin to realise that till we strive to create beauty in our lives and surroundings, and to regain the spirit of community in art, the personal achievements of a few fine talents will not redeem us from general joylessness and the curse of apathy.

(BC 31)

'What a futility is our Art, and all our talk about it,' he wrote in 1907, 'when we build and design and decorate like this!' and hence he stretched his *Saturday Review* column to accommodate arts and crafts, art manufactures, and the key public arts of architecture and

---

[19] *The Times*, 24 June 1908, 14. See Epstein, *Epstein: An Autobiography* (London, 1955), 21–4.

[20] 'Romance and Reality', *SR*, 21 Dec. 1907, 760. See also 'Arts and Crafts; and the Twelve', 104–5.

[21] 'Watts and National Art', *Independent Review*, 5 (Mar. 1905), 201, 203.

city planning.[22] In the same spirit he suggested that 'the most living and best practised art surviving in England' was gardening. In a sane society art is not a luxury to be stored in guarded sanctuaries of beauty amid 'our acres of hideous streets', but 'a function of life, . . . a necessity, . . . part of our common need'.[23]

We fill a museum with fine works from divers countries, and place it in the midst of streets that desolate eye and heart, without an effort to make them part of the beauty we desire. Art is not an end in itself, but a means to beauty in life. This we forget.

(*PFE* 275–6)

The signal event during Binyon's tenure at the *Saturday Review* was Roger Fry's Post-Impressionists Exhibition at the Grafton Galleries from November 1910 to January 1911, which sparked a bloody and richly comic civil war in the British art world and has come to be seen as a watershed in British cultural life, inspiring Virginia Woolf's famous dictum that 'In or about December, 1910, human character changed.'[24] The way the story is usually told pitches the youthful white knights of modernism against the older generation of reactionary, xenophobic Victorians struggling to keep out that deadliest of French exports, the twentieth century. If the Post-Impressionists show is the infallible litmus test it is often been made out to be, Binyon would appear to be stranded on the wrong side of this yawning generation gap. Reality, as ever, resists such neat critical polarities. The exhibition was admired and detested for good and bad reasons on both sides. As Eric Gill told Rothenstein, the sheep and goats were all mixed up, and those who disliked the show displayed 'either great intelligence or else great stupidity'.[25] Balanced enough to draw complaints from both pro and anti lobbies, Binyon's review shows that not everyone who responded unfavourably was a mummified Royal Academy reactionary. Although he felt both evinced 'more struggle than mastery', he found things to admire in Van Gogh and Gauguin, who had driven many critics apoplectic, and he liked Maurice

---

[22] 'Chardin and Ruskin', *SR*, 30 Mar. 1907, 389. See e.g. 'Town-Planning, and the New Bridge', *SR*, 29 Oct. 1910, 543.

[23] 'Ideas of Design in East and West', *Atlantic Monthly*, Nov. 1913, 645, 644.

[24] 'Mr. Bennett and Mrs. Brown', *Collected Essays*, 4 vols. (London, 1966–7), i. 320. For reactions to the exhibition, see *Post-Impressionism in England*, ed. J. B. Bullen (London, 1988).

[25] 5 Dec. 1910, letter 18, *Letters of Eric Gill*, ed. Walter Shewring (London, 1947), 55.

Denis and Jules Flandrin. The artist who impressed him most was Picasso, whose *Nude Girl with a Basket of Flowers* was 'painted and modelled with wonderful subtlety', and he urged visitors to study his drawings in the end room (Pl 610). All of these he found more remarkable than Cézanne, the master Post-Impressionist who had transformed Fry from staid Morellian *Kunstforscher* into England's foremost avant-garde aesthetician. Binyon was sympathetic to Cézanne's aims but unconvinced by his performance. He felt much as he had two years earlier when reviewing the 1908 International Society show: 'Every one must feel conscious of the artist in Cézanne; but the intentional rawness and hardness of his still-life pieces . . . should have been an experimental stage, out of which a really fine austerity might have developed.'[26]

He saw Post-Impressionism as a necessary U-turn out of the cul-de-sac of Impressionism, and applauded its rediscovery of formal rigour as 'a healthy reaction, a movement in the right direction' (Pl 609). His own writings on Western and Oriental art had urged the claims of expressive 'rhythmical design' and an art capable of getting 'behind the appearances of things, to render the dynamic forces of life and nature', the 'primal energies and realities' (Pl 609). 'Form', 'design', 'rhythm'—the keywords of Post-Impressionist theory were a natural part of his vocabulary. If the problem facing Fry and Clive Bell was to introduce a new set of critical criteria to replace the outmoded traditional formulae that had made representation the end of art, Binyon had been engaged in the same project throughout the decade in his work on Oriental art, and, as Fry was well aware, his writings had helped prepare the ground for the acceptance of radical aesthetic ideas in Britain.[27] The year 1910 was notable not only for the Post-Impressionists but also for the great Japan–British Exhibition at Shepherd's Bush and the exhibition of Chinese and Japanese painting Binyon organized at the Print Room. One commentator noted that these exhibitions gave English artists a 'golden opportunity for reform':

[26] 'Two Exhibitions', *SR*, 1 Feb. 1908, 136–7.
[27] S. K. Tillyard suggests that Fry recruited LB 'as an unwitting advocate of the new painting' on the eve of the Post-Impressionist Show by shrewdly placing a Meyer-Riefstahl essay on Van Gogh immediately after one on Chinese art by LB in the November 1910 issue of the *Burlington Magazine*. See *The Impact of Modernism 1900–1920: Early Modernism and the Arts and Crafts Movement in Edwardian England* (London, 1988), 98.

Since the opening of the Chinese Exhibition the Prints and Drawing Gallery in the British Museum has been thronged with students, and one could fancy that one noted them going hence with determination in their eyes, and eagerness to express themselves anew plucking at their right wrists.[28]

Ironically, a month before the Post-Impressionists exhibition Binyon was himself savaged in the *Edinburgh Review* for helping to undermine the 'life of the West' with his writings on Oriental art.[29] Similarly, while the *Athenaeum* hailed *The Flight of the Dragon* (1911) as a harbinger of a European 'spiritual renaissance', G. K. Chesterton in a *Daily News* article entitled 'The Slime of the Dragon' accused 'that admirable poet' Binyon of 'plotting the destruction of England and of Europe' by promoting the philosophy of the Oriental 'Heathens'.[30]

Given this track record, we might have expected Binyon to welcome Cézanne and company with open arms. Instead the exhibition left him 'sad' because the Post-Impressionists did not seem 'strong enough to carry out the programme' (PI 609). He identified more strongly with British artists striving to find solutions to the same problems. During the Grafton show's first month another controversial exhibition opened at the Chenil Gallery in Chelsea, an Augustus John show which included a series of oil sketches painted that spring and summer in Provence. With their daringly simplified forms and areas of flat, unmodelled, decorative colour, these 'Provencal Studies' speak a revolutionary pictorial language akin to that of the Post-Impressionists at the Grafton. 'What does it all mean?' asked *The Times*. 'Is there really a widespread demand for these queer, clever, forcible but ugly and uncanny notes of forms and dashes of colour?'[31] Binyon again proved John's most perceptive critic:

One can see the summary outline under the colour, which is brushed in with hasty decision, abruptly, with a hand contemptuous of suavity, scorning to caress or subtilise the pigment. Two dots will serve for eyes; modelling is disregarded, shadow scarcely used. Yet somehow everything lives. Even the paint, rudely dashed on the canvas, seems to be rebelling into

---

[28] E.M., 'Art Notes', *Illustrated London News*, 2 July 1910, 28.

[29] 'Eastern Art and Western Critics', rev. of *PFE*, *Edinburgh Review*, 434 (Oct. 1910), 476.

[30] *Athenaeum*, 7 Oct. 1911, 429; *Daily News*, 18 Nov. 1911, 6.

[31] 'Mr. Augustus John', *The Times*, 5 Dec. 1910, 14, qtd. Malcolm Easton and Michael Holroyd, *The Art of Augustus John* (London, 1974), 18–19. See also Holroyd, *Augustus John*, i. 360.

beauties of its own. . . . I do not know how it is, but these small studies . . . make an extraordinary impression and haunt one's memory. A tall woman leaning on a staff; a little boy in scarlet on a cliff-edge against blue sea; a woman carrying bundles of lavender: the description of these says nothing, but they themselves seem creatures of the infancy of the world, aboriginals of the earth, with an animal dignity and strangeness, swift of gesture, beautifully poised. That is the secret of Mr. John's power.[32]

He linked John with the Post-Impressionists in his similar sweeping away of mimetic clutter, paring down to essential, expressive forms, and compared John's primitivist-symbolist 'natural instinct' with Gauguin's but found it conjoined with richer technical resources, a judgement which looks foolish now only because John squandered his extravagant gifts. Two months later he showed similar advanced taste in reviews of new work by Epstein and Eric Gill, whose sculptures at the Chenil Gallery were a revelation of 'primitive symbolic form'.[33]

What Binyon was attacking in December 1910 was not so much Cézanne and Matisse, whom he later praised when he came across works he liked, as 'the bluff and bunkum which seem fated to surround every Parisian art movement' (PI 609) and an incipiently totalitarian criticism which sought for one form of avant-garde art hegemony over all others, threatening, as he once said of Julius Meier-Graefe, 'a tyranny of criticism more intolerant than the old prejudices of academies against "vulgar" subjects, a tyranny of doctrinaire catchwords'.[34] Binyon diagnosed Post-Impressionism as a symptom of a more pervasive sea-change in the European mind, a desire to recover the spirituality Western art had lost in its obsession with mimesis: 'We crave for an art which shall be more profound, more intense, more charged with essential spirit, more direct a communication between mind and mind.' This ran 'much deeper than any transplantable French fashion in painting', and hence Binyon's concern that the base of native British art, fragile enough in 1910, might be further eroded by a fetishization of innovation which encouraged young artists to abandon the slow, painfully difficult task of developing their own unique vision in order to compete in mimicking the latest imported formulae, fritter-

---

[32] 'Romney; Raeburn; Mr. John', SR, 10 Dec. 1910, 747.
[33] 'Portraits and Sculpture', SR, 11 Feb. 1911, 171–2.
[34] 'The New Barbarism', rev. of Meier-Graefe's Modern Art, SR, 28 Nov. 1908, 663.

ing away a potential spiritual renaissance in an endless succession of entrepreneurial, critically manipulated 'isms'.[35]

Aware that he was making himself vulnerable to charges of Little Englandism, Binyon stressed his profound admiration for French art but argued, like Delacroix and Baudelaire before him, that 'the English genius' was very different from that of France and that it was better to develop our own, perhaps lesser but unique gifts rather than 'trying to engraft qualities in which our native tendencies will not allow us to excel'.[36] Now that the dust of international modernism has settled and British art is no longer pilloried for failing to be French or conforming to critical shibboleths like Bell's Significant Form, we are in a better position to understand Binyon's desire to nurture a native tradition of mythic, visionary painting, such as was soon to emerge in the work of Stanley Spencer, Paul Nash, and the Neo-Romantic artists. Belated recognition of Binyon's contribution to art criticism during this confusing period comes in an essay David Fraser Jenkins wrote for the catalogue of the *Last Romantics* exhibition at the Barbican in 1989, which sees Binyon as laying the intellectual basis for what Jenkins calls 'Slade School Symbolism', a style that 'can be traced through several clearly distinctive phases, first appearing in the early figure groups of Augustus John, continuing with artists who had been pupils at the Slade School from Orpen to Stanley Spencer, persisting in the underlying arrangement of figures in the Vorticist paintings of Bomberg and Nevinson, and reviving after the war with the academic competitors for the Rome Scholarship in the 1920s'.[37]

As Jenkins adds, 'The difference of personality between Binyon and Fry—and the former's employment at the British Museum—prevented his becoming the champion of this symbolist style as Fry had for the followers of Post-Impressionism.'[38] In fact, he had other priorities. A month after the Post-Impressionists show closed he gave up his *Saturday Review* column, concluding his final review with the highly revealing, if unfulfilled, wish that he would be

[35] 'E pur si muove', *SR*, 31 Dec. 1910, 840–1.

[36] 'E pur si muove', 841. For a fine modern critic's similar assessment of the situation, see Robert Rosenblum, 'British Painting vs. Paris', *Partisan Review*, 24 (1957), 95–100.

[37] 'Slade School Symbolism', *The Last Romantics: The Romantic Tradition in British Art, Burne-Jones to Stanley Spencer*, ed. John Christian (London, 1989), 71.

[38] Jenkins, 76.

free to 'maintain about art and the problems of art a beautiful, restorative silence'.[39]

Binyon's main reason for leaving the *Saturday Review* was to make space for his own creative writing. In January 1911 he wrote to Edmund Gosse:

I have a great long poem brewing in my head these three or four years, and several plays, but am always in arrears and haunted by the dread that I shall be dead or worn-out before I can get the things written. So you can imagine that the desire to get time for original work is sometimes overwhelming—I am giving up my 'Saturday' articles on this account, though I can't afford to do so.[40]

He could look back on some limited success. Among the theatrical people to whom Eleanor Calhoun introduced him in 1902 was the Australian-Norwegian actor Oscar Asche and his wife Lily Brayton, alumni of Benson's Shakespearean company and now with Tree at His Majesty's. With them in mind, in 1904 he wrote a four-act verse drama about Attila, dramatizing the events leading up to his assassination by his Gothic bride Ildico in 453 CE. Seeing the play as an admirable vehicle for his bravura, heroic acting style, Asche wanted to produce it, but as this would be no £15 Literary Theatre Society affair a backer had to be found. In July 1906 Binyon approached the 26-year-old Lord Howard de Walden, one of those rare aristocrats who actually fit the Sidney mould, soldier, yachtsman, and Olympic fencer, admirer of Yeats and himself an aspiring verse dramatist who would go on to write dramas and operas under the pseudonym T. E. Scott-Ellis. One of the richest men in England, he was just embarking on his career as a patron of the arts. 'I have now met him, & told him I wanted 3000£,' Binyon informed Ricketts, already enlisted as *Attila*'s designer. 'Though taken aback, he did *not* say "You be damned", but thought "something might be arranged".'[41]

[39] 'At the National Gallery', *SR*, 18 Mar. 1911, 327.
[40] ALs, 7 Jan. 1911, Sir Edmund Gosse Papers, Brotherton Collection, Leeds University Library (hereafter EG–BC).
[41] ALs, n.d. [July 1906], Add. MS 58090, fos. 69–70, R&S–BL.

Something was, and a year later Lancelot Speed posters featuring a moustachioed Hun sprouted dramatically on walls all over London announcing the arrival of *Attila*. Chosen by Asche to mark his debut as manager of His Majesty's Theatre in the Haymarket, magnificently rebuilt by Tree in 1897, it was the most ambitious and eagerly awaited new play of the 1907 autumn season. The press delighted in contrasting the craggy Asche and the neuralgic poet–scholar who, as the *Sketch* put it, had 'hitherto lived in the rarefied clouds of high art and higher literature'.[42] There was great interest in the production as a spectacle. Sir Charles Stanford, who had not written for the theatre since Irving's Lyceum production of Tennyson's *Becket* in 1893, composed an overture, entr'actes, dance, and war chorus, with leitmotifs for the main protagonists, and conducted the first night performance. Even more tantalizing following his sensational Literary Theatre Society *Salome* a year earlier, *Attila* marked Ricketts's debut in the commercial theatre, with Asche promising 'an elaborate scheme of colour, extraordinary costumes, and a novel setting of scenes unlike anything that's been witnessed before'.[43]

Nobody was disappointed on that score when *Attila* opened for its scheduled run of thirty-two performances on 4 September 1907. Stanford's music perplexed some critics in its attempt to suggest archaic, 'barbaric' musical modes, but Ricketts's work was universally lauded as a landmark in theatre design. It climaxed in the famous all-red final scene with Attila, the tributary kings gathered for his wedding feast, Ildico's attendants, and the dancing girls all in blood-red among red pillars and against a red backdrop, and amid this sea of blood Ildico, preparing to murder Attila with his own sword, standing like a sword herself in a silver and white wedding dress with a long silver train, her hair ornamented with horns and shells, her arms entwined with golden snakes. Harold Child in the *Burlington Magazine* wrote that 'the spectacle is so beautiful and so different from the common glare and riot as to come as a revelation of what may be done with the material means at the disposal of every theatre'.[44] He was particularly moved by Ricketts's symbolic use of colour in costumes, set, and lighting,

---

[42] 'People in the Public Eye', *Sketch*, 7 Sept. 1907, 216.
[43] 'The Asche–Brayton Season at His Majesty's: An Interview at Rehearsal', *Pall Mall Gazette*, 28 Aug. 1907, 6.
[44] '"Attila" and the Art of Stage-Production', *BM*, 12 (Oct. 1907), 5.

from the icy-blue light bathing the early scenes to that all-red climax. As in the Japanese prints whose influence permeated Ricketts's design aesthetic, non-naturalistic colour helped generate a transpersonal psychology in which the protagonists absorb emotions from their environment rather than acting out of any coherent centre of self. As Child put it, 'Ildico begins by hating Attila; she hates him in blue. She goes on to love him, and loves him in red.'[45] As an intrinsically non-illusionistic genre, verse drama naturally tends in the same direction, its protagonists mediums for the poetry flowing through them rather than autonomous novelistic characters. Thus while Child thought *Attila* a 'beautiful play', it presented problems for critics attuned to naturalistic drama, who tried to untangle Ildico's confused motives, debating whether she kills Attila out of sexual jealousy, patriotism, or to avenge her murdered brother.[46]

The *Daily Telegraph* critic praised Binyon's blank verse for bringing 'back some of the rhetorical swing and fire of our Elizabethan stage', while *The Times* spoke of its 'haunting beauty' and commended Binyon for indulging 'in no preciosities, no glittering digressions, no descriptions for description's sake'.[47] Nobody pretended it was a great play. *Paris and Oenone* had hardly prepared him for the structural complexities involved in an ambitious four-act tragedy, and Yeats, who liked the play, empathized with the problems he had inevitably encountered.[48] Nevertheless, to get a poetic drama staged in the commercial theatre was quite a feat, and most critics saw *Attila* as the first step in a promising theatrical career.

In fact, he did not have another play performed until 1919. 'It was one of the misfortunes of Victorian London that no theatre existed for genius such as his,' John Masefield wrote years later. 'His instinct for the theatre was sure; had the machine existed, that instinct might have been fostered and encouraged to results of great beauty.'[49] Masefield was one of his most persistent encouragers,

[45] Child, 6.

[46] See e.g. E. A. Baughan, '"Attila": Laurence Binyon's Play Produced at His Majesty's Theatre', *Daily News*, 5 Sept. 1907, 4.

[47] '"Attila": His Majesty's Theatre: Mr. Binyon's Poetic Play', *Daily Telegraph*, 5 Sept. 1907, 9–10; 'Attila', *The Times*, 5 Sept. 1907, 8.

[48] To Sturge Moore, 4 Oct. 1907, *W. B. Yeats and T. Sturge Moore: Their Correspondence 1901–1937*, ed. Ursula Bridge (London, 1953), 13.

[49] 'The Poet Laureate's Tribute', *The Times*, 13 Mar. 1943, 7.

writing shortly after *Attila*: 'You must not be discouraged, even by the want of leisure, for you have greater gifts than any of us, and an ideal of work which inspires us all.'[50] Binyon needed no urging and was already working on two new verse dramas in the interstices of his crowded life. The first was *King Horn*, a three-act play loosely based on a thirteenth-century Middle English romance. Before its completion in December 1909, nine notebooks of drafts show Binyon striving to break up the iambic flow of his blank verse with staccato sentences and a more flintily monosyllabic vocabulary, seeking a flexible, speech-based idiom. Structurally sounder than *Attila* and dramatically and thematically more powerful, the play was admired by the brilliant romantic actor Henry Ainley, but in the absence of a subsidized theatre no one wanted to risk staging it. In 1910 he entered it for a competition run by the Shakespeare Memorial Theatre at Stratford; it was one of the two plays selected by the reading committee for submission to the Duke of Argyll for his final decision, but he chose the other play and *King Horn* remained unstaged.

Binyon was slipping into a pattern familiar to contemporary verse dramatists, of plays read and admired but never staged. In November 1911 he completed *Ayuli*, a three-act verse play based on one of the most famous events in Chinese history, the disastrous infatuation of the T'ang emperor Ming-huang for his mistress Yang Kuei-fei (Ayuli) and her murder in a coup in 755 CE. The play was admired by both Gordon Craig and Granville Barker, the two innovators who could, Binyon felt, lead British drama into a new era of symbolist drama. Seeing the first of Barker's epoch-making Shakespeare productions at the Savoy, the famed 'Post-Impressionist' *Winter's Tale*, that autumn, Binyon thought it the finest verse drama production he had seen. He wrote ecstatically to Barker that in its 'briskness & continuity', minimal non-illusionistic staging and swift ensemble playing it was 'a revelation'.[51] He had equally high hopes of Craig, whom Rothenstein thought would have staged *Attila* even more effectively than Ricketts.[52] Binyon found Craig's dramaturgical theories in tune with his own views on Oriental art. In January 1910, while he was working on *King Horn* and *Ayuli*, he was Craig's fellow dinner guest at Yeats's rooms in Woburn

---

[50] ALs, 7 June 1908.
[51] Qtd. Lillah McCarthy, *Myself and My Friends* (London, 1933), 159.
[52] *Men & Memories*, ii. 150.

Buildings on the evening when Craig showed them designs for his revolutionary new staging system involving double-jointed folding screens that could be rearranged and lit in different ways to suggest any imaginable space or atmosphere during a performance, making elaborate sets redundant.[53] The following year he was a member of the committee which organized a dinner in Craig's honour at the Café Royal on 16 July 1911, and he sat on the English Advisory Committee formed to raise funds for Craig's proposed School for the Art of the Theatre, which was established in 1913 with financial backing again supplied by de Walden, not in London as originally planned but in the Arena Goldoni in Florence.[54]

Binyon's *Saturday Review* colleague Max Beerbohm had rightly noted that far from indulging in the 'besetting sin of the Victorian school of poetic drama, verbosity', *Attila* evinced an austere 'mistrust of words'.[55] Binyon agreed with Craig that movement, not words, was the source of theatrical magic. The *King Horn* drafts show him struggling to write poetic drama rather than dramatic poetry, subordinating his written text to the symbolic, gestural power of the stage. As he put it in a lecture on verse drama in New York in 1912:

The playwright should think in terms of movement and of relations. It has been a fault of poetic drama that too much emphasis has been placed on fine written speeches, for the very reason that the playwright has not studied the value of setting and of gesture. . . .

I believe with Gordon Craig that drama is more a thing to be seen than to be heard. Everything visible on the stage can be made significant. . . . The recent revival of pantomime, the success of the wordless play, marks a tendency in the right direction.[56]

The key scenes in *King Horn* are designed for maximum visual impact, especially those where the blinded Viking Ragnar, disguised as a palmer, wanders among the quicksands beside the North Sea, creeping in circles on the stage. While obviously echoing *King Lear*, these scenes also have something of the numinous,

[53] See Liam Miller, *The Noble Drama of W. B. Yeats* (Dublin, 1977), 148.

[54] See Edward Craig, *Gordon Craig: The Story of his Life* (London, 1968), 263–4, 282–3.

[55] 'Attila', *SR*, 14 Sept. 1907, 327.

[56] '"We Need More Emotional Understanding in Our Art": Laurence Binyon, Poet, Playwright, Critic and Expert on Oriental Art Says this is True of the Drama as well as of Painting. "Chinese Art Ten Centuries Ago was more Modern than Ours To-day"', *New York Times*, 15 Dec. 1912, 14.

otherworldy quality of Japanese Nō drama, which would soon influence Yeats and Gordon Bottomley, as perhaps does the epilogue to the otherwise overwordy *Ayuli*, where the grieving emperor, also disguised as a wandering mendicant, returns to the ruined palace where Ayuli died in a hail of arrows and is comforted by her ghost in the moonlight. Significantly, when Binyon tried again to get *Ayuli* performed after the war he wanted it designed by Edmund Dulac, who designed Yeats's *At the Hawk's Well* in 1916.

In November 1911, just after the completion of *Ayuli*, the Binyons moved from Tite Street to 118 Belgrave Road, a house bought for £500 on a twenty-three-year lease to accommodate their young family, swelled by the arrival of a third daughter, Nicolete, in July, and Cicely's mother, who spent half the year with them. The 'twins Twinyon', as one wit dubbed them, were growing rapidly, so much that when Charles Shannon started a portrait of Cicely in 1908 he had had to paint the twins out behind a bowl of red flowers when they outgrew his slow work, leaving their beautiful mother, wearing Ricketts's wedding jewel, in sole possession of the canvas.[57] Between his Museum work, potboiling jobs, and poetic drama, Binyon was stretched to and sometimes beyond his physical limits. Close friends worried about a permanent breakdown in his health. This took nothing away from his personal happiness, however. He had little creative energy left for poetry, but at the heart of *England and Other Poems* (December 1909), his first book of poetry for four years, lay a series of lyrics inspired by his wife and children which led the *Morning Post* critic to write that 'as a poet of marriage Mr. Binyon has few equals'. Commenting on the reviewer's surmise that 'the beauty of his emancipation seems to have been due to something little short of revelation', he wrote to Cicely: 'You & your love have indeed been a "revelation", a glory to me. And I am going to write still better now, I feel it; bigger things & more enkindled.'[58] The best poem in the volume is 'Sirmione', a meditative love poem which extends and deepens the themes of *Dream-Come-True*. In a long front-page review the *TLS* thought this 'the finest poem Mr. Binyon has yet written' and the volume his 'youngest book of poems'.[59]

[57] The portrait is in the possession of one of LB's grandsons, Mr Andrew Higgens.
[58] 'Recent Verse', *Morning Post*, 9 Jan. 1910, 2; ALs to CMB, postmarked 10 Jan. 1910.
[59] 'Mr. Binyon's New Poems', *TLS*, 30 Dec. 1909, 513.

When the historian G. M. Trevelyan congratulated Binyon on the book's being 'in the central tradition of English poetry and yet up to date',[60] he could hardly have realized the extent to which the two were rapidly becoming mutually exclusive in the volatile literary and artistic milieu of 1910. Six years earlier Gosse had classed Binyon 'among les jeunes', but at 40 he was rapidly being pushed into middle age by a rising generation of aggressively avant-garde poets such as T. E. Hulme's secessionist group, which met at the Eiffel Tower restaurant in Percy Street to plot a revolution in English poetry. To these poets Binyon must have epitomized the traditionalism and amateurism of the Poet's Club from which they had seceded. In an era when Hulme was calling for 'dry, hard classical verse', Binyon remained a walking definition of 'damp' Romanticism.[61]

In April 1910 the Royal Society of Literature in conjunction with the Society of Authors established an Academic Committee of English Letters on the lines of the Académie Française to encourage fellowship among writers and award literary prizes. Binyon was one of the thirty founding members alongside Bridges, Conrad, Hardy, James, Gosse, Yeats, Murray, Newbolt, G. M. Trevelyan, and other prominent men of letters. He did not, however, any more than Yeats, see himself as part of any entrenched Edwardian literary establishment. Although his belated Romantic poetry was out of step with both Hulme's proto-Imagists and Marsh's *Georgian Poetry* poets, he was fully caught up in the euphoria of this heady pre-war period, out of whose optimism, not out of post-war despair, British modernism was born. The sense of an imminent renaissance in the arts cut across generational and ideological divides, and in books such as his influential *Flight of the Dragon* Binyon was very much part of this.

His ardour is best captured in the brief essay 'The Return to Poetry', published in spring 1912 by John Middleton Murry in the fourth issue of his avant-garde magazine *Rhythm*, widely seen as the 'official organ' of Post-Impressionism.[62] The essay welcomes the twentieth century: 'We are breathing a different air. We are no longer *fin de siècle*. We are being changed, and the world with us.

[60] ALs, 30 Jan. 1910.
[61] Hulme, 'Romanticism and Classicism', *Speculations: Essays on Humanism and the Philosophy of Art*, ed. Herbert Read (London, 1924), 133, 126–7.
[62] See Falkenheim, 29.

Horizons open and allure us.' The Newtonian 'prose view of the world', where 'all is fixed, matter is finality', is crumbling before the 'poetic view' adumbrated by contemporary science, where 'all is energy, relation, change'. 'The nightmare of a mechanical universe . . . is passing.' Anticipating the concerns of books such as Fritjof Capra's *The Tao of Physics* by sixty years, Binyon linked this with the revelation of Oriental art and philosophy: 'The secret of this art is all in the paradoxes of Lao-tzu, and in his doctrine of the Tao,—the Way,—the ever-moving, ever-changing, eternal and universal rhythm of life.' We must discover for ourselves a comparable mode of spirituality and being in the world, otherwise—and Binyon suspected this in much contemporary art—we are in danger of merely faking it by purely formal means. 'We must feel it in ourselves before we can express it.' This requires a radical restructuring of Western modes of thought, for 'not till our minds change will our art change'.[63] When he made his first trip to the United States that autumn, he repeated this message, celebrating Taoism for having known for over two millennia what Western scientists were only now discovering: 'Science is beginning to tell us that the essence of things is movement; ultimate realities are expressed nowadays in terms of force and energy and rhythm.' Twentieth-century art would flower from this new vision of reality. He dismissed Cubism as 'rot' but credited the Futurists with at least 'the idea of getting at the underlying rhythm and meaning of things', and thought the movement would 'produce a lasting benefit . . . by the shock that it gives to a public which demands mere imitation of external things.'[64]

On the one hand Binyon the traditionalist poet and art critic, not a political conservative but a cultural conservationist, recycling the resources of the past; on the other hand the Taoist who saw that the 'principle of change . . . underlies all life' and aspired to a philosophy of 'continual movement, constant fluidity'.[65] If this is a paradox, and at a deeper level perhaps it is not, it is one that prevented him from ever ossifying into a reactionary, fuelled the 'faith in youth' which kept him encouraging the work of young poets and artists, kept him experimenting in his own work, and ensured that his last poems would be his best.

[63] *Rhythm*, 4 (Spring 1912), 1–2. See also 'Ideas of Design', 652–3.
[64] 'We Need More Emotional Understanding', 14.   [65] Ibid. 14.

BULLDOGS

One man alive to the Binyon paradox was Ezra Pound. When the 22–year-old American arrived in London in September 1908 with £3 in his pocket, Binyon was one of the first literary friends he made in the capital. They met through their mutual publisher, Elkin Mathews, at his Vigo Street bookshop in early February 1909.[66] Binyon invited Pound to the Print Room, whose Visitors' Books record his first visit on 9 February, and for several months thereafter he dropped in about once a month. One morning in 1909 Binyon took him to lunch at the Vienna Café on a day when Wyndham Lewis was also lunching at the 'club', and so set up one of the most famous meetings in Anglo-American modernism.

Lewis had known Binyon since his Slade School days, when he was a regular visitor at the Print Room, dispatched by Henry Tonks to copy *cinquecento* drawings but, every inch a man of his age, was mesmerized by the 'more savage symbols' of the Museum's primitive art collections.[67] He fell in with the 'Museum set' of Streatfeild, Squire, Binyon, and Sturge Moore, who encouraged his literary as well as his artistic ambitions. He was a regular visitor at the Vienna Café and occasionally dined with the same crowd at Roche's, where Holmes remembered 'his romantic face, his crumpled, gloomy sonnets and fine Slade-School drawings'.[68] 'Middle-aged scholars' though they were, Lewis found them an 'entertaining group of people', and looking back on the London scene of 1910 three decades later he compared them favourably with the detested Bloomsbury clan:

I have always thought that if instead of the really malefic 'Bloomsburies,' who with their ambitious and jealous cabal have had such a destructive influence upon the intellectual life of England, something more like these Vienna Café habitués of those days could have been the ones to push themselves into power, that a less sordid atmosphere would have prevailed.

[66] See J. J. Wilhelm, *Ezra Pound in London and Paris 1908–1925* (London, 1990), 6–8, 19; Patricia Hutchins, *Ezra Pound's Kensington: An Exploration 1885–1913* (London, 1965), 59.
[67] Lewis, 'History of the Largest Independent Society in England', *Blast*, 2 (July 1915), 80; to James Thrall Soby, 9 Apr. 1947, letter 363, *Letters of Wyndham Lewis*, ed. W. K. Rose (London, 1963), 407. See also Jeffrey Meyers, *The Enemy: A Biography of Wyndham Lewis* (London, 1980), 10.
[68] *Self and Partners*, 188; Lewis, *Blasting*, 273.

The writing and painting world of London might have been less like the afternoon tea-party of a perverse spinster.[69]

The future architect of the Great London Vortex was an admirer of Binyon's and Sturge Moore's poetry, as late as 1907 writing from Paris asking his mother to forward his copies of Binyon's *Odes* and *Porphyrion* and Sturge Moore's *Vinedresser* and *Absalom*.[70]

In his darkest days in the American prison camp outside Pisa almost forty years later, elegiacally recreating Edwardian London in his *Pisan Cantos*, Pound recalled this dramatic first encounter with Lewis under the Vienna's mirrored ceiling in 1909:

> And also near the Museum they served it mit Schlag
> in those days (pre 1914)
> the loss of that cafe
> meant the end of a B. M. era
> (British Museum era)
> Mr Lewis had been to Spain
> Mr Binyon's young prodigies
> pronounced the word: Penthesilea
> There were mysterious figures
> that emerged from recondite recesses
> and ate at the WIENER CAFE
> which died into banking. . . .
> .   .   .   .
> So it is to Mr Binyon that I owe, initially,
> Mr Lewis, Mr P. Wyndham Lewis. His bull-dog, me,
> as it were against old Sturge M's bull-dog.[71]

Binyon and Moore took wry delight in bringing together these two fiery young modernists and steepling egos. In calling Moore 'old Sturge M'—he was only 39, a year younger than Binyon—Pound emphasized the generation gap between Lewis and himself and the older poets, but the obvious affection of the 'bull-dog' image reflects, as Timothy Materer has said, 'the lifelong loyalty and respect the younger men felt for the older. Both Binyon and Sturge Moore stood for creativity polished by learning and seemed to represent a time when talent had ample time to ripen.'[72]

---

[69] *Blasting and Bombardiering*, 279.
[70] Letter 34, *Letters*, 35; see also letter 15, p. 16.   [71] *Cantos* 89/506–7.
[72] *Pound/Lewis: The Letters of Ezra Pound and Wyndham Lewis* (London, 1985), 3.

Art & Thought in East & West :

Parallels and Contrasts.

SYLLABUS OF A COURSE OF FOUR LECTURES,
illustrated with Lantern Slides, to be given in the Small Theatre
of the ALBERT HALL, KENSINGTON, at 5.30 on
WEDNESDAY AFTERNOONS, MARCH 10th, 17th, 24th, and 31st,

By LAURENCE BINYON.

I. SCULPTURE AND RELIGIOUS ART.

Alexander in India. Contact of Greek and Indian art. Two ideals. Common ground. Transforming power of the religious idea in Europe and in Asia. Mediæval sculpture compared with the sculpture of India, China, and Japan. Recent discoveries in Central Asia. The "grotesque" in East and West. The classic tradition in Europe. Primitive painting in the two continents.

II. THE RENAISSANCE IN EUROPE AND IN JAPAN.

Coincidence in time. Similar inspiration of both movements ; contrast in mode of expression. Splendour and austerity. Great patrons of art : Lorenzo de'Medici ; Maximilian ; the Ashikaga Shoguns. Difference in temperament and conditions of life. Contrasted conceptions of personality. Portraiture in East and West. Spirit of the early Reformation, and that of Zen Buddhism. Ideal of intellectual freedom. Gaiety. A change of mood. Materialism. Academic tradition.

III. LANDSCAPE AND THE FEELING FOR NATURE.

Gradual growth of landscape art in Europe. The nineteenth century. Deep feeling for nature in early Chinese poetry and painting. Dualism ; the Tiger and the Dragon. Elemental qualities in landscape of Asia. Treatment of the sea ; Korin and Turner. Perspective in East and West. Drawings by Claude, and Chinese monochromes. Passion for flowers and birds. Pisanello and Oriental art.

IV. POPULAR ART AND REALISM.

Painting of daily life in Venice, the Netherlands, France, and England. Comparison with Japanese colour-prints. Peculiar conditions under which these were produced. Harunobu. Watteau. New treatments of old subjects. Utamaro. Manet. Different conceptions of realism. European art of the present day. Conclusion.

TICKETS for the Course may be obtained from MR. J. STEPNEY,
24, BURY STREET, ST. JAMES', S.W. *Price,* ONE GUINEA.
Admission to single Lectures (pay at the door), 6/-.

Good, Ltd., Burleigh St., Strand, W.C.

Handbill for lecture series, March 1909 (by permission of the Houghton Library, Harvard University). See p. 161.

Pound's English instructor at the University of Pennsylvania, Cornelius Weygandt, had praised Binyon's poetry in the *Sewanee Review* in 1905 and corresponded with him, so Pound probably knew his work before arriving in London. If so, it is safe to assume that, unlike another great modern American poet in the making, Wallace Stevens,[73] he was lukewarm about it. Much as Pound liked Binyon, Maurice Hewlett, Selwyn Image, Ernest Rhys, and other denizens of the Edwardian literary scene, the only poet of the older generation worth attending to was Yeats. He associated Binyon's poetry with that modernist *bête noire*, Milton. In 1934 he recalled:

I found [Binyon] in 1908 among very leaden greeks, and in youthful eagerness I descended on the British Museum and perused, it now seems, in retrospect, for days the tales of . . . demme if I remember anything but a word, one name, Penthesilea, and that not from reading it, but from hearing it spoken by a precocious Binyonian offspring. MR. BINYON'S ODE, poster of, was it THE EVENING STANDARD 'Milton Thou shoulds't,' or whatever it was. 'Of Virtuous sire egregious offspring great!'.[74]

The ode, parodically overmiltonized, is the poem Binyon wrote for recitation at the memorial service for Milton's tercentenary on 9 December 1908, published in the *TLS* in November, but it was hearing *Penthesilea* recited by one of Binyon's daughters ('Mr Binyon's young prodigies') that led him to lament Binyon's 'sad youth, poisoned in the cradle by the abominable dogbiscuit of Milton's rhetoric'.

Although the Binyons' appointments diaries record several visits to and from Pound, including three in one week in March 1912, they were never close friends, yet Binyon, 'BinBin' as he christened him, retained a special place in Pound's memories of these pre-war London years. They were quietly amused at each other, Binyon at the American's turquoise ear-ring and Whistlerian costume, Pound at this grave-faced, ascetic scholar—'You cd. dress him and pass him off for one of Noll's troopers'[75]—who yet revealed a quiet integrity, a rootedness, and lack of personal egotism that he admired, perhaps because it contrasted with his own self-dramatizing persona. Thus when Dorothy Shakespear, whose cat was named

---

[73] Weeks after Pound met LB in London, Stevens sent copies of two love lyrics from *Lyric Poems* to his fiancée Elsie Moll, describing Binyon as 'a very clever chap'. 9 May 1909, *Letters of Wallace Stevens*, ed. Holly Stevens (London, 1967), 143.
[74] 'Hell', 382–3.   [75] 'Hell', 383.

'Binny' after him, described for Pound Binyon's speech welcoming Max Beerbohm into the Academic Committee on 28 November 1913 she noted that he celebrated Beerbohm, not himself: 'Bin bin . . . surpassed himself—he began solemnly and without humour, his mouth minute, about The Comic Muse—Then gave us a really exquisite appreciation of Max—Max & not Bin bin, he gave us—and the Eagle [Yeats] was awfully pleased!'[76] He crops up in unexpected places in Pound's poetry, in the *haiku*-like 'Pagani's, November 8':

> Suddenly discovering in the eyes of my beautiful
> Normande cocotte
> The eyes of the very learned British Museum
> > assistant,

and in the *Rock Drill* Cantos (1955):

> Only sequoias are slow enough.
> BinBin 'is beauty'.
> 'Slowness is beauty.'[77]

By far the most important thing Binyon did for Pound was to introduce him to Oriental art. When they lunched together for the first time in early spring 1909 Binyon talked about Chinese art and gave him a ticket for one of an important series of four lectures he was giving at the Albert Hall on 'Art & Thought in East & West'. Pound found the lecture 'intensely interesting',[78] and there is little doubt he first heard here ideas which concerned him all his life. Pound knew where he was with the Gosses and Newbolts of the Edwardian literary establishment but Binyon had him puzzled. Here was a man whose insight into Oriental art placed him in the van of contemporary aesthetics, whose 1911 book *The Flight of the Dragon* read at times like a Vorticist manifesto,[79] yet whose own poetry remained manacled to the nineteenth century. What Donald Davie rightly calls the 'mingled exasperation and admiration'

---

[76] 29 Nov. 1913, letter 199, *Ezra Pound and Dorothy Shakespear: Their Letters 1909–1914*, ed. Omar Pound and A. Walton Litz (London, 1984), 280. For 'Binny' see p. 336 n.

[77] *Collected Shorter Poems* (London, 1952), 180; *Cantos* 87/572.

[78] See Noel Stock, *The Life of Ezra Pound* (London, 1970), 78.

[79] See Richard Cork, *Vorticism and Abstract Art in the First Machine Age*, 2 vols. (London, 1976), i. 393–4; Timothy Materer, *Vortex: Pound, Eliot, and Lewis* (Ithaca, NY, 1979), 116–17.

Pound felt for him is encapsulated in his affectionate, chiding essay 'Lawrence Binyon' in the second and last issue of *Blast* in July 1915:

We regret that we cannot entitle this article 'Homage to Mr. Lawrence Binyon,' for Mr. Binyon has not sufficiently rebelled. Manifestly he is not one of the ignorant. He is far from being one of the outer world, but in reading his work we constantly feel the influence upon him of his reading of the worst English poets. We find him in a disgusting attitude of respect toward predecessors whose intellect is vastly inferior to his own. This is loathesome. Mr. Binyon has thought; he has plunged into the knowledge of the East and extended the borders of occidental knowledge, and yet his mind constantly harks back to some folly of nineteenth century Europe. . . . Ah well! Mr. Binyon has, indubitably, his moments. Very few men do have any moments whatever, and for the benefit of such readers as have not sufficiently respected Mr. Binyon for his, it would be well to set forth a few of them.

Then follows a set of nine quotations from *The Flight of the Dragon*, including:

P.17. Every statue, every picture, is a series of ordered relations, controlled, as the body is controlled in the dance, by the will to express a single idea.

P.18. In a bad painting the units of form, mass, colour, are robbed of their potential energy, isolated, because brought into no organic relation.

P.21. FOR INDEED IT IS NOT ESSENTIAL THAT THE SUBJECT-MATTER SHOULD REPRESENT OR BE LIKE ANYTHING IN NATURE; ONLY IT MUST BE ALIVE WITH A RHYTHMIC VITALITY OF ITS OWN.

P.21. You may say that the waves of Korin's famous screen are not like real waves: but they move, they have force and volume.[80]

Pound thought enough of this essay to reprint it in *Pavannes and Divagations* (1958), his last volume of prose. Two Pound scholars, Carroll F. Terrell and Woon-Ping Chin Holaday, have shown that Binyon's writings on Oriental art exerted a subtle influence on Pound's aesthetic and the *Cantos*. Terrell suggests that *The Flight of the Dragon* influenced Pound's 'developing concepts of "absolute rhythm", organic form, and the hieratic and spiritual qualities of landscape as evocations of "the process"', the Tao, and his

---

[80] Davie, 'Ezra Among the Edwardians', *Paideuma*, 5 (Spring 1976), 12; *Blast*, 2 (July 1915), 86, but quoted from corrected version reprinted in *Pavannes and Divagations* (Norfolk, Conn.: New Directions, 1958), 149–50.

actual practice in the *Cantos*.[81] Binyon was an eager proselytizer for Asian art, always keen to show his friends the collections under his care, and at least some of Pound's visits to the Print Room were for this purpose. In January 1913, for example, he wrote to Dorothy Shakespear: 'I contemplated mediaeval japanese prints at the [British Museum] & feel ages older & wiser. The Paradisal calm & *aura dolce*.'[82] The paintings he saw in the Print Room almost certainly included pictures of the *bodhisattva* Kuan-yin, which inspired one of Binyon's poems and provided the first images for Pound's profounder invocations to the 'compassionate bisexual bodhisattva', the 'Kuanon of all delights' in the *Cantos*.[83] Binyon and Pound both associated Oriental art with 'Paradise'. While helping Binyon with his Dante translation in 1934, Pound remarked: 'All your work on Oriental art is bound to profit you when you get to the lighting of the *Paradiso*.'[84] Whatever the brash young Pound of 1909 may have made of it, the poet of the *Pisan Cantos* would have understood why Binyon, after Blake, called art 'a means of conversing with Paradise' (*SMAA* 217).

[81] 'The Na-Khi Documents I: The Landscape of Paradise', *Paideuma*, 3 (Spring 1974), 95; Holaday, 'Pound and Binyon: China via the British Museum', *Paideuma*, 6 (Spring 1977), 32–3.

[82] 4 Jan. 1913, letter 130, *Pound/Shakespear*, 177.

[83] See Terrell, 93; Holaday, 34–5.

[84] 6 Mar. [1934], Letter 277, *Letters of Ezra Pound 1907–1941*, ed. D. D. Paige (London, 1951), 340.

8 Sung Landscapes and Romantic Poets

The BinBin Pound met in 1909 was overworked and hemmed in by financial worries, a man near the end of his tether. When his deputy Arnold O'Donoghue retired that summer, Colvin stepped in on his protégé's behalf. The Assistant Keepership would normally have gone to Dodgson as Binyon's senior, albeit by a mere four months, but in a private memorandum to the Director Colvin recommended Binyon on personal grounds:

> Mr. Dodgson is a bachelor and a man of means. Mr. Binyon is a married man with two children and no private income. In official hours a close and most conscientious worker, he has to work very hard also in his private time in order to earn enough to make both ends meet. The strain has lately been telling on his health, and he has been in serious danger of a breakdown. To avoid it he must either be promoted here or find work better paid elsewhere. The loss of his services to this department would be almost irreparable.[1]

This unusual arrangement was ratified by the Trustees, and Binyon was appointed at an annual salary of £520 in August 1909, a few days after his fortieth birthday.

It is hardly surprising that Colvin should have insisted that the loss of his services would be 'almost irreparable'. Not only had he emerged as one of the foremost authorities on British drawings, an expert on the English watercolour tradition and on Blake, Calvert, and Palmer, but he was also the driving force behind the growth of the Oriental art collection, whose interest to students, Colvin reported, was growing daily. These were the years during which Colvin and Binyon built the Museum's fine *ukiyo-e* collection, but the first decade of the century also saw a deepening and broadening

[1] Memorandum to E. Maunde Thompson, 3 July 1909, Original Papers, CE4/208 (1909), BM.

of Binyon's sympathy with and knowledge of all forms of Oriental art, including Chinese, Indian, and Persian art. Much as he admired *ukiyo-e*, he did not fall prey to the European misconception that the genre represented the apogee of Asian art. His deepest sympathies, as both poet and scholar, were engaged by the ink paintings in the older classical tradition of China and Japan, which he saw as holding profound significance for the West at the beginning of the twentieth century.

As early as February 1897 Binyon was sending reproductions of classical Japanese art to Ghose in India. He had begun studying the Japanese ink paintings in the Anderson collection with the help of Anderson's *Catalogue* and its companion volume *The Pictorial Art of Japan* (1886). The collection was large but patchy, with its full quota of misattributed works, copies, and forgeries, but his visual education was enriched by superb reproductions in the *Kokka* and other Japanese publications. His guide to the philosophy behind this art was Okakura Kakuzo, especially in *The Ideals of the East* (1903), which he reviewed enthusiastically in the *TLS*,[2] and *The Book of Tea* (1906), both of which introduced him to facets of Taoism and Zen Buddhism that would colour his own writings on Oriental art and his thinking in general.

His understanding was deepened by contact with Japanese scholars and artists, including Okakura's protégé, the young painter Shimomura Kanzan, who lived in England from 1903 to 1905. The first Japanese Binyon got to know well was Kohitsu Ryōnin, scion of a family who had been art experts to the Shōgun's court in Edo for 300 years until the Meiji Restoration in 1868. Sent by the Tokyo Imperial Museum to investigate European museums, he lived in London from December 1901 to July 1903. A poet and lover of nature, he struck up a warm friendship with Binyon. Through Binyon he gained a wide circle of friends, in marked contrast to the reclusive Sōseki Natsume, later to become one of Japan's greatest novelists, who was also living in London at this time, enduring two years of loneliness that left a permanent mark on his work. We get a brief glimpse of Binyon and Kohitsu together when Sturge Moore described to Trevelyan a dinner party at a Japanese restaurant with the Pissarros and other guests in 1903,

[2] *TLS*, 6 Mar. 1903, 73–4.

when 'Kohitsu & Binny were both in fine form, and set all the others laughing'.[3]

Kohitsu went through the Anderson collection with Binyon, revising the more optimistic attributions and giving him his first lessons in Japanese connoisseurship. It was a foundation for a representative collection but no more, and to encourage students to study this art Binyon removed reproductions from the *Kokka*, mounted them, and arranged them by school. The Department held only some 200, mostly mediocre, Chinese paintings. In 1903, however, the Department acquired its single greatest treasure, when a naval officer, Captain C. Johnson, brought an old Chinese handscroll into the Department of British and Medieval Antiquities and asked Hercules Read to value the jade toggle used to fasten it. Read was more intrigued by the scroll itself and took it to Colvin and Binyon in the Print Room. Unrolled under their disbelieving eyes, the eleven-foot brown silk scroll was signed by the almost legendary fourth-century artist Ku K'ai-chih (Gu Kaizhi). It was acquired, and drew scholars from all over Europe, who argued among themselves but eventually reached a consensus that if the scroll was not by Ku K'ai-chih himself it was a very early copy and one of the most important Chinese paintings in existence.[4]

Four years later in May 1907 the explorer Aurel Stein arrived in the remote Central Asian outpost of Tun-huang on the ancient Silk Road in Western China and discovered a unique hoard of perfectly preserved paintings, manuscripts, and artefacts in a sealed cave among the Caves of a Thousand Buddhas.[5] As the British Museum had contributed two-fifths toward the cost of the Stein expedition, it received two-fifths of this fabulous cache, the remainder being earmarked for the new National Museum in New Delhi. The entire collection was shipped to the Museum, where Binyon supervised the six-year task of unpacking, chemically treating, and mounting the fragile silk banners, streamers, printed silks, and paper paintings, which proved a revelation of pre-T'ang Chinese art. 'To his unfailing knowledge and care', Stein wrote later, 'all students of

[3] ALs, n.d. [June 1903], box 16/496, TSMP–LU. See also Ricketts, *Self Portrait*, 73; 75; 79; 97.

[4] See Basil Gray, '"Admonitions of the Instructress of the Ladies in the Palace": A Painting Attributed to Ku K'ai-chih', *Studies in Chinese and Islamic Art*, 2 vols. (London, 1985), i. 178–95.

[5] Stein recounts the story in vol. ii, ch. 22 of *Serindia: Detailed Report of Explorations in Central Asia and Westernmost Asia*, 5 vols. (Oxford, 1921).

these fine remains of Buddhist art owe gratitude for the ease with which they can now be examined.'⁶

Binyon devoted considerable energy to building up the Museum collection of Chinese art, with the instincts less of a connoisseur than of an educator. In 1910 he orchestrated the purchase of 145 paintings collected in China by Olga-Julia Wegener. The bulk of the £7,500 asking price had to be made up through gifts and private subscriptions via the National Art Collections Fund. Hopeless at getting money for himself, Binyon proved adept at eliciting it for the Museum, writing to Robert Ross: 'Colvin seems unable to get money. I (to my own surprise) have done much better than he has.' 'I want to impress people with the fact that here is a chance for England to show herself the foremost to appreciate an art that is going to be more & more valued,' he told Rothenstein. 'It will be a tragedy if we have to let it go.'⁷

Two years later he again needed all his persuasive fund-raising skills, this time without Colvin's aid, to engineer the acquisition of Arthur Morrison's collection of some 600 Japanese paintings, which was, he wrote Edward Marsh, 'the finest private collection in Europe, & will play the Museum beyond reach of rivalry'. As Winston Churchill's private secretary, Marsh was a useful contact in cases like this where Binyon needed advice on winkling 'a baronetcy or something of that sort' out of the Government to dangle before a prospective donor, since Colvin had tried this once before only for the parliamentary whips to refuse to reward 'any services except contributions to party funds'.⁸ As a result of Binyon's efforts, the collection was bought for the Museum by Sir William Gwynne-Evans through the National Art Collections Fund in 1913.

Binyon did not enjoy this side of Museum business, especially cultivating wealthy patrons—'I seem to myself to have become quite a pushing person,' he remarked to Edmund Gosse⁹—but it was something he steeled himself to do accomplish his twin goals of nurturing students' interest in Asian art and, as far as cramped

---

⁶ *Serindia*, ii. 832. See also LB, 'Essay on the Art of the Tun-Huang Paintings', *Serindia*, iii. 1428–31, and Roderick Whitfield's splendid 3-vol. *The Art of Central Asia: The Stein Collection in the British Museum* (Tokyo, 1982).

⁷ *Robert Ross: Friend of Friends*, ed. Margery Ross (London, 1952), 175–6; ALs to Rothenstein, 9 Nov. 1909, BMS Eng. 1148 (126) fo. 83, WRP–HH.

⁸ ALs, 11 June [1912]; 1 Aug. 1912.

⁹ ALs, 8 Oct. 1912, EG–BC.

exhibition space allowed, extending the appreciation of Asian art beyond the élite cadres of collectors and connoisseurs by mounting imaginative, well-documented exhibitions aimed at progressively broadening the British public's aesthetic horizons. The exhibition of Chinese and Japanese paintings he staged in the Prints and Drawings Gallery in 1910 was a landmark in British appreciation of Far Eastern, and especially Chinese, art.

Even more influential were Binyon's own writings and lectures. He had launched his lifelong lecturing career with a lantern-slide lecture on Oriental art in January 1903. Four months later Roger Fry commissioned him to write a series of articles on Chinese art for the newly founded *Burlington Magazine*, although this plan foundered when the magazine ran into temporary financial difficulties in October and the only one published was a January 1904 article on the Ku K'ai-chih scroll.[10] While Binyon was writing this article, Herbert Giles, Professor of Chinese at Cambridge, asked him to write lengthy captions for the twelve reproductions in his pioneering *Introduction to the History of Chinese Pictorial Art*, to be published in Shanghai in 1905. This Giles–Binyon collaboration was as emblematic as the Binyon–O'Brien Sexton co-authorship of *Japanese Colour Prints*. Whereas Giles's approach was almost wholly textual, his book a collage of biographical and other translated materials, Binyon's mini-essays speak from another world of aesthetic discourse, focusing on the paintings as objects of philosophical contemplation.

Described by Giles as 'illuminating notes, entirely in keeping with his high reputation as an art critic',[11] these were the seeds of the book that appeared three years later as *Painting in the Far East*, the first book in a European language on the Far Eastern pictorial tradition as a whole, treating it as a continuous tradition with shared technical, aesthetic, and religious resources. 'Henceforth', wrote Morrison, 'it is to Mr. Binyon that the student of the future must come to learn all that must be understood before the Eastern half of the world's pictorial art can yield him the elevated delights which it so abundantly exhales.'[12] *Japanese Art*, a handsome volume devoted to the traditional Kanō school, followed in 1909,

[10] 'A Chinese Painting of the Fourth Century', *BM*, 4/10 (Jan. 1904), 39–49.
[11] Giles, *An Introduction to the History of Chinese Pictorial Art* (Shanghai, 1905), pp. vi, x.
[12] 'Chinese and Japanese Painting', *BM*, 14 (Dec. 1908), 160.

and 1911 saw the publication of one of the finest of all Binyon's books, *The Flight of the Dragon*, which went through many re-prints in Cranmer-Byng's Wisdom of the East series, the last in 1972. During its long lifetime, it has been quietly but widely influential, introducing non-Western ideas and broadening the sympathies of artists and writers as different as Pound and Paul Nash.[13]

These years marked Binyon's entry into the small, intimate world of Western scholars of Oriental art, a community certainly not without its rivalries, both personal and national, but one which retained something of the openness and co-operative spirit of a pioneer generation compared to the internecine warfare endemic among European art scholars in the Berenson era. He first met the French scholar Edouard Chavannes, for example, when he came to the Museum to inspect the Ku K'ai-chih scroll. In 1905 Chavannes published an article by Binyon on one of the Museum's better Chinese paintings, a Chao Mêng-Fu handscroll, in *T'oung Pao*, the sinology journal he edited with Henri Cordier.[14] Others, like Gaston Migeon, Paul Pelliot, Victor Goloubew, and Adolf Fischer, he met on visits to Paris, Berlin, Cologne, and other cities, and still others when a small army of international scholars descended on the Museum to study the Stein collection.

Binyon's closest friend was Chavanne's protégé Raphael Petrucci. Three years Binyon's junior, a Belgian of Italian extrac-tion, Petrucci was a Renaissance figure, his talents encompassing science, engineering, and literature as well as Oriental art and religion. He was, Binyon later wrote, 'one of the ablest and most devoted students and interpreters of the art of the Far East', his *La Philosophie de la nature dans l'art d'extréme oriente* (1910) a classic.[15] The two young scholars shared a similar approach to Oriental art, convinced that in order to understand it you had to be personally responsive to its philosophical and religious dimensions.

[13] For Nash, see Mary Beal, 'Paul Nash's "Event on the Downs" Reconsidered', *BM*, 131 (Nov. 1989), 748–54, and George Wingfield Digby, *Meaning and Symbol in Three Modern Artists: Edvard Munch, Henry Moore and Paul Nash* (London, 1960), 140–6.

[14] 'A Landscape by Chao Mêng-Fu in the British Museum', *T'oung Pao*, 2nd ser., 6 (Mar. 1905), 56–60.

[15] Biographical Note, *Chinese Painters: A Critical Study*, by Raphael Petrucci, trans. Frances Seaver (London, 1922), 7. See also Basil Gray, 'The Development of Taste in Chinese Art in the West 1872 to 1972', *Transactions of the Oriental Ceramic Society*, 39 (1971–3), 22–3.

Between 1908 and 1909 Petrucci translated *Attila* into French and tried to get it produced in Brussels in the hope of earning enough money to take the two of them to Japan. Asche agreed to lend Ricketts's scenery and costumes, but the quixotic project did not get off the ground.

In 1908 Binyon finally met Ernest Fenollosa, who arrived in London in September and wrote asking to be shown the Department's collections. He made his first visit to the Print Room on 12 September, but it was a tragically brief friendship. Nine days later Fenollosa died of a heart attack, and his ashes were sent to Japan. Binyon helped Mary Fenollosa make final revisions to the manuscript of her husband's long-planned magnum opus, *Epochs of Chinese and Japanese Art*, published in London in 1912. According to Fenollosa's own recollections, it was either Binyon or the publisher William Heinemann who introduced her to Pound, a meeting which changed the course of twentieth-century poetry and drama when she entrusted her husband's remaining manuscripts to the young poet.[16]

Fenollosa had brought greetings from the American collector Charles Freer, a self-made millionaire who had been inspired by Whistler to build the great collection of Oriental art which now resides in the Freer Gallery of Art in Washington. Freer was impressed by *Painting in the Far East*. 'In writing this book you have done great service to "Painting in the Far East"', he wrote in 1908, 'and have placed all of its English-reading lovers and students under deep obligation.'[17] Shortly afterwards Freer dined with him in London on his way to China and Japan, where, in September 1909, he attended the ceremony in which Fenollosa's ashes were interred at Miidera, a Tendai temple overlooking Lake Biwa where he had studied Buddhism. Beneath the pine trees in the quiet garden, Freer had arranged for the erection of two stone lanterns, a flower vase, and an incense burner, with a tablet stating that they had been dedicated to Fenollosa's memory by Binyon, Migeon, Arthur Wesley Dow, and Freer himself.[18]

---

[16] See Lawrence W. Chisolm, *Fenollosa: The Far East and American Culture* (New Haven, 1963) 222. In fact, they met at the home of the Indian poet Sarojini Naidu, although LB may have been involved. See Wilhelm, 124–5, 129.

[17] ALs, Christmas 1908.

[18] See Thomas Lawton and Linda Merrill, *Freer: A Legacy of Art* (Washington, DC, 1993), 77, 87 150–1; and Chisolm, 211–12.

Freer urged Binyon to visit him in Detroit, but he could not take up his invitation until November 1912, in the middle of his first, two-month trip to the United States, financed by lectures and poetry readings. Binyon and his wife stayed over a week in Freer's Ferry Avenue home, where he spent long hours poring over his superb collection in the steel fireproof vaults beneath the staircase and in the two large, naturally lit galleries. In these beautiful art spaces, unlike anything available in the Print Room, he studied works of a quality to which the British Museum could probably never aspire. 'I am working hard at Freer's magnificent collection,' he told Rothenstein. 'It takes one's breath away.' Freer, who had donated his entire collection to the Smithsonian Institution in 1906, was 'a wonderful man—very American, & the best type. His public spirit is magnificent.'[19] Freer also showed him 5,000 slides of Oriental artworks Fenollosa had taken in Japan, and lent him a caseful for his lecture to the Japan Society of New York. During two weeks in Boston, Binyon spent most of his time at the splendid new Museum of Fine Arts in Huntington Avenue, studying the magnificent Fenollosa–Bigelow collection and musing on the contrast between its spacious Japanese-style exhibition rooms and the cramped Print Room gallery back home. His lecture at the Museum was attended by an audience of over 500, including the legendary Mrs 'Jack' Gardner—'immeasurably old and extraordinarily ugly', according to Cicely[20]—who invited them to lunch at Fenway Court to see the Renaissance paintings acquired for her by Berenson.

Much as he liked America, however, this was not the trip Binyon most wanted to make. The abortive *Attila* project shows how eager he and Petrucci were to visit Japan. Back in 1903 Binyon had confided to Cicely his 'great longing to go out to the Far East': 'Will you come, if we get the chance? . . . O why is life so short! I could do so much, & there is so little time, & one is so hampered. What wouldn't I give for five years freedom *now* instead of at the end!'[21] Over dinner at Roche's in 1903, Emil Hovelaque had regaled him with tales of Japan, telling him that 'the harmony pervading all they do, & the fineness of their senses, makes life in any other country, after one has been there some time, almost impossible, so coarse

---

[19] ALs, 17 Nov. [1912], BMS Eng. 1148 (126) fo. 61, WRP–HH.
[20] 'Journal of Visit to Boston', AMS notebook, n.d. [1912], n.pag. In the possession of Mr Edmund Gray.
[21] ALs, 7 Oct. [1903].

and blundering & confused seems our kind of existence'.[22] Freer wrote from China in 1909, wishing Binyon were beside him to see the artworks he was being shown. Several other friends travelled to India during these years, including Oswald Sickert, Rothenstein, Hugh Fisher, and Robert Trevelyan. 'How I envy you going East,' Binyon wrote to the latter in 1912.[23]

Not only was Binyon's natural *wanderlust* frustrated, but he rightly felt that his lack of firsthand experience in Asia hampered his studies of Oriental art. Museums in Europe and the USA were sending their key staff to the East, friends like the young American scholar Langdon Warner, but there was no hint of this at the British Museum. Through Binyon's efforts, by 1912 the Department had acquired a collection of Asian art as good as any in Europe, but in terms of staff, facilities, exhibition space, and the value it set on Asian art, the Museum was falling behind those of the United States, Germany, and France. Just as the Museum's Asian antiquities, ranging from Chinese ceramics to the Amaravati reliefs, remained in the Department of British and Medieval Antiquities, so Oriental prints and drawings were refugees in a Department dedicated to Western art, looked after by a man with no staff, no separate funding or exhibition space, and pressing responsibilities to the European collections.

With Colvin's retirement looming in 1912, Binyon and Dodgson both had strong claims to the Keepership. Dodgson had agreed to Binyon getting the Assistant Keepership in 1909 on the strict understanding that this would not prejudice his chances of being Keeper. Binyon had mixed feelings. He was not a natural administrator, took no pleasure in exercising power, and wanted to devote his best energies to poetry rather than the responsibilities the Keepership entailed. '[O]fficial ambitions do not really lie near my heart,' he told Gosse, and Dodgson was 'an exceptionally good man, from the Museum point of view'.[24] On the other hand, he needed the higher salary for his young family. In his nuanced confidential report to the Trustees, Colvin was even handed but, as he had done three years earlier, noted Binyon's superior personal qualities, his financial problems, and the damage his departure would cause the Department should he leave to find a more lucrative post elsewhere, probably in America.[25] The three Principal Trustees finally decided,

[22] LB, ALs to CMB, 9 Dec. [1903].   [23] ALs, 5 Sept. 1912.
[24] ALs, 7 Jan. 1912, EG–BC.   [25] TLs, 3 June 1912, BM.

however, that Dodgson's four months seniority had to count, and he was appointed. When the Director, Sir Frederick Kenyon, broke the news, Binyon wrote to Newbolt:

This forces me very seriously to think of my future. I cannot consent to pass my whole life in my present slavery, even if my health would stand it. The whole of this year, for instance, I am prevented from writing a line of poetry, though I have plenty in my head, because even though working at pot-boiling things practically all my evenings, & most of my Sundays & holidays, I can only just make both ends meet (& hardly that).[26]

Quite apart from its impact on Binyon's financial situation, Dodgson's appointment threw into question the status of Asian art within the Department. Although the two men got on well enough, 'the Dodger', as Binyon called him, had no interest in the Oriental collections. Binyon told Gosse that he wanted 'to be independent of Dodgson, as it is most inconvenient to have a Keeper who knows and cares nothing about a whole important side of the collection he controls. I feel I could make something really interesting and that would open people's eyes if I only had scope.'[27]

Binyon now played his last card. In late 1913 the Department was due to leave the White Wing for roomier quarters in the new King Edward VII Galleries. In September 1912 he wrote to Kenyon suggesting the opportunity be used to create 'a new *small* department' of Oriental Prints and Drawings:

I feel every day the need of more freedom to concentrate on my special studies. The Continental museums are having special sections—& beginning to have special museums—for the subject: the French, Germans, & Americans have spent largely on missions to the East for purposes of study & collection: & I feel that, while our collection of Far Eastern paintings & drawings is the most important in Europe, I cannot keep up to the mark myself while I have to give so much of my time, as Assistant Keeper, to other things. Quite apart from my own affairs I am sure it would be far better for the collection if I were able to devote my whole energies to it & have real control.[28]

Such a department might have made a significant difference, providing both a geographical and psychological focus for the serious study of Asian art in Britain before the Great War. It was too big a step for the Museum to contemplate, however, and

[26] ALs, n.d. [June 1912].   [27] ALs, 8 Oct. 1912, EG–BC.
[28] ALs, n.d. [Sept. 1912], uncatalogued papers, BM.

a compromise was achieved with the establishment of a semi-autonomous Sub-Department within the Department of Prints and Drawings under Binyon's control. He was awarded a £100 special allowance, which prompted him to write to Kenyon that it would be 'an intense relief not to be always worrying and doing pot-boilers',[29] although if he really believed this he was being over-optimistic. The arrangement was not ideal, especially as Binyon had no separate acquisitions fund. With Dodgson rather than Colvin controlling the Department's tight budget, acquisitions slowed to a trickle. Still, it was a start, a seed planted.

Even after the Department of Prints and Drawings moved to the Edward VII Galleries in early 1914, the Sub-Department was in no sense physically separate from the rest of the Department, but it soon earned itself a distinct identity. Binyon was allotted a staff of two, one Boy Attendant and one Assistant. The latter, appointed in June 1913, turned out to be a taciturn, intense 24-year-old Cambridge graduate named Arthur Schloss, who had never read a word of Chinese or Japanese. In the Great War he would change his name to Waley and become, with Ezra Pound, the co-inventor of Chinese poetry for the English-speaking world and, in his versions of the *Tale of Genji*, *The Nō Plays of Japan*, and *Monkey*, a translator of genius.

ROMANTIC SCHOLARSHIP

The difficulties facing even the most well-intentioned would-be scholar of Chinese painting in the West in the late nineteenth century were immense, ranging from the paucity of fine, or even authentic, paintings to the lack of reliable translations of Chinese texts and accurate knowledge of the philosophical background, especially Taoist, Ch'an (Zen), and Neo-Confucian thought. To become a true scholar of Chinese painting, a student should shed his or her Western aesthetic preconceptions through study of good paintings and immersion in traditional Chinese connoisseurship, and be intimately familiar with the nuances of brush technique, preferably through years using the brush him/herself. None of this was available in London in the 1890s, when Binyon first became

---

[29] ALs, 24 Nov. 1912, uncatalogued papers, BM.

interested, or by 1905–8, when he sat down to write *Painting in the Far East*.

Most obstructive of all, and quite different from the situation with *ukiyo-e* prints, was the lack of good specimens of Chinese painting and the classical Japanese painting inspired by it. Binyon's problem in writing *Painting in the Far East* was the opposite of that facing Fenollosa when he arrived in London in September 1908 while Binyon's book was in press. Whereas Binyon had seen too little, Fenollosa had seen and experienced so much during his years in Japan that he was unable to finally draw it all together. Hours before his death he was studying Eskimo carvings in the British Museum, adding one last brick to the vast edifice of his knowledge, while back home in New York, untouched since 1906, lay the fragmentary, pencilled rough drafts of his magnum opus, *Epochs of Japanese and Chinese Art*. These manuscripts stand in the Romantic tradition of the epic fragment, unfinished because coterminous with the writer's own life, although, as Fenellosa implied in his 'Ode on Reincarnation', as a Buddhist he could perhaps look forward to completing it in his next rebirth:

> All that was inchoate, incomplete, ungarnered, coming late in life,
>   dissipated by multiplicity of aim,
> Shall be concentrated in early maturity for the balanced genius.[30]

Far from Fenollosa's embarrassment of riches, Binyon's knowledge of great Chinese and Japanese art in 1908 was largely confined to reproductions in the *Kokka*, which were no substitute in an art form whose touchstone is brushwork. Given these disadvantages, it says much for Binyon's natural sympathy with this art that he could write about it as intelligently as he did. He was, moreover, writing primarily for readers in the same boat: paintings he knew mainly in reproduction had to be passed on to the reader in reproduction, seeing through two glasses darkly. The book's muted collotypes leave the full thrust to be carried by the text, which has to work far harder and in more difficult territory than in today's lavishly illustrated art histories. It is this that makes *Painting in the Far East* necessarily a literary work: the paintings have to be coaxed into presence through the spell of words. One corollary of this is an unexpected intimacy between writer and reader, for whom the

---

[30] Akiko Murakata, 'Ernest F. Fenollosa's "Ode on Reincarnation"', *Harvard Library Bulletin*, 21/1 (Jan. 1973), 64.

re-creation of images becomes a shared experience, a mutual act of clairvoyant imagination. A remarkable example of this, leagues outside current canons of scholarly objectivity, comes in a discussion of the great T'ang artist Wu Tao-tzu:

Alas! of all the mighty works of Wu Tao-tzu none now is known certainly to survive. Once, in a dream, I myself beheld them all, but awoke with the memory of them faded in a confusion of gorgeous colour, all except one, which remained with me, strangely distinct. A goddess-like form was standing between two pillars of the mountains, not less tall herself. I remember the beauty of the drawing of her hands, as their touch lingered on either summit; for her arms were extended, and between them, as her head bent forward, the deep mass of hair was slowly slipping to her breast, half-hiding the one side of her face, which gazed downward. At her feet was a mist, hung above dim woods, and from human dwellings unseen the smoke rose faintly. . . . May I be permitted the impertinence of this intrusion? since only in dream can we ever hope to see most of those lost masterpieces of one of the world's great artists.

(*PFE* 1908, 69–70)

Binyon often dreamed of pictures, seeing them in great detail as if studying them in the Print Room. He had had this dream five years earlier in October 1903, when he had also dream-examined unknown drawings by Lorenzo di Credi and Dürer, which he described in a letter to Cicely.[31] Four months later he sent her a draft of the poem 'A Picture Seen in a Dream', which was published shortly after *Painting in the Far East* in *England and Other Poems* (1909):

I saw the Goddess of the Evening pause
Between two mountain pillars. Tall as they
Appeared her stature, and her outstretched hands
Laid on those luminous cold summits, hung
Touching, and lingered. Earth was at her feet.
Her head inclined: then the slow weight of hair,
In distant hue like a waved pine-forest
Upon a mountain, down one shoulder fell.
She gazed, and there were stars within her eyes;
Not like those lights in heaven which know not what
They shine upon; but like far human hopes,
That rise beyond the end of thwarting day
In deep hearts, wronged with waste and toil, they rose;

[31] ALs, 16 Oct. [1903].

And while beneath her from the darkening world
A vapour and a murmur silently
Floated, there came into those gazing eyes,
What should have been, were she a mortal, tears.

(CPi.145–6)

Wary of exoticism in his poetry, Binyon suppressed the origin of the image at the cost of making it opaque, since the second half of the poem can be understood only if we know that, despite features closer to G. F. Watts than Wu Tao-tzu, Binyon's 'Goddess of the Evening' is a Pre-Raphaelite cousin of Kuan-yin, the Chinese version of Avalokitesvara, one of Mahayana Buddhism's major *bodhisattvas*, beings who have gained enlightenment after countless incarnations but vow to postpone their final liberation until all humanity achieves release.[32] That Binyon not only included this dream in 1908 but retained it in all editions except the last in 1934 shows how personal, and how Romantic, a work *Painting in the Far East* is.

Binyon called it his 'learning book', since it began life as a way of making sense of his own fragmentary knowledge and experience, then went through three revised editions in 1913, 1923, and 1934, each incorporating the fruits of current research. The four editions thus comprise a potted history of Oriental art scholarship in the West during these crucial decades of its first flowering. As late as 1934 Morrison still considered it 'the best conspectus of the subject yet available',[33] but this was debatable even then, and as a work of scholarship it has long been superseded. Systematic study of the history of Chinese painting waited upon the series of books, rich in previously unreproduced artworks in Chinese and Japanese collections, published by the indefatigable Osvald Sirén between 1929 and 1958, culminating in his magisterial seven-volume *Chinese Painting: Leading Masters and Principles* (1956–58).

Binyon did not set out to compile an exhaustive history larded with dense listings of schools and artists, even had that been possible in 1908. It was not written for collectors or scholars, although, as Morrison suggested, 'it is to this book that the scholar must have first recourse before entangling himself in the complicated histories of the schools'.[34] His aim was to provide an introduction to the field

---

[32] See C. N. Tay, 'Kuan-yin: The Cult of Half Asia', *History of Religions*, 16/2 (Nov. 1976), 147–77.
[33] *BM* 66 (Jan. 1935), 50.   [34] 'Chinese and Japanese Painting', 159

simple yet compelling enough to induce its readers to study the paintings themselves, rather than suffocating their interest under blankets of undigested data. He set out his modest aims and desired audience in the preface to the 1908 edition:

I hope that meanwhile this volume, in spite of all the deficiencies occasioned by limited opportunities, may not be thought too presumptuous an attempt to survey the achievement and to interpret the aims of Oriental painting, and to appreciate it from the standpoint of a European in relation to the rest of the world's art. It is the general student and lover of painting whom I have wished to interest. My chief concern has been, not to discuss questions of authorship or of archaeology, but to inquire what aesthetic value and significance these Eastern paintings possess for us in the West.

(*PFE* 1908, p. viii)

That last clause is crucial. The significance this art holds for the West goes beyond the aesthetic. Like *The Flight of the Dragon*, *Painting in the Far East* attacks the materialist philosophy which underpins Western science and has permeated European culture since the Renaissance. We forget, Binyon says, that the 'scientific' formulae of Western art are merely conventionalized ways of seeing, not structures of reality. Victorian scholars raised on one-point linear perspective had been appalled by the apparent lack of perspective in Oriental art, but we must learn to see that its multi-polar perspective is part of an alternative, equally coherent set of pictorial conventions, rooted in a profoundly non-Western mode of vision whose implications run deeper than the organization of pictorial space. Asian art is not imperfectly mimetic but radically non-mimetic. Far from being too primitive to develop European illusionistic techniques like modelling, foreshortening, and chiaroscuro, it has no need of them, since as an idealist, spiritual art of linear rhythm it seeks not to duplicate outward form but to participate in and incarnate the 'Rhythm' of all life:

In this theory it is Rhythm that holds the paramount place; not, be it observed, imitation of Nature, or fidelity to Nature, which the general instinct of the Western races makes the root-concern of art.

In this theory every work of art is thought of as an incarnation of the genius of rhythm, manifesting the living spirit of things with a clearer beauty and intenser power than the gross impediments of complex matter allow to be transmitted to our senses in the visible world around us. A picture is conceived as a sort of apparition from a more real world of essential life.

(PFE 11)

'Rhythm' was Binyon's favourite word. The best gloss on the way he uses it here is the first of the Six Canons of Chinese painting formulated by the sixth-century artist–aesthetician Hsieh Ho: 'Rhythmic Vitality, or Spiritual Rhythm expressed in the movement of life' (*FD* 11). Compressed into four characters, *ch'i-yün shêng-tung*, this is an extremely fluid, suggestive concept, and in *The Flight of the Dragon* Binyon gives several translations, his favourite being Okakura's 'The Life-movement of the Spirit through the Rhythm of things'. His own suggestion is 'The fusion of the rhythm of the spirit with the movement of living things' (*FD* 11).[35] At any rate,' he concludes, 'what is certainly meant is that the artist must pierce beneath the mere aspect of the world to seize and himself be possessed by that great cosmic rhythm of the spirit which sets the currents of life in motion' (*FD* 11–12).

The pictorial conventions of Asian art are grounded in a quite different, and in Binyon's view saner, vision of the world and man's place in it:

This difference is rooted in philosophy of life, in mental habit and character. An opposition between man and Nature has been ingrained in Western thought. It is the achievements, the desires, the glory and the suffering of man that have held the central place in Western art; only very slowly and unwillingly has the man of the West taken trouble to consider the non-human life around him, and to understand it as a life lived for its own sake: for centuries he has but heeded it in so far as it opposed his will or ministered to his needs and appetites. But in China and Japan, as in India, we find no barrier set up between the life of man and the life of the rest of God's creatures. The continuity of the universe, the perpetual stream of change through its matter, are accepted as things of Nature, felt in the heart and not merely learnt as the conclusions of delving science.

(PFE 23–4)

Thus while European art is obsessed by the human body as 'the noblest and most expressive of symbols', Asian art explores 'all thoughts that lead us out from ourselves into the universal life' (*PFE* 24).

[35] See also Osvald Sirén, *The Chinese on the Art of Painting* (Peiping, 1936), 21–2, and Michael Sullivan, *Symbols of Eternity: The Art of Landscape Painting in China* (Oxford, 1979), 31.

Binyon was interested in the way in which the treatment of landscape in art and poetry reflects the philosophical orientation of different races and epochs. In general, he saw the pre-nineteenth-century European landscape tradition as dominated by the anthropocentric 'conception of earth as the home of the human race', 'an accessory to human life and a background to human events' (*FD* 31–2), while in Chinese and Japanese landscapes nature lives its own life, for its own sake. When human beings appear they are tiny figures, dwarfed by the mountains through which they journey, the lakes on which they fish, not owners and masters but creatures among earth's other creatures, knit into the web of life.

These landscapes are free from the 'sentiment of ownership' (*PFE* 157), the 'property-feeling' which Binyon saw infusing not only much European landscape art but also paintings of animals, birds, and flowers, in contrast to Sung bird and flower paintings, another of his great loves. One thinks of the acres of European canvases peopled only by dead birds, slaughtered game, and flowers in vases, aptly named still life, still apter in the French *nature morte*. Sung art catches geese on the wing, grasses growing, verbs in 'the perpetual stream of change' of the Tao. In these paintings seemingly insignificant fragments of nature, a glimpse of misty rock, or a tuft of flowers, are not fragments at all; like pieces of a hologram, they contain everything, because the same seamless life energy flows through them. As Binyon read in *The Ideals of the East*, 'the whole universe is manifest in every atom'.[36] The repercussions of this spread beyond the realms of art: when he says that in Sung painting 'The life of nature and of all non-human things is regarded in itself; its character contemplated and its beauty cherished for its own sake, not for its use and service in the life of man' (*PFE* 164), he is calling for an attitude to the planet we now call green.

By stepping outside our narrowly human selves through imaginative empathy with the rest of creation, we become not less but more human, since we can understand ourselves only when we understand what we are part of: 'Man is lord of the world, but only because he has gone out into humbler existences than his own and has understood them, and, returning to his own life, has found in that the supreme expression of the life which animates all things' (*FD* 21). By relinquishing our exploiting, manipulative 'sentiment

---

[36] Okakura Kakuzo, *The Ideals of the East, with Special Reference to the Art of Japan* (London, 1903), 111.

of ownership' we regain our rightful relation to the earth: 'It is not man's earthly surrounding, tamed to his desires, that inspires the artist; but the universe, in its wholeness and its freedom, has become his spiritual home' (*FD* 20).

For Binyon the supreme expression of this view of the world was the Taoist- and Zen-inspired landscape art of China during the Sung period (960–1279) and the Zen landscapists of Ashikaga or Muromachi Japan (1392–1573). These were, he thought, the richest 'flowering times of the Asian genius' (*PFE* 277). He had seen reasonable examples of Ashikaga art in the Museum and in Morrison's collection, including paintings attributed, if somewhat optimistically, to Sesshū, Shūbun, and Sesson. The Museum held no authentic Sung paintings, however, and Binyon's high opinion of Sung art—by 1905 he considered it 'the greatest school of land-scape which the world has seen'[37]—was based largely on repro-ductions in the *Kokka* and other Japanese publications. Along with these reproductions came the critical emphases of traditional Japanese connoisseurship, which saw Chinese landscape art as rising to its apogee in the artists of the Southern Sung Academy at Hangchow, especially Ma Yüan (Ma Yuan) and Hsia Kuei (Xia Gui), many of the finest examples of which had been brought to Japan during the Ashikaga period and remained in Japanese collec-tions. Binyon's admiration for Ma Yüan and Hsia Kuei was con-firmed and deepened when he saw examples of their work, or so it was thought, at Freer's Detroit home in 1912. Among these was a silk landscape handscroll which Freer had bought in Beijing in 1911. It was attributed to Ma Yüan, though, almost inevitably, it has since been identified as a Ming work based on a scroll by Hsia Kuei now in the National Palace Museum in Taipei.[38] When he first saw it in 1912, however, Binyon thought it the greatest landscape in world art (pl. 8).

A long horizontal handscroll—this one measures over 42 feet—is unlike any other art form. You stand at a long table, unroll 2 or 3 feet and study it at leisure, then move on through the scroll, unrolling and rerolling at your own pace. Rather than standing humbled before a masterpiece behind glass on a museum wall, you help create the images by your pace and the way you 'frame' each section, not a passive spectator but a participant. Working your

---

[37] Caption facing p. 112 in Giles.   [38] See Lawton and Merrill, 82.

way through a scroll 42 feet long becomes itself a journey through the unfolding ink landscape of mountains, valleys, and lakes, crossing rivers and climbing winding paths, making you a companion of the tiny figures journeying through the landscape itself. The Tao, literally 'way' or 'path', defined by Binyon as 'the ever-moving, ever-changing, eternal and universal rhythm of life', finds its perfect medium here, for nothing is static, not even the scroll itself. Mountains flow into valleys, rivers into lakes, foreground into background, areas of densely worked detail into infinitudes of misty space, vigorous calligraphic brushwork into transparent ink washes, all within a scroll which is itself a fluid, dynamically open text offering a different experience to each reader. Like life itself, such a scroll is a path to be taken, a journey to be experienced, not a possession to be owned.

Unable to use reproductions to convey the special power of the handscroll, Binyon enacts as well as describes it in his prose:

We enter into this enchanted world and are played upon by every mood of nature. Now the sunlight steeps the distance, and soft ripples break at our feet; now we are climbing dizzy paths, the immense crags tower menacing above us; we are shut within the walls of a ravine, we are liberated with the opening glimpse of wide horizons; sails gleam on winding waters; villages sleep under the hills; reeds tremble in the mist, tall pines drink the sun—it is a world in which, once entered, we can wander for ever, and find new springs of delight.

(*PFE* 155–6)

The passage is a tissue of verbs—active and passive, transitive and intransitive—in which human actions fold seamlessly into the verbs of natural process, embodying his key argument that Oriental art takes us out of our narrowly human selves into the wider, non-human life of nature. It is in this deeper sense that *Painting in the Far East* is a literary work.

A detailed, coherent history of the evolution of landscape painting in China, along the lines of James Cahill's books or Michael Sullivan's *Symbols of Eternity*, was impossible in 1934, let alone 1908, and Binyon's account is sieved with lacunae. There is little on pre-T'ang and T'ang landscapes and the crucial Five Dynasties period is dealt with in a few lines, important artists like Ching Hao, Kuan T'ung, and Tung Yuan missing even from the list of artists in the appendix. Even in the chapter on Sung art 'the deficiencies occasioned by limited opportunities' bulk large. Lack of genuine examples of Northern Sung landscape prevented Binyon forming any coherent idea of its pictorial grandeur and intellectual power. Outdated as scholarship, *Painting in the Far East*, like Fenollosa's *Epochs*, remains a vivid testament to a crucial moment in Western cultural history. Both books hum with an excitement that derives from the fact that both writers felt they were handling dynamite. It was literally headline news: a *New York Times* report on Binyon's lectures in 1912 carried the sub-headline 'Chinese Art Ten Centuries Ago Was More Modern Than Ours Today'. Nobody now would have the critical bad taste to dream a painting, let alone describe it in print, but it was part and parcel of the missionary fervour that inspired Binyon and Fenollosa to introduce Chinese art to a sceptical Western audience.

In our increasingly global culture we are so acclimatized to a bombardment of multicultural images that it takes some effort to imagine how alien such paintings seemed to Binyon's original audience. They were scorned because they seemed so slight and unfinished, more misty space than painted form. Binyon taught two generations of readers and audiences to see that the space in which these paintings are so rich is not static, empty, Newtonian space, a mere absence of objects, but dynamic, the main 'protagonist in the design', the formless out of which form emerges, 'not a final peace, but itself an activity flowing out from the picture into our minds, and drawing us up into a rarer atmosphere' (*SMAA* 98). His crucial insight was that the very slightness of these Sung and Ashikaga landscapes is central to their purpose, which is to enlist the viewer as an active participant in the creative process. A Zen ink painting like Sesshū's *Haboku Landscape* (colour pl. 5) is not 'a completed piece of workmanship' but 'a communicating spark between mind and mind', not a statement but a fluid, open-ended field of activity, 'a hint, a suggestion which the spectator must himself complete' (*PFE* 185, 154), not a thing but an event, a transaction between artist and viewer, awakening and engaging the imagination rather than doping it with 'the satiety of completed forms' (*PFE* 161).

Skill and science in a work of art are, let us never forget, utterly valueless in themselves except as a means to awake emotion of worth and power in ourselves, the spectators. And these painters found that mind could speak to mind by suggestion more intimately than by elaboration.

(*PFE* 185)

This was of central importance to Binyon, who returned to it time and again in books, articles, and lectures throughout his career. Here he is speaking at the Royal Academy during the great Chinese Exhibition of 1936:

Through a true work of art the spectator enters into the mind of the artist, and through that, again, into the depth of space, the boundless horizon of the universal life. Until this chain of relations is completed the painting is, in a sense, only half-existent. Only in the minds of us who contemplate it does it assume its perfect life. The thought of the artist is to flower in us; in ourselves is to be born his masterpiece. Hence the emphasis laid on the importance for the spectator of preparing himself for the work of art by becoming empty to receive the fullness of the impression by sweeping from the mind all extraneous distractions.[39]

You could not ask for a clearer statement of Binyon's own approach to art as a meditative discipline. Zen-inspired Sung and Ashikaga painting is a deeply spiritual art, its aim 'liberation, enlightenment, self-conquest' (*PFE* 185). Every mountainscape is a mindscape, 'a state of the soul' (*PFE* 159), not in the sense that these artists projected their own mental states onto nature, rather the reverse: in meditation the artist achieves 'impassioned self-forgetfulness' (*FD* 28), a state of transparency beyond conceptual thought, in which his own mind and the landscape are expressions of the same all-pervading 'Rhythm'. The paintings in turn induce in those who approach them in a spirit of openness an analogous meditative state of mind, stilling their thoughts and enabling them to re-enact the artist's original experience of liberation. The circuit is complete when what the artist

put into his work comes out from it and flows over into our minds; and we recognize something which cannot be called intellectual only, or sensuous only, or emotional only; it is a wholeness of spirit which goes out, free and unafraid, into the wholeness of the universe.

(*SMAA* 104)[40]

It is characteristic of the man and the age that Binyon saw in all this affinities with some of the central preoccupations of English Romanticism. For him Blake's lines 'To see the world in a grain of

---

[39] 'Chinese Painters', *Journal of the Royal Society of Arts*, 84 (14 Feb. 1936), 378.
[40] See the context in which Chang Chung-yuan approvingly quotes this and other passages from *SMAA* in his *Creativity and Taoism: A Study of Chinese Philosophy, Art, and Poetry* (1963; New York, 1970), 92–6.

sand I And a heaven in a wild flower' crystallize 'what was at the heart of the poet-painters of Sung' (*PFE* 164). (Like all natural Romantics, Binyon unconsciously misquotes Blake's '*a* world' as '*the* world', one small step for grammar, one giant leap for philosophy.) Elsewhere he finds Taoist analogies in Keats's concept of Negative Capability and poems like Shelley's 'The Cloud', but the poet he finds closest in spirit is Wordsworth, who in his apprehension of the One Life shares with the Sung painters 'a rare sense of the solidarity of the universe'. Wordsworth's 'wise passiveness' 'seems to echo Lao-tzu with his doctrine of Inaction' (*FD* 28–9), 'Inaction' being Lionel Giles's inadequate translation of *wu-wei*, literally 'nonaction' but with the connotation of 'not forcing', 'going with the grain of things'.[41] Also invoked is George Meredith, whose 'reading of Earth'

> might have been inspired by the Zen doctrine of Contemplation, that phase of Buddhist thought which drew so much of its ideal from the doctrines of Lao-tzu. For to the Zen votaries the contemplation of the life of nature was, above all, an effort towards the realisation of one's self. They too, contemning book-lore, held, like Wordsworth, that 'one impulse from a vernal wood may teach you more of *man* than all the sages'. By passing out into the non-human world, the life of trees and flowers and animals, man could get rid of his devouring egoism, his belittling self-aggrandisement, realise his true place in the universe, and be braced thereby and fortified. For the Zen sages, as for Meredith, the contemplation of nature was no sentimental indulgence, but an invigorating discipline.
>
> (*FD* 30)

Such analogies were not confined to Europeans. Yone Noguchi, for example, also considered Wordsworth 'the first Easterner of English literature', while in 1903, in one of Binyon's favourite books, Okakura spoke of the 'Oriental Romantistic ideal'.[42] Nevertheless, innocuous as they seemed in the 1900s, we have become uneasy reading this kind of thing since Edward Said has sensitized us to the subtle ways in which Orientalism has historically managed and even produced the 'Orient' by defining, limiting, and authorizing views of it.[43] Binyon distrusted academic 'orientalism' for

[41] Lionel Giles, *The Sayings of Lao Tzu* (London, 1904), 30–2; Alan Watts and Al Chung-Liang Huang, *Tao: The Watercourse Way* (London, 1976), 75–6.

[42] Noguchi, foreword, *Selected Poems* (London, 1921), p. xvi; Okakura, *Ideals of the East*, 168.

[43] See *Orientalism: Western Conceptions of the Orient* (1978; London, 1991), 3, 67.

reasons analogous to Said's, but within Said's inclusive definition of Orientalism as a discourse he cannot escape the net, and is guilty here of 'conversion', distorting and denaturing the Other by assimilating it to European modes of thought.

Binyon admitted this in his preface to *Painting in the Far East* in stating his aim as being 'to appreciate' Asian art 'from the standpoint of a European' (*PFE* 1908, p. viii). Yet there was no manipulative will to power over the Other in this. Binyon consistently confronted Eurocentrism and took every opportunity to attack what he called the West's 'conviction of superiority, & obstinate determination to impose its own standards'.[44] He realized that Romantic nature-mysticism differs from Taoism or Zen in important ways, but he also believed that there were genuine, and valuable, analogies. The Chinese concept of *ch'i* for example, defined by Sirén as 'the life-breath of everything, be it man, beast, mountain or tree', made the Wordsworthian analogy a natural, if partly mistaken, one.[45] Such assimilation was inevitable during this early phase of Western contact with these startling philosophies. Okakura was an inspiring but by no means uniformly accurate guide to Eastern thought. Suzuki Daisetz published his first book in English, *Outlines of Mahayana Buddhism*, only months before *Painting in the Far East* and it took many more years for a real understanding of Zen to develop in England in the wake of Suzuki's three-volume *Essays in Zen Buddhism* (1927–34). The world was not a global village in 1908 and Binyon had to take his knowledge as and where he could find it and interpret it as best he could. Such analogies helped him keep his writings in the realm of public, nonspecialist discourse and—his constant aim—to involve his readers in Asian art as something with vital implications for their own lives by relating it to familiar modes of thought and then pushing beyond them.

It is no coincidence that when his feelings were most deeply engaged Binyon discovered such analogies, for he belonged to the Wordsworthian tradition and his poetry shares some of the preoccupations of Sung landscape as he interprets it. Poem after poem re-enacts the pattern of 'The Renewal', in which in meditating on a

---

[44] 'Chinese Painting', MS of lecture delivered 12 Apr. 1937 at the British Institution in Florence, n.pag.
[45] Sirén, 21. On Wordsworth and Zen, see the scattered comments in R. H. Blyth's *Zen in English Literature and Oriental Classics* (Tokyo, 1942), esp. 212–24.

landscape the poet's individual self merges with the greater Self, the 'one infinity of life that flows . . . I Out into these unnumbered semblances I Of earth and air, mountains and beasts and trees' (*CP*i.40). The *Morning Post* reviewer rightly saw 'A sense of the oneness of things' pervading *England and Other Poems*, the volume contemporaneous with *Painting in the Far East*. Moreover, his writings on Oriental art were themselves extensions of his poetry, as Frank Rinder saw in his 1911 review of *The Flight of the Dragon*: 'Of our writers on art, particularly Oriental art, Mr. Binyon is pre-eminently the poet. Here the material with which he deals is in profound accord with the temper of his own outlook, mental, emotional, spiritual.'[46]

Approaching Chinese landscapes with a mind steeped in Romantic thought and rhetoric, he saw at times what he wanted to see, what, in terms of his own cultural situation, he needed to see. The poignant fact for Binyon was that Wordsworth, Blake, Keats, and Shelley were all 'isolated minds and personalities' (*FD* 28), alienated from the mechanistic Western *Weltanschauung* but without recourse to any viable, coherent alternative philosophy. As a late Romantic himself, marooned in a era when Romanticism was under attack from all sides, Binyon could point to China and Japan as two great, longlived, deeply cultured civilizations inspired by attitudes to nature and the human spirit which he saw, rightly or wrongly, as analogous to those which had marginalized Wordsworth. In an era when Hulme was lambasting Romantics for going on about the 'infinite',[47] he could celebrate a culture for which 'the highest effort of art was to suggest infinity, the infinity that belongs to the free mind of man' (*FD* 23).

Binyon did not expect Oriental art to change all this. Despite Chesterton's fears, he was not trying to convert England *en masse* to Taoism or Zen. As he said in his *Rhythm* article, the West must find its own way. Nevertheless, from Asian art and thought Westerners could gain experiences which, combined with those pioneered by contemporary artists, writers, thinkers, and scientists, could perhaps create a new, profounder, more humane, and genuinely international paradigm for the twentieth century.

[46] 'Appreciation of Art', *Daily News*, 14 Nov. 1911, 3.
[47] 'Romanticism and Classicism', 119–20.

9 For the Fallen

For Binyon, as for Britain as a whole, the months leading up to the Great War were business as usual. He kept up his many and varied friendships—Ricketts's diary for 1 May 1914 records: 'Binyon Yeats in Evening discussion about spiritualism'[1]—but the centre of his life was family and work. Commissioned to write on Botticelli for Macmillan, in *Botticelli: An Essay in Pictorial Criticism* (1913) he used the Florentine artist as a focus for what the art historian David Peters Corbett has described as 'an extended critique of Western culture since the Renaissance', with its insatiable will to power and rejection of spiritual for materialist values.[2] Pound, Lewis, and other young avant-garde artists and writers, who had been influenced by Binyon's critique of Western culture, had gone on to espouse a violent rejection of tradition which Binyon himself could not endorse. *Botticelli* called for contemporary artists and writers to 'make it new', a phrase Pound later re-invented in modernist rhetorical terms,[3] but as a recycling of the tradition in new, contemporary forms rather than a violent and complete rupture with the past:

We cannot discard the past; we cannot throw away our heritage, but we must remould it in the fire of our necessities, we must make it new and our own. . . . What is needed now is the fusion of one imaginative effort that shall make art again a single language expressing the whole modern man.

(BC 17)

By 1913 the London art world had further fragmented into warring factions akin to the real armies building on the Continent, with propagandists for Futurism, Vorticism, and other competing art movements already on a war footing. What worried Binyon was

[1] *Self-Portrait*, 194.

[2] 'Late Romantic Poetry, Criticism and the Visual Arts and Early Modernism in Britain', unpublished paper, p. 12.

[3] Corbett suggests that Pound may have been recalling LB's phrase when he used it in the *Cantos* and the 1934 *Make it New*, ibid. 18 n. 6.

'the increasing tendency' among contemporary artists and critics alike not only 'to become enslaved to doctrinaire theory' but to impose it on everyone else: 'A single method is proclaimed the only right one, and all others are warred on with an almost theological bitterness' (*BC* 29). He largely kept out of these wars, encouraging Slade students as different as Paul Nash and William Roberts, the brilliant future Vorticist he sent to the Omega Workshops with a letter of introduction to Fry in 1913. In 1912 he was the first literary figure to befriend the young East End painter–poet Isaac Rosenberg. He encouraged both sides of his talent, and bought several copies of his pamphlet *Night and Day* in 1912 to send to influential friends, including Edward Marsh, then editing the first *Georgian Poetry* anthology.[4]

Binyon's tenth volume of poetry, *Auguries*, published in December 1913, contained several ambitious meditative poems, including 'Malham Cove' and 'Thunder on the Downs', whose English landscape darkening under towering thunderheads seemed to anticipate something of the coming holocaust. The *TLS* found the book characterized by 'Gravity, serenity, restraint' and an 'austerity that is far indeed from any kind of insensitiveness or inhumanity . . . an austerity that is in the deepest and gravest sense of the word public-spirited'.[5] When people start saying things like that you have to start worrying they might make you Poet Laureate, and indeed Binyon's was one of the names touted when Alfred Austin died in June 1913. The *Daily Graphic*, for example, carried pictures of Hardy, Masefield, Kipling, Watson, Meynell, Phillips, and Binyon, though not of the poet eventually chosen, Robert Bridges.[6]

At the Museum, the establishment of Binyon's Sub-Department in January 1913 was followed by the move to the new King Edward VII Galleries. For the inaugural exhibition of the new Gallery in May 1914 he chose Chinese and Japanese works from the Morrison and Stein collections. At last it seemed he was about to get out to the East. With the help of Hovelaque in Paris, he was in line for an Albert Khan travelling fellowship of the kind which had

---

[4] For Roberts see Cork i. 158; for Rosenberg see LB, Introductory Memoir, *Poems by Isaac Rosenberg*, ed. Gordon Bottomley (London, 1922), 1–4.

[5] *TLS*, 11 Dec. 1913, 601–2.

[6] 'The Late Poet Laureate, Alfred Austin, and a Glimpse at his Possible Successors', *Daily Graphic*, 7 June 1913, 929.

enabled Goldsworthy Lowes Dickinson to travel to India, China, and Japan in 1912–13. On 11 July he laid before the Trustees a detailed plan for a Museum 'mission to the East' in 1915, taking in China and Japan and costed at a modest £250, and it was provisionally approved.[7]

The timing could hardly have been worse. Two weeks earlier Gavrilo Princip had gunned down the Archduke Franz Ferdinand in Sarajevo, setting in motion a chain of events which, improbable as it seemed in the summer of 1914 would destroy four great empires and kill more than ten million men. Britain's declaration of war following the German invasion of Belgium on 4 August put paid to both schemes. The Treasury refused to finance the mission and the Khan fellowships were suspended. 'Come and see for yourself!', Hamilton Bell wrote cheerily from Tokyo in September.[8] It would take Binyon another fifteen years to do so.

Binyon's disappointment was swallowed up in the catastrophic events of August 1914, especially the invasion of Belgium, a country to which he felt particularly close. The Flanders he had lovingly evoked in the poetic prose of *Western Flanders* (1899) was a land autumnally at peace after centuries of war and turmoil, its ancient battlefields reclaimed by nature and agriculture. As the tragedy of the Western Front unfolded, turning Flanders into the abattoir of Europe, Binyon must have remembered with bitter irony his description of Ypres's scarred, lichened ramparts as 'unconsciously impregnable to the agitations of this modern age':

To be a citizen of Ypres is to have wandered out of time; to have come into an indefinite region, where the rising of the sun is but a casual device of nature, where the seasons make no dates, and events never happen. . . . The earth begins to claim this town, to cover it up with soft mosses and silence; and all of which it was composed, buildings and shaped timbers and wrought metal, to be resigned to the elemental stuff of this ever-germinating world.

(WF 3–4)

Ypres was destined to be effaced by forces less benign than ever-germinating nature, as the darker undertones of *Western Flanders*, its side-glances at 'armed and murmuring Europe, restless in huge camps' (WF 46), were realized on a scale undreamt of in 1899. The destruction of much of the ancient Flemish university town of

---

[7] Minutes, lvii (11 July 1914) p. 3266, BM.
[8] ALs, 11 Sept. 1914.

Louvain between 25 and 29 August deeply distressed him because this was where one of his best friends in the 1890s, the poet Olivier Georges Destrée, had entered a Benedictine monastery, living quietly as Dom Bruno in this 'house of love and living peace', as Binyon described it in his poem 'Louvain'. When he wrote these words he did not know whether or not Destrée was one of the many priests killed during those savage five days, but a month later Petrucci wrote from Holland to say he was dead.[9] One small death among what was to become so many, but it brought the war very close.

Binyon's first war poem, 'The Fourth of August', appeared in *The Times* a week after Britain entered the war. It is very much in the spirit of August 1914, all 'Spirit of England, ardent-eyed', but its last-line invocation of the 'Soul of divinely suffering man' (CPi.205–6), while commonplace in later Great War poetry, sounded a slightly discordant note in August 1914 when the war was almost universally seen as an over-by-Christmas bash, typically expressed by Hewlett's 'To Strike Quickly' in the following day's *The Times*: 'Strike, England, quickly, make an end | Of him who seeks to trade with thee.'[10] Ricketts commended Binyon for having written a poem that was a 'great contrast to the schoolboy thought & verse of the Laureate, the editorial leader by W. Watson & the patriotic rubbish I have chanced to see in verse'.[11]

Binyon's response to the outbreak of war was sober, with little of the euphoria felt by some of his friends. He did not attend the secret 2 September 1914 meeting of distinguished British writers at the War Propaganda Bureau in Wellington House to discuss how they could contribute to the Allied war effort, but he was among the fifty signatories to the Authors' Declaration which appeared in *The Times* and the *New York Times* on 18 September. Stressing that they were 'men and women of the most divergent political and social views, some of them having been for years ardent champions of good will towards Germany, and many of them extreme advocates of peace', the writers declared that after the invasion of Belgium they 'were nevertheless agreed that Great Britain could

---

[9] ALs, 24 Sept. 1914; 'Louvain', *The Winnowing-Fan: Poems on the Great War* (London, 1915), 18.
[10] LB, *The Times*, 11 Aug. 1914, 7; Hewlett, *The Times*, 12 Aug. 1914, 7.
[11] ALs, 11 Aug. 1914.

not without dishonour have refused to take part in the present war'.[12]

Three days later *The Times* printed what would become one of the most famous and best-loved poems of the war. Perhaps the most remarkable thing about 'For the Fallen' is that date, 21 September 1914, with the Great War less than seven weeks old. In fact the poem had been written several weeks earlier, just after the retreat from Mons, where the heavily outnumbered British Expeditionary Force became the first British army to fight on Western European soil since Waterloo.[13] Dark days certainly, with the German armies having swept through most of Belgium and with Paris under threat, but the war had not yet revealed its true nature. The cost in human life was already enormous, but little of this had filtered back home. In its gravitas, its tenderness, and depth of grief, 'For the Fallen' looks as if it should have appeared in *The Times* for 21 September 1918 not 1914. It harmonizes with the tone neither of *The Times* war reports nor of other poems appearing at this time. From the beginning Binyon privately called these stanzas his 'requiem-verses', and that is what they are. While other early Great War poems sounded hollow when the true scale and nature of the war slowly permeated the national consciousness, this poem grew in stature with each defeat, each abortive push, and pyrrhic victory. In a curious symbiotic process, it deepened, accommodating itself to the scale of the nation's grief, so that by 1918 it was an infinitely better poem than it had been in 1914.

The poem's seven stanzas chart in advance Britain's changing mood from 1914 to 1918. The first two stanzas are dignified,

---

[12] *The Times*, 18 Sept. 1914, 3. See Peter Buitenhuis, *The Great War of Words: Literature as Propaganda 1914–18 and After* (London, 1989), 14, 18–19; and Samuel Hynes, *A War Imagined: The First World War and English Culture* (New York, 1991), 26–7. Unlike Masefield and others, LB did not write propaganda, with the possible exception of the curious one-act drama *Bombastes in the Shades*, published in 1915 in the Oxford Pamphlets series, a series of mainly historical treatises published by Oxford University Press and distributed by the Central Committee for National Patriotic Associations. For the background, see Buitenhuis, 16.

[13] John Dugdale's suggestion that, having attended the Wellington House meeting, 'For the Fallen' was LB's 'dutiful contribution to the war effort' ('Just How do we Remember Them?', *The Times*, 9 Mar. 1993, 37) seems wrong on both counts: not only was LB not at the 2 Sept. meeting (Buitenhuis, 14), but the poem had probably already been written. LB told John Drinkwater his 'requiem-verses' were written 'some weeks before' their appearance in *The Times*, their publication delayed by that fact that he had originally sent the poem to the *Morning Post*, who had rejected it (ALs, 28 Oct. 1914, BRBM).

solemn, full of sonorous abstractions, while the third is pure late
summer 1914, a mixture of journalese and proto-Rupert Brooke:

> With proud thanksgiving, a mother for her children,
> England mourns for her dead across the sea.
> Flesh of her flesh they were, spirit of her spirit,
> Fallen in the cause of the free.
>
> Solemn the drums thrill: Death august and royal
> Sings sorrow up into immortal spheres.
> There is music in the midst of desolation
> And a glory that shines upon our tears.
>
> They went with songs to the battle, they were young,
> Straight of limb, true of eye, steady and aglow.
> They were staunch to the end against odds uncounted,
> They fell with their faces to the foe.
>
> (CPi.210)

This was standard rhetoric in early Great War poetry. Fair enough
for late August 1914 perhaps, but after Ypres and Loos, after 1915
dragged into 1916 and the nightmare of the Somme, it would
become obvious, to the combatants at least, that in industrialized
trench warfare, which pitted expendable flesh against mass-
produced metals and chemicals, to be 'straight of limb, true of eye,
steady and aglow' meant little. There was no chivalric significance
in whether victims of artillery, machine gun fire, or chlorine gas 'fell
with their faces to the foe', or even had faces left at all. The terrible
realities of the war undermined abstractions such as 'Death august
and royal', washed words clean of their time-hallowed associations
more ruthlessly than any modernist poet. 'Flesh of her flesh they
were', biblical in 1914, echoing Adam's wonder at the creation of
Eve—'This is now bone of my bone, and flesh of my flesh' (Gen. 2:
23)—took on different connotations in the killing fields of Flanders,
where men rotted for weeks on the barbed wire. In the last four
stanzas, however, these romantic clichés gradually give way to a
clairvoyant sense of the sheer scale of the grief that would need to
be consoled, given a bearably human shape:

> They shall grow not old, as we that are left grow old:
> Age shall not weary them, nor the years condemn.
> At the going down of the sun and in the morning
> We will remember them.
>
> They mingle not with their laughing comrades again;
> They sit no more at familiar tables of home;

> They have no lot in our labour of the day-time;
> They sleep beyond England's foam.
>
> But where our desires are and our hopes profound,
> Felt as a well-spring that is hidden from sight,
> To the innermost heart of their own land they are known
> As the stars are known to the Night;
>
> As the stars that shall be bright when we are dust,
> Moving in marches upon the heavenly plain,
> As the stars that are starry in the time of our darkness,
> To the end, to the end, they remain.
>
> (CPi.210)

These stars, natural imagery for any Romantic poet, here add to their qualities of brightness and permanence their sheer number: by implication, the dead are uncountable as the stars in the Milky Way. This gives a cosmic dimension to the tragedy of the war before that tragedy fully revealed itself. Clairvoyant too is the imagery of dawn and sunset: 'At the going down of the sun and in the morning'. Sunrises and sunsets would become central to British poetry of the Great War, from Rosenberg's 'Break of Day in the Trenches' to Owen's 'Anthem for Doomed Youth', and in *The Great War and Modern Memory* Paul Fussell remarks on Binyon's 'uncanny prescience' in using this imagery with the war only weeks old.[14]

The poem hinges on its central stanza, later carved on thousands of gravestones and cenotaphs, and recited at Armistice Day ceremonies and the British Legion Festival of Remembrance, lines that have accrued the power and resonance of a mantra through four generations of utterance:

> They shall grow not old, as we that are left grow old:
> Age shall not weary them, nor the years condemn.
> At the going down of the sun and in the morning
> We will remember them.

Composed in Cornwall as Binyon sat with Cicely gazing out over the ocean,[15] this most public of quatrains is, like the poem that grew from it, deliberately choric, so densely laminated with allusions that the poet recedes into anonymity, allowing the literature-saturated

---

[14] *The Great War and Modern Memory* (1975; Oxford, 1977), 56.
[15] In a 15 Aug. 1919 letter LB told CMB he would never forget 'that it was through Beloved that it was written, on the little cliff at Polseath'.

English language to speak as if of itself. There are the obvious biblical and Shakespearean echoes—Enobarbus's lines on Cleopatra, for example: 'Age cannot wither her, nor custom stale' (*Ant* II.ii, 235)—but beneath these lie powerfully echoic cadences, rhythmical structures of loss and consolation seeded deep in the language by the King James Bible. When the editor of the *Jewish Chronicle* wrote in 1935 asking whether he had had in mind the words 'And there was evening and there was morning, one day' (Gen. 1: 5), Binyon replied:

> The words you quote from Genesis were not in my mind. In seeking for the *rhythmical basis* of my poem, I was, however, influenced by the Bible language. I wanted to get a rhythm something like 'By the waters of Babylon we sat down and wept' or 'Daughters of Jerusalem, weep not for me' for that particular verse; & having found the kind of rhythm I wanted varied it in other stanzas according to the mood required.[16]

All traces of the poet's personal signature are subsumed within these sacramental cadences. The quatrain Eric Gill carved at the Front Entrance of the British Museum in 1921 does not carry Binyon's name, only those of the Museum staff who died, a perfect image of the poetic self's submergence in communal experience.

'For the Fallen' is one of the few great war poems to include in its tragedy those 'that are left'. It takes Henry's St Crispin's Day speech from *Henry V* IV.iii, the key text of English chivalric patriotism, and turns it inside out, seeing the war and its aftermath from the point of view of those at home, the older generation too old to fight, including those who found their jingoist platitudes stilled in their throats by the surreal nightmare the war had become. Henry's shielded citizenry quietly 'a-bed' did not wake each morning to War Office telegrams, appalling newspaper casualty lists and the aftermath of Zeppelin raids, did not, as Binyon did, tend the wounded in France and spend their nights manning a Lewis machine gun. In this war, Binyon wrote in 1918, 'there is no sitting at ease, a remote and indifferent spectator, as in older days'.[17] Binyon's 'we' were deeply implicated in the war, increasingly, as the poem predicts, not through armchair patriotism but shared grief. The poem is prophetic in its sense of 'we that are left' as somehow small, the bereaved parents and grandparents left behind when, through an

[16] S. Levy, 'For the Fallen', letter, *TLS*, 23 Nov. 1946, 577.
[17] 'And What of Art?', *Dial* (Chicago), 31 Jan. 1918, 93.

escalation nobody dreamt of when Binyon composed the poem, Henry's happy few swelled into an entire generation. This is the point behind that awkward inversion 'They shall *grow not old*', which anthologists often accidentally untangle. It is not drafted in for metrical effect but to create a grammatical fluidity within the line which enables 'not' to negate 'old' as well as 'grow'. In the poem, in curling photographs, in the minds of the bereaved older generation, the dead grow steadily younger as their ageing relatives recede from them toward their own deaths.

Days after it appeared in *The Times* Cyril Rootham, organist and director of music at St John's College, Cambridge, wrote asking Binyon's permission to write a choral setting for the poem. He agreed before sailing to the United States in late October on a study and lecture tour organized in happier days to raise money for his trip to the East. He returned in mid-December just as Mathews issued *The Winnowing-Fan*, a slim volume of war poems. One of the many moved by this book was the composer Sir Edward Elgar, who sketched settings for 'For the Fallen', 'The Fourth of August', and 'To Women' in early 1915. When he learnt of Rootham's work-in-progress, however, he modestly withdrew. 'I know you will be disappointed', he wrote Binyon in March, 'but your disappointment is not so great as mine for I love your poem & love & honour you for having conceived it.'[18] Binyon replied:

Your words about my poem touch me deeply. My disappointment matters nothing, keen as it is: but think of England, of the English-speaking peoples, in whom the common blood stirs now as it never did before: think of the awful casualty lists that are coming, & the losses in more & more homes; think of the thousands who will be craving to have their grief glorified & lifted up & transformed by an art like yours. . . . Surely it would be wrong to let them lose this help & consolation.[19]

Colvin and other mutual friends implored Elgar to complete what they were convinced would be one of his great works. They prevailed, and during the dreadful spring of 1915, through the Second Battle of Ypres and the Gallipoli disaster, Elgar worked on *The Spirit of England*, which slowly grew into one of his profoundest, most inward, and deeply imagined choral works, akin to his 1900 masterpiece *The Dream of Gerontius*. The war brought

[18] ALs, 24 Mar. 1915, qtd. in Jerrold Northrop Moore, *Edward Elgar: A Creative Life* (Oxford, 1984), 674. For the full story, see Moore, 674–82, 704–5.
[19] 27 Mar. 1915, qtd. in Moore, 674–5.

out characteristics Elgar and Binyon shared, not only a shared vocabulary of late Romanticism but also its dominant moods of loss, nostalgia, and a vague autumnal sadness, now focused by the war into a very tangible grief. The *Morning Post* in 1916 was only half correct in seeing the 'haunting sense of a cosmical tragedy' as having 'transfigured [Binyon's] temperament',[20] for the war deepened and provided a suitable context for an innate elegiac quality traceable ultimately to Matthew Arnold. Already by 1909 one reviewer had divined that he was naturally 'a consoling poet'.[21]

Parts Two and Three, 'To Women' and the climactic 'For the Fallen', were completed first and performed with *Gerontius* under Elgar's baton by the Leeds Choral Union in Leeds on 3 May 1916. The London première followed five days later at the Queen's Hall, with Clara Butt, the most famous concert singer of the period, taking the soprano part in six performances in aid of the Red Cross, one of which was attended by King George V. Described recently as 'one of the most extraordinary musical events of the war', these concerts helped crystallize the sombre mood of Britain in these weeks leading up to the Somme offensive, a mood very different from the Kiplingesque euphoric jingoism of *Land of Hope and Glory*. As Jeremy Crump has written, in his Binyon cycle and *Gerontius* 'Elgar was considered to have explored and consoled the English soul at a time of national grief.'[22] The music critic Ernest Newman wrote: 'Here in truth is the very voice of England, moved to the centre of her being in this War as she has probably never been moved before in all her history.'[23]

The day after the Queen's Hall recital, a wounded officer wrote attacking 'all the people writing about war & soldiers when they haven't a notion of either. Sensible people like Yeats keep quiet, or express the feelings of non-combatants in the most touching & poignant terms imaginable, as Elgar & Binyon.'[24] One man eager to hear Elgar's setting was the composer-poet Ivor Gurney, who considered 'For the Fallen' 'a great poem' and attempted a setting of his

[20] E.B.O., rev. of *The Anvil*, *Morning Post*, 17 Feb. 1916, 2.

[21] 'Mr. Binyon's New Poems', *TLS*, 30 Dec. 1909, 513.

[22] 'The Identity of English Music: The Reception of Elgar 1898–1935', *Englishness: Politics and Culture 1880–1920*, ed. Robert Colls and Philip Dodd (London, 1986), 176.

[23] '"The Spirit of England": Edward Elgar's New Choral Work', *Musical Times*, 1 May 1916, 239.

[24] Qtd. in Michael Kennedy, *Portrait of Elgar*, 2nd edn. (London, 1982), 180.

own at the Front in 1917.[25] Other soldiers had come across the poem in *War Poems from The Times*, a supplement issued with *The Times* in August 1915. Wilfred Owen had a copy in his luggage when he returned to Britain to enlist a month later, his verdict 'Binyon all right!'[26] Twenty years later, just before Armistice Day 1936, Owen's mentor Siegfried Sassoon, who thought longer, harder, and more bitterly about the war than almost any man in England, wrote to Binyon that ' "For the Fallen" remains as the finest expression of a certain aspect of the war'.[27]

FOR DAUNTLESS FRANCE

When Katharine Tynan wrote in March 1915 thanking him for writing 'the most beautiful poetry of the war', Binyon replied that he wished he 'were younger & could be fighting in France'.[28] Overage and in a reserved occupation, he joined the Second Battalion County of London Volunteer Regiment (Inns of Court Companies) and spent Easter training at Arundel. 'We hope we may be used in some humble way before the war is over,' he told Freer,[29] but he was determined to be of more practical use. On 25 July he took his annual leave and went to France as a Red Cross volunteer ambulancier and orderly assigned to the Hôpital Militaire in Arc-en-Barrois, 15 miles west of Chaumont in the Haute Marne, following in the footsteps of Masefield and Henry Tonks, who had worked there months before. The hospital, staffed by English doctors, nurses, and orderlies, was housed in the Château d'Arc, which the Duc de Penthièvre had donated to the French government early in the war. The château stood in a spacious park laced with trout streams crossed by wooden bridges, set among the pinewoods of the forest of Arc, as sylvan a setting as any ironist could invent with the Argonne front some 40 miles to the north, the guns audible, their effects all too visible in the 110 beds

[25] See Gurney, *War Letters*, ed. R. K. R. Thornton (Manchester, 1983), 73, 81, 104, 110, 122, 126.

[26] Qtd. Jon Stallworthy, *Wilfred Owen* (1974; Oxford, 1977), 125.

[27] ALs, 9 Nov. 1936.

[28] Tynan ALs, 31 Mar. 1915; LB ALs, 13 Apr. 1915, BL–HRC.

[29] ALs, 16 Apr. 1915, Charles Lang Freer Papers, Freer Gallery of Art/Arthur M. Sackler Gallery Archives, Smithsonian Institution, Washington, DC (hereafter Smithsonian).

crammed in six wards on two floors of the château. If Paris had
been uncannily normal, here Binyon found himself in a world for
which nothing in his previous life had prepared him. Straight after
breakfast on his first morning he attended a series of operations,
wheeling patients in from the wards and assisting in the theatre.
The third patient had extreme unction before the operation and
died under anaesthetic. One of his first tasks was to turn a room
into a mortuary chapel with a small altar decked with flowers from
the garden, where he laid out the dead.

The life of an orderly at hospitals like these with no hot water
system, gas, electricity, or lifts was tough, exacting, and often
unpleasant. As a jack-of-all trades at everyone's beck and call at all
hours, it took a while for his muscles to get used to the great variety
of unaccustomed tasks, but he welcomed the challenge. His thir-
teen-hour working day began with a brisk walk from his billet in a
former inn on the Latrecey road to arrive at the château in time to
serve the *blessés* their coffee and bread at seven. He then swept the
ward and emptied the slops before eating his own breakfast. Operations began at nine, followed by X-rays till noon. In good weather
the less severely wounded spent the afternoons in a makeshift
outdoor ward in the garden, where the midsummer limes smelled
sweet after the chloroform of the wards. It was heavy work, hefting
them on stretchers and sometimes beds up and down the winding
stairs. Meanwhile there were rooms to be fumigated, clothes and
blankets disinfected ('three brews a day, very savoury'),[30] mat-
tresses stuffed with straw, sand collected for sandbags, windows
cleaned, stores shifted, meals served, wine brought up from the
cellars. He went to bed exhausted, but nights were often inter-
rupted by telephone calls from the field hospital which sent him and
his fellow orderlies off in the early hours of the morning to collect
fresh batches of wounded off the Red Cross trains at Latrecey. In
odd spare hours he learnt basic carpentry. The château had been
stripped of furniture and so, with wood freely available from a
sawmill nearby on the river Aujon, the orderlies furnished the
wards with simple home-made tables, chairs, cupboards, and
shelves, as well as splints and fracture-beds, 'works of faith and
enthusiasm' at first bow-legged and fragile but slowly gaining in
sturdiness and sophistication (*FDF* 178). He took a quiet joy in

[30] ALs to CMB, postmarked 3 Aug. 1915. Other details are drawn from LB's
letters and the chapter 'The Day of an Orderly', in *FDF* 171–90.

this, absorbed in manual tasks, learning new skills, his scholar's hands hardened by real labour and the making of useful things. His bedside tables were his 'pride and delight. They stood square. They held things' (*FDF* 178).

He was deeply impressed by the *blessés'* fortitude and quiet courage, their hatred of the war combined with a willingness to see it through. They came from all over France, but many were Breton *cultivateurs*, brawny, sunburnt, bearded men, though Binyon was shocked to find many of them, an increasing number, mere boys. There was an occasional hesitant English speaker, such as Raymond Belin, who later wrote to him in London: 'Good shake hand. I say also "Long lived at the good, big and journey England!" Hip! Hip! Hip! Hurrah!'[31] Another found out that he was a poet and engaged him in long conversations about poetry and drama. For the most part, however, these were countrymen whose dialects he at first found difficult and with whom he communicated in a mixture of French and sign language, which seemed in a way to deepen the intimacy, since it limited speech to primal realities, food, pain, laughter, fear. His old wish 'to have elemental things near in [his] life' was fulfilled in ways unimaginable when he had voiced it eleven years earlier. He discovered here a camaraderie based on modes of communication deeper and more eloquent than intellectual discourse, small gestures, the care that went into making a bedside table or feeding a young soldier with both hands amputated, the stealing of roses for those too ill to make it down to the garden.

This intimacy made the operations even harder to bear, despite the patients' robust black humour faced with repeated visits to *le billard*, as they christened the operating table. Under anaesthetic many returned to the trenches, struggling and yelling until the chloroform took effect. The simpler, cleaner operations were sometimes 'fascinating', like the patient who had shrapnel removed from his arm in the X-ray room, 'in the dark just lit up in ghostly fashion by the bluish rays',[32] but the amputations were dreadful, especially as one of his tasks was burning the amputated limbs in the furnace. 'Oh Beloved; it is horrible,' he wrote home after his first amputation. 'I would give something to escape this part of the work, but it has to be gone through.'[33] So good was he with the patients that by the third week, when a lull in fighting in the Argonne gave way

[31] ALs, 12 Sept. [1915?].   [32] ALs to CMB, 7 Aug. [1915].
[33] ALs, postmarked 3 Aug. 1915.

to a series of engagements which brought waves of new patients, he was given rubber gloves and promoted to swabbing, the first orderly to take over these nursing duties. 'It is horrible all the maiming of young men,' he wrote in the middle of a seemingly endless series of 'heartbreaking' cases, '& to think of what is being endured all over Europe!'[34]

These weeks put Binyon back in touch with things, physical things, real people, taught him to see, hear, and smell more clearly. This comes across in a poem like 'Fetching the Wounded', which describes a midnight drive to Latrecey to meet the Red Cross train, picking up wounded French soldiers and returning to Arc at dawn. The poem has an immediacy and presence new in Binyon's poetry. The old Romantic impulse to fly up 'into the eternal gases', as Hulme would put it,[35] is still there, but the focus keeps coming back to the physical details of the scene, the plants illuminated in the headlights, so clear he can see the 'powdery white bloom' on their stems, the 'stale odour of blood' which 'mingles with keen | Pure smell of grass and dew' as they carefully load the *blessés* into the ambulances. Looking at their faces in the lantern light and thinking of the vacant beds in 'far homes | Lost in deep country' where they belong, he says 'I touch the world of pain | That is so silent,' and the visceral verb 'touch', among all those abstracts, persuades us that he does (*CPi*.219–21). Aptly described by a later reviewer as 'flawless in its tenderness of handling', it conflates the poetic and paracletic acts, the physical tenderness involved in carrying the wounded somehow woven into the texture of the poem.[36] The short sentences, clinging close to the action—

> The Chief
> Gives every man his order, prompt and brief.
> We carry up our wounded, one by one.
> The first cock crows: the morrow is begun.
>
> (*CPi*.221)

—hint at one direction in which his poetry might have developed had he been a younger man fighting at the front.

Returning to London very reluctantly in early September, he put the finishing touches to his Japanese print *Catalogue*, and worked on a monograph to accompany a fine photographic facsimile of

---

[34] ALs to CMB, 19 Aug. [1915].   [35] 'Romanticism and Classicism', 120.
[36] Rev. of *The Four Years*, *TLS*, 18 Sept. 1919, 496. The experience is described in an ALs to CMB, 13 Aug. [1915].

Freer's Ma Yüan scroll which Freer was having made in New York for distribution to European and American museums as a means of fostering interest in Chinese art. In February 1916 Mathews issued *The Anvil*, another slender volume of war poems which was enthusiastically reviewed and sold well.[37] The book included 'Fetching the Wounded', 'The Healers', a celebration of battlefield medics and stretcher bearers, and 'Orphans of Flanders', written in snatched moments at Arc for Edith Wharton's fundraising anthology *The Book of the Homeless* (1916), joining a stellar list of contributors which included Henry James, Conrad, Hardy, Verhaeren, Maeterlinck, Monet, Stravinsky, Cocteau, and Santayana.

Nevertheless, Binyon found it difficult to settle back into Museum routines. He devoted time to fund-raising for Arc, writing a letter to *The Times* calling on 'Those who love France, who feel the debt all Europe owes to her, who understand how precious a gain among all these miseries of loss is the experience of human sympathy and friendship between the two great nations.'[38] 'I fret greatly here, & long to be back at the hospital, but I fear they won't let me go,' he had written to Freer in October. 'I dare say you think that I am to be envied being at peaceful work, but that is not how one feels here. The war is a horrible slaughter but we have to go on to the bitter end; and so one's great longing is to be made use of in some way or other.'[39] In January he applied to the Trustees for paid leave to work for the Red Cross in France, but was turned down. The Museum eventually agreed to three months leave but the Treasury refused to pay his salary, without which it was impossible for him to maintain his family and pay for his board and lodging at Arc. 'I keep having letters and telegrams imploring me to come if possible,' he told Marsh. 'I shall be most bitterly disappointed if I don't get out.'[40] In his letters, the Museum becomes a 'prison', a bureaucratic enclave tending its own interests in a disintegrating world, especially when the government closed it to the public from March 1916, a decision Binyon described as 'the kind of thing that makes one ashamed of one's country'.[41]

---

[37] See e.g. Francis Bickley, 'Laurence Binyon and Others', *Bookman*, 50 (Apr. 1916), 17.
[38] 'An English Hospital for French Soldiers', Letter, *The Times*, 6 Nov. 1915, 10.
[39] ALs, 7 Oct. 1915, Smithsonian.   [40] ALs, n.d. [1916].
[41] ALs to Marsh, 25 Jan. 1916.

Using his annual leave again, he returned to Arc in May and found things dramatically changed for the worse. The appalling losses suffered by the French Second Army at Verdun demanded that all hospital procedures be speeded up and patients treated as quickly as possible to free beds for fresh batches of badly injured soldiers. At first incessant rain kept the *blessés* cooped up indoors, adding to the conveyor-belt mentality. 'It is a different atmosphere from last year,' he wrote Cicely, and the tone of his letters darkens, not for himself, although he suffered badly with lumbago in the 'eternal wet' and was laid up for two guilt-racked days, but for the French soldiers and for Europe itself: 'But oh, the misery, the wasting & maiming!'[42] The most serious cases came to Arc, men who had endured the most murderously intense artillery bombardments of the war, with over 2,000 German guns concentrating their fire on barely 8 miles of front.[43] 'Verdun, the name of thunder, | Is written on their flesh,' he wrote (*CP*i.227–8).

East met West in macabre ways far removed from the aesthetics of *Painting in the Far East* when he studied Islamic rites in order to bury an Arab soldier. Binyon shared his Westward Ho tobacco and befriended the longer-term patients, but much of his time was spent assisting at seemingly endless operations. Again he was moved by the *blessés*' fortitude in the face of appalling wounds and appalling memories. 'I love these men,' he told Cicely.[44] The long working day was extended through increasingly frequent midnight drives to Latrecey to fetch more wounded, and it is hardly surprising that in his letters descriptions of the wounded and dying sometimes give way, when this became too painful, to quiet moments alone at night, keeping his inner world of memory and love intact amid the carnage of a world seemingly falling apart. 'Venus was indescribably brilliant. I thought of you across the sea,' he wrote on 3 June. Six days later a landscape pristine as a Sung ink painting until the last, telling detail:

Yesterday after dinner I went for a little walk on the hill. Millions of grasshoppers rustling, a distant bell now & then, white mist in the valley, a young moon above,—a feeling of everything washed clean after the

---

[42] ALs to CMB, 30 May [1916].
[43] For Verdun, see Alistaire Horne, *The Price of Glory, Verdun 1916* (London, 1962).
[44] ALs to CMB, 5 June [1916].

rain—& at intervals a little shock in the air, like a pulse beating—the guns at the front.[45]

This became the poem 'The Distant Guns'. Other poems such as 'Men of Verdun' and 'La Patrie' describe his maimed patients, but the full horror of this hospital overflowing with victims of what some military historians consider the most brutal battle in history, is kept from his poetry. Binyon just did not have the vocabulary.

Letters came fairly regularly, preserving a parodic normality. Verhaeren sent him his latest book. Freer, sensing he needed it, sent a generous £100 cheque for the Ma Yüan monograph. Parisian friends described Mme Bartet of the Comedie Française reciting his poem 'Edith Cavell' at the Grand Amphitheatre of the Sorbonne on 15 June. Waley sent proofs of the *Catalogue*, while Dodgson angered him by sending a letter 'all about prints & drawings', as if there were no war on at all—'how can he?' he asked Cicely.[46]

He reluctantly returned to London early in July, 'caged in this closed Museum' by day, as he described it to Freer, at night taking his turn on the rota to stand sentry duty at Hyde Park Corner.[47] Cicely, whose most recent books were *Historical Dialogues* (1914) and *The Reign of Edward VII* (1915), also had two jobs. In addition to night shifts at the Woolwich Arsenal canteen, in March she had become an examiner in the postal censorship office, sifting through French, German, Dutch, Swedish, and Norwegian letters for coded messages. Binyon worked on the *Catalogue* proofs, an essay on Cozens, an edition of Keats, and literary reviews for the *Bookman*, and in March 1917 wrote enthusiastically about Epstein in the first in a two-year series of art reviews for the *New Statesman*, which would include empathetic accounts of the work of war artists such as C. R. W. Nevinson, Eric Kennington, William Roberts, and especially Paul Nash. At the Museum, Waley was proving a real boon to the fledgling Sub-Department. Binyon told Freer his young Assistant was forging ahead and would become a 'first-rate scholar'.[48] Inspired by Waley's rapid mastery of written Chinese and impressed by the Chinese poems he had read in Pound's and Waley's translations, he started learning Chinese himself.

---

[45] ALs, 3 June [1916]; 9 June [1916].   [46] ALs, 30 June [1916].
[47] ALs, 4 Aug. 1916, Smithsonian.   [48] ALs, 31 Aug. 1916, Smithsonian.

Instead of sending Binyon back to Arc in 1917, the Red Cross dispatched him on a month-long journey through central, eastern, and southern France to report on all aspects of the work being done by British volunteers for the French wounded, refugees, and other victims of the war. He arrived in Paris on 4 May and spent several days arranging permits and transport, spending the evenings with Henri de Regnier, Andre Chevrillon, and other literary friends. After visiting hospitals in Lyons and Nevers, he travelled by train to Belfort in eastern France and was driven north up into the mountains through a landscape turning from summer back into spring to Gérardmer, close to the German border. From here he toured the sectors of the Vosges front served by British ambulances, visiting first-aid posts and dug-outs often close to the German trenches. On 15 May he drove through the Vosges to Remiremont, visiting British canteens staffed by volunteers, then up along the Moselle to Nancy via Gerbéviller and other villages devastated by the Germans in August and September 1914. The next day he took the train to Bar-le-Duc and was driven up to the shattered town of Verdun, eerily silent now after the carnage of 1916. In the shell-cratered lunar landscape beyond Verdun spread the battlefields whose names he knew only too well from countless conversations at Arc: Fleury, Fort Vaux, Douaumont, Mort Homme, Hill 304, 'scenes of hideous slaughter and of indescribable valour; fought for with desperate tenacity, lost and won, and lost and yet again won, in the hugest and most fiercely protracted battle that this earth had ever seen' (*FDF* 285). This was the emotional heart of Binyon's journey, culminating in a vision of a single blue-uniformed French soldier on the Sacred Way near Verdun, a solitary figure amid the immense landscape of annihilation. 'Alone on that famous, empty highway,' he wrote later, 'he seemed the symbol and incarnation of the enduring soul of France' (*FDF* 286).

By contrast, the real industrialized nature of the Great War revealed itself as he travelled through the Champagne region, especially in a trip to the front line in an area wrested from the Germans in bitter fighting weeks earlier. Here he watched a routine artillery bombardment, appalled, he wrote later, by 'the sinister solitariness of it all. War seemed an insanity of boredom, an earnestness of idiots, looked at close.'[49] In his poem 'Guns at the

---

[49] ALs to CMB, 18 May [1917].

Front', the huge guns that impersonally confound 'flesh with dirt' mindlessly chant 'Nothing, Nothing, Nothing!' (CPi.236). The landscape of mud, churned-up hills and splintered trees was 'extinct. It had lost all its native life. . . . Men, as men, appeared no longer to exist. A vast and horrible impersonality pervaded this world' (FDF 231-2). Binyon remembered this landscape weeks later when he wrote about 'the sense of hurt in the landscape' hauntingly expressed in Paul Nash's Ypres drawings,[50] the war a crime against not only humanity but the sustaining web of life itself. Struggling to imagine the depth of misery the soldiers must have plumbed in these mud-choked trenches under full-scale bombardment, he 'experienced a sort of humiliation at coming on this scene as a spectator' (FDF 233), brought face to face with the guilt which he, like all non-combatants with any moral imagination at all, felt throughout the war. Months later he wrote in the *New Statesman* that if Britain had to have a War Museum

let it tell the truth about the war; not only the incomparable bravery and daring and endurance, which will never be forgotten, but the horrible cost in pain, desolation, and waste which the world has in the past contrived to forget so easily.[51]

These experiences helped condition his response to the last leg of his journey, by train from Paris south to the Riviera to visit convalescent hospitals near Nice and Cannes. Compelled by the timetable to break his Mentone–Nice rail journey at Monte Carlo, he spent an hour on the Casino's trim terraces, glad that the luckier wounded were being medicined by this expensive Mediterranean sunlight but troubled by this stark evidence of the inequalities of the world the French *poilu* and English tommies were dying to save:

How this coast smells of riches!
To eyes fresh from the ruined homes of Eastern France, from the ghastly desolations and sublime endurances of the Front, this previous world of moneyed idleness, these innumerable villas perched on the hills and clouded with flowers, these glowing white walls and basking blue bays, the crowd of monstrous hotels, parasites of that glaring gamblers' Paradise in the middle of them—all seemed a transplantation from another planet, a projection of dreams into the sunlight. This was not France; it was some cosmopolitan country, detached from reality and now in some way

[50] 'Three Artists', *NS*, 30 June 1917, 304.
[51] 'War Pictures and the War Museum', *NS*, 20 Apr. 1918, 53.

inexpressibly exposed and forlorn, as if inhabited by ghosts of purposeless rich people driven in phantom automobiles on endless circles.

(*FDF* 294)

'Even the landscape appeared still to have an obsequious and subservient air', he wrote, '... like a box of toys set out with glittering and the most expensive neatness—for whom?' (*FDF* 294). Not for the *poilu*. In his quiet, understated way, he was almost as horrified by this moneyed landscape, choreographed by the 'sentiment of ownership' he had excoriated in *Painting in the Far East*, as he was by the devastated landscapes of the Front, as if they were, ultimately, part of the same process.

Returning to London in early June, Binyon spent most of his spare time researching and writing the Red Cross fundraising book from which this and the other passages come, *For Dauntless France*, brief excerpts from which appeared in *The Times* as a Bastille Day 'Homage to France'.[52] Despite its dry subtitle—*An Account of Britain's Aid to the French Wounded and Victims of the War, Compiled for the British Red Cross Societies and the British Committee of the French Red Cross by Laurence Binyon*—this ranks with 'For the Fallen' and 'Fetching the Wounded' as Binyon's major contribution to the non-combatant literature of the Great War. Opening with a dedicatory poem to 'France, dear to men that honour human things' and a panoramic aerial view of the Western Front reminiscent of Hardy's *The Dynasts* and closing with a statistical index and lists, its 372 pages encompass many of the documentary and literary modes in between. It carries its weight of detail lightly, and manages in a way characteristic of Binyon to be both self-effacing and profoundly personal. It has, inevitably, a literary substructure, surfacing in symbols like the lone soldier at Verdun and, recurring through Binyon's springtime journey, the fruit-trees, emblems both of the brevity of human life and its endless capacity for rebirth. The last hospital he describes in *For Dauntless France* is a maternity hospital at Châlons, close to the Front and often under bombardment. Faced with this surreal interface between life and death, his prose modulates into ritual cadences:

> There, was nothing but ends; here, all was beginning.
> There, was shattering mechanism; here, was growing life.

[52] *The Times*, 14 July 1917, 9.

I seemed to see, out of all this blood, and all these tears, young France
re-risen.

(*FDF* 311)

Ricketts designed the dust jacket, while Dulac and other artist
friends donated illustrations, including a stark image of shattered
trees at Fresnes by Rothenstein, now an official War Artist. When
Rothenstein called it a 'beautiful' book, 'one of the fine books of the
war', however, he was referring neither to its pictures nor its prose
but its humanity.[53]

By 1917 'For the Fallen' had become a widely loved poem,
appearing on postcards and in an elaborate volume whose mistily
symbolic illustrations made it a war memorial in book form.[54]
Elgar finished setting 'The Fourth of August' in June 1917, and
the completed *Spirit of England* was performed at the Royal
Albert Hall on 24 November,[55] by which date it must have
seemed to Binyon a requiem not only for those fallen in battle
but also for older friends and contemporaries who had died
during the war, as if infected by its poison. Verhaeren had been
killed in an accident at Rouen station on 27 November 1916, days
after sending Binyon his latest book inscribed 'au très cher Binyon
avec mon admiration vive'. Binyon mourned his death in the *TLS*
ten days later.[56] Petrucci, whom Binyon saw both in Paris and Arc
during the war, died in Paris after an operation in June 1917, worn
out by his work in an ambulance corps at La Panne. The essay on
mandalas Petrucci had been writing for Stein's *Serindia* was sent to
Binyon and Waley for completion by Chavannes, who himself died
months later.

Among Binyon's friends at the Front were several writers, including Wyndham Lewis, whose commission papers he had signed,[57]
and Frederic Manning, the young Australian Galton had brought
back from Sydney in 1897. In 1916 he had received from Isaac
Rosenberg what would become one of the most famous letters of
the Great War:

[53] ALs, 4 Sept. 1918.
[54] *For the Fallen and Other Poems* (London, 1917). See Brian Murdoch, *Fighting
Songs and Warring Words: Popular Lyrics of Two World Wars* (London, 1990),
56–8.
[55] See Ernest Newman, 'Elgar's "Fourth of August" ', *Musical Times*, 1 July 1917,
295–7.
[56] 'Verhaeren', *TLS*, 7 Dec. 1916, 584.
[57] See *Pound/Lewis Letters*, 84–5; LB, 'What is Art?', 93.

I am determined that this war, with all its powers for devastation, shall not master my poeting. . . . I will not leave a corner of my consciousness covered up, but saturate myself with the strange and extraordinary new conditions of this life, and it will all refine itself into poetry later on.[58]

A war poet Binyon had never met, Siegfried Sassoon, wrote to him from the Denmark Hill hospital in May 1917 about his elegiac poem 'The English Youth':

I am not writing to you as a 'regular reader' of your poetry. But your poem on 'The English Youth' is so beautiful, & so true that I cannot deny myself the pleasure of writing to thank you for it. It is a most noble poem.

I wish that those, who, like myself, have had their full share of the 'loathed business', could also say that 'blessed are our eyes because they have seen'—But it is not so. For us it is mostly boredom & stark horror & fear.[59]

By February 1918 and the publication of his third book of war verse, *The Cause*, Binyon's London life had changed out of all recognition. The Print Room and Gallery were occupied by the Registry of Friendly Societies, leaving the curatorial staff cooped up in the offices on the mezzanine floor below. Binyon's skilled mounter, Stanley Littlejohn, had been killed in action in September 1917.[60] The erosion of Binyon's late Victorian Museum world was symbolized by the demise of the Vienna Café, which had closed when the Austrian owner and several of his waiters were interned. As Pound would write,

> the loss of that cafe
> meant the end of a B. M. era
> (British Museum era).

Back home, Belgrave Road had 'lost some of its dismal aura of respectability' now the houses opposite had become soldiers' hostels and canteens. Lance Corporal Binyon was a trained machine gunner, manning a Lewis gun alternately at Holland Park and Woolwich, scanning the skies 'in the distant hope of a chance of firing on Bosche raiders'. At Woolwich, he told Gordon Bottomley,

we have a hut on the river bank in the most sinister & deserted landscape; steamers going by on the tide, mysterious lights, old jetties, the amazing

---

[58] Qtd. in LB, Introductory Memoir, *Rosenberg*, 38.
[59] 8 May [1917].
[60] See LB and Sidney Colvin, 'The Late Stanley William Littlejohn', *BM*, 32 (Jan. 1918), 16–19.

labyrinth of the Arsenal—buildings full of cordite close by with a moat around them—a wonderful scene altogether, suggesting the last chapter of a detective story.[61]

In May he told Freer he was considering joining the Army as a volunteer machine gunner.[62] After the breaking of the Hindenburg line in late September he was sent to France in mid-October to join the Allied forces for the final push against the crumbling German armies, ironically not to fight but to lecture to British and American troops on, of all things, Chinese civilization. Being up in 'the liberated country' was, he told Cicely, 'very wonderful and *emotionnant*',[63] but his poems of these weeks are elegiac, focusing on the devastated natural, urban, and human landscapes of the Arras Road, mourning the dead strewn in the wasteland of 'Heaped mud, blear pools, old rusted wire' (CPi.247). In the ravaged French town of Cambrai, liberated by British troops nine days earlier, 'the one human sound | In the silence' was the melancholy song of a Chinese labourer working among the ruins, a moment captured in his poem 'An Incident at Cambrai', where, remembering Pound's *Cathay* and Waley's translations, he imagined the song to be one of the ancient Chinese elegiac poems lamenting 'The desolation of Han', the distilled sorrow of war in all eras and all countries (CPi.248–9).

In the moment of 'victory', the longed-for end of the carnage, all thought was for the dead. He wrote in 'The Arras Road': 'I think not on the battles won; | I think on those whose day is done' (CPi.247). The Chinese dirge might well have been for Cicely's brother Dick, who died at La Basée, and Calderon, killed at Gallipoli, both in spring 1915, and for Rosenberg, killed in action in April 1918, having, as Binyon later wrote, 'endured the inhuman horror of modern war with a great heart'.[64] When John Bateson, son of Binyon's close friend William Bateson, the great Cambridge geneticist who shared his passion for Blake and Chinese art, was killed within days of the Armistice, his mother wrote to Cicely about the comfort they derived from Binyon's poems: 'I think we both feel a sort of humility of gratitude to him for having written them.'[65] Another man who felt this was Kipling, whose only son had died at Loos in 1915. In 1919 he recommended that the 'For

---

[61] ALs, 22 Apr. 1918 [CMB transcript].   [62] ALs, 6 May 1918, Smithsonian.
[63] ALs, 18 Oct. [1918].   [64] LB, Introductory Memoir, Rosenberg, 11.
[65] Beatrice Bateson, ALs, 1 Nov. 1918.

the Fallen' quatrain be inscribed on Lutyens's Cenotaph in White-
hall, writing to Sir Frederick Kenyon: 'Immeasurably above all
stands Binyon's quatrain. . . . It is written in the heart.'[66] The two
men had never met and Binyon was no admirer of Kipling's imperialism, but a few days later they met by chance at the home of
Lady Sophy Hall, who recalled the scene years later:

Mr. Kipling did not speak but on hearing Laurence Binyon's name walked
quickly up to him, put his arm through his and walked away with him to
a distant part of the garden, where they remained together for a long time
in earnest conversation. We could see that Mr. Kipling was suffering from
great emotion—it was a hallowed moment for the great man of letters who
had lost his only son in the war to be brought face to face with the poet
whose lines 'For the Fallen' he thought the most beautiful expression of
sorrow in the English language.[67]

Kipling told Binyon that when a soldier at the Front sent him the
poem shortly after his son's death in 1915, it had 'cut him to the
heart'. He had thought the lines 'were old,—something classic,—
"and then I realized they were just It." '[68]

It was symbolic that when Binyon sent Elgar a draft of his 'Peace'
ode during the last days of the war, the composer replied:

I think your poem beautiful exceedingly—but I do not feel drawn to write
peace music somehow—I thought long months ago that I could feel that
way & if anything could draw me your poem would, but the whole
atmosphere is too full of complexities for me to feel music to it: not the
atmosphere of the poem but of the time I mean.[69]

Although Binyon the man may not have realized it, Binyon the poet
felt the same way. 'Peace' falls far short of 'For the Fallen', lacking
its tragic dimension, the elegiac lyricism Binyon shared with Elgar,
who now distilled it in chamber music and his Cello Concerto.
Gosse spoke for many when he told Binyon that during the war he
had 'been the real national Laureate',[70] but if so he was the Laureate of the nation's grief, not its peace.

[66] Qtd. in ALs, Kenyon to LB, 13 Aug. 1919.
[67] 'Dr. Laurence Binyon', letter, *The Times*, 18 Mar. 1943, 7.
[68] ALs from LB to CMB describing the event, 17 Aug. 1919.
[69] ALs, 5 Nov. 1918, qtd. in Kennedy 277.   [70] ALs, 2 Dec. 1918.

10   Sirens in the Waste Land

INDIAN ART

In August 1919 the Binyon family moved into one of the houses in the East Wing of the Museum overlooking Montague Street. These five-storey houses were normally reserved for Keepers, but since Dodgson preferred his own Montagu Square residence Binyon gratefully accepted the rent-free Museum house. He was now really 'Binyon of Bloomsbury', as *Punch* dubbed him in a 1923 cartoon,[1] and the Museum became in every sense the centre of his world.

Binyon's life during the 1920s was hectic but immensely productive. In addition to his day-to-day work at the Museum he continued to write and lecture widely on Oriental art. His work on British art included *The Engraved Designs of William Blake* (1926) and *The Followers of William Blake* (1925), an influential introduction to the work of Calvert, Palmer, and the visionary school, and in 1927 he helped organize and write the catalogue for the Blake Centenary Exhibition. More reluctantly, he turned anthologist to edit the *Golden Treasury of Modern Lyrics* (1924) and the *Golden Treasury* Book Five (1926). Lectures, literary reviews, and other articles ate further into his time, as did his work for the Academic Committee of the Royal Society of Literature, but throughout the decade he worked dedicatedly at poetry and verse drama and embarked on a *terza rima* translation of Dante that would take the rest of his life.

Honours began to roll in, starting in May 1921 with an honorary doctorate from Glasgow University. 'Is this the beginning of the end? Being laid on a respectable shelf?' he asked Bottomley. 'Do I look like a Doctor of Laws?'[2] In his speech the Dean described him as 'a poet of world-wide influence',[3] a wild exaggeration but one which was nearer the truth than it had been before or would be again. As Kipling had prophesied, 'For the Fallen' had become

---

[1] 'Curiosities of Literature', *Punch*, 14 Nov. 1923, 464.
[2] ALs, 10 May 1921 [CMB transcript].
[3] LB to CMB, ALs, n.d. [May 1921].

enshrined in post-war national culture. Its central quatrain was carved on thousands of gravestones and cenotaphs, and from the early 1920s it became an integral part of the British Legion's annual Festival of Remembrance and other Armistice Day ceremonies and services throughout Britain. In itself non-Christian, it was incorporated in a liturgical rite, intoned like a prayer, with the line 'We will remember them' repeated by the congregation, just before the two-minute silence for the dead.

As the 1920s wore on, however, Binyon felt that outside the ritual confines of Remembrance Sunday the fallen were not being remembered in the way his 1914 poem had pledged. He had assumed that a catastrophe as great as the war would radically reshape the priorities of whatever peacetime government emerged, but as post-war Britain looked less and less like becoming a land fit for heroes, he began to feel that the appalling loss of life had been rendered meaningless. In an essay for the seventh anniversary of the Armistice he wrote:

Our time is disheartened because the sense of failure is on the world's conscience. Is all that immense sacrifice in the war, vivid to each of us personally in the image of someone lost out of our lives, but in its full immensity quite beyond power of any imagination really to conceive, to go for nothing or worse than nothing? The thought is unbearable, and stirs a longing for action.[4]

'O you dear Dead, pardon!' he had pleaded in 'Wingless Victory', published in the *Observer* on 11 July 1920:

> Worms feed upon the bodies of the brave
> Who bled for us: but we bewildered see
> Viler worms gnaw the things they died to save.
>
> .   .   .   .
>   . . . old greeds unconfined
> Possess men, sick at battle's blood hot-spent
> Yet sleek and busy and righteously content
> To wage war, safe and secret, on their kind.
>   (CPi.255)

While Cicely Binyon was an active member of the Women's International League for Peace and Freedom, founded in London in 1915, taking her daughters on peace marches, Binyon sympathized with the peace movement without being himself a pacifist. He

---

[4] 'The Revolt of Reason', *St Martin's Review*, Nov. 1925, 566.

saw the root problem as being the inherently predatory nature of the Western industrialized nations, whose commercial activities were 'but a less candid kind of war, which after all is only the brutal outward sign of the hidden greeds within us, producing the horrors of peace'.[5] Poverty, unemployment, inadequate housing and education at home were matched by continued exploitation abroad.

All Binyon's post-war work, spread over an impressive range of fields, is best seen as his quiet response to the moral and spiritual crisis in European civilization, which he felt as keenly as Eliot, though his response was different. His hopes lay with the people. The courage and endurance displayed by combatants and non-combatants on both sides of the conflict reinforced his conviction that, whatever mischief 'those idols called States and Governments' got up to, ordinary men and women worldwide preserved a 'vast reservoir of good-will, of devotion, of courage'.[6] Thus, in pursuit of his ideal of a common culture, one of his major concerns was to try to keep the arts in the realm of public discourse rather than allow them to shrink into a rootless subculture accessible only to an educated, socially privileged élite served by an equally élitist, inspeak-ridden criticism. He was only geographically 'Binyon of Bloomsbury'.

Moreover, after the first *world* war, in which Indians had died alongside Englishmen, Arabs alongside Frenchmen, it was even more imperative that the West shed its Eurocentrism and begin to feel part of one world, sharing aims and interests with its fellow inhabitants of a fragile planet. Binyon put his trust in art as the best medium of intercultural understanding. He was convinced, as he told an Indian audience in 1929, that 'the art of a race is a very sure index of what that race has most deeply felt about life and imagined about the universe'.[7] Through books, articles, lectures, and exhibitions he continued to make Asian art accessible to as wide an audience as possible. When the Civil Service 'interlopers' finally vacated the Students Room and Gallery in 1920, he mounted a major exhibition of Japanese prints, the first in a series of five winter shows illustrating in detail the history of the genre. In 1923 his twenty years' work on *ukiyo-e* culminated in the classic

---

[5] 'the Revolt of Reason', *St Martin's Review*, Nov. 1925, 566.   [6] Ibid.
[7] 'Indian Art and Literature: Mr. Laurence Binyon's Address at the Oxford Majlis Dinner', *Bharat*, 14 (Trinity term 1929), 4.

Japanese Colour Prints. His continuing research in Chinese and Japanese art was embodied in the revised third edition of *Painting in the Far East* (1923), *Chinese Art in English Collections* (1927), and other books.

These years also saw a broadening of his interests in Asian art, most notably in Persian and Indian painting. His interest in Persian culture dated back to 1890 and a chance meeting in Wales with an Indian Muslim, Mahomed Shah Din, who introduced him to Persian and Hindustani poetry. In the 1890s he began to admire the flat patterns and vibrant, jewel-like decorative colour of the Persian miniatures he found in the Print Room and in the collections of friends such as Ricketts and Shannon, Goloubew, Koechlin, and Migeon. He never claimed to be a Persian art expert, but he did much to broaden the base of appreciation for this unfamiliar art through Print Room exhibitions, lectures, articles, and books. Among his more important studies were *The Poems of Nizami* (1928), an annotated reproduction of the Museum's sixteenth-century illustrated manuscript of Nizami's *Khamsa* and, in collaboration with J. V. S. Wilkinson, *The Shāh-nāmah of Firdausī* (1931).[8]

Binyon's interest in Indian culture had, of course, even older roots. Ghose had been appointed to a professorship at Presidency College, Calcutta, in 1903, but soon afterwards mysteriously stopped corresponding. He wrote one sad letter in 1916 describing his 'utter friendlessness', but it was not until years later that Binyon heard the full story of his wife's sudden paralysis in 1905 and the way his career had been blighted by his brothers' anti-British activities.[9] After his wife's death in 1918, he planned to return to England on his retirement. He even booked his passage for March 1924, but died two months before sailing, still only 54, his last words 'I want to rest in peace. I long for the beautiful.'[10] Binyon heard all this from Ghose's daughter Lotika, who visited England in 1924 to show him her father's manuscripts. He made a selection and had them published as *Songs of Love and Death*, prefaced by his poignant memoir, by Blackwells of Oxford, who had published *Primavera* in happier days.

---

[8] For an appreciation of LB's work on Persian art, see Basil Gray, 'In Memoriam: Laurence Binyon', *Ars Islamica*, 11–12 (1946), 207–9.

[9] See Lotika Ghose, *Manmohan Ghose* (New Delhi, 1975), 37–8.

[10] Lotika Ghose, *Ghose*, 53–4; LB, MG 20.

'To know personally a man like Mᵣ Binyon I consider one of the greatest honours that can befall anyone,' Lotika Ghose later wrote to Cicely. 'I have never before met such simplicity and nobility coupled with such greatness.'[11] This is how Binyon himself felt about another Bengali poet, Rabindranath Tagore. He had heard about Tagore from Ghose as early as 1897 but they first met at Rothenstein's house in June 1912, on the trip to England which led to the publication of *Gitanjali*, Tagore's 1913 Nobel Prize, and his meteoric rise to world fame. Binyon was struck by his 'inward serenity', even among the 'jostling straphanging London crowd' as they went home by tube, and was captivated by his melodic chanting of his own Bengali lyrics, full of rhythmic expressiveness and 'rippling lightness of movement'.[12] In 1940, long after Tagore had fallen out of fashion in the West, Binyon still considered him 'the greatest poet now living in the world'.[13]

To Binyon and friends interested in Indian art it was a scandal that despite India being the jewel in Britain's imperial crown its art was the last of the major arts of Asia to achieve recognition. The Victorian–Edwardian view, moulded by colonialist prejudice, was that although India produced superlative handicrafts it had never aspired to fine art. It was to rectify this situation that the India Society was established in 1910, with Rothenstein and Binyon among its founder members. One of Binyon's friends in the Society was the Ceylonese art historian and philosopher Ananda Coomaraswamy, a key figure in the wider acceptance of Indian art in the West during these crucial years. They shared among other things a love of Blake, having arrived independently at the view that of all European artists he was the closest in spirit to Asian art and thought. As an Indian nationalist and conscientious objector, Coomaraswamy came under suspicion in wartime England and in order to obtain permission to leave for the United States in 1916 he turned to Binyon, the most unimpeachable of his friends, who assured the authorities that 'Dr. Coomaraswamy has rendered services of the greatest value to the world by his pioneer work which has done much to promote a truer understanding between

[11] ALs, 4 Aug. 1926.
[12] LB, speech at Rabindranath Tagore Memorial Meeting at the India Society in 1941, *Indian Art and Letters*, NS, 15/2 (1941), 59.
[13] 'Homage to India', *Indian Art and Letters*, NS, 14/2 (1940), 112.

India and the West.'[14] In 1917 he became the first Curator of Indian Art at the Boston Museum of Fine Arts.

The Museum owned a fine collection of Mughal miniatures, and Binyon's admiration for this Persian-influenced Indian art form found expression in *The Court Painters of the Grand Moghuls* (1921). The beautiful paintings of the Rajput schools which flourished in the minor princely courts of Rajasthan and the Punjab hills from the sixteenth to the nineteenth centuries, however, were almost unknown in England until 1910 when Coomaraswamy returned from India with a fine collection of paintings and missionary zeal for making them known, most fully in his two-volume *Rajput Painting* (1916). 'These miniatures were a revelation, with their sensitive, delicate line and their lyrical feeling,' Binyon recalled. 'They had a kind of radiance which charmed at once.'[15] From the lyrical, erotically charged paintings of the Krishna cycle to the exquisite *ragamala* paintings, which evoke through colour, typology, and symbolic gesture the atmosphere of the modes of Indian music, Rajput art helped make Indian culture more widely accessible. From 1912 Binyon set about building a collection for the Museum, including some acquired from Coomaraswamy, and mounted and wrote guides for a series of important exhibitions.

With the older forms of Indian painting, however, things took longer. Binyon longed to visit India, aware that his lack of firsthand experience of Asia was a particular handicap here, for the greatest Indian art needs to be seen *in situ*. The Amaravati reliefs and other Indian sculpture in the British and Victoria and Albert Museums conveyed little idea of the enormous power such works generate in their original setting, as Rothenstein discovered on his trip to India in 1910,[16] and as anyone who has visited Ellora, Elephanta, Mamallapuram, and other great sites can testify. The four editions of *Painting in the Far East* chart Binyon's gradual awakening to the genius of classical Indian art and the grandeur of Indian spirituality, especially in its Mahayana Buddhist phase exemplified by the frescoes in the Ajanta 'Caves', thirty Buddhist temples and meditation halls, dating from the first century BC to the seventh century CE, cut into the rocky sides of a remote crescent-shaped gorge in Western

[14] Qtd. in Roger Lipsey, *Coomaraswamy*, 3 vols. (Princeton, 1977), iii. 123–4.
[15] 'Tributes to Abanindranath Tagore', *Visva-Bharati Quarterly*, May–Oct. 1942, 2–3.
[16] See Rothenstein, *Men and Memories*, ii. 228–53.

India. Encountering them first in oil copies made by John Griffiths during 1875 and 1885, Binyon found the designs 'crowded and incoherent' in the 1908 edition of *Painting in the Far East* (36). He persuaded the artist Christiana Herringham to go to Ajanta in the winters of 1906/7, 1909/10 and 1910/11, and the full-scale copies she and her assistants made were exhibited at the Crystal Palace in 1912, and reproduced in an annotated portfolio published by the India Society with essays by Binyon and Rothenstein.[17] Another friend, the young Bengali artist Mukul Dey, also copied some of the frescoes for him. However, the full power of Ajantan art was not revealed until a complete colour and monochrome photographic record of the frescoes was published with an introduction by Binyon in 1930. By now he had realized that the unity he had found lacking in these teeming frescoes in 1908 must be sought in their deep structures:

The unity attained is not so much like the decorative unity we are accustomed to expect in works of pictorial art, as like the deep congruity we find in nature, the continuity of relation between the hills and the trees and the flowers, the shadows and the light: it satisfies in the same large and silent way. . . . Man is seen in the midst of nature, not using her as something vanquished and subservient to his needs and pleasures, but emerging among those kindred forms of life as the most eloquent form she has created. The more the mind steeps itself in this art, the more it is aware of the profound conception of the unity of all life which pervades it.[18]

Here was an art which fulfilled everything Binyon had desired in his 1903–4 letters to Cicely, a paradisal vision of life before 'the disastrous division into sacred and profane'.[19] 'The secret of this art', he wrote in 1915, 'is a deep recognition of the spiritual element in man, conceived not as an essence apart, to be cloistered and protected from the material world, but as something pervading and refining all the actions and events in which men and women take part.'[20] This humane, mature spirituality found its profoundest expression in the figure of the *bodhisattva* Padmapani in Cave 1,

[17] See Christiana Herringham, 'The Frescoes of Ajanta', *BM*, 17/87 (June 1910), 136–8; Sir Wilmot Herringham, 'The Expedition', *Ajanta Frescoes* (London, 1915), 16.

[18] Introduction, *Ajanta: The Colour and Monochrome Reproductions of the Ajanta Frescoes Based on Photography*, by G. Yazdani, 8 vols. (London, 1930), i. p. xii.

[19] ALs, 10 Jan. [1904].

[20] 'Indian Art', *Quarterly Review*, 443 (Apr. 1915), 516.

which he described as 'one of the greatest creations in the art of the world' (*PFE* 40).[21]

Binyon had both Ajantan and Rajput art on his mind shortly before the Armistice in November 1918 when he met another Bengali, Kedar Nath Das Gupta, friend of Tagore and charismatic organizer of the Union of the East and West, established to foster East–West understanding through art, philosophy, music, and drama. Das Gupta wanted to arrange a London production of Kalidasa's fifth-century poetic drama *Sakuntala*, the apogee of classical Sanskrit drama and one of the world's great works of literature. He had abridged the text for performance and made a rough English translation, and Binyon agreed to rewrite it for the English stage. Based on a minor episode in the vast Sanskrit epic, the *Mahabharata*, *Sakuntala* explores the nature of human love through the story of King Dushyanta and Sakuntala, their courtship, marriage, separation and, thanks to the gods, eventual reunion.[22] Binyon found constant analogies between the play and the contemporary Ajanta frescoes, 'the same pervading tenderness of feeling, the same spirituality, undetached from a deep sensuous enjoyment', the same seamless interweave of sacred and quotidian:

We are transported to a world in which men and women are not enclosed and engrossed in their humanity. There is no separation of human life from the life above it and the life below it. Gods, spirits, demons, animals, birds, trees, flowers and streams; these all share in the one living whole.

This was, he added, 'an attitude to the universe' that 'we may some day learn to imitate'.[23]

Staged without scenery and relying heavily on the audience's imagination, classical Sanskrit drama was theatre after Binyon's own heart. He commissioned Rothenstein to create three symbolic screens or curtains based on Rajput paintings, but as he was still on Official War Artist duty in Belgium his drawings were delayed and the design was entrusted to Bruce Winston. Produced by Lewis Casson, with Sybil Thorndike as Sakuntala and Arthur Wontner as King Dushyanta, *Sakuntala* was performed under the auspices of

[21] Reproduced in *The Arts of India*, ed. Basil Gray (Oxford, 1981), 25.

[22] See LB, *Sakuntala: By Kalidasa, Prepared for the English Stage by Kedar Nath Das Gupta in a New Version Written by Laurence Binyon* (London, 1920).

[23] LB, 'Kalidasa and the Sanskrit Drama', *Shakuntala or The Lost Ring: An Indian Drama Translated into English Prose and Verse by Sir Monier Monier-Williams* (London, 1929), 8, 12.

the Indian Art and Dramatic Society for two matinées on 14 and 21 November 1919 at the Winter Garden Theatre, Drury Lane. Warmly received by the Aga Khan, the Maharaja of Baroda, and a cosmopolitan full house, it was a great success. Ricketts found it 'enchanting' and told Binyon it had 'interested him more than anything he had seen in the theatre for a long time'.[24] In a further attempt to make Indian drama better known, the text was published in 1920 with an introduction by Tagore.

The Indian writer Ranjee G. Shahani thought Binyon's version 'excellent', conveying 'the ecstasy of love with consummate art'. Shahani was writing in 1947, the year of India's independence, an event Binyon would have loved to have lived to see. He remembered Binyon with great affection as one of India's 'real friends—one who tried to interpret our thought and feeling without any prejudice or postjudices', with 'a deep insight into our spiritual make-up'. He recalled Binyon once saying to him:

The cosmic energy that India holds is immeasurable. She will soon startle the world. . . . There is more poetry, mystery, and vision in the Vedas and the Upanishads than in any other books. Shakespeare, had he known them, would have adored them.[25]

'I hope to visit India before I die,' Binyon told the members of the Majlis, the Oxford University India Society, in 1929, concluding his guest-of-honour speech with a typical and revealing trope:

India is in my mind like a great mountain seen from far away. I know that if I came near to it, if I explored its valleys and recesses, it would yield riches of comprehension and knowledge, from which distance shuts me out. Yet I know that there are streams flowing past me which have their springs in that far mountain, and if I know it only by its majestic outline on the sky, still remote and ignorant, I am conscious of its presence, and salute it with veneration.[26]

ARTHUR

While working on *Sakuntala* in 1919, Binyon was exploring a darker love story in his verse drama *Arthur: A Tragedy*, set in a

---

[24] LB to Bottomley, ALs, Jan. 1920 [CMB transcript]. See '"Sakuntala": Worthy Performance of a Great Play', *The Times*, 15 Nov. 1919, 14; *Era*, 19 Nov. 1919, 6.
[25] 'Some British I Admire: VII, Laurence Binyon', *Asiatic Review*, NS, 43 (Jan. 1947), 93–4.
[26] 'Art and Literature', 4, 7.

1. Edmund Dulac, caricature of Laurence Binyon after a kabuki actor print by the *ukiyo-e* artist Sharaku, watercolour, 24 x 17 cm, *c.* 1912. 'BM' in the *mon* crest on LB's kimono stands for 'British Museum' (see p. 70).

2. (*above*) Kitagawa Utamaro, *Colours and Scents of Flowers of the Four Seasons*, woodblock (diptych print), 37.5 × 25 cm each, *c.* 1784 (see p. 84).

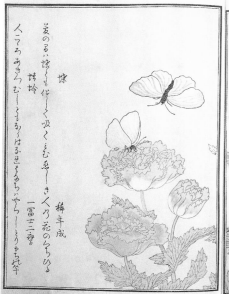

3. (*above*) Kitagawa Utamaro, 'Dragonfly, Butterflies and Poppies' from *Ehon Mushi Erabi*, woodblock with mica and gauffrage, 18.5 x 27.1 cm, 1788 (see p. 73).

4. (*left*) *Rabbits and Autumn Grasses* (detail), 6-fold screen, ink, colours and gold leaf on paper, 154 x 327 cm, Rimpa School, 18th century (see p. 266).

5. Sesshū, *Haboku Landscape* (detail), hanging scroll, ink on paper, 149 x 33 cm, dated 1495 (see p. 183).

world where no benign gods intervene. The *Arthur* project dated back to 1912 when, at the pinnacle of his career as Oedipus in Max Reinhardt's famous Covent Garden Opera House production of *Oedipus Rex*, the great romantic actor John Martin-Harvey conceived the idea of a drama based on Malory's *Morte d'Arthur* performed on the same scale in the same theatre:

What would be more glorious than to produce a play on the great British theme of Arthur, written by a British poet, in settings by a British artist, in the foremost British theatre? Laurence Binyon for the poet, my old friend Professor Robert Anning Bell for the designer, and Covent Garden Opera House for the production![27]

Although he had reservations about tackling 'so pawed over & "stock" a subject',[28] the project chimed with Binyon's wish to see drama, poetry, and the visual arts reinterpreting the nation's rich historical and mythological heritage. In *Painting in the Far East* he argued that in groping for a shallow, amnesiac 'originality', modern European artists were actually less free than the traditional Asian artist, whose 'subject belongs to his race, and therefore to mankind. It partakes of the universal; it has been sifted by the choice of many generations; it has struck root in the imagination of a people' (*PFE* 150). What British myth fits this description better than the Arthurian cycle?

The war intervened before the project got fully under way, but Binyon worked on the play intermittently during the war, occasionally spending weekends with Martin-Harvey and his wife Nina de Silva at their cottage in Bonchurch on the Isle of Wight. The Covent Garden project was revived soon after the Armistice. Reading Binyon's play in July 1919, Martin-Harvey, now 56, decided to play Arthur rather than Launcelot and the play was partially rewritten to focus on the King. The result was a play in nine scenes dramatizing the final tragic collapse of the Arthurian world, from Elaine's fatal love for Launcelot to Guenevere's retirement to Amesbury and the climactic battle between Arthur and Mordred.

The Covent Garden production was scheduled to open in December 1919. Anning Bell designed sets and costumes, which were executed by a large staff at the Opera House. When Nina de Silva told Binyon they were 'going Nap on the play',[29] she was not

[27] *The Autobiography of Sir John Martin-Harvey* (London, 1933), 494.
[28] ALs to Gordon Bottomley, 22 Apr. 1918.
[29] LB to CMB, ALs, 9 Aug. 1919.

exaggerating: Martin-Harvey spent £1,600 on costumes alone. Robert Loraine was engaged to play Launcelot, thus bringing together two of the most charismatic actors of their generation. Loraine had also distinguished himself as an air ace during the war, however, and this proved the production's undoing. At the last moment his war-weakened health broke down, his doctor insisted he take a long sea voyage to recuperate, and *Arthur* was hastily replaced by a revival of Martin-Harvey's famous *Hamlet*. 'The postponement of *Arthur* was a great disappointment to us all,' Martin-Harvey recalled in 1933, but despite his admiration for and huge investment in Binyon's play, *Arthur* was never staged as he had envisaged it. The last great actor–manager in the Irving tradition, his grandiose plans for *Arthur* had been designed for the opulent, unashamedly spectacular pre-war theatre, conceived on an Irving–Tree–Reinhardt scale. By the 1920s this form of epic pictorial theatre had migrated to its true home, Hollywood, and the *Arthur* project died under its own weight. Binyon was disappointed but his regret was tempered by recognition that Martin-Harvey's proposed treatment ran counter to his own theatrical aesthetic and indeed the play itself, for *Arthur* is the antithesis of such grandly rhetorical drama. It is more intimately scaled, its language deliberately non-operatic, an austere idiom stripped of Tennysonian glamour. When Arthur confronts the adulterous Guenevere we get not passionate arias of blame and regret but a language bleakly beyond emotion:

GUENEVERE.   I am past tears. All I have done and been,
Been and endured, I see from far away,
As if another in my shape were there
Moving through storm and fire.—Have you no word,
No reproach for me?
ARTHUR.   All my thoughts are stript
As trees after the tempest, and life's bare
As winter to the homeless.[30]

The verse is already elegiac, anticipating the battle to come and, subtextually, reliving those just ended. These final scenes were written during and immediately after the Great War, and Malory's grief at the destruction of the Arthurian world merges with that of 'For the Fallen', grief for 'the young men | . . . fallen in their blood'

[30] *Arthur: A Tragedy* (London, 1923), 113–14.

in an even more apocalyptic, epoch-ending conflict.[31] In the final scene at Amesbury, where the convent has become a hospital as crowded as Arc during Verdun, Binyon drew on his own experiences:

> Cloister and ante-chapel both are filled;
> And still they bring them in, dying and dead.
> Never was seen such a slaughter in the world[32]

The 'grieving' convent bell tolls for the fallen in both wars. A chivalric, patriotic text when Martin-Harvey envisioned it in 1912, by 1919 in Binyon's hands *Arthur* had become an implicit elegy for another lost generation of English youth.

Various attempts were made to stage *Arthur*. Henry Ainley was interested, and there were moves to produce it in New York, but in March 1923 it found its predestined home in the theatre at the opposite end of the spectrum from the splendours of Covent Garden, Lilian Baylis's Old Vic among the pubs, cafés, and cheap boarding houses of the Waterloo Road. 'It really is the *only* theatre!' Binyon enthused when Robert Atkins told him he wanted to produce *Arthur*,[33] and indeed it was, with an eager cast skilled in the ensemble playing of verse drama and the most committed and knowledgeable audience in London. Atkins was in the middle of his five-year career at the Vic, setting new standards in Shakespearean production and trying to establish contemporary verse drama as part of its repertoire. He had staged Bottomley's *Britain's Daughter* months earlier and hoped that *Arthur* would help make it 'the home of modern poetic as well as of classical drama'.[34]

Like everything the Vic did, *Arthur* was a shoestring affair, mounted at a total cost of £15.10s. In fact, this was more in keeping with Binyon's play. As the *Nation* remarked, 'scenic poverty is a great aid to fancy in the right type of mind' with 'a production designed in the mood of creative imagination'.[35] Wilfrid Walter played Arthur, Florence Buckton Guenevere, and Douglas Burbidge Launcelot. Much to everyone's surprise, since he had composed virtually nothing since his wife's death in 1920, Elgar wrote eight

---

[31] *Arthur*, 120. See also Hynes, 392.   [32] *Arthur*, 123.

[33] ALs to CMB, 17 Sept. 1922.

[34] Desmond Mountjoy, 'Laurence Binyon's Arthur', *Old Vic Magazine* 4/6 (Mar. 1923), 2.

[35] D.L.M[ountjoy], 'Round Table and Retort', *Nation and Athenaeum*, 24 Mar. 1923, 964.

interludes and incidental music for the Old Vic production and conducted Charles Corri's tiny orchestra on the first night. Smoking his pipe while fine-tuning the score at rehearsals, Elgar was, Binyon told Percy Withers, 'absolutely charming, & just like a boy'.[36] Together they watched as, despite getting through only half the play at dress-rehearsal, the Old Vic's unique blend of enthusiasm, creativity, and genius for making do conjured order out of chaos in time for *Arthur* to open for its ten-night run on 12 March.

Binyon always remembered that 'glorious' opening night as one of the high points of his career. The Old Vic 'has never seemed more like our National Theatre than it did last night,' the *Express* declared. S. R. Littlewood agreed: 'It was an altogether beautiful, distinguished, memorable, and successful evening, for which the gratitude of a crammed audience went out in full measure to everyone concerned.'[37] No one doubted the success of the occasion and the enthusiasm of the Old Vic *cognoscenti*, who greeted *Arthur* with 'a storm of applause so genuine, so warm-hearted, so unanimous',[38] but opinion was divided on the play itself. E. A. Baughan of the *Daily News* praised Binyon's skilful handling of caesuras, enjambment, and end-stopped lines to create a 'plastic dramatic speech' with the fluency and naturalness of prose while retaining 'the lilt of verse', but the *Daily Telegraph*'s W. L Courtney, while agreeing that the play was 'a fine piece of work, nobly designed and carried out with no little literary skill', none the less felt that *Arthur* was 'a heroic enterprise in which success is nearly won', an austere work that all would respect but few love.[39]

One critic suggested that *Arthur* would have had more theatrical vitality if Binyon had written it 'for the Old Vic. Company even as Shakespeare wrote for his players',[40] and he was undoubtedly right. However, the era of subsidized theatres and resident playwrights was still decades away, and dramatists like Binyon, Bottomley, Moore, and Abercrombie were writing in limbo between the

[36] ALs, 19 Mar. 1923. See Moore, *Elgar*, 762–4.

[37] '"King Arthur": Weighty Production at the Old Vic', *Daily Express*, 13 Mar. 1923, 8; '"Arthur": Mr. Laurence Binyon's Play at the Old Vic', *Pall Mall Gazette*, 13 Mar. 1923, 4.

[38] W. L. Courtney, '*Arthur*: Laurence Binyon's Play', *Daily Telegraph*, 23 Mar. 1923, 17.

[39] '"Arthur": Laurence Binyon's Work at the Old Vic', *Daily News*, 13 Mar. 1923, 5; Courtney, '*Arthur*', 17.

[40] '*Arthur*', *Weekly Westminster Gazette*, 17 Mar. 1923, 15.

commercial 'Theatre Outworn', as Bottomley called it, and the 'Theatre Unborn'.[41] Before a performance of *Everyman* during *Arthur*'s run, Lilian Baylis invited Binyon onto the Old Vic stage to deliver a passionate defence of the theatre as an art of the people. 'Drama cannot be great, nor even fully alive, unless it draws its sap from the deepest springs in the nation of its birth,' he declared. 'We want our drama to be completely representative, to represent the whole nation & not merely a section of it.' Not until the nation recognized the value of drama would 'the theatre take the vital place in our civilization that it should take'.[42] As a founding member of the British Drama League in 1919, a member of its Council and one of the speakers at its inaugural meeting at the Haymarket Theatre on 22 June 1919, Binyon had high hopes for the League's support for the National Theatre campaign and its socially-oriented plans to encourage drama at the grassroots level through schools, trade unions, worker's education authorities, women's institutes, and village drama groups. Given both the reluctance of theatre managers to risk staging contemporary poetic drama and Binyon's interest in amateur theatre, it is not surprising that his next play made its debut in an amateur production.

The Young King dramatizes the struggle for power between Henry II and his son Henry, known as the Young King because the 15-year-old prince had been crowned at Westminster in 1170 to ensure political stability for the Plantagenet regime. Under the influence of the Queen, Eleanor of Aquitaine, he led his brothers in a rebellion against their autocratic father, was defeated, and died of fever in 1183. Binyon saw *The Young King* as a psychological rather than a historical drama, however, and chose the story while seeking a suitable subject for exploring father–son rivalry and 'the antagonism between two generations'.[43] Young Henry hates not only his father but the entire older generation. Entering Anjou after a battle, he declares: 'My quarrel's less with those I That fought, than with the old men that spurred them on I So they might sit safe.'[44] Like *Arthur*, *The Young King*, written between 1919 and 1923, is saturated with echoes of the Great War, in this case the antagonism between the generations it inspired, the hatred of the old home-front warmongers in Sassoon's war poetry, expressed

---

[41] *A Stage for Poetry: My Purposes with My Plays* (Kendal, 1948), 3.
[42] 'Speech at Old Vic', AMS, n.d. [1923], 6 pp., n.pag.
[43] LB, Preface, *The Young King* (London, 1935), n.pag. [44] *Young King*, 43.

most devastatingly in Owen's 'The Parable of the Old Man and the Young'. When young Henry dies, his father mourns that 'the old should bury the young',[45] a line with a deeper resonance in this immediately post-war context, written by a poet who had himself buried countless young men, physically at Arc, symbolically with 'For the Fallen'.

In 1924 Masefield chose *The Young King* to inaugurate the Music Room, a small theatre with seating for 150, fine acoustics, and a split-level stage he had built in the garden of Hill Crest, his house on Boars Hill.[46] Boars Hill had changed considerably in the thirty years since Binyon used to hike up to visit the Woods. By the early 1920s it was home to Masefield, Bridges, Gilbert Murray, the archaeologist Sir Arthur Evans, and the young poets Robert Graves and Robert Nichols. Here *The Young King* played for three nights from 13 November 1924, acted enthusiastically by a cast of experienced amateurs and Boars Hill residents, including the actress Lillah McCarthy, who made a guest appearance as the Prologue, confirming Masefield's view of it as a profound play with 'scenes of very great beauty'.[47]

Lillah McCarthy was not the only major actress in Binyon's circle, for he had a lifelong friend and admirer of his poetry in Sybil Thorndike, who had played the title role in *Sakuntala* and recited a poem Binyon had written to welcome Tagore to England. She inspired him as much as Duse had done years before. After seeing her mesmeric Beatrice in Shelley's *The Cenci* in November 1922, he wrote 'I feel I was born to do dramatic poetry, & I will'.[48] *Sakuntala* was in fact the only play on which they worked together, but this was certainly not for want of trying. In spring 1923, seeking 'some one heroic & resisting' as a vehicle for her unique talents, Binyon chose Joan of Arc, who had been canonized three years earlier. Feeling destined to play Joan, Thorndike commissioned him to write the play. 'He was such a beautiful writer,' she later recalled. 'We had great talks about it.' He was hard at work on the play, which was to focus almost exclusively on Joan's

---

[45] *Young King*, 135.

[46] See Smith, *Masefield*, 186–8; 'A Country House Theatre', *Country Life*, 58 (8 Aug. 1925), 233–4.

[47] 'A Little Theatre at Boars Hill: A House for Poetic Drama: Interview with Mr. John Masefield', *Oxford Chronicle*, 7 Nov. 1924, 13. See also *The Times*, 15 Nov. 1924, 8; *Daily News*, 15 Nov. 1924, 4.

[48] ALs to CMB, n.d. [Nov. 1922].

trial, when he opened his *Observer* on 29 April and read: 'Mr. Bernard Shaw is engaged on a play of Joan of Arc'. Thorndike was equally surprised. The two playwrights reacted in opposite and characteristic ways to the discovery that they were both writing a play on the same subject for the same actress. Shaw was typically combative, booming 'Nonsense! Of course Sybil plays my *Saint Joan*. Let so-and-so do the other one. I warned off Masefield and Drinkwater, but I forgot Binyon.'[49] Binyon just as characteristically withdrew, despite Thorndike urging him to press on, quietly dropping his own play because he felt Shaw would create a better vehicle for her unique talents. After seeing the play, he knew he had been right and wrote to Shaw: 'I am glad to be contemporary with it, and rejoice in its success. I think you have done a great service to the cause of tragedy.'[50]

While Thorndike went on to the triumph of her career in *Saint Joan*, Binyon turned to Boadicea, a warrior queen in the mould of his first heroine, Penthesilea. Thorndike was again keen, but *Boadicea* too made its debut at Boars Hill on a snowy 14 January 1926.[51] Binyon wrote to Lillah McCarthy about the play: 'Ostensibly the subject is remote of course, but the real theme is the problem of Imperialism, & contemporary.'[52] *Boadicea* is about imperialism in both its political and sexual forms. Key scenes in *The Young King* explored Eleanor's frustration at being compelled by a patriarchal culture to act indirectly through her menfolk, and in Boadicea Binyon chose a woman even more loth to sit quiet 'While men grapple for mastery'.[53] In the broader scheme of the play, Boadicea's Britons embody the female principle, imaginative, intuitive, animist, open to the mysteries of earth, in direct opposition to Roman culture, male, ratiocinative, regimented, using its bureaucratic and military technology to exploit natives and nature alike. 'We have to build, and bridge, drive through moor and forest, to make something durable and habitable for men that use their

---

[49] Elizabeth Sprigge, *Sybil Thorndike Casson* (London, 1971), 153–4. See also Michael Holroyd, *Bernard Shaw 1918–1950: The Years of Fantasy* (1991; London, 1993), 79.
[50] ALs, 3 July 1924, Add. MS 50519, fos. 147–8, BL.
[51] See '"Boadicea": Tragedy Produced at Oxford', *The Times*, 16 Jan. 1926, 8; '"Boadicea": Mr. Laurence Binyon's New Play in Verse', *Morning Post*, 16 Jan. 1926, 8.
[52] ALs, 6 Aug. 1934, BL–HRC.
[53] *Boadicea: A Play in Eight Scenes* (London, 1927), 12.

reason and their will,' Seutonius complains, shouldering the white man's burden. 'We need all our time for this: to keep the world going.'[54] Only snow-numbed brains among the Boars Hill audience could have failed to hear contemporary echoes. In contrast to the Britons' blank verse, among themselves the Romans speak in prose, the devious language of imperial *realpolitik*, justifying the empire with sonorous platitudes like 'justice', 'order', and 'discipline'.

Ricketts agreed to design a professional production and Thorndike was eager because she felt that the play 'has things in it that are good to be heard *today*, it's for now as much as in those days'. Persuading a theatre manager to stage it, however, was a different matter. 'I *despair*,' she wrote, 'I ask manager after manager & they say these poetic plays are no use, not human. I point out they're far more human than the bilge we usually have to play.'[55]

Disappointments such as these convinced Binyon that Bottomley was right about the 'Theatre Outworn'. This, and his sympathy with the burgeoning post-war amateur theatre movement, persuaded him in the later 1920s to write several short, experimental one-act verse plays requiring very small casts and little or no scenery. The first of these, *Love in the Desert*, was based on the Arabian story of the tragic lovers Laila and Majnun, the subject of one of the poems in Nizami's *Khamsa* retold by Binyon in *The Poems of Nizami*.[56] Binyon's brief play dramatizes the scene where the love-crazed Majnun comes to Laila's tent and runs away on seeing her. We do not see Majnun, only his effect on Laila. The only other character is Laila's nurse and the only action is the symbolic action of their verse dialogue, in which Laila lyrically explores the nature of love, while the nurse acts as a chorus, narrating and commenting on the action. Freed from the necessities of character and plot, this brief, intense play is drama stripped down to lyrical speech. Written for pairs of verse speakers, it was first performed on 24 July 1928 at the Oxford Recitations. Here, according to Gordon Bottomley, 'it evoked a performance of deep significance to the art of performed poetry, in which the two women suggested

[54] *Boadicea*, 55.
[55] ALs to LB, 22 July 1926; ALs, Thursday, n.d. [1926?].
[56] See *The Poems of Nizami, Described by Laurence Binyon* (London, 1928), 21–7.

setting, story, and personal relationship by plastic groupings which had something of the quality of fine statuary'.[57]

The Oxford Recitations was an annual verse-speaking festival inaugurated by John Masefield in 1923. Held over two, later three, days, these highly successful festivals consisted primarily of verse-speaking contests in various classes in the Oxford University Examination Schools, with recitals by the best speakers on the final evening. The aim was to help free poetry from the straitjacket of print culture and restore it to its ancient origins in living speech and performance; to encourage the unmannered recitation of poetry as an art in its own right; and to create a body of skilled verse speakers to act in poetic dramas. Binyon was involved from the start, one of the five judges in the first festival on 24 and 25 July 1923, when more than 500 competitors came from all over Britain, private individuals and schools as well as more expert entrants like students of the Central School of Speech and Drama at the Albert Hall, founded in 1906 by another friend, Elsie Fogerty, who taught many of the finest actors and actresses in Britain. Judging was arduous work, but Binyon found it 'a really exhilarating experience'.[58] The large audience was 'spellbound', he reported, sitting 'in absolute stillness, enchanted' by great poetry naturally spoken.[59]

He returned every summer and became President of the Festival Committee from 1928. He was himself a masterly reader of poetry. In a *Guardian* interview in 1966, looking back over forty years, the poet and verse-speaking expert Wallace Nichols remembered Binyon as an unselfdramatizing, moving reader of his own poetry, 'much the best poetry reader of any of the poets' he had heard, including Yeats with his 'too chanty . . . half-and-half speech and song'. He continued:

I think of all the poets I've ever met, he was the man of biggest integrity as an artist and as a critic. And I think he was a much better poet than has been admitted. His ode, 'The Syrens,' is surely one of the best odes in the English language.[60]

---

[57] *Stage for Poetry*, 25. See also John Masefield, preface, *The Oxford Recitations* (New York, 1928), 8–9.
[58] ALs to Masefield, 28 July [1923], HRC. See also Masefield, preface, *Oxford Recitations*, 5, and Smith, *Masefield*, 189–91.
[59] LB, 'The Speaking of Verse', *Torchbearer*, 1/1 (June 1924), 21.
[60] Derek Parker, 'Poet of the Theatre', *Guardian*, 3 Aug. 1966, 7.

The latter reference probably had the *Guardian* man puzzled. In 1966 few remembered *The Sirens*. In 1925, however, it had been another story.

SYMPHONIES

Given the paucity of time he could devote to it during the 1920s, it says much that rather than dwindling imperceptibly into the pastime of an all-round man of letters, poetry became if anything even more central to Binyon's life, increasingly essential as his ongoing dialogue with his deepest self. When his old tutor H. E. D. Blakiston, now President of Trinity, wanted to nominate him for the Oxford Professorship of Poetry in 1928, he declined, explaining:

my one consuming desire, which grows on me every day, is to write poetry & not criticism. For twenty years I have nursed in my mind the theme of a magnum opus, which I have never had the leisure seriously to attack. . . . Hence I want to retire from the Museum as soon as I can, before old age or fatigue—or death—overtake me. . . . I'm quite aware that comparatively few people believe in my poetry, & nearly everybody seems to think I should be better employed in doing other things. . . . All the same it is what I live for. I have no other ambitions whatever. And I can't describe how intensely I long to be doing at last the work I want to do.[61]

His first book of post-war poetry, *The Secret* (1920), was the most varied he ever published, ranging from extended meditative lyrics like 'The Secret' and 'Initiation' to 'The Wharf on Thames-Side: Winter Dawn', a pictorial urban study more crisply focused than anything in *London Visions*, and love poems like 'The Dream House' and 'Westward'. He published two other volumes of verse during the 1920s, a book of translations, *Little Poems from the Japanese* (1925), and *The Wonder-Night* (1927), but he invested most of his energy in two long, ambitious poems, *The Sirens* (1924–25) and *The Idols* (1928). Both have the same subtitle: *an Ode*. Since the 1890s the groundswell in modern poetry had been against rhetoric, particularly the grand style epitomized by the ode form, which for most young poets in the 1920s, Georgian, modernist, or otherwise, was a relic of an outmoded literary tradition.

[61] ALs, 22 Oct. 1928, Trinity College Archives.

Binyon was fully aware of the problems, and the risks, involved. In November 1921 he delivered an English Association lecture on 'The English Ode', in which he traced the complex history of the form in British literature. While conceding that 'Rhetoric and abstraction are the peculiar bane of the ode', he nevertheless concluded by suggesting that even today 'great things might yet be done' in 'the heroic ode' on 'a great human theme'.[62]

He was already at work on an ode which would be published three years later as *The Sirens*. In the true Romantic tradition, he was haunted by the idea of writing a great long poem, and had spoken to friends of his desire to get down to a 'big work' after the war. Although he had served his poetic apprenticeship in the symbolist 1890s, he had continued to admire the larger rhetorical forms of poetry. Theodore Maynard had already detected in Binyon's poetry a 'persistent odic quality' rare in this age 'of small things exquisitely done', which he traced to an equally atavistic vatic strain, describing Binyon as 'one of the few poets who has dared to take upon himself the ancient prophetic office of the bard'.[63]

The Sirens began life on 15 June 1919, seven months after the Armistice, when Binyon passed a London newspaper placard announcing the safe arrival in Ireland of Alcock and Brown's Rolls-Royce-powered Vickers Vimy biplane after a 16-hour, 1,960-mile flight from America. The first non-stop transatlantic flight, this was one of the great landmarks of early aviation. Here, Binyon thought, was a truly epic modern subject, an adequate symbol of the post-war world. Around this core image grew other contemporary icons of epic heroism, such as Scott of the Antarctic, who in March 1912 'quietly | Sitting in his Polar tent | Found so great a way to die' (CPi.334). Behind these doomed heroes—Alcock was killed six months later—stands their archetype, Odysseus, not Homer's homesick mariner but the restless, visionary quester who recounts his final voyage and death in Dante's *Inferno*, canto 26, the first canto of the *Divina Commedia* Binyon translated. Binyon saw Dante's Ulysses as the archetypal Occidental man, personifying, he claimed in a 1936 lecture, 'the passion for knowledge which has driven Western man with ever-increasing ardour on the road of

---

[62] *Essays by Divers Hands*, NS, 2 (1922), 13, 21.
[63] 'Laurence Binyon: A Prophet without a God', *Our Best Poets* (London, 1924), 128, 135, 129.

scientific discovery'.[64] Nothing, he tells Virgil in Binyon's trans-
lation, 'Could conquer the inward hunger that I had | To master
earth's experience.'[65]

Over a thousand lines long, *The Sirens* comprises a Prelude and
three parts, each divided into four sections. The rhapsodic Prelude
establishes the lyric voice at the core of the poem and introduces
the central theme, the restless, hungry 'star-watching eyes of the
venturer, Man' (*CP*i.324). Part I, 'The Victories', explores this
'inward hunger' for adventure, beginning with the haunted psyche
of world conquerors like Alexander, dying in Babylon with visions
of unconquered lands gnawing his 'unsated mind' (*CP* i. 327). Then
Binyon turns to contemporary heroes, with a remarkable Shelleyan
hymn to mountaineers and their realm of pristine 'unascended
solitudes', climbers like George Mallory and A. C. Irvine, who
disappeared 600 feet below the summit of Everest in June 1924.
E. G. Selwyn, a friend of Mallory's at Cambridge, thought this the
perfect epitaph for his friend's lost grave on Everest.[66] Mountains
lure such men because they preserve a saving, uncontaminated
otherness, but they cannot sate their desire for the infinite. Having
scaled the highest peak, the climber 'Stands in the vast air, stricken
and insatiate, | Wingless, a spirit craving wings to soar.' The moun-
taineer's secret dream is fulfilled by the aviator, who breaks away
from the earth altogether in his fragile biplane, 'a free rider of the
undulating silences':

> Careless of death is he, riding in the eagle's ways
> Above the peak and storm, so dear a sting
> Drives him unresting to strive beyond the boundaries
> Of his condition, being so brief a thing,
> Being a creature perishable and passionate,
> To drink the bright wine, danger, and to woo
> Life on the invisible edge of airy precipices,
> A lover, else to his own faith untrue,
> Giving the glory of youth for flower of sacrifice
> Upon the untried way that he must tread,
> So that he savour the breath of life to the uttermost,

[64] *The English Romantic Revival in Art and Poetry: A Reconsideration* (London,
1936), 15.
[65] *Inferno xxvi, 97–8, Dante: The Divine Comedy Translated by Laurence
Binyon*, ed. Paolo Milano (1947; London, 1979), 141.
[66] See Selwyn's review of *The Sirens* in *Theology*, 12/7 (Jan. 1926), 35, and his
ALs to LB, 30 July 1925.

Breath only sweet when all is hazarded.
Is it that, moving in a rapture of deliverance
From chains of time and paths of dust and stone,
Serving a spirit of swiftness irresistible,
He makes his pilgrimage, alone, alone,
Seeking a privacy of boundlessness, abandoning
A self surpassed, yet other worlds to dare?

(CPi.330–2)

Whether it be the Alexander dying in his tent in Babylon in 323 BC or Scott freezing to death in his tent at the South Pole in 1912, man's 'inward hunger' for adventure in all its different guises is, Binyon suggests, really the soul's quest for transcendence.

The fourth section diagnoses this yearning for transcendence as the driving force behind science and technology, which from the first apelike hands fashioning primitive tools to contemporary atomic research reveals the hunger of the human 'mind that seeks behind | The world for the befriending Mind' (CP i. 333).[67] Binyon felt that the enormous scientific achievements of his age, in all their complexly inwoven positive and negative aspects, were an important, if difficult, subject for contemporary poetry. He had seen the traumatic results of a modern technological war in France. Alcock and Brown's epic 1919 flight had been made in a Vickers Vimy bomber. Part II, 'Penumbra', explores the darker side of these victories of spirit over matter, their twisted misuse in industrialized warfare and the slower peacetime destruction of nature through exploitative technologies. 'Insatiable of ransacked worlds', man seeks to become 'Master of earth, the world's sole will', but in the process is destroying the planet itself, our only home.[68]

If the urge for adventure celebrated in Part I is the universal evolutionary 'hunger of Eternity' expressing itself through humanity, the 'Supreme articulate voice of nature's striving', the task now is to rechannel it into spiritual evolution. The 'Undiscovered World' of Part III is not a supernatural heaven but an inner state of

---

[67] Six years later the mathematician and theoretical physicist Sir James Jeans suggested that as the new physics eroded the mechanistic Newtonian model 'the universe begins to look more like a great thought than like a great machine'. *The Mysterious Universe* (Cambridge, 1930), 148.

[68] *The Idols* mourns the forests felled to provide pulp for the newspaper industry. The life of the forest trees, intricately knit into the web of all life, has been sacrificed for a very different kind of web, not of life but of death, the newspapers' 'web of lies and of half-lies | And lying silences' (CPi.364).

enlightenment which empowers a new vision of the world, with the sacred not monopolized by an anthropomorphic God, really a projection of man's own dominating will, but permeating all life in its wholeness and unity, 'All things living, joined and whole, I Bloomed with light of Paradise' (CPi.341). The root evil is not desire, which Binyon sees in Blakean terms as the essential grammar of life, but the urge to possess, a verb that rings through *The Sirens*, coupled with 'Man' in an implicit critique of patriarchal Western scientific culture, which 'makes of Earth an enemy' by 'aching to possess her' (CPi.342). The next, necessary stage is to stop treating reality as a realm of alien objects to be subjugated and learn to experience it as an ever-unfolding process in which we are participators, not masters. Only love for all life, not just the narrow human band on the life spectrum, can create a

> world where no possession is of men's,
> Where the will rages not with fever to destroy
> Differing wills, or warp another life to its use,
> But each lives in the light of its own joy!
> In one wide vision all have share, and we in all,
> Infinitely companioned with the stars, the dust,
> Beasts of the field, and stones, and flowers that fall!
> (CPi.347)

Beneath huge differences in idiom, passages like this reveal a fundamental continuity with Binyon's writings on Oriental art, especially his analysis of the 'property-feeling' endemic in Western attitudes to nature, and his sense of the unity of all being as the manifold expression of the Tao, 'the ever-moving, ever-changing, eternal and universal rhythm of life'.

So too does its 'companion ode', *The Idols*, which appeared in 1928. The title derives from Francis Bacon's *Novum Organum* and its 'Idols of the Mind', the images, fictions, philosophies, dogmas, and mental and linguistic habits which prevent the human mind making naked contact with reality. While *The Sirens* explores mankind's insatiably questing spirit, *The Idols* examines the human mind's equal propensity to stiffen into illusory 'frozen certainties' (CPi.352). In religion, the questing human spirit opens up new spiritual paths only to see them ossify into institutionalized dogma: 'The God departs, the Idol stays' (CPi.362). The living spirit flows on, shedding dead husks of meaning which we inhabit and call truth. The reality which eludes our systems and 'Lives lost in its own light' (*CP*i.352) can be approached only through a difficult process of unlearning conditioned emotional, perceptual, cognitive, and linguistic habits:

> *Break the word and free the thought!*
> *Break the thought and free the thing!*
> (*CP*i.367)

By attending to the silences between words, the spaces around objects, the formless from which form emerges, we quieten the mind until it attains the perfect, selfless receptivity of a mirror: 'Let spiritual Silence brim again | The mind's well to a mirror virgin-clear' (*The Sirens, CP* i. 344). *The Idols* is ultimately about liberation, in the sense that Binyon called Zen a way of 'liberation, enlightenment, self-conquest'. It cannot be bestowed by institutionalized religion, with its reality-distorting 'imagery, form, ritual' (*PFE* 185), but must be earned by soul work:

> Alone the soul has knowledge of release;
> Only in the soul is stillness,
> Poised to receive a universe in peace.
> (*CP*i.380)

In a 1929 review K. E. Curzon saw *The Idols* as an important contribution to the Western mystical tradition, but suggested a closer modern parallel in the campfire talks given by the young Indian spiritual teacher Krishnamurti at summer camps at Ommen in Holland in 1926, 1927, and 1928.[69] In these talks Krishnamurti increasingly warned his listeners against dogmas, gurus, and ceremonies, culminating in 1929 when he formally renounced the role of 'World Teacher' for which his Theosophist sponsors had groomed him, and spoke of 'Truth' as 'a pathless land' which cannot be approached through any religion, because once a belief is organized 'it becomes dead and crystallized, it becomes a creed, a sect, a religion, to be imposed on others'.[70] Published only months earlier, *The Idols* inhabits a different rhetorical and mental world from Krishnamurti's subtle meditations but shares a similar concern with the way we corral fluid reality in structures which must

---

[69] *Poetry: Past and Present*, 1/1 (Winter 1929), 24.
[70] Qtd. in Mary Lutyens, *Krishnamurti: The Years of Awakening* (London, 1975), 272. Several 1928 Ommen talks appeared in Krishnamurti's *Life in Freedom* (Ommen, Holland, 1928).

be dismantled if we are to break through into a genuine, lived experience of the oneness of life.

Several critics saw *The Idols* as 'a sustained mystical poem'.[71] Mystical experience certainly lay behind some of Binyon's intensest poetry. In 'The Secret' he had explored one of the key experiences of his life, an epiphanic moment in Kew Gardens in May 1895 when 'the mystery of the world seemed to be solved, with a sense of absolute rapture'.[72] 'Mystical' is a slippery term, especially when applied to literature, since pure mysticism is innately hostile to language, whereas poetry, however it may chafe against its limitations, has no other medium. But this perhaps was Binyon's problem, the key to the paradox of this superbly lucid prose writer whose meditative poems too often dissolve into a thingless, eventless vacuum, an atmosphere too rarefied for ideas to take flesh.

By the 1920s Binyon had realized this, and this was one of the reasons he began translating Dante. It was, as he told T. S. Eliot in 1930, for his 'own private discipline'.[73] It is no coincidence that *The Idols* and *Episodes from the Divine Comedy* appeared within months of each other in 1928. With its Dantean epigraph, *Luce intelletual, piena d'amore* ('intellectual light, full of love'), *The Idols* shows Binyon struggling to incarnate the spiritual in fully visualized visionary experience. It originated in a Dantean experience one summer night in August 1911 when he found himself lost in a Hertfordshire wood,[74] a memory explored at the beginning of the poem. In its lyric journey from this dark wood towards the unconditioned 'Light', the ode moves through visions like the dream of 'the Door' and culminates in a mystical experience triggered by the play of sunlight on water in a May garden, an 'Eternal Moment' in which he ceases to identify with his individual life and is freed to participate in the 'Spiritual Rhythm': 'When I am not, then I am: | Having nothing, I have all'. In that moment, 'The Idols fade: the God abides' (*CP*i. 381).

By the lights of Binyon's generation these odes were stylistically experimental. He thought of calling them 'symphonies' and constructed them on symphonic lines, 'built up in repeated and con-

[71] E. G. Twitchett, *London Mercury*, 19/3 (Jan. 1929), 319.
[72] ALs to Hope Bagenal, 24 Oct. 1940. In the possession of Mr John Bagenal.
[73] ALs, 13 May 1930. In the possession of Mrs Valerie Eliot.
[74] LB, ALs to James Smith, 9 Sept. 1942.

trasted movements'.[75] *The Sirens* in particular is a virtuoso display, employing a wide variety of metrical forms ranging from passages approaching free verse, through accentual metres to quantitative verse based on Bridges's metrical experiments, giving each section its own distinctive speed, weight, and texture, each poised and balanced against the next. With lines running from seventeen syllables to one, irregular and constantly shifting rhyme and metrical patterns, *The Sirens* formally mirrors its theme of the human spirit's restlessly inventive spirit. Nevertheless, the question arises as to whether the unique pressures of the post-war world could be embodied in poems so saturated with the traditions of English poetry, so apt, at their weakest moments, to slide into pastiche Shelley, or, at even weaker moments, pastiche Milton. Can a rhetoric which doggedly preserves poetic archaisms ('Yon sail'), inversions ('foot superb', 'world august'), Miltonic latinisms ('leaves depending still'), and personifications ('Time's heir . . . Doubt's dim future') meaningfully interpret the contemporary world of transatlantic flight and atomic physics? The answer for many of Binyon's generation was, amazingly, yes.

Despite Frank Kendon's prediction that they would be read 'in the future with comfort by millions',[76] *The Sirens* and *The Idols* have dropped out of literary history so completely that it comes as a surprise to learn how enthusiastically they were received. *The Sirens* was seen by some as a landmark in modern poetry. James Smith was convinced it was 'the greatest lyric . . . since Shelley'.[77] 'Nothing finer has ever been said to the minds of this country,' wrote Masefield. 'It is just the sort of poem to fill the needs of this time.'[78] Newbolt wrote that it was more than he could 'find words for, much the loftiest rhyme built by anyone in this century', while G. M. Trevelyan asked simply: 'where did you get the fire?'[79] The forty-page poem was first published in September 1924 in a handsome limited edition of 200 copies, hand-printed by Richard and Elinor Lambert at their Stanton Press in Chelsfield. This edition quickly sold out and the following summer Macmillan published a revised second edition, which was widely and positively reviewed. 'Let the bells ring to the city to announce a great poem,' wrote

[75] Ibid.   [76] 'The Idols', *Bookman*, 76 (May 1929), 122.
[77] ALs to LB, 18 Nov. 1923.   [78] ALs to LB, n.d. [1924].
[79] ALs to LB, 11 June 1925; ALs to LB, 30 Mar. 1925.

Darrell Figgis in the *Sunday Times*, calling it 'as great a poem as this century has produced.'[80] The *Contemporary Review* declared: 'This great poem, for it is no less, strikes the note of that hunger of soul which is, perhaps, the justification of our modern civilisation in Heaven.'[81] Looking back over the poetic output of 1925, another critic wrote that in *The Sirens* 'The year has yielded one great achievement in verse which, if it is not the only one, is the only one whose greatness is unchallengeable.'[82]

The reviews that give us the clearest insight into a critical mindset that could praise *The Sirens* in such lavish terms two years after *The Waste Land* were written by Lascelles Abercrombie, who felt so keenly the importance of *The Sirens* that he reviewed it twice, the 1924 edition in the *Manchester Guardian* in February 1925 and the Macmillan edition in the *Weekly Westminster* seven months later. In February he wrote: 'There is nothing . . . that can be put in the same order of achievement with this noble poem of Mr. Binyon's unless we go back to Wordsworth and Shelley.'[83] In September: 'In the poetry of today it stands by itself; for any valid comparison we should go back, probably, to Wordsworth.'[84] This was no hack reviewer churning out snap judgements for a newspaper deadline. Abercrombie was a poet, dramatist, and scholar of profound, if highly uneven, talents. As Professor of English Literature at Leeds University (and later at the Universities of London and Oxford), it was as an academic literary historian, critic, and theorist, as well as a practising poet, that Abercrombie praised the architectonics of *The Sirens* and predicted that future academics would churn out dissertations on subjects like 'Free verse and the metre of "The Sirens"' and 'Binyon's *Weltschmerz* and the science of his age'.[85]

The Sirens was, Abercrombie contended, a thoroughly contemporary poem, crystallizing the mood of the time:

here, for once, a poet has truly identified himself with his age, and has become the speech—no, not the speech, the music—of his age. . . . I at any

---

[80] 'What Song the Sirens Sang', *Sunday Times*, 5 Apr. 1925, 10.

[81] J. E. G. de M., 'Mr. Binyon's New Poem', *Contemporary Review*, 287 (Aug. 1925), 253.

[82] C.P., 'Verse in 1925', *Manchester Guardian Weekly* (Supplement), 4 Dec. 1925, p. xi.

[83] 'A Great Ode', *Manchester Guardian*, 9 Feb. 1925, 7.

[84] 'A Great Poem', *Weekly Westminster*, NS, 4/20 (12 Sept. 1925), 503.

[85] 'A Great Ode', 7.

rate feel, while I am reading 'The Sirens,' that I am in the very presence of the spirit of the age.[86]

Other commentators agreed. Frank Kendon felt that 'it achieves an expression, which has not I think been surpassed, of the mood of the world at this time'.[87] The *TLS* described it as 'one of the finest attempts at expressing in poetry the spiritual experience of our generation'.[88] Another critic, who considered *The Sirens*' 'greatness ... unchallengeable', described Binyon as 'a reconciling force between the old poetry and the new'.[89] One wonders what he meant by 'new'. Yeats aside, no such *rapprochement* was possible in the polarized literary world of the 1920s. The years during which Binyon wrote *The Sirens*, 1921–5, stand for us now as the high-water mark of modernist poetry, with *The Waste Land* (1922), Wallace Stevens's *Harmonium* (1923), Pound's *A Draft of XVI Cantos* (1925), and William Carlos Williams's *Spring and All* (1925) redrawing the map of twentieth-century Anglo–American poetry. Looking back on the early 1920s, it seems obvious to us today that *The Waste Land* was the poem which expressed 'the mood of the world at this time'. Yet, just as obviously many in Binyon's generation interpreted the mood of the age quite differently.

In any era the overlapping generations see and interpret the world in different ways. Their poetry, music, art, and politics are all aspects of a fuller, richer story each generation tells itself about the world in which it lives, the world it creates and calls reality. Since the world that is dead to one generation is very much alive for its elders, these generational narratives necessarily conflict, both in their content and in the rhetoric in which they are told. In the chasmic generation gap between the late Victorians and the modernists immediately after the war, however, this amounted to a total rupture, a mutual incomprehension, and the critical reception of *The Sirens* was a minor but exemplary skirmish in this larger intergenerational conflict.

The language of these reviews echoes Binyon's own, revealing poet and reviewers locked into a mode of discourse natural and meaningful for one generation, but gaseous, hollow rhetoric to the next. The word 'noble', for example, recurs constantly, as in Mark

---

[86] 'A Great Poem', 503.   [87] 'The Idols', *Bookman*, 76 (May 1929), 122.

[88] *TLS*, 23 July 1925, 492.   [89] C.P., 'Verse in 1925', p. xi.

McNeal's description of *The Sirens* as 'a noble poem, probably the noblest yet produced in the twentieth century'.[90] Did anyone ever describe *The Waste Land* as 'noble'? The word was all but expunged from the modernist lexicon, a rhetorical casualty of the war. If we continue the Abercrombie passage quoted above—

I at any rate feel, while I am reading 'The Sirens,' that I am in the very presence of the spirit of the age, pitilessly examining itself, soberly encouraging itself, knowing itself, shamed and exalted by its hunger for eternity, to be that humble and glorious paradox, 'earth for ever mingled with unearthliness.'[91]

—it becomes obvious that his experience of 'the spirit of the age' was quite different from, say, Ezra Pound's. *The Sirens* and *The Idols* are echo chambers of Romantic thought and rhetoric, steeped in Wordsworth and Shelley and their own great father, Milton, and critics who admired the poems did so in terms of the same shared heritage. It almost goes without saying that Milton and Shelley, closely followed by Wordsworth, were the English poets most routinely savaged by Pound, Eliot, and their fellow modernists. What remained for many of Binyon's generation a living, viable tradition was to the rising generation an exhausted seam.

This view was vigorously expressed by the young poet and critic Edgell Rickword, reviewing *The Sirens* in his iconoclastic *Calendar of Modern Letters*, a short-lived but influential magazine which helped to create a new style of literary criticism more attuned to modernist poetry. The only positive thing he had to say of *The Sirens* was that it was marginally more contemporary than Alfred Noyes's scientific epic *The Torch-Bearers*. At least Binyon and his audience were 1900 minds compared with Noyes's '1880 minds' (not bad when you consider that Binyon was eleven years older than Noyes). Attacking Binyon in terms prepared by Hulme and Pound, exemplified by Eliot, and soon to become critical orthodoxy, Rickword deplored the lack of 'contemporary speech in his idiom, or of contemporary life in his imagery', the absence of irony, and his cloudily idealist view of language, in which 'words mean states of the soul, not things or sensations'.[92] Seven years later in his seminal *New Bearings in English Poetry*, F. R. Leavis conceded Binyon's 'skilled craftsmanship' but echoed Rickword's strictures

[90] 'Laurence Binyon', *America*, 7 July 1928, 307.   [91] 'A Great Poem', 503.
[92] *Calendar of Modern Letters*, 2 (Sept. 1925), 67.

in rejecting *The Sirens* as a superannuated relic adrift in the age of Eliot.[93]

In the 1920s Eliot himself thought of Binyon as a reactionary anti-modernist, as did Pound, who muttered darkly to Eliot about 'the Binyon faction' in 1922.[94] When Binyon chaired a meeting at which he spoke in 1919, Eliot complained to his mother of having 'both a hostile chairman and a hostile audience'.[95] His assumption that this 'middle aged poetic celebrity' had not read his poetry may have been correct in 1919, although Binyon read more widely and sympathetically in contemporary poetry than his conservative editing of *The Golden Treasury of Modern Lyrics* (1924) would suggest. With *The Waste Land*, however, we are on sure ground. Binyon could hardly have missed it, since, in one of the minor ironies of literary history, it first appeared in the inaugural issue of Eliot's *Criterion* right after an essay by Sturge Moore praising Binyon's 1902 poem 'The Death of Tristram'.[96] Eliot might have been surprised. To friends who angrily dismissed it out of hand, he defended it as baffling but interesting, and he continued to study it until at least 1940, when he spoke about the impact of the war on this 'remarkable poem': 'The Great War had come like some abrupt and appalling tidal wave, invading, upheaving, destroying. Its slow subsidence left a landscape of ruin, the Waste Land of the poem.' He could understand this—he had seen the horrific effects of the war in a way Eliot and Pound in London had not—but despite this the war had not shattered his liberal humanism, nor instilled in him the 'sense of desolation & sterility and confusion' he heard in *The Waste Land*'s 'jangled music and deflated rhythms'.[97]

In a lecture a year after the publication of *The Idols*, Binyon admitted that the contemporary 'division between the Traditionalists and the Modernists' was deeper than that between any previous pair of generations, but he suggested that this antagonism would be resolved in time:

Mr Eliot's poetry can probably be appreciated justly only by one of his own generation. But he is a serious mind; and I think the serious poets of the

---

[93] *New Bearings in English Poetry* (1932; London, 1972), 24.

[94] Letter to Eliot, 29 July 1922, *Letters of T. S. Eliot*, ed. Valerie Eliot, i. *1898–1922* (London, 1988), 590.

[95] Letter, 10 Nov. 1919, *Letters of T. S. Eliot*, i. 346.

[96] 'The Story of Tristram and Isolt in Modern Poetry. Part 1', *Criterion*, 1 (Oct. 1922), 34–9.

[97] 'Poetry of Today', AMS, n.d. [Athens, 1940], 10, 13.

younger school are seeking, through mental trouble and disillusion, to find a new harmony between the human spirit and the world. Poets cannot go on making poetry out of disillusion and a sense of the futility of life. That can only be a passing phase.[98]

When we consider Eliot's journey from *The Waste Land* to *The Four Quartets*, Binyon was perhaps right, and, as we shall see, this particular rift was healed. But this was in the future. As far as the early 1920s were concerned, Binyon and Eliot gazed at each other across perhaps the deepest generational divide in English cultural history. In 1922 the 53-year-old Binyon was not, like the 34-year-old Eliot, a man shoring fragments against ruin. He belonged to the last generation that could speak without irony of 'the Spirit of Man'. 'Here, in fact, held in a vessel of lovely words, is the quintessence of our world today,' wrote Abercrombie.[99] That is just the point: for many in the younger generation the quintessence of the traumatized post-war world could not by definition be 'held in a vessel of lovely words'. Alienated, fragmented, spiritually barren, it could only be expressed in a fractured, ironic, densely allusive text such as *The Waste Land*.

[98] 'English Poetry & Drama of To-Day and To-Morrow', *Studies in English Literature* (Tokyo), 10 (Jan. 1930), 12.
[99] 'A Great Ode', 7.

11 *East and West*

The 'great longing to get out to the East' of which Binyon wrote to Aurel Stein in Kashmir in 1919 seemed doomed to frustration.[1] Six weeks after the Armistice he had applied for leave and funds to revive his pre-war 'mission to the East' but the Treasury rejected the plan.

He was particularly keen to get to Japan. By the late 1920s he was well known in Japan as a poet and influential champion of Japanese culture. He had numerous friends, many of whom had visited England as young men and women. Among these was the art historian Yashiro Yukio, who arrived in London in 1921 to study European art and was adopted by the Binyons and their three schoolgirl daughters. Binyon became his English *sensei*, a model of the scholar–artist he himself wished to become. 'It seems that I am walking in the same road, following you,' he wrote in 1922. 'I look up to you as my predecessor, teacher.'[2] Yashiro considered himself 'not a historian, but a humble disciple of the Beautiful', and that is the phrase he used for Binyon years later, a *bi-no-shito*, a dedicated apostle of beauty.[3] Unlike Noguchi and Markino, his Whistlerian compatriots of the 1890s generation, Yashiro found the London fogs depressing, and with Binyon's help he settled in Florence and embarked on the research that resulted in his magnificent three-volume *Sandro Botticelli* in 1925.

When Yashiro returned to Japan and became Director of Tokyo's Institute of Art Research, he joined Taki Seiichi, Dean of the Faculty of Letters at Tokyo Imperial University, and other friends of Binyon in a concerted effort to bring him to Japan. As a result, in 1928 Binyon was invited to lecture on British art at Tokyo

---

[1] ALs, 6 Sept. 1919, MS Stein 410, fos. 131–2, Bodleian.

[2] ALs, 29 Nov. [1922]. See my 'Anglo–Japanese Friendships: Yashiro Yukio, Laurence Binyon and Arthur Waley', *Fukuoka University Review of Literature & Humanities* (Japan), 23 (March 1992), 997–1022.

[3] ALs to LB, 6 Oct. 1921; 'Nihon bijutsu no onjintachi: Laurence Binyon', *Bungei-shunju* (Tokyo), 30 Sept. 1961, 65.

University. The Treasury refused funds to expand this into a full-scale Museum mission, but authorized special leave for the trip 'provided that no extra cost fell on Imperial funds'.[4] Money was the problem, as it had always been, but this was solved in Japan with the organizing of a Binyon Reception Committee to finance and co-ordinate his visit.

And so on his sixtieth birthday, 10 August 1929, Binyon sailed out of Southampton on the *Empress of Scotland* on the first leg of a journey that would bring him to the Far East in a role for which the last thirty years had uniquely fitted him, that of cultural ambassador. The Binyons took the Western route via Canada, sailing from Vancouver on the *Empress of France* on 29 August and arriving at Yokohama in torrential late summer rains eleven days later. They stayed only a few hours before sailing on south-west through a typhoon to Kobe, then travelled overland to Shimonoseki and crossed the Japan Sea to Korea. Apart from fleeting glimpses of Japan on this hurried journey—the mountainous coastline from the ship looked exactly like Hiroshige's rainswept landscapes—Binyon's first experience of Asia was of the mainland, a world in the process of being radically reshaped by Japan's imperial ambitions in the aftermath of its stunning victories in the 1894–5 Sino-Japanese war and Russo-Japanese war of 1904–5. Korea had been a Japanese colony since 1910. From Seoul they took a crowded train through a harsh, unhiroshigean landscape to Mukden (now Shenyang), the industrial centre of southern Manchuria. By late 1929 Manchuria was a powder keg, with fierce fighting between Chinese and Soviet troops on the northern border, and in the south, nominally under Chinese control, a power struggle between the Nationalist army, Manchurian warlords, and the Japanese Kwantung Army in the South Manchuria Railway Zone, the latter secretly planning the military takeover that would lead to Japan's annexation of Manchuria between 1931 and 1932. A year earlier in Paris fifteen leading nations, including China, Japan, and the Soviet Union, had signed the Kellogg–Briand Pact for the Renunciation of War, the high point of post-war international idealism, but here in north-east China Binyon had his first glimpse of a world darkening towards another world war.

[4] Minutes, vol. lxii, CE3/62, p. 4501, BM. LB was accompanied by R. L. Hobson, the Museum's expert on Oriental ceramics, but his expenses were covered by the collector and Museum benefactor Oscar Raphael, who also joined the party.

Further south, travelling was difficult and risky, the cities stiff with troops, tense and apprehensive. It was hardly an ideal time to visit China. Following the collapse of the Ch'ing dynasty in 1911, the fragile new Republic had been racked by civil wars. By 1929 Chiang Kai-shek's Nationalist regime in Nanking was recognized as the national government, but it was under continual threat from the Soviets to the north, Chinese Communists, warlord coalitions, and Japanese expansionism. Nevertheless, when they arrived in Peking (Beijing) on 16 September, despite what Binyon described as 'the prevailing atmosphere of mystery and apprehension',[5] they found it one of the most beautiful cities they had ever seen. Staying at the Grand Hotel de Pékin in the Legation Quarter just inside the walls of the Inner City, they enjoyed an unaccustomed 'Arnold Bennett millionaire style of life' and spent ten days exploring the city.[6] Binyon's main priority was to study art collections, but even with good contacts this often proved difficult, as many of the finest private collections had been removed for safekeeping to banks in Tientsin. The National Museum collection was also something of a disappointment, but at the Palace Museum he had much better luck. In a private room here, case after case of paintings from the fabulous imperial art collection was unsealed for his perusal, then resealed, as was the room itself after his departure.

The revelation of Peking lay not in individual artworks, however, but the city itself, especially the Forbidden City with its sweeping palace roofs of curved yellow tiles, the Temple of Heaven with its lapis-lazuli tiled roof, 'the deepest, densest blue you ever saw', and its vast, empty courtyards and fine trees. 'The Chinese are marvellous in their sense of scale,' he wrote to his youngest daughter, Nicolete. 'The walls, towers, gates & huge roofs are stupendous; but you don't feel that they are simply made to impress by size: it is the space–design that is so wonderful. . . . Altogether Peking has a sort of legendary grandeur.' Even more than this imperial architecture, he enjoyed visiting the homes of Chinese friends. He found the Chinese 'charming, natural people', living in 'the most delightful houses in the world—one courtyard after another, with

---

[5] LB, AMS report to Director and Trustees of the British Museum, 28 Jan. 1930, Original Papers, CE4/239 (1930) no. 432, p. 1, BM.

[6] LB to Helen and Margaret Binyon, 17 Sept. 1929. In the possession of Mrs Harriet Proudfoot.

flowering trees, pomegranates, etc, in the middle & verandahs all round'.[7]

Binyon wrote this while sailing in the Inland Sea, 'a paradise of waters' and misty islands, after a rough voyage back across the Japan Sea. When they finally arrived in Tokyo on 1 October, they found a city very different from the museum-like Forbidden City quarter of Peking. Six years earlier, the great Kanto earthquake of September 1923 had destroyed three-fourths of the city and killed more than 140,000 people, most of them in firestorms that swept through the dense neighbourhoods of wooden houses. Rebuilt at great speed, it was now re-emerging as an even bigger, more dynamic and chaotic metropolis. 'Tokyo is a quite enormous town,' Binyon wrote home. 'London is a dream of beauty compared with it. It is very ugly.' What struck him most, however, was the amount of the old Hokusaian Edo street life that was still visible

as if through chinks and holes in the cheap American façade of sprouting telegraph poles & shoddy houses: coolies with naked legs & big black hats like mushrooms, women in native dress & with babies on their backs, going through the mud in their clogs, with paper umbrellas, in fact a number of figures that had just stepped out of colour-prints.[8]

They stayed in one of the few major buildings to survive the earthquake unscathed, Frank Lloyd Wright's Imperial Hotel, built in 1922 and now one of the most famous hotels in Asia, although Cicely thought it 'quite quite mad . . . full of jagged ends of concrete & weird contorted forms everywhere'.[9]

Here in Tokyo, in a relentless month-long round of official receptions and dinners at the British Embassy and in royal, aristo-cratic, and literati circles, Binyon experienced some of the many facets of modern Japan. He made almost daily visits to Japanese and Chinese art collections, not only those of the Imperial Museum and other institutions but the wonderful private collections of old aristocratic families and industrial magnates. Here he at last came face to face with the handscrolls, album leaves, and hanging scrolls that had changed his life when he had discovered them decades earlier in the pages of the *Kokka*. Yashiro, who accompanied him on many of these forays, was 'greatly touched by the sight of

[7] ALs, 1 Oct. 1929 (Harriet Proudfoot collection).
[8] ALs to Margaret and Helen Binyon, 10 Sept. 1929.
[9] ALs to Helen and Margaret Binyon, 4 Oct. 1929 (Harriet Proudfoot collection).

Binyon's joy at seeing, for the first time, the originals of those things he had admired for so long, a joy which was really that of meeting old familiar friend[s]'.[10] Here, in the tatami-floored rooms of traditional Japanese houses like Nezu Kaichirō's estate in Tokyo or the lovely Yokohama home of his old friend, the artist Shimomura Kanzan, for the first time he was seeing Japanese paintings, screens, statues, and ceramics in their natural context. As several of his hosts were masters of the *chanoyu* tea ceremony, the Zen-inspired meditative art form he had first encountered in Okakura's *Book of Tea* in 1906, Binyon was served tea in tea rooms where many of the great Zen art forms, from ink painting and calligraphy to ikebana flower arranging, were combined in a complete aesthetic–spiritual experience.

The Binyons took every opportunity, in Tokyo and later in Kyoto, to experience the performing arts, especially theatre, attending performances of bunraku puppet theatre, kabuki, and Nō. It was thirty years since he, Yeats, and Moore had first dreamed of a theatre dedicated to poetic drama, non-naturalistic scenery, and symbolic gesture. Here, in Nō, was its archetype. 'O Nik,' he wrote to Nicolete:

the No plays were too wonderful for words. Just the theatre itself, the spotless fine unpainted wood of the stage (uncurtained) with its fine proportions & the big pine-tree painted on the back, was ravishing to look at. And then the utter remoteness from realism, the slow movements, the gorgeous dresses![11]

This world of traditional culture was not as divorced as it might have seemed from the struggles of contemporary Japan. The committee organized to finance and co-ordinate Binyon's visit included not only Tokyo University academics but also powerful political figures like Makino Nobuaki, Lord Keeper of the Privy Seal, and Dan Takuma, head of the massive Mitsui financial, industrial, and commercial combine.[12] Binyon met Dan often and studied his fine collection of Japanese art, and through him met his mentor Masuda Takashi, the man who had built the Mitsui empire. Now 82 years old, Masuda had amassed a priceless collection of Asian art, the

[10] 'Lawrence Binyon', *Bulletin of Eastern Art* (Tokyo), 7–8 (July–Aug. 1940), 20.
[11] ALs to Nicolete Binyon, 18 Oct. 1929.
[12] See preface by the Binyon Reception Committee in LB, *Catalogue of the Loan Collection of English Water-Colour Drawings Held at the Institute of Art Research, Ueno, Tokyo, October 10–24th, 1929* (Tokyo, 1930), p. xi.

finest items of which he laid out in various rooms for Binyon to study when he visited his Gotenyama estate on 20 October. A dedicated connoisseur of *chanoyu*, he made tea for his guest and they exchanged extemporary poems. Binyon's poem was to be translated, written on a calligraphic scroll, and kept for tea ceremonies. Masuda's own poem, translated by Yashiro, read: 'Although this is the first encounter, yet it is not only I that feel you a friend of 100 years.' Binyon wrote home: 'You should have seen the dear old Baron beam with happiness.'[13] In men like Masuda and Dan, however, the seemingly timeless ritual world of the tea ceremony and the complex, sometimes violent power struggles of contemporary Japanese politics met. Two years later, in March 1932, Dan would be gunned down by members of the ultranationalist League of Blood in a wave of assassinations as Japan slid towards militarism and war.[14]

From Yashiro and other Japanese friends, as well as old Tokyo hands like the diplomat and historian George Sansom, Binyon learnt something of the social and political tensions that lay behind these future events, with the New York Stock Market crash on 24 October adding to the anxieties of a nation already in recession. Everywhere he met with the same warmth, however, welcomed as a poet by a poetry-loving race. He was surprised at how well known his poetry was. As guest speaker at the first Congress of the English Literary Society of Japan at Tokyo University on 19 October, he was welcomed with a remarkably comprehensive lecture on his poetry by Professor Okada Tetsuzō, who, he told the twins, 'knew much more about the subject than I do, & had read & studied everything I ever wrote. It was quite embarrassing.'[15]

In his own lecture, Binyon surveyed contemporary British poetry and drama,[16] and he gave other talks and poetry readings, but the core of his official program in Tokyo was the series of six 90-minute lectures on *Landscape in English Art and Poetry* that he

---

[13] LB, ALs to Helen and Margaret Binyon, 20 Oct. 1929 (Harriet Proudfoot). See Christine M. E. Ruth's *Art, Tea, and Industry: Masuda Takashi and the Mitsui Circle* (Princeton, 1993), 146.

[14] See LB, 'Baron Takuma Dan', *The Times*, 11 Mar. 1932, 19.

[15] ALs to Helen and Margaret Binyon, 20 Oct. 1929. See Okada Tetsuzō, 'An Approach to the Poetry of Laurence Binyon', *Studies in English Literature* (Tokyo), 10 (Jan. 1930), 16–25.

[16] 'English Poetry & Drama of To-Day and To-Morrow', *Studies in English Literature* (Tokyo), 10 (Jan. 1930), 1–15.

delivered at Tokyo Imperial University during the middle fortnight of October. Having immersed himself in Japanese culture, here his task was to interpret British culture for the Japanese. These lectures, published in book form in Tokyo and London the following year, reveal one of Binyon's best qualities as a lecturer and prose writer, his sensitivity to his audience. In their distilled simplicity, conveying complex ideas in eloquent, unknotted English, they were perfectly attuned to the needs of his Japanese audience. 'The language seemed to be no barrier between him and his audience,' Hobson reported. '[T]he large hall was filled to its utmost capacity with eager Japanese students who listened with rapt attention.'[17] Reading the book much later in London, the art critic John Russell wrote: 'It is the mark of Binyon that . . . a vast repertory of learning and allusion is disposed so skilfully as to lie upon the page as lightly as one eyelid upon another.'[18]

It was a subject close to Binyon's heart. The history of the treatment of landscape in art and poetry is, he argued in his opening lecture, a major 'aspect of the history of the human spirit' (*LA* 1), one that addresses the most vital questions confronting the human race:

> What account does the spirit of man make of this wonderful world in which he is placed; these bountiful riches, this intricate profusion of beauties, these vast energies, these overwhelming grandeurs and terrors? What account does he make of all that wild life, not his own, which animates this earth and air? What do they mean to Man? Are they altogether outside him? Are they something to be conquered for his use, his service, and his pleasure? Or are they rather to be understood, as things having a kindred life with our own, as sharers of the universal life?
>
> (*LA* 3–4)

We are back in familiar Binyon territory, the world of *Painting in the Far East*, *The Flight of the Dragon*, and, in a different idiom, his own poetry. The first lecture explored the difference between Western and Eastern approaches to landscape and distinguished between the anthropocentric Mediterranean 'classic spirit' and the northern, Celtic spirit, given to dreams, contemplation, and communion with numinous nature. It was from this northern romantic spirit, Binyon argued, that Western landscape developed. The six

[17] 'A Journey to the Far East', *BMQ*, 5/1 (1930), 37.
[18] 'Laurence Binyon as Art Critic', rev. of *English Water-Colours*, by LB, *Listener*, 5 Oct. 1944, 384.

lectures then explored the way these two spirits interweave in English art from the medieval illuminated manuscripts to Paul Nash, and in English poetry from Chaucer to Blunden, as well as the cross-fertilizations between the pictorial and literary arts, the affinities between, say, Turner and Shelley, who both 'saw the world in terms of energy' (*LA* 226). At key points he introduced analogies with Japanese and Chinese art and philosophy, both to help clarify unfamiliar issues for his Japanese audience and to reveal the subtle affinities between, say, Girtin and J. R. Cozens and the Sung landscapists, Rowlandson and Utamaro, Cotman and the Kōrin school, between Wordsworth and the Zen poet-painters, Shelley and the Taoist sages.

Binyon had brought with him a collection of English water-colours for an accompanying exhibition mounted by Yashiro at his Institute of Art Research in Ueno Park. The fifty-four pictures ranged from eighteenth-century watercolours by Wilson, Gainsborough, Alexander and J. R. Cozens, Francis Towne, Rowlandson, and Romney, through the great Romantics Blake, Constable, Girtin, Turner, and Cotman, to twentieth-century artists such as Vanessa Bell, Paul Nash, Stanley Spencer, and David Jones. Binyon had borrowed all the pictures from private collectors, mostly friends such as Edward Marsh and Michael Sadler. Prime Minister Ramsey MacDonald loaned a Rowlandson. Binyon himself contributed Gainsborough's radiant *On the Coast* and Wilson Steer's *The Shadow of the Trees*, while Nash's pencil, chalk-and-wash drawing *The Grove of Trees* belonged to his daughter Nicolete. It was a representative selection embodying a wide range of styles, but also a personal one, its profoundest works chosen to reveal deep-lying affinities between the English and Japanese attitudes to nature, such as Cotman's expressive, near-abstract ink painting *A Shipwreck*, which in the exhibition catalogue Binyon compared with the Zen *haboku* 'flung ink' style.[19] His purpose in both lectures and exhibition was to show that certain insights into the nature of reality are universal, transcending the barriers of nation, creed, and ideology, that East and West can meet, in fact have met countless times without knowing it. Such affinities are, Binyon wrote later, 'wonderful testimony to the solidarity of mankind'.[20] He concluded his final lecture: 'I hope I have shown that,

---

[19] *Catalogue of the Loan Collection of English Watercolours*, 10.
[20] 'Chinese Painting', *Asia*, 35 (Nov. 1935), 670.

divided as we are by half the world, with a totally different inheritance of mind, in art we share a like ideal and speak in a tongue that
either can understand' (*LA* 294–5).

In this he seems to have been remarkably successful. Yashiro felt
that he 'had never heard a lecture given in such beautiful language
before except the one by the Indian poet Tagore'.[21] Nippon Columbia recorded him reading excerpts from the lectures, together with
'For the Fallen' and other poems, and sold a souvenir two-record
set as 'the essence of the pure nobility of the English language'.[22]
Almost two years later Taki wrote: 'I still now hear it told everywhere that no foreigner had yet made lectures of such deep impression here as those you delivered at the Imperial University.'[23]
George Sansom's wife recorded in her diary that Binyon 'has had a
wonderful success. He is probably as good an ambassador as we
have ever had.'[24] The British Ambassador, Sir John Tilley, wrote: 'I
hope you realize that we are all extremely proud of the impression
that you have made in this country. From my point of view you
have achieved unconsciously I think a great purpose.'[25] He also
submitted a special report to Arthur Henderson, the Secretary of
State for Foreign Affairs:

Mr. Binyon's success has been most remarkable. Each lecture has been
attended by an audience of nearly one thousand persons, including a very
large proportion of students. . . . I am told by Professor Anesaki, the head
of the Library of the Imperial University and a very reliable witness that the
impression made in this country by Mr. Binyon, not merely on his actual
audiences, but on cultivated society in general has been quite extraordinary. . . . Among the elements of Mr. Binyon's success have been his modesty, his obvious deep love of Japanese art, the beauty of his language and
his enunciation. The success of the lectures exceeds all expectation.[26]

Sir Frederick Whyte wrote to the Prime Minister that while Binyon
had long enjoyed 'a unique position in the admiration of the
Japanese', these lectures 'have not only raised his personal prestige,

---

[21] 'Lawrence Binyon', 21–2.
[22] Sleeve note (in Japanese), Nippon Columbia, J12303/J12304 (Tokyo, 1929)
(Harriet Proudfoot collection).
[23] ALs, 30 July 1931.
[24] Katharine Sansom, *Sir George Sansom and Japan: A Memoir* (Tallahassee, Fl.,
1972), 42.
[25] ALs, 13 Nov. 1929.
[26] TLs, 17 Dec. 1929, copy sent to the Trustees of the British Museum, Original
Papers, CE4/238 (1929), no. 4207, BM.

but have done us as a nation great service'.[27] Ramsey Macdonald himself wrote later telling Binyon he had heard 'from all sides of the great success you scored'.[28]

On 31 October the Binyons left Tokyo for the autumnal mountains and lakes of Hakone, where scarlet maples in the mist made him wonder whether he had visited these mountains before 'in a different birth'.[29] Via the castle town of Nagoya they travelled south to Nara, capital of Japan during the eighth century, now a quiet town of temples and shrines, a treasure house of early Japanese Buddhist art. Nara was, he told Nicolete, 'one of the most enchanting places I have ever seen'.[30] One of the highlights of his stay was Hōryūji, a temple founded by Prince Shōtoku in 607 CE, one of the most atmospheric places in the Buddhist world. In the adjoining nunnery of Chūgūji they saw the seventh-century Miroku Bosatsu, a small lacquer-on-wood statue profoundly expressive of the tenderness and compassion Binyon admired in Mahayana Buddhism (*SMAA* pl. 47). He was so moved by another ancient wooden statue, the willowy, attenuated, Korean-style Kudara Kannon, that he commissioned a famous Nara craftsman to make an exact replica for the British Museum. It would be two-and-a-half years before it reached London, due to the search for the right camphor tree for what the Japanese, and Binyon himself, considered not a Museum replica but a sacred image. A Shintō service was held in the forest to beg the tree's pardon before felling it.[31]

On 9 November they moved to nearby Kyoto, capital of Japan for eleven centuries before Emperor Meiji moved to Tokyo in 1868, and still the heart of traditional Japanese culture. Apart from giving two lectures at Kyoto Imperial University, Binyon spent most of his fortnight visiting Kyoto's hundreds of temples, monasteries, shrines, and gardens. In temples he was shown rarely displayed treasures of Chinese and Japanese art in their most perfect setting, not museum specimens but aids to meditation in a living Buddhist environment.

[27] Qtd. in TLs to LB from Rose Rosenberg, Prime Minister's Secretary, 20 Jan. 1930.

[28] ALs, 10 April 1930.

[29] 'Hakone', *Koya San: Four Poems from Japan* (London, 1932), 15.

[30] ALs, 11 Nov. 1929.

[31] See LB, 'Replica of a Statue of Kwannon', *BMQ* 7/1 (1932), 1. See also 'The Odd Side of Things: Asking a Tree's Pardon for Felling It', *Illustrated London News*, 26 Mar. 1932, 467.

Twice, in September and November, the Binyons visited Miyajima, a small island off Hiroshima in the Inland Sea. With its sixth-century Itsukushima Shrine dedicated to the daughters of Susano-o-no-Mikoto, the Shintō god of moon and oceans, the island was so sacred that no one was allowed to be born or to die there. 'I have lost my heart to this island,' he told Nicolete.[32] With its misty forested Mount Misen and deer wandering along the beach, it was, he told Yashiro, 'just dreamy', an almost technical term in Binyon's vocabulary. It was because he himself was 'too dreamy' that he succumbed to an aural mirage while walking alone one night. Yashiro recalled:

He lost his way and as it began to get dark from a little house he heard strains of music that, to his mind, fitted in with the whole atmosphere of the Island. He was filled with admiration, thinking that Japan indeed was a country of art when one could hear such beautiful music in the humble home of the farmers or fishermen. Filled with the emotion of the moment he composed a sonnet which he flattered himself was really very good. Well pleased he continued walking in the moonlight. Presently again from another little house came that same beautiful music, then from another and another until at last the truth of it all flashed across his dreamy mind. Even on this remote, old-fashioned Island there was such a thing as radio and this was the source of the music. The disillusionment amused him and he finished the story with a laugh saying, 'A poem had been made and I like it nevertheless.'[33]

It is a typical Binyon story, mocking himself as the earnest japanophile eager to have his dreams fulfilled, yet also covertly affirming the dreamy misprision of reality in which poems are born. The lyric, 'Miyajima', celebrates this island where 'All paths lead upward to the sky':

> This sacred isle has banished death;
> And yet I would that my last breath
> Might amid ocean-murmur cease
> On such an isle, in such a peace.

> (*NS* 27)

A far better poem resulted from a trip to the sacred mountain Koyasan, south-east of Kyoto on the Kii peninsular, a vast complex of temples and monasteries founded by Kōbō Daishi early in the ninth century as the headquarters of the esoteric Shingon sect of

---

[32] ALs, 20 Nov. [1929].   [33] 'Lawrence Binyon', 21.

Buddhism. After Kōbō Daishi's death the mountain became a major pilgrimage destination, and what moved Binyon was this sense of a place made holy by the footsteps and prayers of generations of pilgrims, a feat of communal spiritual imagination. After a vegetarian supper at the temple where they lodged, the Binyons walked the final 2 kilometres of the ancient pilgrimage trail, a path up through the huge forested Okunoin cemetery, past several hundred thousand tombstones and monuments of emperors, shōguns, daimyōs, samurai, priests, and poets, to Kōbō Daishi's tomb, illuminated by lights that have been kept burning since the eleventh century. Binyon's shorthand notes in a hurried note home—

Moonlight & hard frost, & giant cryptomerias (cedars that look like pines), & stone lanterns, & incense from a great cauldron, & a pilgrim saying his prayers aloud before the tomb, & sound of running water. It was most wonderful.[34]

—later developed into one of his most fully achieved meditative poems, 'Koya San', which describes the moonlit walk and the praying pilgrim haloed by 'a veil of trembling light'. Another poet might have played this up as an exotic, 'Japanese' image, but Binyon goes beyond this to reveal the bond of common humanity between himself and the pilgrim, expressed without portentous East-meets-West rhetoric. It is, as Earl Miner has written, 'a remarkable instance of simple and basic humanity, without exoticism, to have appeared just before the Second World War, or perhaps at any period'.[35]

> Bare-headed, sandalled, still that pilgrim prayed,
> Unconscious of all else but his heart's prayer.
> Out of his breast a broken murmur deep
> Came with his frosted breathing on the air
> Before the shrine in its tree-guarded shade
> Where that great Saint continued in his sleep.
>
> It seemed that from Time's beginning he had stood there
> In a hushed vastness,
> Solitary, erect, amid the unimagined motion
> Of worlds unnumbered,
> Absorbed, secure in his small star of light.
> And now that ceaseless, fugitive frail smoke
> Appeared to me like shadowy souls in flight

[34] ALs to Nicolete Binyon, 20 Nov. [1929].   [35] *Japanese Tradition*, 206–7.

Woven together into a veil of breath
That wavered as their little life awoke
And passed for ever into birth or death.

What prayer was his that mingled with the mist
Of the forgotten sighings of the dead?
I knew not; yet in him I seemed to share
Longings that still were patient to persist
Through Time and Death from lips that once were red.
In that one image all my kind stood there.
Lover of the body, lover of the divine sun,
Of earth's replenished
Fullness and change and savour of life rejoicing
Careless of all care,
Me now the Silence for its vessel chose
And filled from wells unsounded by the mind.
No other need I had, and could not less
Than to be wholly to this spell resigned
And dark communion with the spirit that knows
Vigil and frost and solitariness.

Fragments we are, and none has seen the whole.
Only some moment wins us to restore
The touch of infinite companionship.
I that had journeyed from so far a shore
Found at the world's end the same pilgrim soul,
And the old sorrow, no flight can outstrip.

Now in the midst of the irradiated noonday
Suddenly absent,
While in my ear the sound of familiar voices,
Light talk and laughter,
My thought has in an instant flown the seas;
A great remoteness occupies my heart;
And there arises on my inward sight
The shadowy apparition of vast trees.
A pathway opens; I am stolen apart,
And I ascend a mountain in the night.

(*NS* 24–5)

On 27 November the Binyons travelled north to the castle town of Sendai on the Pacific coast for a lecture at Tohoku University, where the poet Ralph Hodgson taught. A boat trip among the pine-clad islands of Matsushima inspired the poem 'Matsushima' celebrating this 'paradise of waters, paradise of isles' (*NS* 26). A final week in Tokyo passed in a welter of official engagements, farewell dinners, and last glimpses of cherished paintings. On 9 December they sailed from Kobe to Shanghai, where Binyon spent three hectic days seeing friends and private collections of Chinese art.

The 'great marvel' of the long voyage home, however, came when the ship docked at Saigon and the Binyons hired a car and Annamese driver for the 'unforgettable' three-day, 600–mile round-trip upcountry to Angkor, the ancient ruined capital of the Khmer kingdom in Cambodia, which Binyon had dreamed of visiting for thirty years. The lure was the huge twelfth-century Hindu temple complex of Angkor Vat and the slightly later Angkor Thom, dominated by the towering mass of its central shrine, the Bayon. Since the sacking of Angkor by Siamese armies in 1437, these masterworks of religious art had been almost submerged by the Cambodian jungle, a process being slowly reversed in some ruins by French archaeologists, who had been working on Angkor Vat since 1921 under the direction of Binyon's old friend, Victor Goloubew. This is what most deeply impressed Binyon at Angkor, the sight of rampant nature reclaiming these arrogantly human artefacts, a dynamic interface between two kinds of energy, the human rage for order and the jungle's ceaselessly procreative green life:

> Invented order and scruple of willed proportion,
> The strong square, all the lineaments of reason,
> Lost in the green extravagance, the strangling
> Young embraces of a pitiless desire.
>
> (NS 29)

The quatrain comes from 'Angkor', one of Binyon's most ambitious late poems, written fifteen months later. A year before Binyon reached Angkor, Aldous Huxley's 1928 essay 'Wordsworth in the Tropics' wittily mocked Wordsworth for his parochially northern vision of nature, geared to 'the cosy sublimities of the Lake District', and prophesied: 'The Wordsworthian who exports this pantheistic worship of Nature to the tropics is liable to have his religious convictions somewhat rudely disturbed.'[36] In Binyon's 'Angkor' we have precisely that, a Wordsworthian in the tropics, indeed hypnotized by this display of slow-motion sexual violence, the cry of the seed to the sun 'Through million miles of

---

[36] *Life & Letters*, I (1 Oct. 1928), 342–55.

air', 'Multiplying, bursting, swelling to burst afresh, | Writhing and wrestling to mount into the light.' The 'wild' sap

>   races into
> The boughs, and the boughs stream out into the leaves.
>
> Roots thrust downward into the black heat of earth;
> Boughs descend, thicken, and root themselves afresh;
> The builded fabric is seized and is enfolded
> In the tightening of these fibres, passive as a victim.
>
>   (NS 29)

This undomesticated, non-human nature seems physically and allegorically to undermine the pacific serenity of the cryptically smiling stone faces on the Bayon's towers, reversing the human task of transfiguring 'ancient stone to breathing mind' (NS 30). Binyon later told Percy Withers he was 'entirely possessed by the theme. I am still haunted by the sight of those ruins gripped by the jungle; & the thought of the tyranny of the life-instinct, of sex, over the mind & its creations seemed a natural transition.'[37] The poem imagines a naked hermit sitting cross-legged among the ruins, intent on achieving a yogic victory over 'the tyranny of the life-instinct', seeking to break the karmic cycle of 'Desire born of desire, breeding desire' (NS 28). Amid all that surging biological life and death he sits 'Motionless contemplating the eternal motion', 'Still as a flame is still in a windless place', 'Still . . . like the emptiness a whirlpool | Furiously encompasses' (NS 35). Meditating on emptiness, attuned to 'the communion of silence' and 'dipt into a central stillness', he ignores nature and human art alike as delusions of *maya*, 'obstructing shadow and apparition'. The poem implies, however, that his ruthlessly disciplined meditation is itself a higher expression of the desire that drives the green world, 'the wild | Energy leaping into boughs and leaves'. The seed yearns towards the physical sun, the yogi towards the 'Universal Sun':

> But from what desire, O Solitary, dost *thou* come?
> From what seed sown in the abysses of the stars
> Was that strong engendering of the passion of thy stillness,
> Desire surpassing all the desires of mortals,
>
> Secret in the anchored body's immense surrender,
> A strange, transforming vision, a strange excess,

[37] ALs, 21 July 1931.

>   Prisoned in the heart's beat, and out of its prison
>   Crying to the glory of the Universal Sun?
>
>   (*NS* 36)

If nothing later quite matched Angkor, the entire voyage vouch-safed 'a hint of the glory of the earth'.[38] They spent New Year's Eve on a day trip up through the rubber and tea plantations to Kandy in Ceylon, and then, by the slow acclimatizing degrees allowed by pre-jet-age travel, they passed westwards through the climatic and cultural zones and arrived back in London on 19 January 1930.

END OF A BM ERA

The Museum house the Binyons returned to in January 1930 was the centre of social and artistic activity spanning three generations. Their three daughters, the twins Helen and Margaret, and Nicolete, were all variously talented. Six years younger than her sisters, Nicolete had inherited from her father a profound love of art, and would become a leading designer, teacher, and historian of letter-ing. Aged 18, she was now reading history at Lady Margaret Hall, Oxford. Margaret had read chemistry at Oxford, while Helen had studied at the Design School of the Royal College of Art, headed by William Rothenstein. Here she was taught by Paul Nash, who, himself influenced by her father's writings on Asian art, now in turn inspired Helen. Her fellow students included some of the most talented artists of their generation, including Barnett Freed-man, who illustrated Binyon's slim volume of poems *The Wonder Night* in 1927, and Eric Ravilious, with whom she would later fall in love. Helen's own work, honed by periods in Paris and the United States, was in watercolour and wood engraving, especially book illustration.[39]

It was characteristic of Binyon family life that the twins wel-comed their parents home from Japan with a puppet show, with words written and recited by Margaret and sets and marionettes made by Helen, using wood-carving skills she had learnt at the Central School of Art. This led to the creation of the Jiminy Puppets (from gemini: twins), a leading portable puppet theatre which gave

[38] ALs to Withers, 24 Jan. 1930.
[39] For a concise account of Helen's life, see 'Eric Ravilious and Helen Binyon', Richard Morphet's preface to Helen Binyon, *Eric Ravilious* (London, 1979), 7–20.

performances throughout the 1930s. Equally characteristic was *Sophro the Wise*, a verse play for children Binyon had written between 1923 and 1924 as light relief from *The Sirens*. Performed by Nicolete and friends at the Museum house, and published in 1927 with designs by Helen and tunes by Margaret, *Sophro* is a playful comedy in which Binyon mocks himself as an absent-minded, philosophical father eager to get his young daughters married off:

> A daughter off my hands! A little more
> To spend on books; good. Both must marry soon,
> And then I'll have my leisure for my own—
> Peace without interruptions.[40]

'Peace without interruptions' was a luxury Binyon had looked forward to for years. He had long planned to retire from the Museum on his sixtieth birthday to devote himself to poetry, but this plan was dashed when Arthur Waley decided to leave the Museum himself at the end of 1929 to concentrate on translation, spelling the end of the remarkable two-poet Sub-Department. Waley and Binyon were not close friends, but they were certainly not the antagonists they might have been. Nicolete had attended a Dalcrozean dancing class taught by Waley's companion, the remarkable Beryl de Zoete, but this was one of the few points of contact between their worlds. Waley stood firmly on the far side of the late Victorian–modernist generation gap, both physically and spiritually at home in Bloomsbury (Gordon Square), a friend of Eliot and intimate with the Sitwells. As an orientalist, too, he belonged to a new generation of scholars who read Chinese, were influenced by Chinese rather than Japanese canons of taste, and looked askance at the Romantic attitudes of the Fenollosa–Binyon generations. Nevertheless, the two men had developed a sympathetic working relationship based on mutual respect for each other's areas of expertise. Looking back on his Museum career, Waley remembered Binyon as 'an ideal friend and chief'.[41]

His successor was the 25-year-old Basil Gray, who would develop into one of the outstanding Oriental art scholars of his

[40] *Sophro the Wise: A Play for Children* (London, 1927), 14.
[41] Introduction, *One Hundred and Seventy Chinese Poems*, rev. edn. (London, 1962), 4. See also Basil Gray, 'Arthur Waley at the British Museum', *Madly Singing in the Mountains: An Appreciation and Anthology of Arthur Waley*, ed. Ivan Morris (London, 1970), 37–44; and Hatcher, 'Anglo–Japanese Friendships'.

generation. Gray had read Binyon's poetry as an Oxford undergraduate, admired *The Flight of the Dragon*, and was, according to a later colleague, 'manifestly under [Binyon's] spell'.[42] Binyon postponed his retirement in order to give Gray time to add experience to his natural flair. Determined that Gray would not suffer the disadvantages under which he had laboured, in his report to the Trustees on his Far East trip he urged that his successor be given leave and funds to study in Asia.[43] The Treasury's parsimony in allowing Binyon's trip to be funded by the Japanese epitomized successive British governments' apathy towards Asia except where trade or imperial security was at stake. This myopic Anglocentrism was a source of acute frustration for Binyon, especially as on visits to the United States he had witnessed the enormous growth in the public collections and the facilities built to house them, which he interpreted as less a matter of Yankee millions than a different attitude to Asian culture. Britain seemed content to treat its Asian treasures as imperial booty, hoarded in museums lacking the space to adequately display them, let alone create an environment in which visitors could enter into a creative dialogue with the art of non-European cultures. In his report on Waley's retirement, Binyon urged the Trustees to implement the recommendations of the Royal Commission on National Museums and Galleries 1927–8, which had discussed the creation of an independent Museum of Oriental Art in London. His own memorandum to the commissioners had stressed the educative value of the national collections, the way in which imaginatively exhibited Oriental art could inspire in the British public a new, enriching vision of Asia:

I believe everyone would be astonished if these collections could be adequately displayed in a related scheme so as to be intelligible and eloquent to the eye. It would be an event and a revelation. . . . Since the barrier of language is insurmountable, save for the very few, the creative art of these countries is the most direct approach for the western public to the understanding of oriental history, religion and ideals of life. . . . This country has had a longer and closer connexion with the East than any other: it seems fitting that it should take the lead in this matter.[44]

[42] William Watson, 'Scholar of the Orient', obituary, *Guardian*, 20 June 1989, 39.
[43] AMS report, 28 Jan. 1930, Original Papers, CE4/239 (1930), no. 432, BM.
[44] Great Britain, Parliament, *Parliamentary Papers (Commons), 1929–30*, vol. 9 (*Reports*, vol. 16), 20 Sept. 1929, 'Royal Commission on National Museums and Galleries: Final Report. Part 1: General Conclusions and Recommendations', 61–2.

The Commission concluded that organizational difficulties and prohibitive cost made the creation of a new museum impracticable, but recommended the development of a Department of Far Eastern Antiquities at the British Museum, which 'might be a stepping stone to the larger scheme for a Museum of Asiatic Art and Antiquities which might be realized at a later date'.[45] After returning from Japan, Binyon worked towards this goal.

Binyon and Gray worked together closely on the landmark International Exhibition of Persian Art in Burlington House from January to March 1931. As Chairman of the Selection Committee, Binyon worked throughout the autumn and winter, helping sift through English, European, and Asian collections to amass the largest and finest collection of Persian miniatures ever displayed in Europe, as well as publicizing the exhibition with essays, newspaper articles, and lectures, including a brilliant talk at the Royal Society of Arts. After attending a lecture on Persian art at the Athenaeum, Gordon Craig wrote thanking him for 'the most delightful evening' of his sojourn in London.[46]

Binyon's enthusiasm for Oriental art remained undimmed, but his patience with administration frayed as he found it increasingly frustrating having to postpone working on poems which, especially since his re-energizing Far East trip, were queuing up to be written. In December 1930 he confided to his fellow poet Wilfrid Gibson:

for months I have had not an hour of leisure: committees, lectures, articles, rows & worries, visits to collections—all this on the top of all my ordinary work—I am desperately tired & sick of it all. . . . How I long to get back to poetry! But in a year or two I shall retire, and then—I hope.[47]

When in November 1928 Macmillan suggested publishing his collected poems, he was unenthusiastic, preferring to concentrate on his new work, but eventually agreed. The appearance of his two-volume *Collected Poems* in 1931 provided an opportunity for critics and friends to assess his career. Bottomley was convinced that it placed him 'among the major British poets for good', while G. M. Trevelyan, now Regius Professor of Modern History at Cambridge, described it as 'intellectually massive'.[48] In the *Listener*

---

[45] Royal Commission, 61.

[46] ALs, n.d. [1930]. See LB, 'Persian Painting', *Journal of the Royal Society of Arts*, 79 (28 Nov. 1930), 52–65.

[47] ALs, 14 Dec. 1930.

[48] Bottomley, ALs to LB, 24 Feb. 1932; Trevelyan, ALs to LB, 16 Mar. 1932.

Abercrombie argued that by revealing the scope and variety of his poetry, 'its weight of significance and its noble imagination, and its consistently scrupulous and beautiful craftsmanship', it had gained him an 'assured place in the great tradition of English poetry'.[49]

Several critics, like Frederick T. Wood with his twenty-five-page essay in the *Poetry Review*, treated the chronologically arranged *Collected Poems* as one continuous text through which they traced a gradual evolution in thematic and technical resources culminating in *The Sirens* and *The Idols*.[50] A year earlier, E. G. Twitchett had embarked on a similar retrospective by re-reading all Binyon's books for an essay in the *London Mercury*. Twitchett saw Binyon as a mystic in the classical Western tradition, one who 'sees his flights as journeys into a great radiance, where sublunary details and distinctions are lost in the oneness of the light'. He traced Binyon's slow self-education in combining 'ecstasy with accuracy' from the early lyrics through 'A Mirror', in which Binyon first attained 'the real ecstasy of revelation, the first touch of "otherness"', to 'The Secret', and culminating in the odes. For sustained visionary power and 'sheer verbal beauty' *The Idols* was the pinnacle of Binyon's career to date, the 'new music' which 'came into [his] power towards the sixtieth year of his age'.[51] Other critics also portrayed Binyon as a mystical poet, the more perceptive seeing this as inextricably linked with his vision of love, which through the slow accumulations of the *Collected Poems* emerged as an abiding presence and source of power. In an insightful review in the *Observer*, Basil de Selincourt wrote: 'Many a poet has shown us how he would remake the world for the woman of his love; none has shown us more beautifully than Mr. Binyon how a man and a woman can make their world together.' He summarized Binyon's 'mystical' thought:

the substance of the world—the earth, the sea, and the sky to its furthest constellations, are, in his apprehension, one spiritual presence; whose quality we finally realise in our human intercourse, since we are all aiming, individually and collectively, at a completer life, to which the complete beauty summons us. To that beauty we respond . . . by a never-ceasing

[49] 'Laurence Binyon', *Listener*, 18 Nov. 1931: supplement, p. vii.
[50] 'On the Poetry of Laurence Binyon', *Poetry Review*, 23 (Sept.–Oct. 1932), 349–74.
[51] 'The Poetry of Laurence Binyon', *London Mercury*, 22 (Sept. 1930), 425–7, 431.

spending of self, which is at once denial and surrender, the renewal of creative love within us in submission to the love which continually creates all.[52]

It is no accident that the *Collected Poems* ends with Binyon's translation of *Paradiso*, canto 33 and Dante's great vision of 'The Love that moves the Sun and the other Stars' (*CP*ii.310).

But did this make Binyon a major contemporary poet, as had seemed certain to many in 1925? Many of the older generation felt so, but the *TLS* critic expressed the nagging doubt felt by others: 'We feel that we have been in contact with a great poet, and yet we do not feel that we have been reading great poetry.'[53] Sturge Moore too felt that his old friend was 'more primordially poetical' than his actual poems.[54] Binyon's mentor Robert Bridges had divined this in the 1890s; when Newbolt asked him about *Porphyrion* he had replied enigmatically 'The great thing about Binyon is that he has such a beautiful mind.'[55] Twitchett's suggestion that Binyon was more opposed to the Eliotic spirit of the age 'than any considerable poet now writing' except Yeats was taken up polemically by James Southworth in a long 1935 *Sewanee Review* essay celebrating Binyon for heroically resisting the fashionable post-war malaise:

In contrast to the poetry of Mr. T. S. Eliot, Mr. Binyon affects a reconstruction of beauty against the forces of disintegration—forces against which Mr. Eliot seems powerless to act. Mr. Eliot's poetry is a balm to the contemporary who lacks the strength to combat the anti-cultural forces of the present day. He sees that in spite of the apparent chaos of twentieth century civilization, beauty, serenity, and the abundant life are still attainable.[56]

In fact, by 1935 Binyon's own reading of Eliot was more subtle and positive than Southworth's. The two poets were now on friendly terms, brought together by their mutual love of Dante. Since the publication of *Episodes from the Divine Comedy* in 1928, friends, including several Italians, had urged Binyon to undertake a translation of the complete *Commedia*. Among these was the brilliant young scholar Mario Praz, a family friend since the early 1920s, who read the translations in manuscript in 1927 and

[52] 'Heir to Poetry: Mr. Binyon's Collected Poems', *Observer*, 29 Nov. 1931, 6.
[53] 'Mr. Binyon's Poems', *TLS*, 21 Jan. 1932, 41.
[54] ALs to LB, 25 Nov. 1931.   [55] Newbolt, *My World*, 189.
[56] Twitchett, 'Binyon', 423; James Granville Southworth, 'Laurence Binyon', *Sewanee Review*, 43 (1935), 341.

described them as 'good poetry, and even poetry of the highest order'.[57] After reading Eliot's *Dante* pamphlet in May 1930, Binyon sent him *Episodes from the Divine Comedy*, writing: 'I agree with you that Dante is the best of all poets to train oneself by: indeed I have made my translations with that object, for discipline and exercise.' He told him Praz had encouraged him to begin a complete translation, but doubted he would do so except for his 'own private discipline'.[58] Eliot seconded Praz's suggestion: 'I do not know of anyone living who could translate Dante as well as that. Ezra could do parts, but he will never understand the whole pattern.'[59] He also sent Binyon *Ash Wednesday*, a poem he came to admire greatly. It suggested he had been right six months earlier in Tokyo when he had prophesied that Eliot and 'the serious poets of the younger school' would go beyond 'making poetry out of disillusion and a sense of the futility of life' to seek 'a new harmony between the human spirit and the world'.[60]

The reception of the Dante translations in his *Collected Poems* brought further encouragement. Abercrombie told *Listener* readers:

they translate Dante's sense with extraordinary closeness and precision, and yet with equal fidelity provide an English equivalent for the grave ardour of Dante's Italian and for its poetic form. They are not only model versions of the Divine Comedy: they are models of what ought to be accomplished in any poetic translation.[61]

Bottomley wrote: 'This proves you are the first among English Dante translators, and that you owe it to your country and race to do the Commedia complete.'[62]

In fact Binyon was already at work on the *Inferno*, published by Macmillan in 1933. By the time his *Collected Poems* appeared in late 1931, Binyon looked anything but a man preparing for retirement. As well as embarking on the herculean task of a *terza rima* translation of the complete *Commedia*, he had published *Three Short Plays*, *Landscape in English Art and Poetry*, several works on Persian art, and an edition of Blake's poetry that E. M. Forster reckoned provided 'the best approach to Blake likely to be made in

[57] ALs to LB, 12 Jan. 1928.
[58] ALs, 13 May 1930. In the possession of Mrs Valerie Eliot.
[59] TLs, 16 May 1930.
[60] 'English Poetry & Drama of To-Day and To-Morrow', 12.
[61] 'Laurence Binyon', p. vii.   [62] ALs, 24 Feb. 1932.

our generation'.[63] He was editing his Japan poems for publication in *Koya San* (1932), and preparing for the culmination of his life's work on the English watercolourists, *English Watercolours* (1933). His interest in Indian art and history had also led him to embark on *Akbar* (1932), an acclaimed short biography of the enigmatic Mughal emperor which G. M. Trevelyan described as 'a little masterpiece'.[64] Yet another horizon opened up in July 1931 when Gilbert Murray, as Chairman of the Executive Committee of the League of Nations Union, invited him on behalf of the Chinese government to accept the chair of English Literature at Nanking University.

Binyon was mulling this over and was two-thirds through *Akbar* when, the day after writing to Moore 'I suppose one ought to feel old, but I don't,'[65] he entered Guy's for a prostate operation and spent the next two months in hospital, dangerously ill from pneumonia after a blood clot in a lung. He was allowed home in December but the wound kept re-opening and complications set in, necessitating a second operation. On 28 March *The Times* reported that he was 'still seriously ill'. Nomura Yōzō wrote to Cicely from Japan: 'He is a treasure of mankind and God should certainly take a special care of him.'[66] Perhaps he did, or perhaps it was the *bodhisattva* Kannon, for in March the Kudara Kannon replica finally arrived from Nara. Binyon found it, like the original, 'of extreme beauty'.[67] By mid-April he was back working at the Print Room a few hours each day.

On 16 July, on Dodgson's retirement, Binyon became Keeper of the Department of Prints and Drawings, but only for a little over a year, as he himself was at last able to retire on 9 September 1933. The *Burlington Magazine* found it 'difficult to think of the Print Room without him'.[68] The socialist academic Harold Laski spoke for many when he celebrated Binyon's forty-year career serving the Museum 'in a spirit worthy of its own life' as 'one of the great temples of the human spirit'. He recalled scholar friends from all over the world who returned from consulting Binyon

---

[63] 'An Approach to Blake', *Spectator*, 2 Apr. 1932, 474.
[64] ALs to LB, 29 May 1932.   [65] ALs, 26 Oct. 1931, 62/15/2, TSMP–LU.
[66] ALs, 26 Dec. 1931.
[67] ALs to Rothenstein, 19 Mar. [1932], BMS Eng. 1148 (126), fo. 92, WRP–HH.
[68] 'Laurence Binyon', editorial, *BM* 62 (Apr. 1933), 153.

with the same grateful admiration for his infinite patience, his kindly courtesy, his eager anxiety that the full resources of the Museum should be available to any genuine searcher after knowledge.

In Harvard and in Munich, in Paris and Chicago and Madrid, I have heard men speak of what they owed to Mr. Binyon, the official and the scholar. He has been a living demonstration of the great ideal that a scholar's work—if he be a true scholar—makes him part of a great fellowship which knows no boundaries of race or class or creed.[69]

Honours of various kinds rolled in. In the King's Birthday Honours List the year before he had been appointed to the Order of the Companions of Honour, invested by George V at Buckingham Palace on 21 June 1932. Now he became an honorary Fellow of Trinity College and was awarded an honorary D. Litt. by Oxford University in June. That spring and summer saw big changes in the family. On 19 April Margaret married Humphrey Higgens, followed on 20 July by Nicolete, who, after what the newspapers dubbed a 'Museum romance', married Basil Gray, the man her father was grooming to assume responsibility for Asian art. When her parents moved out of the Keeper's House, Helen moved into a flat in Belsize Park with an artist friend.

A large group of friends and admirers clubbed together to present gifts to the Museum in Binyon's name in a ceremony on 29 September, including an early fourteenth-century Persian miniature, a seventeenth-century Rajput drawing, and an eighteenth-century Japanese screen, the latter especially moving for Binyon as it had belonged to Ricketts, who had died two years earlier (colour pl. 4). To Binyon himself they gave a Turner watercolour, which would be, he told his old friend Walter de la Mare, who had sat beside him at his farewell party, his 'most precious & cherished possession'.[70]

On 30 September Binyon boarded the *Scythia* at Liverpool and sailed to the United States as Charles Eliot Norton Professor of Poetry at Harvard University. He had been invited to deliver the Norton lectures for the 1927/8 academic year, their second year of operation, a signal honour that he had reluctantly declined for Museum and family reasons. In January 1933, however, he was invited to succeed Eliot, who had delivered *The Use of Poetry and*

---

[69] 'Scholar–Poet', *Daily Herald*, 11 Sept. 1933, 8. See also 'Mr. Binyon Retires: 40 Years in the British Museum', *Observer*, 24 Sept. 1933, 11.
[70] ALs, 6 Oct. 1933.

the Use of Criticism as the 1932-3 Norton Lectures, and gladly accepted. Settled in a quiet flat in the Commander Hotel, the Binyons spent eight months in Cambridge, through a radiant New England fall and then a record winter that saw Boston harbour frozen over for only the third time since the seventeenth century. 'Did you know you could get your *eyeballs* frozen?' he asked de la Mare.[71] As well as old Harvard and Boston friends such as Langdon Warner, Paul Sachs, Edward Forbes, and Ananda Coomaraswamy, he gained many new friends, including John Livingstone Lowes and the man he admired most among contemporary philosophers, Alfred North Whitehead, whom he found 'a really enchanting old man, so wise & sweet & witty'.[72] 'Really,' he wrote Newbolt, 'it would be hard to find anywhere so many interesting & able & delightful people.'[73]

Apart from his Norton lectures, he gave lectures and talks on almost every subject in his repertoire, including Blake as poet, painter, and seer, English watercolours, various aspects of Oriental art, Shakespeare, 'English Poetry in its Relation to Painting and the Other Arts', 'On Translating Dante', and 'The Magic of Form in Poetry', as well as poetry readings, not only in Cambridge and Boston but New York, Philadelphia, Washington, Chicago, Cleveland, Yale, Princeton, and Vassar. Exhibitions of English watercolours at the Fogg and of Blake at Boston and the J. Pierpont Morgan Library in New York were mounted to coincide with his lectures.

At the heart of all this activity lay the six slide-illustrated Norton lectures on *The Spirit of Man in Asian Art* delivered between 15 November 1933 and 28 February 1934, and published by Harvard University Press in 1935. The culmination of his lifetime's work in Oriental art, these lectures concentrated mainly on the art traditions of India, China, Japan, and Persia, the philosophies informing them, and the implications of these alternative visions of the world for his Western listeners. They were written for a general audience, not scholars, aimed at broadening the base of appreciation of Asian art and thought. Reviewing them in book form in 1935, Coomaraswamy thought they provided 'undoubtedly for the general reader the best available introduction to the inner life of Asiatic peoples as it has found expression in art. It is the work of a

[71] ALs, 11 Feb. 1934.   [72] ALs to Percy Withers, 3 Dec. 1933.
[73] ALs, 3 Dec. 1933.

poet, perfect in its kind.'[74] The Nobel prizewinning novelist Pearl S. Buck, who knew China as well as any Westerner, wrote in her review in *Asia* magazine:

I like to fancy that Laurence Binyon's long living among the finest objects of Asian art, the years of his custody over exquisite paintings and carvings and prints, have imbued him with their essence. His writing makes one think of a Chinese painting, apparently simple to the point of artlessness, yet profound with knowledge and feeling where simplicity is in reality the subtlest of eliminations, the stripping away of all but the purest and most essential form. . . .

. . . The last chapter . . . is Binyon at his best. It leads us on beyond art into speculations on the relation of art to the meaning of life, and that leading on of the spirit is again an essential of oriental art. This is a very beautiful book, not profound in any technical sense, and perhaps of no supreme value for the museum world or the collection of many pieces. But it is profound with feeling and with human comprehension of its subject.[75]

'The difficulty is to make it fresh, not to repeat what I have said elsewhere,' Binyon told Cicely while composing the lectures.[76] He succeeded by making them movingly personal, not in the sense of being egoistically self-advertising but by conveying his obvious, deeply matured love for this art. The slide-illustrated lecture was his perfect medium, almost an allegory for his own work, because it foregrounds the artworks themselves, the glowing images on the screen, companioned by an eloquent voice in the dark. The ability to share aesthetic joy, to convey a sense of living engagement with art, is a rare gift, even among art scholars, but it is a constant presence in *The Spirit of Man in Asian Art*. It is a poet's book, embodying the shifting tones of voice of a man responding to particular works of art, the description of his thirty-year relationship with the Ku K'ai-chih scroll (*SMAA* 22–9), for example, or his pleasure in a Rajput drawing (Ibid. 140–1). Here he is on the thirteenth-century hanging scroll *Nachi Waterfall*, profoundly 'expressive of the inner spirit of Japanese art' and, for Binyon, 'one of the most beautiful landscapes in the world'. In Japan he had studied this scroll in Nezu Kaichirō's superb collection on his first visit to Tokyo, and then returned one last time before sailing home, knowing it would be the last painting he would ever see on Japanese soil:

[74] *Journal of the American Oriental Society*, 55 (1935), 325.
[75] *Asia*, 35 (Oct 1935), 635.   [76] ALs, 22 Aug. 1933.

It was a December afternoon when I took leave of this picture in its owner's house, hanging in the alcove. The brief daylight was going, the early dusk coming on; but I could not help begging Mr. Nezu that the picture might remain, and not be rolled up like the others. I wanted to see the last of it, while any light lingered.

As perhaps you know, the Japanese temples have bells of enormous size which are struck by great suspended beams of wood; and when they are struck, the sound goes out through the pine-woods and into the surrounding air with deep-toned vibrations that only after an incredibly long time are re-absorbed into silence. The effect of these vibrations on the hearer is powerful and strange; it is a kind of disembodying of material things, a momentary initiation into some world beyond range of sight or touch. And contemplating the picture, I felt as if I were listening to those prolonged tones of the evening bell. The waterfall now glimmering in the twilight seemed to be purged of all the accidents of appearance; to be an essence, a spirit, a symbol. I seemed to be in presence of something hidden from the outer world, the continuing soul of a race.

(*SMAA* 181)

'SLOWNESS IS BEAUTY'

The Binyons returned to England in June 1934, but did not make the familiar trip back to Bloomsbury. For over half a century Binyon had enjoyed living at the centre of things, had loved and hated London, cared passionately about its architecture and its people, but he had also long dreamed of retiring to a quiet place in the country where he could, literally and figuratively, cultivate his own garden. As early as 1918 he had written to Gordon Bottomley: 'What would I not give to be able to retire to a cottage in the country & write all the poetry schemed ahead of me! The older I grow the more passionately I care for poetry & would let all else go hang.'[1] London friends were sceptical that the poet of *London Visions* would ever actually leave. Metropolitan to the core, Ricketts had been aghast at the idea of his old friend retiring to 'the gloom & damp of the country' and urged him to find a comfortable flat in town.[2]

The dye had been cast years earlier, however, at least as early as the love poem 'The Dream House':

> Often we talk of the house that we will build
> For airier and less jostled days than these
> We chafe in
>
> (CPi.311)

A few months before his retirement in 1933, after months of searching, he and Cicely had found an old farmhouse on the Berkshire Downs, high above the Thames villages of Streatley and Goring south of Oxford. It was austere country, surprisingly remote in those pre-motorway days. Continuously inhabited since Palaeolithic times, marked by earthworks, hill camps, dykes, and other ancient British and Roman remains, it was, as he told Walter de la Mare, 'old, old country'.[3] On the opposite ridge, across a long

---

[1] ALs, 5 Feb. 1918 [CMB transcript].   [2] Ricketts to LB, ALs, n.d. [1931].
[3] ALs, 13 June 1933. See LB, 'From a Corner of Rural England', *Britain To-day*, 20 Sept. 1940, 9–12.

valley, the prehistoric Ridgeway, the oldest road in England, ran along the crest of the downs. With their sweeping horizons, the downs were made for a man who loved Cornwall because its bareness left him 'free for the sky', who dreamed of a house on 'a green hill | That gazes over alluring distances' (CPi.311). The same sensitivity to the empty spaces of Sung landscapes, where tiny humans work or wander amid the vastness of nature, informed his feeling for this primeval landscape. 'O the width & the solitude, the space & the light!'[4]

Westridge Farm House had the 'garden to companion us' he had envisaged in 'The Dream House', and if it was a wilderness overrun with weeds that gave them the pleasure of creating it themselves. They planted hundreds of daffodils, anemones, jonquils, tulips, and other flowers, and letters emanating from Westridge contained increasingly detailed reports on garden and orchard in all weathers and seasons. After reading his book *Science Lends a Hand*, he wrote to his friend Sir Frederick Keeble that he was 'dazzled by so much new light but fascinated by the world of wonders you disclose. I look now with awe on our herbaceous border, thinking of all the invisible events going on in the soil and in the roots; and I shall think now of plants as persons, . . . each a character, and all life one.'[5] When Yashiro visited him in 1936, he found him 'dressed as the ordinary farmer of the district', 'a good-natured old man of the country' accompanied by his cocker spaniel Genji named after the hero of *The Tale of Genji*.[6]

Behind the garden was a neglected orchard which became his special joy. In war-torn France, the human suffering of soldiers and refugees had been compounded for him by the sight of orchards destroyed by German troops, which he read as the expression of a deeper hatred of nature itself. At Westridge he now learnt how to plant and care for fruit trees. Nothing would shake Binyon from his ingrained idealism—flowering trees remained for him, as for Persian artists, 'thoughts springing from, and unfolding in the eternal mind'[7]—but the apple, cherry, plum, pear, and almond trees now under his care were also living, growing things, daily realities

[4] ALs to Percy Withers, 11 Aug. 1933.   [5] ALs, 5 Dec. 1939, HRC Texas.
[6] 'Lawrence Binyon' 19. See Hatcher, 'Anglo-Japanese Friendships', 20–1.
[7] LB, 'The Qualities of Beauty in Persian Painting', *Survey of Persian Art: From Prehistoric Times to the Present*, ed. Arthur Upham Pope, 6 vols. (London, 1938–39), iii. 1917.

known to the hands and muscles through long hours of work. In poems such as 'Sowing Seed' and 'Autumn Song' he explored his new-found sense of rootedness in one beloved place known in all seasons and weathers, of participation in the process of growth and decay, and trust in

> The strong slow patience of the living earth
> And the apple ripening on the apple-tree
> Almost as if I felt it in my flesh.
>
> ('August Afternoon', *NS* 13)

As he put it in a letter to Cicely, 'I feel our roots are going down into the good earth'.[8]

If Westridge was to be a place of work, care, and craftsmanship in gardening, Binyon hoped to bring the same qualities to the poetry he planned to write here. A year before leaving the Museum he had written to Henry Tonks: 'Still poetry to me is the one great joy, & I hope soon to retire & do nothing else.'[9] He was retiring to, not from, work, inspired by a sense of urgency not usually associated with rural retirement. 'There's so much, so much to do, & so little time', he told Cicely in 1932, promising her 'lots of poems. You shall have them all if I live.'[10]

He was, however, far from doing 'nothing else'. When a writer for *Homes and Gardens* magazine tracked him down to Westridge, he headlined his article 'Mr. Laurence Binyon at Home: An Old Farmhouse Provides a Peaceful Retreat for the Distinguished Author and Poet after a Busy Life in Town',[11] but in fact he continued to be heavily in demand as a lecturer and essayist, so much so that by April 1935 he complained: 'I should like to be forgotten and just think & read & wrestle with poetic problems, instead of having to fight for just a little peace.'[12] His old love of travelling had not retired either. Even while they were searching for their 'cottage of dreams' in 1932, he had hinted to Cicely about another, highly Binyonian possibility, musing 'I sometimes feel I would like to wander with you & have no possessions'.[13] She did not take to the prospect of becoming a 1930s hippy, but her husband's wanderlust took them on trips and lecture tours to many parts of Europe and

---

[8] ALs, 15 Aug. 1933.   [9] ALs, 29 Sept. 1932, HRC Texas.
[10] ALs, n.d. [June 1932].   [11] *Homes and Gardens*, Sept. 1937, 115–18.
[12] ALs to Mary Winslow, 16 Apr. [1935], Houghton Library, Harvard (hereafter Houghton).
[13] ALs, Thursday n.d. [June 1932].

once, in spring 1935, to Egypt (where he was offered the post of Director of Fine Arts), Palestine, Turkey, and Greece.

Two of his major plays were interestingly revived in the mid-1930s. A year before Eliot's *Murder in the Cathedral* was first performed at the Canterbury Festival of Music and Drama, the centrepiece of the 1934 Festival was a shortened version of *The Young King*, produced by Eileen Thorndike and performed in the Cathedral's Chapter House every evening from 9 to 16 June.[14] The following year Lillah McCarthy played the lead in two well-received performances of *Boadicea* at the Oxford Playhouse on 30 July 1935.[15] 'You will never know what it means to play a really great part,' she wrote, '—why did we not give "Boadicea" before, when I was younger?'[16]

The play was staged by Elsie Fogerty to inaugurate the 1935 Oxford Verse Speaking Festival, the successor to John Masefield's Oxford Recitations. Since 1932 the annual festival had been organized by the English Verse Speaking Association, of which Binyon was elected President in 1934. When the Association folded in 1936, Binyon, Bottomley, Richard Church, and Wallace Nichols ran the festival independently and the annual summer competitions, switched now to the Taylorian Institution, grew in size and popularity until the war brought them to a halt in 1941. Binyon, who remained President until the end, was more convinced than ever that poetry needed to be revived as a spoken art, a communal experience closer to poetry's bardic origins. 'Listening to a poem many times over', he told Edmund Blunden, 'is in effect a searching & illuminating criticism of it.'[17] It increasingly informed his own poetic practice, and he wrote 'Shelley's Pyre' expressly for choral speaking. In an era when poetry was becoming increasingly marginalized, he was happy to see it being read, listened to, and enjoyed by so many people, especially young people, over these three Oxford summer nights. As he told Walter de la Mare, 'I have learnt a lot from the festivals, as a writer of verse, and in these days it is rather heartening to live for a short time in the exhilaration of poetry & find everybody more or less intoxicated with it.'[18]

---

[14] See 'The Friends of Canterbury', *The Times*, 11 June 1934, 9.
[15] See '"Boadicea": Mr. Binyon's Play at Oxford', *Guardian*, 31 July 1935, 10; *The Times*, 31 July 1935, 10.
[16] ALs, 5 Aug. 1935.   [17] ALs, 21 Jan. 1936, HRC Texas.
[18] ALs, 29 Jan. 1936. See also LB, 'Learning to Speak and Enjoy Poetry: The Latest Oxford Movement', *Times Educational Supplement*, 1 Dec. 1934, 401.

The 1937 Festival was the most successful ever, both in terms of the number and quality of verse speakers, especially choral groups, and the judges, who included W. H. Auden, Victoria Sackville-West, Wilfrid Gibson, Austin Clarke, Clifford Bax, and L. A. G. Strong, while the guests of honour were T. S. Eliot, the newly knighted Edward Marsh, and one of Binyon's heroes, the radical crusading journalist H. W. Nevinson. Binyon was particularly glad to have Auden, whose *Look, Stranger!* he was keen should win that year's Royal Society of Literature's Gold Medal, for which he was one of the judges alongside Masefield, Murray, de la Mare, and I. A. Richards.

Binyon continued to write and lecture on Oriental art until his death, but his last involvement in a major project was the great International Exhibition of Chinese Art at the Royal Academy from November 1935 until March 1936. With 3,080 exhibits covering thirty centuries of Chinese civilization, many of them loaned by the Chinese government, this hugely successful exhibition was a landmark in European appreciation of Chinese art. More than 55,160 tickets were sold in the first fortnight, with a record 6,300 visitors on 12 December.[19] As a member of the Executive Committee, Binyon spent most of the summer, autumn, and winter of 1935 writing the catalogue introduction and articles for journals and newspapers, giving lectures and talks, sitting on committees, and finally hanging by far the richest collection of Chinese paintings ever seen in England. In an article entitled 'The Spirit of Laurence Binyon in Chinese Art', the *China Review* thought it 'a piece of stupendous luck' that the Exhibition opened shortly after the publication of *The Spirit of Man in Asian Art*, the ideal guide 'for spiritual mediation between Orient and Occident'. The Exhibition was, it suggested, in 'a very genuine sense . . . a slightly belated Silver Jubilee of Laurence Binyon's career as exponent of Chinese painting and kindred pictorial arts'.

It is hardly an exaggeration at all to say that Chinese art in England is seen through Mr. Binyon's eyes and is understood through his spirit. Apart from a very small circle of independent connoisseurs, Chinese paintings and bronzes and sculptures . . . are seen and understood by Englishmen as and because Mr. Binyon sees and understands them.[20]

[19] See 'Exhibition of Chinese Art', *China Review*, 5 (Jan. 1936), 9–10; Basil Gray, 'The Royal Academy Exhibition of Chinese Art, 1935–6, in Retrospect', *Transactions of the Oriental Ceramic Society* (1985–6), 11–36.
[20] *China Review*, 4 (Oct. 1935), 28, 27.

This was largely true. Younger scholars were moving away from Binyon's 'Romantic' scholarship, but the way Chinese art was popularly perceived in Britain was largely Binyon's creation. This was particularly true for those, an increasing number, who approached Chinese art from a spiritual perspective. The leading British proponent of Buddhism, Christmas Humphreys, admired Binyon's work, and as late as 1978 quoted Binyon's catalogue introduction when recalling the Exhibition in his autobiography.[21] In his review of the Exhibition in the journal *Buddhism in England*, the 21-year-old Alan Watts had clearly read books such as *The Flight of the Dragon*. With Watts destined to become the hugely influential interpreter of Zen for the Beat and hippy generations in America, Binyon's influence extended well beyond his lifetime.[22]

Binyon's translation of the *Inferno*, dedicated to Mario Praz, was published by Macmillan in May 1933. It was an ambitious undertaking, whose aims he outlined in a brief Preface:

In making this version the aim has been to produce what could be read with pleasure as an English poem. At the same time I have kept as close to the original as I could, and have tried to communicate not only the sense of the words but something of Dante's tone, and of his rhythm, through which in great measure that tone is conveyed.[23]

In addition to accepting the challenge of *terza rima*, with all the strains it puts upon the comparatively rhyme-poor English language, Binyon set himself subtler, even more difficult tasks. Robert Fitzgerald, a modern Italian scholar who considers Binyon's *Commedia* the version 'that most nearly reproduces the total quality of the original poem', explains some aspects of this:

So far as English would permit, and in the decasyllabic line native to English, he had imitated the Dantean hendecasyllable, scanning by syllables rather than feet, but through systematic elisions achieving flexibility in syllable count. The result was a regular but very subtle refreshment and quickening of rhythm. . . . But this was not all, either. By using fine

[21] *Both Sides of the Circle: The Autobiography of Christmas Humphreys* (London, 1978), 88.

[22] 'The Genius of China: Notes on the International Exhibition of Chinese Art', *Buddhism in England*, 10 (Jan.–Feb. 1936), 162–3. *The Flight of the Dragon* also appeared in the 'List of Recommended Reading' in Aldous Huxley's 1945 *The Perennial Philosophy*, a key text for the same young audience which responded to Watts's writings.

[23] *Dante's Inferno, with a Translation into English Triple Rhyme by Laurence Binyon* (London, 1933), pp. vii–viii.

distributions of weight and accent, he had contrived to avoid the beat of pentameters and to even out his stresses on the Italian model.[24]

Reviews were mixed, but encouragement came from the right quarters. Geoffrey Bickersteth, whose own great translation of the *Paradiso* had appeared months earlier, congratulated Binyon on his 'almost incredibly good' *Inferno*: 'You have absolutely mastered *terza rima* and over and over again you simply are Dante writing in his own style in English.'[25] Support came from a more unexpected source when Ezra Pound asked Eliot to send him the *Inferno* to review for the *Criterion*. Binyon had not heard from Pound since he left England in 1920, and the American had spurned few opportunities to excoriate his erstwhile friends in the Edwardian literary world. The *Inferno* changed his mind. Surveying the contemporary scene in January 1934, he lighted on four poets: William Carlos Williams, Yeats, Eliot, and 'old BinBin', who looked 'as if he might have found the light *at last* after 45 years' labour'.[26] In his fifteen-page *Criterion* review in April, a craftsman's detailed appreciation of a fellow craftsman's work, he announced: 'The venerable Binyon has I am glad to say produced the most interesting english version of Dante that I have seen or expect to see'.[27]

The two poets were already corresponding, Pound from Rapallo, Binyon from Harvard and later Westridge. Assured by Binyon 'Venerable I may be, but I have lots of energy left, & hope to go on',[28] Pound urged him to complete the *Commedia*. On 6 March he wrote:

I wonder if you are using (in lectures) a statement I remember your making in talk, but not so far as I can recall, in print. 'Slowness is beauty,' which struck me as very odd in 1908 (when I certainly did not believe it) and has stayed with me ever since—shall we say as proof that you violated British habit; and thought of it.[29]

A slightly different version appeared in *Guide to Kulchur* three years later:

Binyon in 1908 or 1909: 'I cdn't do that. Never can do anything QUICK.' Later, in, I think, *The Flight of the Dragon*, or it might have been in the same conversation, 'Slowness is beauty.'

[24] 'Mirroring the *Commedia*: An Appreciation of Laurence Binyon's Version', *Paideuma*, 10 (1981), 489, 490–1.
[25] ALs, 14 May 1933.   [26] 7 Jan. 1934, letter 269, *Letters*, 334.
[27] 'Hell', 382.   [28] ALs, 8 June 1934, BRBM.
[29] 6 Mar. 1934, letter 277, *Letters*, 340.

The sincere reader or auditor can find in those words a very profound intuition of veracity.[30]

The phrase became his emblem for Binyon and what he epitomized, the slow gestation and maturation empowered by tradition at its rare best. He was still meditating on the theme as late as 1955 in the *Rock Drill* cantos:

> Only sequoias are slow enough.
> BinBin 'is beauty'.
> 'Slowness is beauty.'[31]

Like sequoias, Binyon belonged to an earlier evolutionary epoch in which things had time to grow at their own internal pace. He was a cherishable, 'venerable' anachronism in a speed-driven, increasingly superficial and fragmented culture, some of the best and worst aspects of which Pound had himself helped inspire. Binyon was not blessed with abundant natural gifts as a poet, but through persistence and integrity he had made the very best of what he had. Rather than relaxing into semi-retirement as a distinguished man of letters, he had continued to accept new and risky challenges such as the *Inferno*. He had admitted to Pound, 'The difficulties are so immense—often I was in absolute despair.'[32] The metrical and other tasks he had set himself in attempting a *terza rima* translation as close as possible to Dante's rhythm and tone were of the kind that only a poet set on testing and extending the limits of his own technique would undertake.

'Writing poetry is a terribly difficult art. I always feel to be at the beginning, and old faults crop up just like the thistle and bindweed I battle with in my garden', Binyon admitted to Pound. 'There's nothing for it but persistence.'[33] The translation was for Pound living proof that 'Honest work has its reward in the arts if no other where.'[34] The phrase recurs throughout his *Criterion* review, a coded message to modish, superficially modernist young poets that poetry was indeed 'a terribly difficult art' that required hard work and persistence:

I do not expect to see another version as good as Binyon's. . . . Few men of Binyon's position and experience have tried or will try the experiment. You can not counterfeit 40 years honest work. . . .

---

[30] (London, 1938), 129.   [31] *Cantos* 87/572.
[32] ALs, 18 Feb. 1934, BRBM.   [33] 17 July 1934, BRBM.
[34] *Guide to Kulchur*, 193.

. . . One ends with gratitude for demonstration that 40 years' honest work do, after all, count for something; that some qualities of writing can not be attained simply by clever faking, young muscles or a desire to get somewhere in a hurry.[35]

The *Purgatorio* appeared in September 1938 to fairly general critical acclaim. Stephen Spender, a poet Binyon admired, reckoned he deserved 'the greatest gratitude and admiration' for achieving his 'almost impossible task'. H. B. Charlton saw in it 'the rich austerity, the loaded economy, and the rigorous thrift of Dante's majestic simplicity'.[36] In a dense flurry of correspondence during April and May 1938, Pound dispatched long, detailed letters commenting on the *Purgatorio* proofs, typically exuberant stuff punctuated by animadversions on 'that blighter Milton' and ejaculations like 'Banzai, my dear Bin' and 'Bravo, Bravo, BRAVO.'[37] He wrote an Italian review for *Broletto* and in the *New English Weekly* hailed it as a masterpiece of transparency: 'You can SEE the original through it.'[38] He stressed, however, that the book needed 'campaigning for'. It did indeed, for Macmillan had lost £200 on the *Inferno* and, despite the critical acclaim, the *Purgatorio* looked set for equally sparse sales. Never one to let public indifference get him down, Pound urged: 'And now, Boss, you get RIGHT ALONG with that *Paradiso* as soon as you've stacked up the dinner dishes. . . . Banzai, alalLA!'[39]

TIME FOR STRIPPING THE SPIRIT BARE

Apart from one last isolated letter from Binyon in December 1939, the Binyon–Pound correspondence effectively ceased at the end of 1938, as the storm clouds gathered. Binyon pressed on with the *Paradiso*, glad of the therapeutic discipline of translation as an antidote to events in Asia and Europe, where the three countries he loved most—Japan, China, and Italy—were engaged either as ag-

---

[35] 'Hell', 388, 396.
[36] Spender, 'Dante in English', *New Statesman and Nation*, 14 Jan. 1939, 57; Charlton, 'Mr. Binyon's Dante', *Manchester Guardian*, 25 Oct. 1938, 7.
[37] See *Letters*, 402–14.
[38] 'Purgatory', *New English Weekly*, 29 Sept. 1938, 373. 'Binyon: Salutiamo un a traduzione pregevolissima della Divina Commedia', *Broletto*, 34 (Oct. 1938), 14–15. For a partial translation, see Fitzgerald, 498–9.
[39] 12 May 1938, letter 350, *Letters*, 414.

gressors or victims in the prelude to the greatest war in history. The decade that had started so well for him with the Anglo-Japanese amity of his Tokyo lectures and his April 1931 trip to a Spain 'wild with joy' at the birth of the Second Republic had seen the rise of Nazism in Germany, the Italian annexation of Abyssinia, the Spanish Civil War, and the rise of militarism in Japan. The Japanese invasion of China depressed him profoundly, as he explained to Yashiro in Tokyo: 'Some of our Japanese friends assure us that the only way in which Japan can show her friendship to China & veneration for Chinese culture is to make war on her and reduce her to vassalage. I cannot understand this attitude.'[40] In his study overlooking the garden and orchard he tracked Dante's ascent from Hell through Purgatory to Paradise, while the world followed a precisely opposite course.

Three days after Hitler and Mussolini signed the Pact of Steel in Berlin on 22 May 1939, Binyon delivered Oxford's most prestigious lecture, the Romanes, at the Sheldonian, where half a century earlier he had recited 'Persephone'. He chose for his subject 'Art and Freedom', a theme which would in various guises preoccupy him for the last four years of his life. While Germany made final preparations for the invasion of Poland, he turned 70 on 10 August. 'It doesn't seem long ago that I looked on 70 as an age of remote decrepitude, & now that it is on me I don't feel old a bit,' he remarked to a friend. 'There is so much still that I want to do in poetry, if only I am granted some years more. I don't seem to care what is thought of it, so long as I can get it done.'[41] Three weeks later Britain was at war. He wrote to Percy Withers:

How frightful that we have to go through it all again! I remember how confident we all were in 1918 that there would be no more war—for England at least—in our time. Still in spite of the slaughter & misery, it's better than giving in to the blackmailer once more.... Now that I'm turned 70 I don't suppose I can be of any use, unless some writing sort of job turned up later: so I go on as before. Dante means intensive work which takes one's mind into other regions.[42]

He was wrong. On 13 December the British Council telephoned to ask if he would consider going out to Athens for four months as a stopgap Byron Professor of English Literature on a few days'

---

[40] ALs, 20 July 1940, in the possession of Mrs Yashiro Wakaba.
[41] ALs to Percy Withers, 8 Aug. 1939.   [42] ALs, 3 Sept. 1939.

notice. Despite his age and the uncertainties of travel in a disintegrating Europe, he did not hesitate. As a classicist, he revered Greece as the source of European culture and intellectual freedom. Now, with all that under threat, he was glad to return.

Arriving in Athens on the Orient Express in early January, the Binyons moved into a small suite at the Hotel Grande Bretagne, where he hastily wrote a series of fourteen lectures on English poetry from Wordsworth to Eliot and Auden, a valedictory celebration of the craft and tradition he had followed for sixty years. With enthusiasm for English surging in Athens since the outbreak of war, the lectures were packed with students from among the 5,000 enrolled at the English Institute. It was a strange, luminous time, sequestered from the momentous events to the west and north yet under imminent threat from them. From the city which more than any other had shaped its culture, he watched Europe again tearing itself apart. He wrote to an American friend:

Sometimes out here I ask myself why I am in this lovely country, having all the pleasure, when there is all the slaughter & the torture going on. What I feel most is the degradation of the world. How it has sunk in our lifetime!

I try not to think far ahead, and to take things as they come, the crystal air of Athens among the rest, & the sunshine: at any rate I'm glad not to be on the shelf but to be found of a little use to my country's cause, which I believe is the world's cause too.'[43]

Returning to Britain in May as planned had always seemed likely to be problematic, especially if Italy entered the war. Binyon had been well aware of this, telling Bottomley he would return 'if the ways are open'.[44] By mid-May return by land or sea was impossible with the Swiss cancelling all visas and the Mediterranean closed. On 16 May, a day after the collapse of Holland, the Binyons were flown by flying boat to Marseilles, where they were held up for two days by a mistral, while to the north the Allied armies began withdrawing from Belgium and the Germans entered Brussels. They arrived back in England in time for Dunkirk and the fall of France. 'My mind & heart are all in France,' he wrote to Bottomley. 'I don't lose faith in our final victory, but the agony of France at this moment haunts me all the time. When I was in France in 1917 & 18 I saw the hideous destruction & can never forget it: & to have

[43] ALs to Mary Winslow, 10 Mar. 1940, Houghton.   [44] ALs, 9 Feb. 1940.

to endure it again & much worse, is hard for us in England to imagine.'[45]

Returning from Greece four years earlier, memories of its beautiful, dry, ruthlessly clear landscapes had brought home to Binyon the 'indescribable tenderness' of the English countryside, epitomized by his orchard and garden at Westridge. Now, in a besieged Britain never more conscious of itself as an island, this feeling returned with a power deepened by the threat of imminent invasion. '[H]ere we are on this besieged island, having to fight for our lives', he wrote to Yashiro in July, during the first phase of the Battle of Britain. 'Any day & any hour now we expect to be invaded by the Germans.'[46] Plans were laid to defend the downs, which were considered a possible landing site for paratroopers. The danger intensified his 'sense of the extreme & intoxicating beauty of the earth, the wonder of everything'.[47] He volunteered for the Defence volunteers, but, being well over age, was put on reserve. Surrounded by children and grandchildren at Westridge, he returned to Dante, listened to Churchill's defiant speeches on the radio, weeded the vegetable garden, and tended his orchard. He dug deep, both into the earth and into himself, and entered upon the most intense creative period of his life.

In November Eliot enquired about publishing a selection of his poems in Faber's Sesame series, telling him: 'Indeed I should feel that the series was not what I wished it to be unless you were included.'[48] Binyon agreed with alacrity, but Macmillan refused permission on the grounds that they would later issue a *Selected Poems* themselves. It was, Binyon admitted, 'a real disappointment. . . . I think such a book, with Faber's imprint, might have reached a rather different public.'[49] Impressed by a batch of new poems, Eliot proposed instead that Faber publish his new book. Binyon was surprised and pleased, though, as he told Cicely, 'a little embarrassed by such warmth toward a belated Victorian like me'.[50] When Macmillan again objected, however, his loyalty to the firm for persevering with the loss-making Dante translations won out and the new book went to them.

The North Star appeared in May 1941, at the height of the Blitz. It is a richly varied collection, the last and best published during

[45] ALs, 12 June 1940.   [46] ALs, 20 July 1940.
[47] ALs to Bottomley, 21 Sept. 1940.   [48] TLs, 22 Nov. 1940.
[49] ALs, 10 Jan. 1941 (Valerie Eliot collection).   [50] 29 Dec. 1940.

Binyon's lifetime. There is a tragic symmetry in the fact that the earliest poem in the collection was written for the tenth anniversary of the Armistice while the latest, like 'Airmen from Overseas', are Second World War poems. 'Angkor' and the Japan poems are here, 'Mediterranean Verses', inspired by his 1935 trip to Egypt and Palestine, poems about Greece, and the fine sonnet 'Windows at Chartres'. Several poems express his love for England, such as 'Inheritance' with its celebratory catalogue of English landscapes, while lyrics like 'Sowing Seed' and 'Autumn Afternoon' explore his life at Westridge.

The title poem, 'The North Star', is a typical Binyon lyric meditation, but it is overshadowed by the opening poem, 'In Hospital', a poem Eliot admired when he read it in manuscript and Spender thought 'very fine indeed'.[51] It re-enacts an experience Binyon had waking at dawn one morning during his near-fatal illness at Guy's in the winter of 1931–2:

> Nothing of itself is in the still'd mind, only
> A still submission to each exterior image,
> Still as a pool, accepting trees and sky,
>
> A candid mirror that never a breath disturbs
> Nor drifted leaf,—as if of a single substance
> With every shape and colour that it encloses,—
>
> When, alone and lost in the morning's white silence,
> Drowsily drowsing eyes, empty of thought,
> Accept the blank breadth of the opposite wall.
>
> Lying in my bed, motionless, hardly emerged
> From clouds of sleep,—a solitary cloud
> Is not more vague in the placeless blue of ether
>
> Than I, with unapportioned and unadjusted
> Senses, that put off trouble of understanding,
> Even the stirring of wonder, and acquiesce.
>
> The early light brims over the filled silence.
> Memory stirs not a wave or a shadow within me.
> Only the wall is the world; there stops my sight.
>
> (*NS* 1)

On the blank wall he sees the figure of a 'great Archer', his face turned away, his bow hidden behind his back, an eerie but beauti-

---

[51] *NS*, 12 July 1941, 40.

fully restrained image of the archer Death. Watching him, wondering if he will turn and shoot, the speaker examines his own delicately balanced state of mind—'is it fear, or hope?'—and realizes that it is beyond either, a luminous state of heightened attention outside of time:

> As if all my gaze were fixt on a drop of water
> Suspended, about to fall and still not falling,
> A liquid jewel of slowly increasing splendour
>
> As the rain retreats and the shadow of cloud is lifted
> And all light comes to enclose itself in the circle
> Of a single drop, so is this suspended moment.

III

> The stillness moves. Tripping of feet; shadows;
> Voices. The hospital wakes to its ritual round.
> The moment breaks; the drop, the bright drop falls.
>
> A sponge has prest its coldness over my spirit.
> Shape and colour abandon their apparition,
> Subside into place in the order of usual things.
>
> And another mind returns with the day's returning,
> Weaving its soft invisible meshes around me.
> This is the daylight, bald on the plain wall.
>
> Cracks in the paint, a trickle of random lines,
>
> .   .   .   .
>
> Is it out of these I supposed a towering image
> There on the blankness? Are you gone, my Archer,
> You who were living more than the millions waking?
>
> No, you are there still! It was I released you
> Out of the secret world wherein you are hidden.
> You are there, there; and the arrow is flying, flying . . .
>
> And yet patient, as if nothing were endangered,
> We do small things and keep the little commandments,—
> We and our doings a scribble upon the wall.

> (*NS* 2–3)

Trying to explain why this poem produced in him the same effect 'as a beautiful smiling image of the Buddha', Ranjee Shahani wrote in terms reminiscent of Binyon's own meditations on Zen art: 'We feel, as we read his work, that he writes from a still centre; and, as

we continue, he instils stillness into us.'[52] It is a new voice in
Binyon's poetry, simpler, less rhetorical and with a metrical fluidity
which enacts rather than describes the subtle inflections of thought
and emotion. The poem is the experience, not a report on it. Pound
was at least partly right in seeing the discipline involved in translating Dante as having cured Binyon of his Miltonic 'rhetorical
bustuous rumpus' and helped him break free from his generation's
'doughy mess of third-hand Keats, Wordsworth, heaven knows
what'. He also suspected that Binyon's long immersion in Japanese
art had had a cumulative effect.[53] In the 'Clarity and immaculacy'
of the prose of *The Spirit of Man in Asian Art*, the *China
Review* had seen analogies with Sung ink painting. So had Pearl S.
Buck:

His writing makes one think of a Chinese painting, apparently simple to
the point of artlessness, yet profound with knowledge and feeling where
simplicity is in reality the subtlest of eliminations, the stripping away of all
but the purest and most essential form.[54]

For the first time this could be said with equal truth of Binyon's
poetry. He had congratulated Pound on his 'incessant war on the
indefinite and the decorative' in *ABC of Reading*,[55] and this was his
own programme in these taut, lean poems, a stripping away of
inessentials. Another fine poem in *The North Star*, 'The Way
Home', is an implicit manifesto for the poetry of Binyon's old age
and its search for an unillusioned winter clarity:

> More than soft clouds of leaf
> I like the stark form
> Of the tree standing up without mask
> In stillness and storm,
>
> Poverty in the grain,
> Warp, gnarl, exposed,
> Nothing of nature's fault or the years'
> Slow injury glozed.
>
> From the thing that is
> My comfort is come.
> Wind washes the plain road:
> This is the way home.

                                            (*NS* 55)

[52] 'Laurence Binyon', 95.   [53] 'Hell', 383, 386-7.
[54] 'Spirit of Laurence Binyon', 27; Buck, 635.   [55] ALs, 17 July 1934, BRBM.

In its acceptance of what the Japanese call *sono mama*, the way things are, and in the clarity of those final bare monosyllables, this is the most Zen-like poem Binyon ever wrote.[56]

The North Star was praised by poet–reviewers as different as Blunden, Kathleen Raine, and Spender, who acknowledged that Binyon had 'never received the full recognition which he deserves'.[57] Just about the doyen of English poets by now, a self-acknowledged 'antique Victorian', Binyon confessed to being 'rather pleased not to be classed with outmoded ancients'.[58] De la Mare found them 'so truly and inwardly *shareable*', while other old friends such as Bottomley and Moore were amazed at the resilience and 'sustained power' of his creativity in face of a war which each found, in different ways, inhibited their own work.[59]

It was certainly not that the war did not touch Binyon. If anything, the Second World War hit him harder than the First. 'For the Fallen' had long been enshrined as a secular hymn in Remembrance Day services, so integral a part of official British culture that reciting it at the Festival of Remembrance at the Albert Hall in November 1936 had been one of King Edward VIII's last public engagements before he abdicated in December. Binyon still occasionally lost patience with this ritualized national grief. In one of the poems in *The North Star*, 'Anniversary (November 11)', written in 1928 for the tenth anniversary of the Armistice, he had urged that the nation go beyond anodyne 'remembering tears' and actually build the new world for which a generation died:

> Have we only remembering tears, and flowers to strew?
> They are crying to us with the cry of the unfulfilled,
> Like the earth aching for spring, when frosts are late.
> Are we the answer? Or shall they twice be killed?
>
> (*NS* 6)

By 1941, in a war that was the culmination of twenty years of violence rooted in the same national hatreds and social injustices, the answer to that final question seemed to be yes.

[56] See Daisetz Suzuki, *Zen and Japanese Culture* (1959; Tokyo, 1988), 16, 208, 230–1.

[57] Blunden, 'Poems by Laurence Binyon', *Guardian*, 13 June 1941, 279; Raine, *Spectator*, 12 Sept. 1941, 268; Spender, *NS*, 12 July 1941, 40.

[58] ALs to James Smith, 21 Oct. 1942.

[59] De la Mare, ALs to LB, 16 June 1941; Moore, ALs, 5 June 1941.

BBC wireless broadcasts meant that not even the Berkshire downs was immune from the relentless 'daily tale of slaughter & destruction' from Europe, Africa, and Asia, which Binyon found 'soul-sickening'.[60] Lectures took him to London several times during the height of the Blitz, where more than 250,000 Londoners were bombed out of their homes. From Westridge, 50 miles away, they could see the flashes of anti-aircraft fire during the nightly raids. With babies and young children under their roof, even Westridge was not entirely safe. War-planes droned overhead, and bombs occasionally dropped on nearby fields and farmhouses. Nicolete, 3 years old when the Great War broke out, now had three, four, then five young children of her own, who spent long periods at Westridge. With Margaret and her two, then three children living there since the beginning of the war, they lived, as Binyon put it, 'in an atmosphere of baby-hood'.[61] From 1940 onwards Margaret wrote and Helen illustrated a series of books for children, which were published by Oxford University Press and became known as the 'Binyon books'.

The extended family, often including eleven adults and children, were absorbed in 'a daily round of small things',[62] gardening, salting beans, making jam, canning fruit, and selling greengages and plums to raise money for the Red Cross. By the autumn of 1942 the orchard was yielding two tons of apples and plums, and, with income tax taking half Binyon's pension, they lived frugally, living mainly off home-grown vegetables. Binyon found a hard, resilient joy in craftsmanly labour, whether sitting in his William Morris chair in the upstairs study unteasing the more scholastic *Paradiso* cantos, working in the orchard and garden, or composing poetry by the light of the western sky in his draughty, beloved loggia at the back of the house. For a man who had always been more conservationist than conservative, these activities intermeshed, the cycles of nature and the cyclical human seasons of his family and his own life and creativity all parts of a wider, deeper unity, the 'Spiritual Rhythm' celebrated in his writings on Chinese art.

Binding all this together was his relationship with Cicely. 'To have achieved a beautiful relation to another human being is to

[60] ALs to Winslow, 28 Jan. 1942, Houghton.
[61] ALs to Winslow, 14 Apr. 1942, Houghton.
[62] ALs to Winslow, 28 Jan. 1942, Houghton.

realise a part of perfection', he had written in *The Flight of the Dragon* (*FD* 22). The girl in the hyacinth garden was accessible to Eliot only in memory and vision, but for the 70-year-old Binyon it meant the woman he had grown old with: 'I feel a little dazed & drunk by the beauty of the garden. I keep thinking of it & you in the midst of the flowers. I feel you so young, my lovely wife, & I too feel young on such heavenly days as this.'[63] When she was away from Westridge briefly in the summer of 1942, he wrote: 'But how I miss you in the morning when I go round the garden! Not that I don't miss you all the time. The longing for you is just over-powering some times. . . . I think how wonderful it is that we should have such happiness in each other & in all three of our adorable children.'[64]

The enforced isolation of their life on the downs was a godsend to Binyon's poetry. He completed the *Paradiso* in April 1941, and returned to his other major project of these final years, *The Madness of Merlin*, a long dramatic poem which had been in gestation for at least thirty years. Its subject was not the Merlin of the Arthurian legends but the Welsh prince of Geoffrey of Monmouth's twelfth-century *Vita Merlini*, who joined forces with the North Welsh and the Cumbrians to wage war on the Picts, but, horrified at the slaughter, fled the battlefield to roam the great forest.

Binyon's poem was to have been in three parts, but at his death he had completed only the first. Even in its fragmentary state it is an uncanny, visionary work unlike anything else in Binyon's *œuvre*, creating a bardic speech at once primitive and sophisticated, draw-ing on a monosyllabic Anglo–Saxon vocabulary shorn of almost all 'poetic' and abstract words within a framework of free rhythms playing over a loose accentual base. He told Wilfrid Gibson that he found traditional metres inappropriately glib in face of the horrors of the war: 'in writing myself these days I feel a craving for language that is, so to speak, bruised & hurt or hard & rasping & rhythms to correspond'.[65] The unpublished manuscripts show that instead of pushing ahead with the other two parts, Binyon worked pains-takingly on Part 1, adding to the density and physicality of the text, paring away all inessentials.

[63] ALs to CMB, 20 Apr. 1939. [64] ALs, n.d. [1942].
[65] ALs, 5 Oct. 1941 [CMB transcript]. See also Bottomley, Introduction, *The Madness of Merlin* (London, 1947), p. xi.

> I have sung of the red berry
> In white mist, and the stag
> Crashing through frozen reeds.
> I have sung of the prow carving
> Water into beauty
> In bays where the gulls cry;
> And the flash of the blue spears
> When the chiefs toss their hair
> Riding proud by the hill.[66]

In a review of the published fragment Gwyn Jones noted that some lines 'have the exact air of a translated englyn'.[67] In fact, with advice from a Museum colleague, the Welsh scholar Idris Bell, he had studied translations of early Welsh poetry. Reading the manuscript in 1942, Bell wrote: 'You seem to me remarkably successful in getting . . . the tone & atmosphere of the early Welsh poetry: the verse has the same clearness of outline and brightness of atmosphere, the same economy of statement, especially in the more lyrical passages, as the poetry of the Cynfeirdd.'[68] It was a search for roots, for the *Ap Einion* beneath the Binyon, for (another of Binyon's favourite words) the 'elemental' in both language and human experience. The best gloss on *The Madness of Merlin*, whose 'mystical poetry' has recently been described as 'considerably better than average',[69] is the first of Binyon's Tokyo lectures, where he describes Celtic sensitivity to the numinous otherness of nature, quoting an ode to the wind attributed to the sixth-century Welsh bard Taliesin, who appears as a character in the poem (*LA* 9).

Merlin was to have been an ambitiously philosophical poem, exploring themes he had essayed in 'Asoka', 'The Idols', and 'Angkor' in a manner 'symbolic of our time', including the war.[70] It was a Dantean task for a poet who was no Dante, and the magnum opus was destined to remain an enigmatic fragment, while the great poetry of Binyon's old age was written during periods when he laid the cumbrous epic aside. While revising the *Paradiso* proofs in

---

[66] *The Madness of Merlin* (London, 1947), 37–8.

[67] *Life and Letters To-Day*, 54 (July 1947), 76.

[68] ALs to LB, 19 Mar. 1942; LB to Bell, ALs, 5 Apr. 1942, National Lib. of Wales, Aberystwyth.

[69] Muriel Whitaker, 'Laurence Binyon', *The Arthurian Encyclopedia*, ed. Norris J. Lacey (New York, 1986), 46.

[70] ALs to Sturge Moore, 10 Jan. 1938, box 28/160, TSMP–LU.

March 1942 he began work on 'The Ruins', a long poem in seven sections on the Odes pattern which soon became a sequence of seven, then five separate poems interlinked by theme and imagery, perhaps influenced by the *Four Quartets*, parts of which Eliot sent him as they appeared. He admired the *Quartets*' 'directness and precision', the way 'when symbol & image come, they are enhanced by the bareness which foils them'. In the same March 1941 letter to Eliot, he spoke of his own struggles to purify the dialect of the tribe: 'How tormenting are the problems of expression. I am always wishing that I could start quite fresh—make a new beginning.'[71]

In praising Eliot's 'precision' and unobtrusive symbolism he could be describing his own spare, luminous last poems. Due to the difficulties of wartime travel, letters between Binyon and his closest friends were longer and more numerous than before, and it is possible to chart the growth of 'The Ruins' week by week during the spring and summer of 1942, when it began circulating in manuscript, copied out in letters and handed on from friend to friend. Logan Pearsall Smith wrote: 'I can't tell you how great is the kind of aromatic consolation the *Burning of the Leaves* has given the few of my friends to whom I have allowed myself to show these verses.' Among these friends was Cyril Connolly, founder and editor of *Horizon*, described by Smith as 'that rather wild publication . . . which has become the organ of the younger generation'.[72] Connolly greatly admired the sequence, especially the opening poem, which first appeared in the *Observer* on 11 October:

> Now is the time for the burning of the leaves.
> They go to the fire; the nostril pricks with smoke
> Wandering slowly into a weeping mist.
> Brittle and blotched, ragged and rotten sheaves!
> A flame seizes the smouldering ruin and bites
> On stubborn stalks that crackle as they resist.
>
> The last hollyhock's fallen tower is dust;
> All the spices of June are a bitter reek,
> All the extravagant riches spent and mean.
> All burns! The reddest rose is a ghost;
> Sparks whirl up, to expire in the mist: the wild
> Fingers of fire are making corruption clean.
>
> Now is the time for stripping the spirit bare,
> Time for the burning of days ended and done,

---

[71] ALs to Eliot, 4 Mar. 1941 (Valerie Eliot).   [72] ALs, 5 Aug. 1942.

Idle solace of things that have gone before:
Rootless hope and fruitless desire are there;
Let them go to the fire, with never a look behind.
The world that was ours is a world that is ours no more.

They will come again, the leaf and the flower, to arise
From squalor of rottenness into the old splendour,
And magical scents to a wondering memory bring;
The same glory, to shine upon different eyes.
Earth cares for her own ruins, naught for ours.
Nothing is certain, only the certain spring.

(BL 1)

Connolly published the five-poem sequence as 'The Ruins' in the October *Horizon*, a month before it appeared under its final title, 'The Burning of the Leaves', in the November *Atlantic Monthly*. It made a deep impression on *Horizon* readers, and when the magazine folded in 1949 Connolly told Cicely he thought it the best poem they had printed during its remarkable decade.[73] The poem has either joined or supplanted 'For the Fallen' in good anthologies, rightly so since it is a far better poem. Like 'For the Fallen' it is a war poem, only this time not for the fallen but for the unfallen, for 'we that are left', who did grow old enough to see the world engulfed by an even more destructive war. That Pearsall Smith and others of Binyon's generation could find 'aromatic consolation' in so nakedly honest and unsentimental a poem is indicative of the mood of the war years. 'The Burning of the Leaves' is one of the major lyrics of the home front, and it is remarkable, to say the least, that the poet who produced the most famous consolatory poem of the First World War should also have written during the Second World War what George Gilpin has correctly identified as 'the poem that spoke most poignantly for the besieged and for the era'.[74]

The themes and images of this opening poem recur in redefining contexts in the four poems that follow. In poem II the scene changes to a deserted theatre, for this theatre-loving man a powerful 'symbol of disenchantment & desolation',[75] as on a grey winter morning, silent except for the shuffling mops of two charwomen,

---

[73] TLs to CMB, 30 Dec. 1949. See also Victoria Sackville-West, 'Voices and Visions', *Observer*, 30 July 1944, 3.

[74] '1898–1945: Hardy to Auden', *Columbia History of British Literature*, ed. Carl Woodring and James Shapiro (New York, 1994), 552.

[75] LB, ALs to Withers, 19 July 1942.

only the speaker remembers the voices, 'Beautiful as water, beautiful as fire', that have long since fallen silent. The old man who stumbles about the blitzed house in poem III is a *London Visions* figure forty years on, set in a denser visionary world, while poem IV, a meditation on Michelangelo's 'Slaves' in the Louvre, affirms the final indestructibility of the creative spirit, unquenchable as that of nature itself. 'Beautiful as water, beautiful as fire' is the pivotal line of the entire sequence, balancing across its caesura the harshly cleansing fire which destroys in order to create new life, and its complementary antithesis, the 'living springs' which glide through the 'lunar desolation' of the Blitz, 'Still | Fluent and fresh and pure | . . . As if nothing had died' (*BL* 4). The mysterious waters in poem V 'mirror the ruins a moment' but retain no memory, the self-renewing springs of life indifferent to and uncontaminated by man's insanity:

> The freshness of leaves is from them, and the springing of grass,
> The juice of the apple, the rustle of ripening corn;
> They know not the lust of destruction, the frenzy of spite;
> They give and pervade, and possess not, but silently pass;
> They perish not, though they be broken; continuing streams,
> The same in the cloud and the glory, the night and the light.
>
> (*BL* 6)

One acute reviewer described this as 'a lyrical footnote to some of the sayings of Lao Tzu',[76] rightly so since the water imagery of the *Tao Tê Ching* was in Binyon's mind here, as it had been six years earlier when he had lectured on the Taoist principle of 'the *power* of emptiness, of inaction and of weakness', of the 'secret of fluidity, of aspiring to pervade rather than to resist, to flow rather than to strive'.[77] These waters were for Binyon the operations of the divine made visible, bespeaking no personal God who can be called upon for salvation or to account for a world gone mad, but flowing 'At their own will' from their mysterious source, fructifying and giving life. As he wrote in *The Spirit of Man in Asian Art*:

Tao is the creative cause of the universe; it contains the quintessence of reality. 'It loves and nourishes all things, but does not act as master.'

---

[76] 'Laurence Binyon', rev. of *BL*, *TLS*, 17 June 1944, 298.
[77] 'Chinese Painters', *Journal of the Royal Society of Arts*, 84 (14 Feb. 1936), 377–8.

'Production without possession, action without self-assertion, development without domination; this is its mysterious operation.'

(*SMAA* 72)

Since at least *For Dauntless France*, the planting and nurturing of fruit trees for the benefit of future generations had been Binyon's symbol for 'Production without possession'. In his 'small | Corner of paradise' at Westridge, this became a daily reality. In 'The Orchard', a poem found among his papers after his death, he and Cicely plant trees for their grandchildren, 'No stony monument | But growing, changing things' which will bloom 'In other Junes than ours' (*BL* 14).

These last poems comprise a poetry of old age almost as fine in its understated way as Yeats's. With their unsentimental awareness of mortality, they are essays in non-attachment, loving without clinging to the past or even to life itself, a meditative stripping bare of the spirit in a season of war and death, discarding all the psychic hand-luggage we cannot take on what Binyon called 'the flight of "the Alone to the Alone"' (*SMAA* 102). In his case there seems to have been little excess baggage to discard. Richard Church wrote that his was 'a spirit grave, subtle in its extraordinary sensitiveness, Franciscan in its welcome for poverty'.[78] 'One couldn't live with Laurence without, at any rate understanding his unworldliness & trying to live up to it', Cicely told Rothenstein.[79] A few weeks before Binyon died Sturge Moore wrote to Gordon Bottomley, depressed that his own personality was not more like Binyon's. Bottomley replied:

I agree with all you say of Binyon, and the harmonious beauty of his character. But you need not envy him; his qualities do not further his writing (being always such as expand outward from him) as your inward-moving concentration and intensity of focus do your writing—and always have done.[80]

This is an acute insight. Harmonious beauty of character, integrity, and wholeness translate into good poetry less readily than inner conflict, since, as Yeats knew, poetry comes from the quarrel with ourselves. In these last poems, however, perhaps at last Binyon found the right form, a rhetoric flexible and sensitive enough to

---

[78] 'Poets in War Time', rev. of *NS*, *Listener*, 3 July 1941, 30.
[79] ALs, 12 June [1943], BMS Eng. 1148 (127) fo. 2, WRP–HH.
[80] Bottomley to Sturge Moore, ALs, 31 Dec. 1942, box 17/399, TSMP–LU.

capture his thinking voice and allow us to see in motion the 'beautiful mind' of which Bridges had spoken fifty years before. This is 'Winter Sunrise', the poem Binyon was working on when he died:

> It is early morning within this room; without
> Dark and damp; without and within, stillness
> Waiting for day: not a sound but a listening air.
>
> Yellow jasmine, delicate on stiff branches
> Stands in a Tuscan pot to delight the eye
> In spare December's patient nakedness.
>
> Suddenly, softly, as if at a breath breathed
> On the pale wall, a magical apparition,
> The shadow of the jasmine, branch and blossom!
>
> It was not there, it is there, in a perfect image;
> And all is changed. It is like a memory lost
> Returning without a reason into the mind;
>
> And it seems to me that the beauty of the shadow
> Is more beautiful than the flower; a strange beauty,
> Pencilled and silently deepening to distinctness.
>
> As a memory stealing out of the mind's slumber,
> A memory floating up from a dark water,
> Can be more beautiful than the thing remembered.
>
> (*BL* 16)

To read these last poems and unpublished fragments is to watch, as if in slow motion, a poet steadily growing in sensitivity and power, poem by poem, up to, and in a sense including, his own death. Masefield wrote to Cicely about this 'most beautiful last poem': 'One of the most wonderful things of a rare spirit is that continued growth; it's one of the rarest things in life; yet see how marvellously marked it is in him.'[81] Binyon called it his 'midwinter poem', for the season in which it was written, for his own place in the human seasonal cycle, and perhaps also as a reference to *Little Gidding*, which Eliot sent him with the inscription: 'I have felt some diffidence about offering this: but any experiment in an English variation of *terza rima* ought to be submitted to the censure of you who know more about it than any of us!'[82]

The poem is complete in itself, but it was to have been the opening of a longer poem. The surviving drafts include visions of

[81] ALs, 21 Mar. 1943.
[82] AMS inscription on flyleaf, n.d. [1942] (Harriet Proudfoot collection).

war and apocalypse. Although the tide was slowly beginning to turn the Allies' way in Russia, North Africa, and the Pacific in the winter of 1942–3, dark news was filtering through from central Europe. On 22 December Binyon wrote to Withers about the 'slaughter & torture of Jews & Poles—one can't begin to realize it. It is beyond all imagination,'[83] while in the drafts he pleads 'Let me not be so stunned that I cannot feel.' Finally, however, the poet's attention returns to the present, the redemptive here and now of the shadow on the wall of his bedroom at Westridge:

> My dreaming eyes return
> The flower of winter remembers its own season
> And the beautiful shadow upon the pale wall
> Is imperceptibly moving with ancient earth
> Around the sun that timeless measures sure and silent.
>
> (*BL* 17)[84]

By the time 'Winter Sunrise' appeared in the April 1943 *Horizon*, Binyon was dead. Nine months earlier he had suffered a rupture through an old prostate operation scar and had to wear a truss. He continued working in the garden and at his desk, but during the winter, Cicely recalled later, 'he suddenly began to look much older, to *be* older in his body though his mind was as active as ever & he wrote as well as ever he did'.[85] After an appendix operation in early March, broncho pneumonia set in, leaving him too weak to undergo a needed second operation. On 10 March, days after completing final revisions to the *Paradiso* proofs, he died quietly in a Reading nursing home. His death, announced that night on the 9 o'clock BBC news, came as a shock to all but his family. He had kept the seriousness of his illness from friends, writing them serene, encouraging letters about poetry until a few days before his death. He sent his closest friends a draft of 'Winter Sunrise', which Bottomley later realized had been 'a gift at parting'. Bottomley's last letter, a few days before Binyon's death, had been in response to this 'miracle of a poem', which in its chaste economy reminded him of an early Chinese drawing. 'It made me feel breathless for fear I should disturb the shadow,' he wrote, 'and it left both of us speechless'.[86]

[83] ALs, 22 Dec. 1942.
[84] CMB appended a few of the rough drafts when she published 'Winter Sunrise' in *The Burning of the Leaves*. See CMB's Introduction, p. v.
[85] ALs to Mary Winslow, 9 July [1943], Houghton.
[86] ALs to CMB. 10 Mar. 1943; to LB, 26 Feb. 1943.

Hearing the announcement on the BBC, Sturge Moore wrote to his own wife: 'Alas! alas! Binyon is gone. He was very perfect and very good. One felt all piecemeal patched together beside him. I feel all alone now. . . . He was very complete.'[87] To Cicely he wrote that he was perhaps 'the most complete and perfect man' he had ever known.[88] Walter de la Mare mourned the loss of 'his rare & precious gifts & qualities of mind & spirit. This is a personal loss, but I realize no less how tragic a loss, especially in these days when so much that one values most is in danger, it is for England, which he loved so ardently & served with all his heart.'[89]

After a funeral service in Trinity College chapel on 13 March he was buried near Westridge in the churchyard of St Mary's Church, Aldworth. Among his unfulfilled engagements was a talk at Greek House in aid of occupied Greece, which was delivered by Basil Gray, and Edith Sitwell's charity Poets' Reading at the Aeolian Hall on 14 April, where he had been due to read alongside Eliot, Blunden, de la Mare, Sitwell, H. D., Bottomley, Gibson, and Waley to an audience which included the Queen and the princesses Elizabeth and Margaret. Masefield turned it into a memorial service, making a speech and reading 'For the Fallen' and 'Winter Sunrise'. According to Bottomley, as his 'remarkable and unusual tribute' progressed Masefield

was more and more moved, and he had to control his voice quite hard. . . . [W]hen he came to 'For the Fallen' he was very fine indeed, and again there were suppressed tears in his voice. It is not Laurence's noble voice, and I missed that as the familiar words went on, but before the end I could hear Laurence's voice too by some miracle of sympathy—so clearly that I thought others might too.[90]

Sturge Moore chaired a Poetry Society commemoration in May. In the *New Statesman* Cyril Connolly lamented the passing of 'a wise, poor, happy and incorruptible lover of truth and beauty', a man who had learnt from Chinese culture 'how to be both warm and detached, in fact, a sage'. He would be remembered 'both as the populariser of Chinese painting (his *Flight of the Dragon* is still the best cheap book on the subject) and as the authority on Blake

---

[87] Postcard, postmarked 11 Mar. 1943, 37/158, TSMP–LU.
[88] ALs to CMB, n.d. [1944].   [89] ALs to CMB, n.d. [March 1943].
[90] ALs to CMB, Easter Sunday 1943. See 'The Queen and Princesses at Reading of Poetry', *The Times*, 15 Apr. 1943, 7; Masefield, 'The Poet Laureate's Tribute', *The Times*, 13 Mar. 1943, 7.

and Palmer', and as the poet who 'wrote one of the best poems of
the last war, and "The Leaves," one of the best poems in this'.[91]
Pearsall Smith in *The Times* celebrated Binyon for having written
not only the 'greatest poem of the last Great War' but also his 'even
grander, more tragic, and yet more consolatory' war poem 'The
Burning of the Leaves':

> Such were the thoughts of one of the finest spirits, if not the finest, of our
> time as, a shabbily dressed figure, he raked together for their consumption
> the garden rubbish and fallen leaves of the Berkshire farm of his retire-
> ment. Such a sight of perhaps the last successor of the English dynasty
> of self-devoted servants of the austere Muses, of Milton, of Wordsworth,
> of Robert Bridges, who made their lives, as Milton said they should
> ... into a true poem, was a sight which certainly, to one observer at least,
> made England, made indeed the whole world, seem a better place to live
> in.[92]

Among many other tributes were several from Asia. S. K. Mukerjea
wrote to the *Guardian* reporting that the Oxford Majlis had con-
vened a special meeting to pass a resolution that 'in the death of
Laurence Binyon India has lost a lifelong friend, and she will always
remember him with affection and gratitude.'[93] A Binyon Memorial
Fund was set up to create an Oxford bursary to enable students to
travel abroad to study art. With committee members including
Robert Trevelyan, Eliot, de la Mare, Shaw, Sir Atul Chaterjee,
Masefield, and Waley, the Binyon Prize was inaugurated in 1947, a
fitting memorial for a man who loved youth, travel, and art in equal
measure.

Binyon died a month before his and Cicely's thirty-ninth wedding
anniversary. He had written his last letter to her five weeks before
he died. She was away from Westridge briefly, and he had spoken
of his sense of the spring coming, of having read in *The Times*
about Montgomery reciting his poetry to the troops at Tripoli,
and concluded 'How I long for the sight & the touch of you, &
your voice, my Beloved'.[94] 'When I think of the nearly 40 years
of amazing companionship which I have had', she wrote to
Rothenstein, 'I know that pride & thankfulness must swallow up

---

[91] 'A London Diary', *New Statesman and Nation*, 27 Mar. 1943, 201.
[92] 'Dr. Laurence Binyon', *The Times* 16 Mar. 1943, 6. See also Nowell Smith,
'Thoughts on the Poetry of Laurence Binyon', *English*, 4 (1943), 143–6; Robert
Sencourt, 'Laurence Binyon', *Fortnightly*, May 1943, 337–44.   [93] *Guardian*, 18 Mar. 1943, 4.   [94] ALs, 2 Feb. [1943].

all other feelings.'[95] She kept his spirit alive at Westridge by editing his manuscripts. Macmillan at last brought out the *Paradiso* in November 1943, while his delightful puppet play for children, 'British Museum Diversion', appeared in *Horizon* in September. *The Burning of the Leaves and Other Poems* appeared the following summer with a foreword by Cicely. 'I have read it through with joy and grief, thinking that he was one of the very few whose poetry got better as he grew older,' wrote Masefield. 'He did nothing better than these.'[96] With Gordon Bottomley's help, Cicely edited *The Madness of Merlin*, which was published in 1947. Always much more robust than her husband, she lived on at Westridge Farm House for another twenty years, keeping his study as it was the day he died, until she succumbed to the bitter winter of 1962–3 at the age of 86 and joined her husband in the Aldworth churchyard.

The best tributes to poets always come from other poets. Being no Yeats, Binyon had no Auden, but perhaps, given the collaborative ethic of the 1890s, it is fitting that he shared in a communal elegy. In Chapter 3, we met the young Wilfrid Gibson listening to Yeats, Binyon, and Sturge Moore discuss Tolstoy in a London tea shop. A year after Binyon's death he mourned the loss of all three poets within five years of each other. In the Holborn tea shop Binyon, 'Grave-eyed and gentle,' had sat 'silent, pondering like some Indian god | Rapt in calm introspective meditation', but when Gibson visited him at Westridge in August 1942 he had read to him, and Gibson had listened

> with blood that pulsed
> Responsive to the rhythm and the rapture
> As he to me with undiminished vigour
> Read his last poems in the resonant voice
> Whose organ-tones still echo in my heart.[97]

The finest tribute, the one that captures the essence of Binyon's final weeks by borrowing his own symbolism, was written by his neighbour, the novelist Rosamond Lehmann. In late January 1943 she had come to dinner, and afterwards he had read her 'The Burning of the Leaves', some Dante, and the poem he was working on, 'Winter Sunrise'. Her elegy appeared in the April 1943 *Horizon* alongside 'Winter Sunrise':

[95] ALs, 21 Mar. [1943], BMS Eng. 1148 (127), fo. 1, WRP–HH.
[96] ALs to CMB, n.d. [*c.*June 1944].   [97] 'The Three Poets' 73–4.

Last month, sitting in his armchair, he read—
He who today is dead,
Our honoured love, pride, grief—
Poems: his spring-winter cluster, blossom and fruit in one.
His rich voice lifted that triumphant sheaf.
Bonfires and running waters; ordeals of youth;
Ruin, rebirth; solaces, lucid meditations of old age;
All these were in his words: symbols and images of purifying truth.
He closed the page.
Quiet, gentle he sat. Then, since the hour grew late:
'Goodnight.' He went ahead,
Casting his torch-beam towards the garden gate.
'Goodnight.' Then, 'Wait', he said,
'One moment. You must see
Our winter-flowering tree.'
Across the grass we went. Then suddenly
From dead of dark the apparition! . . . White
Aërial spirit broken from bare wood,
Prunus in bloom. . . . 'How beautiful by this light!'
Over the boughs he threw its mild dim shower.
So thus they stood,—
Sweetly illumined she
By him; but he
Folded in winter dark impenetrably,—
Silently shining one upon the other:
The old man and the young tree, both in flower.[98]

---

[98] 'In Memoriam: Laurence Binyon', *Horizon*, 7 (Apr. 1943), 221–2. Quoted by permission of the Society of Authors on behalf of the Rosamond Lehmann Estate.

Bibliography

This bibliography is selective. For a fuller check-list of writings by LB, manuscript materials, and contemporary reviews, see my doctoral dissertation, 'Laurence Binyon: A Critical Biography' (Oxford, 1991).

CHRONOLOGICAL CHECK-LIST OF SELECTED WRITINGS BY LAURENCE BINYON

Books

Niobe (London, 1887).

Joan of Arc (London, 1888).

Primavera: Poems by Four Authors, with Stephen Phillips, Manmohan Ghose, and Arthur C. Cripps (Oxford, 1890).

Persephone: The Newdigate Poem, 1890 (Oxford, 1890).

Lyric Poems (London, 1894).

Poems (Oxford, 1895).

Dutch Etchers of the Seventeenth Century (London, 1895).

First Book of London Visions (London, 1896).

The Praise of Life (London, 1896).

The Supper: A Lyrical Scene (Edinburgh, 1897).

John Crome and John Sell Cotman (London, 1897).

Porphyrion and Other Poems (London, 1898).

Catalogue of Drawings by British Artists and Artists of Foreign Origin Working in Great Britain, Preserved in the Department of Prints and Drawings in the British Museum, 4 vols. (London, 1898–1907).

Second Book of London Visions (London, 1899).

Western Flanders: A Medley of Things Seen, Considered and Imagined by Laurence Binyon, with Ten Etchings by William Strang (London, 1899).

Thomas Girtin: His Life and Works: An Essay (London, 1900).

Odes (London, 1901).

William Blake, Being All His Woodcuts Reproduced in Facsimile (London, 1902).

The Death of Adam and Other Poems (London, 1904) [1903].

Penthesilea: A Poem (London, 1905).

Dream-Come-True: Poems (London, 1905).

Paris and Oenone (London, 1906).

William Blake: Vol. 1 Illustrations to the Book of Job (London, 1906).

Attila: A Tragedy in Four Acts (London, 1907).

London Visions, collected and augmented (London, 1908).

Pictures by Japanese Artists (London, 1908).

Painting in the Far East: An Introduction to the History of Pictorial Art in Asia, Especially China and Japan (London, 1908; rev. edns. 1913, 1923, 1934).

Japanese Art (London, 1909).

England and Other Poems (London, 1909).

The Flight of the Dragon: An Essay in the Theory and Practice of Art in China and Japan, Based on Original Sources (London, 1911).

The Art of Botticelli: An Essay in Pictorial Criticism (London, 1913).

Auguries (London, 1913).

The Winnowing Fan: Poems on the Great War (London, 1914).

Bombastes in the Shades: A Play in One Act (London, 1915).

The Anvil (London, 1916).

A Catalogue of Japanese and Chinese Woodcuts Preserved in the Sub-Department of Oriental Prints and Drawings in the British Museum (London, 1916).

For the Fallen and Other Poems (London, 1917).

The Cause: Poems of the War (London, 1918).

For Dauntless France: An Account of Britain's Aid to the French Wounded and Victims of the War, Compiled for the British Red Cross Societies and the British Committee of the French Red Cross by Laurence Binyon (London, 1918).

The New World: Poems (London, 1918).

The Four Years: War Poems Collected and Newly Augmented (London, 1919).

Sakuntala: By Kalidasa, Prepared for the English Stage by Kedar Nath Das Gupta in a New Version Written by Laurence Binyon (London, 1920).

The Secret: Sixty Poems (London, 1920).

The Court Painters of the Grand Moguls (London, 1921).

The Drawings and Engravings of William Blake (London, 1922).

Arthur: A Tragedy (London, 1923).

Japanese Colour Prints, with J. J. O'Brien Sexton (London, 1923; rev. edn., ed. Basil Gray, London, 1960).

Ayuli: A Play in Three Acts and an Epilogue (Oxford, 1923).

The Sirens: An Ode (Chelsfield, 1924; rev. edn., London, 1925).

Little Poems from the Japanese: Rendered into English Verse by Laurence Binyon (Leeds, 1925).

The Followers of William Blake: Edward Calvert, Samuel Palmer, George Richmond and their Circle (London, 1925).

Tradition and Reaction in Modern Poetry (London, 1926).

The Engraved Designs of William Blake (London, 1926).

The George Eumorfopoulos Collection: Catalogue of Chinese Frescoes (London, 1927).
Boadicea: A Play in Eight Scenes (London, 1927).
Sophro the Wise: A Play for Children (London, 1927).
A Laurence Binyon Anthology (London, 1927).
The Wonder Night (London, 1927).
The Poems of Nizami, Described by Laurence Binyon (London, 1928).
The Idols: An Ode (London, 1928).
The George Eumorfopoulos Collection: Catalogue of the Chinese, Corean and Siamese Paintings (London, 1928).
Trans. *Dante: Episodes from the Divine Comedy* (London, 1928).
Art and Modern Life (Bristol, 1929).
Three Short Plays: Godstow Nunnery, Love in the Desert, Memnon (London, 1930).
Landscape in English Art and Poetry (Tokyo, 1930; London, 1931).
A Persian Painting of the Sixteenth Century: Emperors and Princes of the House of Timur (London, 1930).
Catalogue of the Loan Collection of English Water-Colour Drawings Held at the Institute of Art Research, Ueno, Tokyo, October 10–24th, 1929 (Tokyo, 1930).
Collected Poems, 2 vols. (London, 1931).
Akbar (London, 1932).
Koya San: Four Poems from Japan (London, 1932).
Trans. *Dante's Inferno, With a Translation into English Triple Rhyme by Laurence Binyon* (London, 1933).
English Water-Colours (London, 1933; 2nd edn. 1944).
With J. V. S. Wilkinson and Basil Gray: *Persian Miniature Painting, including a Critical and Descriptive Catalogue of the Miniatures Exhibited at Burlington House January–March 1931* (London, 1933).
The Young King: A Play (Canterbury, 1934).
The Case of Christopher Smart (London, 1934).
The Spirit of Man in Asian Art: Being the Charles Eliot Norton Lectures Delivered in Harvard University 1933–34 (Cambridge, Mass., 1935).
The English Romantic Revival in Art and Poetry: A Reconsideration (London, 1936).
Trans. *Dante's Purgatorio, With a Translation into English Triple Rhyme by Laurence Binyon* (London, 1938).
Brief Candles (London, 1938).
Art and Freedom, Romanes Lecture (Oxford, 1939).
The North Star and Other Poems (London, 1941).
Trans. *Dante's Paradiso, with a Translation into English Triple Rhyme by Laurence Binyon* (London, 1943).
The Burning of the Leaves and Other Poems, ed. Cicely Binyon (London, 1944).

The Madness of Merlin (London, 1947).

Trans. *The Divine Comedy. Dante: The Divine Comedy Translated by Laurence Binyon, With La Vita Nuova Translated by D. G. Rossetti*, ed. Paolo Milano (New York, 1947), 1–544; reprint edns. (London, 1972 and 1979).

Selected Poems, Articles, Reviews, Editions, and Introductions

'Matthew Arnold's Poetry', *Temple Bar*, 84 (Sept. 1888), 106–11.

'The Garden of Criticism (with Humble Apologies to "The Garden of Proserpine")'. *Oxford Magazine*, 21 Nov. 1888, 107.

'On Certain Confusions of Modern Life, Especially in Literature: An Essay Read, at Oxford, to the Gryphon Club of Trinity College', *Hobby Horse*, NS 18 (Apr. 1890), 58–68.

'The Popularization of Art', *The Civilization of Our Day*, ed. James Samuelson (London, 1896), 320–9.

Rev. of *Christ in Hades*, by Stephen Phillips, *SR*, 20 June 1896, 629–30.

'Mr. Sidney Colvin', *English Portraits: A Series of Lithographs*, by William Rothenstein (London, 1898–9), Part IV, n.pag.

'Mr. Bridges', "Prometheus", and Poetic Drama', *Dome*, NS 2/6 (March 1899), 199–206.

Rev. of *The Ideals of the East*, by Kakuzo Okakura, *TLS*, 6 March 1903, 73–4.

'The Life and Work of John Sell Cotman', *Masters of English Landscape Painting, Studio*, Special Summer Number 1903, JSC, pp. ii–xvi.

Introduction, *Poems*, by John Keats (London, 1903), pp. xi–xxix.

'A Chinese Painting of the Fourth Century', *BM*, 4/10 (Jan. 1904), 39–49.

'The Art of the Nineteenth Century', rev. of *Nineteenth Century Art*, by D. S. MacColl, *Quarterly Review*, 199 (Jan. 1904), 80–99.

'A Reply to Mr. MacColl (1)', letter, *SR*, 13 Feb. 1904, 202–3; 'A Reply to Mr. MacColl (11)', letter, *SR*, 20 Feb. 1904, 232–3.

'The Art of Blake', *Independent Review*, 2 (Apr. 1904), 407–15.

'Note', *Artist–Engraver*, 1 (Jan. 1904), 4.

Preface, *The Society of Twelve: First Exhibition, 1904* (London, 1904), n.pag.

'Three Artists', preface, *Catalogue of an Exhibition of Water-Colours, Pastels, and Paintings by Charles Conder, W. Rothenstein and C. H. Shannon* (London, 1904), 7–10.

'Watts and National Art', *Independent Review*, 5 (Mar. 1905), 201–9.

'A Landscape by Chao Mêng-Fu in the British Museum', *T'oung Pao* (Leiden), 2nd ser., 6 (Mar. 1905), 56–60.

'The International Society', *SR*, 2 Feb. 1907, 137–8.

'Chardin and Ruskin', *SR*, 30 Mar. 1907, 388–90.

' "Max"; and a Peep at the Academy', SR, 4 May 1907, 553–4.
'Old and New English Art', SR, 23 Nov. 1907, 630–1.
'Romance and Reality', SR, 21 Dec. 1907, 759–60.
'Art and Legend', SR, 18 Jan. 1908, 75–6.
'Two Exhibitions', SR, 1 Feb. 1908, 136–7.
'Some Phases of Japanese Art', *Proceedings of the Japan Society of London*, 8 (1907–9), 96–112.
'Reflections on Two Great Movements', SR, 9 May 1908, 589–90.
'National Character in Art', SR, 10 Oct. 1908, 447–8.
'Some Autumn Shows', SR, 24 Oct. 1908, 510–11.
'Whistler', SR, 7 Nov. 1908, 571–3.
'The New Barbarism', Rev. of *Modern Art*, by Julius Meier-Graefe, SR, 28 Nov. 1908, 662–3.
'The New English Art Club', SR, 29 May 1909, 683–4.
'Mr. Strang and Others', SR, 23 Oct. 1909, 497.
'Arts and Crafts: and the Twelve', SR, 22 Jan. 1910, 104–5.
'Japanese Masterpieces in London', SR, 28 May 1910, 686–7.
'Art and Life', SR, 20 Aug. 1910, 229–30.
'Town-Planning, and the New Bridge', SR, 29 Oct. 1910, 543–4.
'Post-Impressionists', SR, 12 Nov. 1910, 609–10.
'Romney; Raeburn; Mr. John', SR, 10 Dec. 1910, 746–7.
'E pur si muove', SR, 31 Dec. 1910, 840–1.
'Portraits and Sculpture', SR, 11 Feb. 1911, 171–2.
'Some Phases of Religious Art in Eastern Asia', *Quest*, July 1911, 654–72.
'The Return to Poetry', *Rhythm*, 4 (Spring 1912), 1–2.
Text. *Admonitions of the Instructress in the Palace: A Painting by Ku K'ai-chih in the Department of Prints and Drawings, British Museum Reproduced in Coloured Woodcut* (London, 1912), 3–30.
'Ideas of Design in East and West', *Atlantic Monthly*, Nov. 1913, 643–54.
'For the Fallen', *The Times*, 21 Sept. 1914, 9.
'Indian Art', *Quarterly Review*, 443, Apr. 1915, 507–26.
'The Art of Asia', *Atlantic Monthly*, Sept. 1915, 348–59.
'The Place of the Ajanta Paintings in Eastern Art', *Ajanta Frescoes* (London, 1915), 21.
'An English Hospital for French Soldiers', letter, *The Times*, 6 Nov. 1915, 10.
Ma Yüan's Landscape Roll in the Freer Collection (New York, 1916).
Ed., *The Poetical Works of John Keats* (London, 1916).
'The Art of Asia', *Transactions and Proceedings of the Japan Society, London*, 14 (1916), 2–23.
'Verhaeren', TLS, 7 Dec. 1916, 584.
'Art and the War', NS, 12 May 1917, 135–6.
'Three Artists', NS, 30 June 1917, 304.

With Sidney Colvin, 'The Late Stanley William Littlejohn', *BM*, 32 (Jan. 1918), 16–19.

'And What of Art?', *Dial* (Chicago), 31 Jan. 1918, 93–5.

'War Pictures and the War Museum', *NS*, 20 Apr. 1918, 52–3.

'English Poetry in its Relation to Painting and the Other Arts', *Proceedings of the British Academy* (1917–1918), 381–402.

'The Spell of Dante's Poetry', *TLS*, 15 Sept. 1921, 585–6.

'The English Ode', *Essays by Divers Hands*, NS 2 (1922), 1–21.

Introductory Memoir, *Poems of Isaac Rosenberg*, ed. Gordon Bottomley (London, 1922).

Biographical Note, *Chinese Painters: A Critical Study*, by Raphael Petrucci (London, 1922), 7–9.

'The Speaking of Verse', *Torchbearer*, 1/1 (June 1924), 21–2.

'The Art of Yoshijiro Urushibara', *Ten Woodcuts, Cut and Printed by Yoshijiro Urushibara after Designs by Frank Brangwyn, R. A.* (London, 1924), n.pag.

Ed., *The Golden Treasury of Modern Lyrics* (London, 1924).

'The Revolt of Reason', *St Martin's Review* (Nov. 1925), 566–8.

Introductory Memoir, *Songs of Love and Death*, by Manmohan Ghose (Oxford, 1926), 7–23.

Introduction, *Burlington Fine Arts Club: Blake Centenary Exhibition Catalogue* (London, 1927), 7–11.

'Eastern Art', *Twenty-Five Years of the National Art-Collections Fund 1903–1928*, ed. D. S. MacColl (Glasgow, 1928), 163–75.

Ed., *Palgrave's Golden Treasury of Songs and Lyrics: Fifth Book (Nineteenth Century)*, Vol. v of *Golden Treasury of Songs and Lyrics* (London, 1928).

'Kalidasa and the Sanskrit Drama', *Shakuntala or the Lost Ring: An Indian Drama Translated into English Prose and Verse by Sir Monier Monier Williams* (London, 1929), 7–14.

'Indian Art and Literature: Mr. Laurence Binyon's Address at the Oxford Majlis Dinner', *Bharat* (Oxford), 14 (Trinity Term, 1929), 4–7.

'English Poetry & Drama of To-Day and To-Morrow', *Studies in English Literature* (Tokyo), 10 (Jan. 1930), 1–15.

Introduction, *Ajanta: The Colour and Monochrome Reproductions of the Ajanta Frescoes Based on Photography*, by G. Yazdani, 8 vols. (London, 1930), i. pp. xi–xix.

Introduction, *The Shāh-nāmah of Firdausī: The Book of the Persian Kings*, by J. V. S. Wilkinson (London, 1931), pp. xiii–xx.

'Baron Takuma Dan', *The Times* 11 Mar. 1932, 19.

Ed., *Poems of Blake*, by William Blake (London, 1931).

'Replica of a Statue of Kwannon', *BMQ*, 7/1 (1932), 1.

'The Artistry of Speech', *Good Speech*, 3/20 (July–Sept. 1933), 5–11.

'Learning to Speak and Enjoy Poetry: the Latest Oxford Movement', *Times Educational Supplement*, 1 Dec. 1934, 401.

Introduction, 'Painting and Calligraphy', *Chinese Art*, ed. Leigh Ashton (London, 1935), pp. ix–xi, 1–30.

'Chinese Painting', *Asia*, 35 (Nov. 1935), 666–72.

'Chinese Painters', *Journal of the Royal Society of Arts*, 84 (14 Feb. 1936), 369–79.

'Chinese Art and Buddhism', *Proceedings of the British Academy* (1936), 157–75.

Introduction, *The Chinese Exhibition: A Commemorative Catalogue of the International Exhibition of Chinese Art, Royal Academy of Arts, November 1935–March 1936* (London, 1936), pp. vii–xi.

'A Tribute to the Genius of Chinese Painting', *China: Body and Soul*, ed. E. R. Hughes (London, 1938), 19–26.

'Gerard Hopkins and His Influence', *University of Toronto Quarterly*, 8 (Jan. 1939), 264–70.

'The Qualities of Beauty in Persian Painting', *Survey of Persian Art: From Prehistoric Times to the Present*, ed. Arthur Upham Pope, 6 vols. (London, 1938–9), iii. 1917.

'Approach to Chinese Art and Poetry', *Asiatic Review*, July 1940, 558–72.

'From a Corner of Rural England', *Britain To-day*, 20 Sept. 1940, 9–12.

'Homage to India', *Indian Art and Letters*, NS 14/2 (1940), 111–12.

Preface, *Leaves from the Sketch Books of Frank Brangwyn Cut by Urushibara* (Leigh-on-Sea, [1940?]), n.pag.

Speech, Rabindranath Tagore Memorial Meeting, India Society, 1941, *Indian Art and Letters*, NS 15/2 (1941), 59.

'The English Lyric', *Journal of the Royal Society of Arts*, 89 (14 Nov. 1941), 786–96.

'Translating Dante', *Mark Twain Quarterly*, 6/1 (Summer–Autumn 1943), 2–3.

'British Museum Diversion: A Play for Puppets', *Horizon*, Sept. 1943, 153–5.

SECONDARY LITERATURE AND CONTEMPORARY REVIEWS

All reviews are listed chronologically.

Primavera (1890).

Wilde, Oscar, *Pall Mall Gazette*, 24 May 1890, 3.

Cambridge Review, 29 May 1890, supplement, pp. lxxxvii–lxxxviii.

Athenaeum, 21 June 1890, 796–7.

Image, Selwyn, *Century Guild Hobby Horse*, 5/19 (July 1890), 119–20.

Symonds, John Addington, *Academy*, 9 Aug. 1890, 104.

Johnson, Lionel, *Church Reformer*, 9/8 (Aug. 1890), 185.

Lyric Poems (1894).
The Times, 16 Feb. 1894, 3.
Gale, Norman, *Academy*, 24 Mar. 1894, 247.
Symons, Arthur, *Athenaeum*, 12 May 1894, 607–8.

First Book of London Visions (1896).
Publishers' Circular, 64 (18 Jan. 1896), 83.
Sketch, 5 Feb. 1896, 53.
Gale, Norman, *Academy*, 29 Feb. 1896, 175.
Bookman, 9 (Mar. 1896), 189.

Porphyrion (1898).
Pall Mall Gazette, 2 Aug. 1898, 4.

Second Book of London Visions (1899).
Dome, 2/4 (Jan. 1899), 88–90.

The Death of Adam (1903).
'Mr. Binyon's New Poems', *Pilot*, 21 Nov. 1903, 504.
'Poetry', *Academy*, 9 Jan. 1904, 33–4.

Dream-Come-True (1905).
Moore, Thomas Sturge, *Academy*, 13 May 1905, 512.
'Some Recent Verse', *TLS*, 25 Aug. 1905, 267.

Penthesilea (1905).
Courtney, W. L., *Daily Telegraph*, 26 Apr. 1905, 13.
'A Tale of Troy', *Outlook*, 14 Oct. 1905, supplement, pp. iii–iv.

Paris and Oenone (performance, 1906).
'Notable New Play: Mr. Binyon on His Version of "Paris and Oenone"', *Daily Chronicle*, 8 Mar. 1906, 10.
Archer, William, 'Savoy Theatre: New One-Act Plays', *Tribune*, 9 Mar. 1906, 9.
Ross, Robert, 'The Drama', *Academy*, 17 Mar. 1906, 263.

Attila (performance, 1908).
'"Attila": His Majesty's Theatre: Mr. Binyon's Poetic Play', *Daily Telegraph*, 5 Sept. 1907, 9–10.
'Attila', *The Times*, 5 Sept. 1907, 8.
Baughan, E. A., '"Attila": Laurence Binyon's Play Produced at His Majes-

ty's Theatre', *Daily News*, 5 Sept. 1907, 4.

Beerbohm, Max, 'Attila', *SR*, 14 Sept. 1907, 327–8.

Child, Harold, ' "Attila" and the Art of Stage-Production', *BM*, 12 (Oct. 1907), 3–6.

London Visions: Collected and Augmented (1908).

Abercrombie, Lascelles, 'Eight Voices', *Nation* (Supplement), 14 Nov. 1908, 282.

Painting in the Far East (1908).

Morrison, Arthur, 'Chinese and Japanese Painting', *BM*, 14 (Dec. 1908), 158–60.

Fry, Roger, 'Oriental Art', *Quarterly Review*, 212 (Jan. 1910), 225–39.

England and Other Poems (1909).

'Mr. Binyon's New Poems', *TLS*, 30 Dec. 1909, 513.

Morning Post, 9 Jan. 1910, 2.

The Flight of the Dragon (1911).

Athenaeum, 7 Oct. 1911, 428–9.

'Appreciation of Art', *Daily News*, 14 Nov. 1911, 3.

Chesterton, G. K., 'The Slime of the Dragon', *Daily News*, 18 Nov. 1911, 6.

Auguries and Other Poems (1913).

Fairfax, Griffith, *Poetry and Drama*, 1 (Dec. 1913), 494–5.

TLS, 11 Dec. 1913, 601–2.

The Anvil (1916).

'Mr. Binyon's Poems', *TLS*, 17 Feb. 1916, 78.

Bickley, Francis, 'Laurence Binyon and Others', *Bookman*, 50 (Apr. 1916), 17.

A Catalogue of Japanese and Chinese Woodcuts (1916).

'Japanese Prints', *TLS*, 3 May 1917, 209.

The Four Years (1919).

TLS, 18 Sept. 1919, 496.

Sakuntala (performance, 1919).

'Sakuntala: New Version of Old Play', *Era*, 19 Nov. 1919, 6.

' "Sakuntala": Worthy Performance of a Great Play', *The Times*, 15 Nov. 1919, 14.

Arthur (1923) (performance and text, 1923).

B[aughan], E. A., ' "Arthur": Laurence Binyon's Work at the Old Vic', *Daily News*, 13 Mar. 1923, 5.

'Arthur', *Weekly Westminster Gazette*, 17 Mar. 1923, 14–15.

' "King Arthur": Weighty Production at the Old Vic', *Daily Express*, 13 Mar. 1923, 8.

Littlewood, S. L. R., ' "Arthur": Mr. Laurence Binyon's Play at the Old Vic', *Pall Mall Gazette*, 13 Mar. 1923, 4.

Courtney, W. L., '*Arthur*: Laurence Binyon's Play,' *Daily Telegraph*, 23 Mar. 1923, 17.

Mountjoy, Desmond, 'Laurence Binyon's Arthur', *Old Vic Magazine*, 4/6 (Mar. 1923), 2–3.

——, 'Round Table and Retort', *Nation and Athenaeum*, 24 Mar. 1923, 964.

The Young King (performance, 1924).

' "The Young King": New Play in a New Theatre: Mr. Binyon's Poetry', *The Times*, 15 Nov. 1924, 8.

'Poet as Play Producer', *Daily News*, 15 Nov. 1924, 4.

The Sirens (1924–5).

Abercrombie, Lascelles, 'A Great Ode', *Manchester Guardian*, 9 Feb. 1925, 7.

Figgis, Darrell, 'What Song the Sirens Sang', *Sunday Times*, 5 Apr. 1925, 9.

TLS, 23 July 1925, 492.

J. E. G. de M., 'Mr. Binyon's New Poem', *Contemporary Review*, 287 (Aug. 1925), 253–6.

Abercrombie, Lascelles, 'A Great Poem', *Weekly Westminster*, NS 4/20 (12 Sept. 1925), 503.

Rickword, Edgell, *Calendar of Modern Letters*, 2 (Sept. 1925), 65–8.

C. P. 'Verse in 1925', *Manchester Guardian Weekly*, 4 Dec. 1925, supplement, pp. xi–xii.

Selwyn, E. G., *Theology*, 12/7 (Jan. 1926), 35.

Boadicea (performance, 1926).

' "Boadicea": Mr. Laurence Binyon's New Play in Verse', *Morning Post*, 16 Jan. 1926, 8.

' "Boadicea": Tragedy Produced at Oxford', *The Times*, 16 Jan. 1926, 8.

The Idols (1928).

Twitchett, E. G., *London Mercury*, 19 (Jan. 1929), 319–20.

Roberts, R. Ellis, 'Mr. Binyon: A Writer in the Grand Manner', *Daily News*, 13 Mar. 1929, 4.

Kendon, Frank, *Bookman*, 76 (May 1929), 121–2.

Curzon, K. E., *Poetry: Past and Present*, 1/1 (Winter 1929), 24–6.

Poems of Blake (1931).
Forster, E. M., 'An Approach to Blake', *Spectator*, 2 Apr. 1932, 474.

Collected Poems (1931).
Abercrombie, Lascelles, 'Laurence Binyon', *Listener*, 18 Nov. 1931, supplement, p. vii.
Selincourt, Basil de, 'Heir to Poetry: Mr. Binyon's Collected Poems', *Observer*, 29 Nov. 1931, 6.
'Mr. Binyon's Poems', *TLS*, 21 Jan. 1932, 41.
Wood, Frederick T., 'On the Poetry of Laurence Binyon', *Poetry Review*, 23 (Sept.–Oct. 1932), 349–74.

Dante's Inferno (1933).
Pound, Ezra, 'Hell', *Criterion*, 13 (Apr. 1934), 382–96.
TLS, 25 May 1933, 353–4.

The Young King (performance, 1934).
'The Friends of Canterbury', *The Times*, 11 June 1934, 9.

Boadicea (performance, 1935).
' "Boadicea": Mr. Binyon's Play at Oxford', *Manchester Guardian*, 31 July 1935, 10.
The Times, 31 July 1935, 10.

The Spirit of Man in Asian Art (1935).
Buck, Pearl S., *Asia*, 35 (Oct. 1935), 635.
Coomaraswamy, Ananda K., *Journal of the American Oriental Society*, 55 (1935), 325–9.
'The Spirit of Laurence Binyon in Chinese Art', *China Review*, 4 (Oct. 1935), 27–8.

Dante's Purgatorio (1938).
Pound, Ezra, 'Purgatory', *New English Weekly*, 29 Sept. 1938, 373.
——, 'Binyon: Salutiamo un a traduzione pregevolissima della Divina Commedia', *Broletto*, 34 (Oct. 1938), 14–15.
Charlton, H. B., 'Mr. Binyon's Dante', *Manchester Guardian*, 25 Oct. 1938, 7.
Spender, Stephen, 'Dante in English', *NS*, 14 Jan. 1939, 57–8.

The North Star (1941).
Blunden, Edmund, 'Poems by Laurence Binyon', *Guardian*, 13 June 1941, 279.

Church, Richard, 'Poets in War Time', *Listener*, 3 July 1941, 30.
Spender, Stephen, *NS*, 12 July 1941, 40.
Raine, Kathleen, *Spectator*, 12 Sept. 1941, 268.

The Burning of the Leaves (1944).
'Laurence Binyon', *TLS*, 17 June 1944, 298.
Alloway, Lawrence, *Sunday Times*, 2 July 1944, 3.
Sackville-West, Victoria, 'Voices and Visions', *Observer*, 30 July 1944, 3.

The Madness of Merlin (1947).
Jones, Gwyn, *Life and Letters To-Day*, 54 (July 1947), 74–6.
Gant, Roland, *Poetry Quarterly*, 9 (Winter 1947–48), 252–3.

GENERAL BIBLIOGRAPHY OF WORKS CITED

ANADOS (see Coleridge, Mary E.).
ANDERSON, WILLIAM. 'A History of Japanese Art', *Transactions of the Asiatic Society of Japan*, 7 (1879), 339–73.
——*Descriptive and Historical Catalogue of a Collection of Japanese and Chinese Paintings at the British Museum* (London, 1886).
——*Japanese Wood Engravings* (London, 1895).
——*The Pictorial Art of Japan* (London, 1886).
ARCHER, WILLIAM, *Poets of the Younger Generation* (London, 1902).
ARNOLD, MATTHEW, *Complete Prose Works of Matthew Arnold*, ed. R. H. Super, 11 vols. (Ann Arbor, 1960–77).
——*The Poems of Matthew Arnold*, ed. Kenneth Allott (London, 1965).
'The Asche–Brayton Season at His Majesty's: An Interview at Rehearsal', *Pall Mall Gazette*, 28 Aug. 1907, 6.
ATKINSON, F. G., 'Unpublished Letters of Laurence Binyon (1): The Years of Struggle', *Notes and Queries*, NS, 29 (Aug. 1982), 335–9.
——'Unpublished Letters of Laurence Binyon (2): The Years of Achievement', *Notes and Queries*, NS, 31 (Mar. 1984), 72–6.
'Mr. Augustus John', *The Times*, 5 Dec. 1910, 14.
'An Auspicious Occasion', *Drama*, 1/1 (July 1919), 22–4.
BEAL, MARY, 'Paul Nash's "Event on the Downs" Reconsidered', *BM*, 131 (Nov. 1989), 748–54.
BECKETT, JOHN, and GARDINER, ANDREW, *Merlewood Grange-over-Sands and the Lancashire Cotton Industry* (Grange-over-Sands, 1987).
BECKSON, CARL, *London in the 1890s: A Cultural History* (New York, 1992).
BENJAMIN, WALTER, *Charles Baudelaire: A Lyric Poet in the Era of High Capitalism*, trans. Harry Zohn (London, 1973).

BERGER, KLAUS, *Japonisme in Western Painting from Whistler to Matisse*, trans. David Britt (Cambridge, 1992).

BICKLEY, FRANCIS, 'Laurence Binyon', *T.P.'s Weekly*, 28 Aug. 1915, 197–8.

BLAKISTON, HERBERT E. D., *Trinity College* (London, 1898).

BLYTH, R. H., *Zen in English Literature and Oriental Classics* (Tokyo, 1942).

BOTTOMLEY, GORDON, *A Stage for Poetry: My Purposes with my Plays* (Kendal, 1948).

BRIDGES, ROBERT, *Ode for the Bicentenary Commemoration of Henry Purcell, with Other Poems* (London, 1896).

—— *Selected Letters of Robert Bridges*, ed. D. E. Stanford, 2 vols. (Cambridge, Mass., 1984).

BUCKLEY, JEROME HAMILTON, *William Ernest Henley: A Study of the Counter-Decadence of the 'Nineties* (Princeton, 1945).

BUITENHUIS, PETER, *The Great War of Words: Literature as Propaganda 1914–18 and After* (London, 1989).

BULLEN, J. B. (ed.), *Post-Impressionism in England* (London, 1988).

CARPENTER, HUMPHREY, *A Serious Character: The Life of Ezra Pound* (London, 1988).

CHANG CHUNG-YUAN, *Creativity and Taoism: A Study of Chinese Philosophy, Art, and Poetry* (1963; New York, 1970).

CHISOLM, LAWRENCE W., *Fenollosa: The Far East and American Culture* (New Haven, 1963).

COLEMAN, VERNA, *The Last Exquisite: A Portrait of Frederic Manning* (Melbourne, 1990).

COLERIDGE, MARY E. [Anados], *Fancy's Guerdon* (London, 1897).

COLVIN, SIDNEY, *Memories and Notes of Persons and Places* (London, 1921).

CONANT, ELLEN P, 'Refractions of the Rising Sun: Japan's Participation in International Exhibitions 1862–1910', *Japan and Britain: An Aesthetic Dialogue 1850–1930*, ed. Tomoko Sato and Toshio Watanabe (London, 1991), 79–92.

CONNOLLY, CYRIL, 'A London Diary', *New Statesman and Nation*, 27 Mar. 1943, 201.

CORBETT, DAVID PETERS, 'Late Romantic Poetry, Criticism and the Visual Arts and Early Modernism in Britain' (unpublished paper, 1991).

—— 'Laurence Binyon', *The 1890s: An Encyclopedia of British Literature, Art and Culture*, ed. G. A. Cevasco (New York, 1993), 59–60.

CORDOVA, RUDOLPH DE, 'Some Phases in Literature and Art: An Interview with Mr. Laurence Binyon', *Great Thoughts*, 23 May 1914, 120–2.

CORK, RICHARD, *Vorticism and Abstract Art in the First Machine Age*, 2 vols. (London, 1976).

CORTAZZI, SIR HUGH, 'The Japan Society: A Hundred-Year History', *Britain and Japan 1859–1991: Themes and Personalities*, ed. Cortazzi and Gordon Daniels (London, 1991), 1–53.

'A Country House Theatre', *Country Life*, 8 Aug. 1925, 233–4.

CRAIG, EDWARD, *Gordon Craig: The Story of his Life* (London, 1968).

CRANE, WALTER, *The Decorative Illustration of Books Old and New* (London, 1896).

CRUMP, JEREMY, 'The Identity of English Music: The Reception of Elgar 1898–1935', *Englishness: Politics and Culture 1880–1920*, ed. Robert Colls and Philip Dodd (London, 1986), 164–90.

'Curiosities of Literature', *Punch*, 14 Nov. 1923, 464.

DARRACOTT, JOSEPH, *The World of Charles Ricketts* (London, 1980).

DAVIE, DONALD, 'Ezra Among the Edwardians', *Paideuma*, 5 (Spring 1976), 3–14.

DELANEY, PAUL, *Charles Ricketts: A Biography* (Oxford, 1990).

DICKINS, F. V., *Fugaku Hiyaku-Kei or a Hundred Views of Fuji (Fusiyama) by Hokusai*, 4 vols. (London, 1880).

DIGBY, GEORGE WINGFIELD, *Meaning and Symbol in Three Modern Artists: Edvard Munch, Henry Moore and Paul Nash* (London, 1960).

DIXON, RICHARD WATSON, *Songs and Odes* (London, 1896).

DOLMETSCH, MABEL, *Personal Recollections of Arnold Dolmetsch* (London, 1957).

DOWSON, ERNEST, *Letters of Ernest Dowson*, ed. Desmond Flower and Henry Maas (London, 1967).

DUGDALE, JOHN, 'Just How Do We Remember Them?', *The Times*, 9 Mar. 1993, 37.

EASTON, MALCOLM, and HOLROYD, MICHAEL, *The Art of Augustus John* (London, 1974).

Editorial, *Pauline*, 2 (Oct. 1884), 263–4.

ELIOT, T. S., *Letters of T. S. Eliot: Vol. 1 1898–1922*, ed. Valerie Eliot (London, 1988).

ELLMANN, RICHARD, *Oscar Wilde* (New York, 1988).

'The Encaenia at Oxford', *The Times*, 26 June 1890, 8.

EMMONS, ROBERT, *The Life and Opinions of Walter Richard Sickert* (London, 1941).

EPSTEIN, JACOB, *Epstein: An Autobiography* (London, 1955).

'Exhibition of Chinese Art', *China Review*, 5 (Jan. 1936), 9–10.

FALKENHEIM, JACQUELINE V., *Roger Fry and the Beginnings of Formalist Art Criticism* (Ann Arbor, 1980).

FENOLLOSA, ERNEST, *Review of the Chapter on Painting in 'L'Art japonais'* (Boston, 1885).

—— *The Masters of Ukioye* (New York, 1896).

—— *An Outline History of Ukiyo-Ye* (Tokyo, 1901).

FENOLLOSA, MARY, Preface, *Epochs of Chinese and Japanese Art: An Outline History of East Asiatic Design*, by Ernest Fenollosa, 2 vols. (London, 1912), i. pp. vii–xxii.

FICKE, ARTHUR DAVIDSON, *Chats on Japanese Prints* (London, 1915).

FITZGERALD, ROBERT, 'Mirroring the *Commedia*: An Appreciation of Laurence Binyon's Version', *Paideuma*, 10 (1981), 489–508.

FLETCHER, IAN, Introduction, *The Complete Poems of Lionel Johnson*, ed. Fletcher (London, 1953), pp. xi–xliv.

—— 'A Note on the Reputation of Elkin Mathews', *Elkin Mathews: Poet's Publisher (1851–1921)* (Reading, 1967), n.pag.

—— 'Poet and Designer: W. B. Yeats and Althea Gyles', *W. B. Yeats and his Contemporaries* (London, 1987), 166–96.

—— *Rediscovering Herbert Horne: Poet, Architect, Typographer, Art Historian* (Greensboro, GA, 1990).

FLUKINGER, ROY, SCHAAF, LARRY, and MEACHAM, STANDISH (eds.), *Paul Martin: Victorian Photographer* (London, 1978).

'French Debating Society', *Pauline*, 6 (May 1888), 663–5.

FROST, PETER, 'The Century Guild Hobby Horse and its Founders', *Book Collector*, 27 (1978), 348–60.

—— 'The Rise and Fall of Stephen Phillips', *English Literature in Transition 1880–1920*, 25/4 (1982), 225–31.

FRY, ROGER, *Bellini* (London, 1899).

—— *The Letters of Roger Fry*, ed. Denys Sutton, 2 vols. (London, 1972).

FUSSELL, PAUL, *The Great War and Modern Memory* (1975; Oxford, 1977).

GALTON, ARTHUR, *Rome and Romanizing: Some Experiences and a Warning* (London, 1900).

GHOSE, LOTIKA, *Manmohan Ghose* (New Delhi, 1975).

GHOSE, MANMOHAN, *Collected Poems*, i, ed. Lotika Ghose, 4 vols. (Calcutta, 1970).

—— *Love-Songs and Elegies* (London, 1898).

GIBSON, WILFRID, *Solway Ford and Other Poems*, ed. Charles Williams (London, 1945).

GILES, HERBERT A., *An Introduction to the History of Chinese Pictorial Art* (Shanghai, 1905).

GILES, LIONEL, *The Sayings of Lao Tzu* (London, 1904).

GILL, ERIC, *Letters of Eric Gill*, ed. Walter Shewring (London, 1947).

GILPIN, GEORGE H., '1898–1945: Hardy to Auden', *Columbia History of British Literature*, ed. Carl Woodring and James Shapiro (New York, 1994), 552.

GONSE, LOUIS, *L'Art japonais* (Paris, 1883).

GORDON, W. R., 'A Poet of Humanity: Mr. Laurence Binyon and the World', *Daily News*, 24 Jan. 1928, 4.

GRAY, BASIL, ' "Admonitions of the Instructress of the Ladies in the Palace": A Painting Attributed to Ku K'ai-chih', *Studies in Chinese and Islamic Art*, 2 vols. (London, 1985), i. 178–95.

—— 'Arthur Waley at the British Museum', *Madly Singing in the Mountains: An Appreciation and Anthology of Arthur Waley*, ed. Ivan Morris (London, 1970), 37–44.

—— 'The Development of Taste in Chinese Art in the West 1872 to 1972', *Transactions of the Oriental Ceramic Society*, 39 (1971–3), 19–43. Rpt. *Studies in Chinese and Islamic Art*, i. 16–38.

—— 'In Memoriam: Laurence Binyon', *Ars Islamica*, 11–12 (1946), 207–9.

—— 'The Royal Academy Exhibition of Chinese Art, 1935–36, in Retrospect', *Transactions of the Oriental Ceramic Society* (1985–6), 11–36.

GRAY, JOHN, 'Les Goncourt', *Dial*, 1 (1889), 9–13.

GRAY, NICOLETE, 'Friends of My Father, Laurence Binyon', *Private Library*, 3rd ser., 8/2 (1985), 79–91.

Great Britain, Parliament, *Parliamentary Papers* (Commons), *1913*, vol. 50 (*Accounts and Papers*, vol. 10), 31 Mar. 1913, 'Accounts, etc. of the British Museum'.

—— Parliament, *Parliamentary Papers* (Commons), *1929–30*, vol. 9 (*Reports*, vol. 16), 20 Sept. 1929, 'Royal Commission on National Museums and Galleries: Final Report. Part 1: General Conclusions and Recommendations'.

GRIFFITHS, ANTHONY, and WILLIAMS, REGINALD, *The Department of Prints and Drawings in the British Museum: User's Guide* (London, 1987).

GURNEY, IVOR, *War Letters*, ed. R. K. R. Thornton (Manchester, 1983).

HALL, LADY SOPHY, 'Dr. Laurence Binyon', letter, *The Times*, 18 Mar. 1943, 7.

HARKER, MARGARET, *The Linked Ring: the Secession Movement in Photography in Britain, 1892–1910* (London, 1979).

HARRIS, P. R., *The Reading Room* (London, 1979).

HARTMANN, SADAKICHI, *Japanese Art* (London, 1904).

HATCHER, JOHN, 'Anglo–Japanese Friendships: Yashiro Yukio, Laurence Binyon and Arthur Waley', *Fukuoka University Review of Literature & Humanities* (Japan), 23 (Mar. 1992), 997–1022.

—— 'Laurence Binyon: A Critical Biography', D. Phil. diss. (Oxford, 1991).

HAWORTH-BOOTH, MARK (ed.), *The Golden Age of British Photography 1839–1900* (London, 1988).

HENLEY, W. E., *The Works of W. E. Henley*, 7 vols. (London, 1908).

—— (ed.) *A London Garland: Selected from Five Centuries of English Verse* (London, 1895).

HERRINGHAM, CHRISTIANA J., 'The Frescoes of Ajanta', *BM* 17/87 (June 1910), 136–8.

HERRINGHAM, SIR WILMOT, 'The Expedition', *Ajanta Frescoes* (London, 1915), 16.

HILLIER, JACK, *Utamaro: Colour Prints and Paintings*, 2nd edn. (Oxford, 1979).

HOBSON, R. L., 'A Journey to the Far East', *BMQ*, 5/1 (1930), 34–9.

HOLADAY, WOON-PING CHIN, 'Pound and Binyon: China via the British Museum', *Paideuma*, 6 (Spring 1977), 27–36.

HOLMES, C. J., *Hokusai* (London, 1899).

—— 'Nature and Landscape', *Dome*, NS, 2/5 (Feb. 1899), 139–47.

—— *Self and Partners (Mostly Self): Being the Reminiscences of C. J. Holmes* (London, 1936).

HOLROYD, MICHAEL, *Augustus John: A Biography*, 2 vols. (London, 1974–5).

—— *Bernard Shaw 1918–1950: The Years of Fantasy* (1991; London, 1993).

HORNE, ALISTAIRE, *The Price of Glory, Verdun 1916* (London, 1962).

HORNE, HERBERT, 'William Morris', *SR*, First Illustrated Supplement (Christmas 1896), 1–4.

HOSMON, ROBERT STAHR, 'Hobby Horse, The', *British Literary Periodicals: The Victorian and Edwardian Age*, ed. Alvin Sullivan (Westport, Conn., 1984), 163–7.

HULME, T. E., 'Romanticism and Classicism', *Speculations: Essays on Humanism and the Philosophy of Art*, ed. Herbert Read (London, 1924), 113–40.

HUMPHREYS, CHRISTMAS, *Both Sides of the Circle: The Autobiography of Christmas Humphreys* (London, 1978).

HUTCHINS, PATRICIA, *Ezra Pound's Kensington: An Exploration, 1885–1913* (London, 1965).

HUXLEY, ALDOUS, *The Perennial Philosophy* (New York, 1945).

—— 'Wordsworth in the Tropics', *Life & Letters*, 1 (1 Oct. 1928), 342–55.

HYNES, SAMUEL, *A War Imagined: The First World War and English Culture* (New York, 1991).

JACKSON, HOLBROOK, *The Eighteen Nineties* (London, 1913).

JEANS, SIR JAMES, *The Mysterious Universe* (Cambridge, 1930).

JENKINS, DAVID FRASER, 'Slade School Symbolism', *The Last Romantics: The Romantic Tradition in British Art, Burne-Jones to Stanley Spencer*, ed. John Christian (London, 1989), 71–6.

JENYNS, SOAME, 'The Franks Collection of Oriental Antiquities', *BMQ*, 18 (1953), 103–6.

KEATS, JOHN, *Letters of John Keats*, ed. Maurice Buxton Forman, 4th edn. (London, 1952).

KENNEDY, MICHAEL, *Portrait of Elgar*, 2nd edn. (London, 1982).

KRISHNAMURTI, JIDDU, *Life in Freedom* (Ommen, Holland, 1928).

LANE, RICHARD, *Images from the Floating World: The Japanese Print, including an Illustrated Dictionary of Ukiyo-e* (Oxford, 1978).

LASKI, HAROLD, 'Scholar–Poet', *Daily Herald*, 11 Sept. 1933, 8.

'The Late Poet Laureate, Alfred Austin, and a Glimpse at his Possible Successors', *Daily Graphic*, 7 June 1913, 929.

'Laurence Binyon' editorial, *BM*, 62 (Apr. 1933), 153.

LAWTON, THOMAS, and MERRILL, LINDA, *Freer: A Legacy of Art* (Washington, DC, 1993).

LEAVIS, F. R., *New Bearings in English Poetry* (1932; London, 1972).

LECKY, WILLIAM EDWARD HARTPOLE, *History of European Morals from Augustus to Charlemagne*, 2 vols. (London, 1869).

LE GALLIENNE, RICHARD, *Limited Editions: A Prose Fancy, together with Confessio Amatis, a Sonnet* (London, 1893).

—— *Robert Louis Stevenson, an Elegy and Other Poems* (London, 1895).

LEGGE, SYLVIA, *Affectionate Cousins: T. Sturge Moore and Maria Appia* (Oxford, 1980).

LEHMANN, ROSAMOND, 'In Memoriam: Laurence Binyon', *Horizon*, 7 (Apr. 1943), 221–2.

LEVY, S., 'For the Fallen', letter, *TLS*, 23 Nov. 1946, 577.

LEWIS, WYNDHAM, *Blasting and Bombardiering* (London, 1937).

—— 'History of the Largest Independent Society in England', *Blast*, 2 (July 1915), 80–1.

—— *Letters of Wyndham Lewis*, ed. W. K. Rose (London, 1963).

LIPSEY, ROGER, *Coomaraswamy*, 3 vols. (Princeton, 1977).

'A Little Theatre at Boars Hill: A House for Poetic Drama: Interview with Mr. John Masefield', *Oxford Chronicle*, 7 Nov. 1924, 13.

LUBBOCK, PERCY, *George Calderon: A Sketch from Memory* (London, 1921).

LUCAS, E. V., *Charles Lamb and the Lloyds* (London, 1898).

—— *The Colvins and their Friends* (London, 1928).

LUTYENS, MARY, *Krishnamurti: The Years of Awakening* (London, 1975).

M., E., 'Art Notes', *Illustrated London News*, 2 July 1910, 28.

McCARTHY, LILLAH, *Myself and My Friends* (London, 1933).

MacCOLL, D. S., 'A Quarterly Reviewer', *SR*, 6 Feb. 1904, 166–7.

—— letter, *SR*, 20 Feb. 1904, 233.

—— *Nineteenth Century Art* (London, 1903).

McDONNELL, MICHAEL F. J., *A History of St Paul's School* (London, 1909).

MADSEN, S. TSCHUDI, *Art Nouveau*, trans R. I. Christopherson (London, 1967).

MARKINO, YOSHIO, *A Japanese Artist in London*, ed. Sammy I. Tsunematsu (1910; Brighton, 1991).

MARTIN-HARVEY, SIR JOHN, *The Autobiography of Sir John Martin-Harvey* (London, 1933).

MASEFIELD, JOHN, Preface, *The Oxford Recitations* (New York, 1928), 5–9.

—— 'The Poet Laureate's Tribute', *The Times*, 13 Mar. 1943, 7.

MATERER, TIMOTHY, *Pound/Lewis: The Letters of Ezra Pound and Wyndham Lewis* (London, 1985).

—— *Vortex: Pound, Eliot, and Lewis* (Ithaca, NY, 1979).

MAYNARD, THEODORE, 'Laurence Binyon: A Prophet Without a God', *Our Best Poets* (London, 1924), 128–38.

MENPES, MORTIMER, *Japan: A Record in Colour by Mortimer Menpes, Transcribed by Dorothy Menpes* (London, 1901).

MEREDITH, GEORGE, *Letters of George Meredith*, ed. C. L. Clune, 3 vols. (Oxford, 1970).

MEYERS, JEFFREY, *The Enemy: A Biography of Wyndham Lewis* (London, 1980).

MEYNELL, ALICE, *London Impressions: Etchings and Pictures in Photogravure by William Hyde and Essays by Alice Meynell* (London, 1898).

MILES, ALFRED H., *Robert Bridges and Contemporary Poets*, vol. vii of *The Poets and the Poetry of the Nineteenth Century* (London, 1906), 621–3.

MILLER, EDWARD, *That Noble Cabinet: A History of the British Museum* (London, 1973).

MILLER, LIAM, *The Noble Drama of W. B. Yeats* (Dublin, 1977).

MINER, EARL, *The Japanese Tradition in British and American Literature*, 2nd edn. (Princeton, 1966).

MOORE, JERROLD NORTHROP, *Edward Elgar: A Creative Life* (Oxford, 1984).

MOORE, T. STURGE, 'A Plea for an Endowed Stage', *Monthly Review*, 16 (Jan. 1902), 119–31.

—— 'The Renovation of the Theatre', *Monthly Review*, 19 (Apr. 1902), 102–16.

—— 'The Story of Tristram and Isolt in Modern Poetry. Part 1', *Criterion*, 1 (Oct. 1922), 34–9.

—— 'Yeats', *English*, 2/11 (1939), 273–8.

MORPHET, RICHARD, Preface, 'Eric Ravilious and Helen Binyon', for Helen Binyon, *Eric Ravilious* (London, 1979), 7–19.

'Mr. Binyon Retires: 40 Years in the British Museum', *Observer*, 24 Sept. 1933, 11.

MUDDIMAN, BERNARD, *The Men of the Nineties* (London, 1920).

MUKERJEA, S. K., letter, *Guardian*, 18 Mar. 1943, 4.

MURAKATA AKIKO, 'Ernest F. Fenollosa's "Ode on Reincarnation"', *Harvard Library Bulletin*, 21/1 (Jan. 1973), 50–72.

MURDOCH, BRIAN, *Fighting Songs and Warring Words: Popular Lyrics of Two World Wars* (London, 1990).

NAYLOR, GILLIAN, *The Arts and Crafts Movement: A Study of its Sources, Ideals and Influence on Design Theory* (London, 1971).

NELSON, JAMES G., *The Early Nineties: A View From the Bodley Head* (Cambridge, Mass., 1971).

—— *Elkin Mathews, Publisher to Yeats, Joyce, Pound* (Madison, Wisc., 1989).

—— 'Elkin Mathews' Shilling Garland Series', *Papers of the Bibliographical Society of America*, 78 (1984), 17–43.

NEWBOLT, SIR HENRY, *Admirals All and Other Verses* (London, 1897).

—— *My World As in My Time: Memoirs of Sir Henry Newbolt 1862–1932* (London, 1932).

—— *Later Life and Letters of Sir Henry Newbolt*, ed. Margaret Newbolt (London, 1942).

NEWMAN, ERNEST, '"The Spirit of England": Edward Elgar's New Choral Work', *Musical Times*, 1 May 1916, 235–9.

—— 'Elgar's "Fourth of August"', *Musical Times*, 1 July 1917, 295–7.

NOGUCHI YONE, *The Pilgrimage*, 2 vols. (Kamakura, Japan, 1909).

—— *Selected Poems* (London, 1921).

—— *The Story of Yone Noguchi: Told by Himself, Illustrated by Yoshio Markino* (London, 1914).

—— *Harunobu* (London, 1927).

—— *Yone Noguchi: Collected English Letters*, ed. Ikuko Atsumi (Tokyo, 1975).

'The Odd Side of Things: Asking a Tree's Pardon for Felling It', *Illustrated London News*, 26 Mar. 1932, 467.

OKADA TETSUZŌ, 'An Approach to the Poetry of Laurence Binyon', *Studies in English Literature* (Tokyo), 10 (Jan. 1930), 16–25.

OKAKURA KAKUZO, *The Book of Tea* (London, 1906).

—— *The Ideals of the East, with Special Reference to the Art of Japan* (London, 1903).

PARKER, DEREK, 'Poet of the Theatre', *Guardian*, 3 Aug. 1966, 7.

'People in the Public Eye', *Sketch*, 7 Sept. 1907, 216.

PEVSNER, NIKOLAUS, 'Arthur H. Mackmurdo: A Pioneer Designer', *Studies in Art, Architecture and Design*, 2 vols. (London, 1968), ii. 132–40.

PHILLIPS, CATHERINE, *Robert Bridges: A Biography* (Oxford, 1992).

PHILLIPS, STEPHEN, *Christ in Hades and Other Poems* (London, 1896).

PLARR, VICTOR, *Ernest Dowson 1888–1897: Reminiscences, Unpublished Letters and Marginalia* (London, 1914).

POUND, EZRA, *The Cantos* (London, 1975).

—— *Collected Shorter Poems* (London, 1952).

—— *Letters of Ezra Pound 1907–1941*, ed. D. D. Paige (London, 1951).

—— *Ezra Pound and Dorothy Shakespear: Their Letters 1909–1914*, ed. Omar Pound and A. Walton Litz (London, 1984).

—— *Guide to Kulchur* (London, 1938).

—— 'Lawrence Binyon', *Blast*, 2 (July 1915), 86. Rptd, *Pavannes and Divagations* (Norfolk, Conn., 1958), 148–50.

PURANI, A. B., *Sri Aurobindo in England* (Pondicherry, India, 1956).

'Quarterly Review', *Morning Post*, 16 Jan. 1904, 9.

'Queen and Princesses at Reading of Poetry', *The Times*, 15 Apr. 1943, 7.

RANSOME, ARTHUR, *The Autobiography of Arthur Ransome*, ed. Rupert Hart-Davis (London, 1976).

—— *Bohemia in London* (London, 1907).

RHYS, ERNEST, *Everyman Remembers* (London, 1931).

—— *Wales England Wed: An Autobiography* (London, 1940).

RICKETTS, CHARLES, 'Outamaro', *Dial*, 5 (1897), 22–6.

—— *Self Portrait: Letters and Journals of Charles Ricketts*, comp. T. Sturge Moore, ed. Cecil Lewis (London, 1939).

ROBINSON, ALAN, *Poetry, Painting and Ideas, 1885–1914* (London, 1985).

ROSENBLUM, ROBERT, 'British Painting vs. Paris', *Partisan Review*, 24 (1957), 95–100.

ROSS, ROBERT, *Robert Ross: Friend of Friends*, ed. Margery Ross (London, 1952).

ROTHENSTEIN, WILLIAM, *Men and Memories: Recollections of William Rothenstein*, 3 vols. (London, 1931–9).

RUSSELL, JOHN, 'Laurence Binyon as Art Critic', *Listener*, 5 Oct. 1944, 384.

RUSKIN, JOHN, *The Works of John Ruskin*, ed. E. T. Cook and Alexander Wedderburn, 39 vols. (London, 1903–12).

RUTH, CHRISTINE M. E., *Art, Tea, and Industry: Masuda Takashi and the Mitsui Circle* (Princeton, 1993).

SAID, EDWARD, *Orientalism: Western Conceptions of the Orient* (1978; London, 1991).

SAMUELS, ERNEST, *Bernard Berenson: The Making of a Connoisseur* (Cambridge, Mass., 1979).

SANSOM, KATHARINE, *Sir George Sansom and Japan: A Memoir* (Tallahassee, Fl., 1972).

SANTAYANA, GEORGE, *Interpretations of Poetry and Religion* (London, 1900).

SATO TOMOKO, and WATANABE TOSHIO, 'The Aesthetic Dialogue Examined: Japan and Britain 1850–1930', *Japan and Britain: An Aesthetic Dialogue*, ed. Sato and Watanabe (London, 1991), 19–25.

SCHMUTZLER, ROBERT, *Art Nouveau* (London, 1964).

SCHUCHARD, RONALD, 'W. B. Yeats and the London Theatre Societies, 1901–1904', *Review of English Studies*, NS, 29 (1978), 415–46.

SEITZ, WILLIAM C., *Claude Monet* (London, 1960).

SENCOURT, ROBERT, 'Laurence Binyon', *Fortnightly*, May 1943, 337–44.

SHAHANI, RANJEE G., 'Some British I Admire: VII Laurence Binyon', *Asiatic Review*, NS, 43 (Jan. 1947), 93–4.

SHARP, WILLIAM (ed.), *Sonnets of this Century, Edited and Arranged with a Critical Introduction on the Sonnet*, rev. edn. (London, 1887).

SIRÉN, OSVALD, *The Chinese on the Art of Painting* (Peiping [Beijing], 1936).

SMITH, CONSTANCE BABINGTON, *John Masefield: A Life* (Oxford, 1978).

SMITH, LAWRENCE, 'History and Characteristics of the Ukiyo-e Collection in the British Museum', English Supplement, *Ukiyo-e Masterpieces in European Collections: British Museum*, supervised by Muneshige Narazaki, 3 vols. (Tokyo, 1987–8), i. 1–2.

—— 'Ukiyo-e Prints in the British Museum', English Supplement, *Ukiyo-e Masterpieces in European Collections: British Museum*, ii. 1.

—— 'Japanese Illustrated Books in the British Museum', English Supplement, *Ukiyo-e Masterpieces in European Collections: British Museum*, iii. 1.

—— (ed.), *Ukiyoe: Images of Unknown Japan* (London, 1988).

SMITH, LOGAN PEARSALL, 'Dr. Laurence Binyon', *The Times*, 16 Mar. 1943, 6.

SMITH, NOWELL, 'Laurence Binyon', *DNB* (1941–50), 79–81.

—— 'Thoughts on the Poetry of Laurence Binyon', *English*, 4 (1943), 143–6.

SOUTHWORTH, JAMES GRANVILLE, 'Laurence Binyon', *Sewanee Review*, 43 (1935), 341–55.

SPRIGGE, ELIZABETH, *Sybil Thorndike Casson* (London, 1971).

STANGE, G. Robert, 'The Frightened Poets', ed. H. J. Dyos and Michael Wolff, *The Victorian City: Images and Realities*, 2 vols. (London, 1973), ii. 475–94.

STALLWORTHY, JON, *Wilfred Owen* (1974; Oxford, 1977).

STEEL, DAVID, Introduction, *Laurence Binyon and Lancaster: An Exhibition Held at Lancaster Museum 28th April–26th May 1979* (Lancaster, 1979), 3–19.

STEIN, AUREL, *Serindia: Detailed Report of Explorations in Central Asia and Westernmost Asia*, 5 vols. (Oxford, 1921).

STEVENS, WALLACE, *Letters of Wallace Stevens*, ed. Holly Stevens (London, 1967).

STEVENSON, ROBERT LOUIS, *Collected Poems*, ed. Janet Adam Smith (London, 1950).

STOCK, NOEL, *The Life of Ezra Pound* (London, 1970).

STORRY, RICHARD, *A History of Modern Japan* (London, 1960).

STREATFEILD, R. A., 'Two Poets of the New Century', *Monthly Review*, 2 (Mar. 1901), 93–114.

SULLIVAN, MICHAEL, *The Meeting of Eastern and Western Art, from the Sixteenth Century to the Present Day* (London, 1973).

—— *Symbols of Eternity: The Art of Landscape Painting in China* (Oxford, 1979).

SUTTON, DENYS, 'Conversing with Paradise', editorial, *Apollo*, Aug. 1980, 74–7.

SUZUKI DAISETZ, *Essays in Zen Buddhism*, 3 vols. (London, 1927–34).

—— *Outlines of Mahayana Buddhism* (London, 1907).

—— *Zen and Japanese Culture* (1959; Tokyo, 1988).

SYMONDS, JOHN ADDINGTON, *The Letters of John Addington Symonds*, ed. Herbert M. Schueller and Robert L. Peters, 3 vols. (Detroit, 1969).

SYMONS, ARTHUR, *The Collected Works of Arthur Symons*, 9 vols. (London, 1924).

—— 'Mr. Henley's Poetry', *Fortnightly Review*, NS, 308 (Aug. 1892), 182–92.

TAY, C. N., 'Kuan-yin: The Cult of Half Asia', *History of Religions*, 16/2 (Nov. 1976), 147–77.

TAYLOR, JOHN RUSSELL, *The Art Nouveau Book in Britain*, 2nd edn. (Edinburgh, 1980).

TERRELL, CARROLL F., 'The Na-Khi Documents I: The Landscape of Paradise', *Paideuma*, 3 (Spring 1974), 94–122.

THESING, WILLIAM B., *The London Muse: Victorian Poetic Responses to the City* (Athens, Ga., 1982).

THWAITE, ANN, *Edmund Gosse: A Literary Landscape 1849–1928* (London, 1984).

TILLYARD, S. K., *The Impact of Modernism 1900–1920: Early Modernism and the Arts and Crafts Movement in Edwardian England* (London, 1988).

TREUHERZ, JULIAN, *Hard Times: Social Realism in Victorian Art* (London, 1987).

TWITCHETT, E. G., 'The Poetry of Laurence Binyon', *London Mercury*, 22 (Sept. 1930), 423–32.

VALLANCE, AYMER, 'Mr. Arthur H. Mackmurdo and the Century Guild', *Studio*, Apr. 1899, 183–92.

WALEY, ARTHUR, *One Hundred and Seventy Chinese Poems*, rev. edn. (London, 1962).

WATANABE TOSHIO, 'Eishi Prints in Whistler's Studio? Eighteenth-century Japanese Prints in the West before 1870', *BM*, 128 (Dec. 1986), 874–80.

—— *High Victorian Japonisme* (Berne, 1991).

WATSON, WILLIAM, 'Scholar of the Orient', obituary of Basil Gray, *Guardian*, 20 June 1989, 39.

WATTS, ALAN, 'The Genius of China: Notes on the International Exhibition of Chinese Art', *Buddhism in England*, 10 (Jan.–Feb. 1936), 162–3.

' "We Need More Emotional Understanding in Our Art": Laurence Binyon, Poet, Playwright, Critic and Expert on Oriental Art Says this is True of the Drama as well as Painting. "Chinese Art Ten Centuries Ago was more Modern than Ours Today" ', *New York Times*, 15 Dec. 1912, 14.

—— and AL CHUNG-LIANG HUANG, *Tao: The Watercourse Way* (London, 1976).

WEAVER, MIKE, *Alvin Langdon Coburn, Symbolist Photographer 1882–1966: Beyond the Craft* (New York, 1986).

—— 'Atmospheric Influence', *The Photographic Art: Pictorial Traditions in Britain and America* (London, 1986), 46–8.

WEISBERG, GABRIEL, and WEISBERG, YVONNE, *Japonisme: An Annotated Bibliography* (New York, 1990).

WEST, PAUL, 'The Dome: An Aesthetic Periodical of the 1890's', *Book Collector*, 6/2 (Summer 1957), 160–9.

WEYGANDT, CORNELIUS, 'The Poetry of Mr. Laurence Binyon', *Sewanee Review*, 13 (July 1905), 279–91.

WHITAKER, MURIEL, 'Laurence Binyon', *The Arthurian Encyclopedia*, ed. Norris J. Lacey (New York, 1986), 46.

WHITE, COLIN, *Edmund Dulac* (London, 1976).

WHITFIELD, RODERICK, *The Art of Central Asia: The Stein Collection in the British Museum*, 3 vols. (Tokyo, 1982).

WHITMAN, WALT, *Leaves of Grass: Comprehensive Reader's Edition*, ed. Harold W. Blodgett and Sculley Bradley, *Collected Writings of Walt Whitman* (New York, 1965).

WICHMANN, SIEGFRIED, *Japonisme: The Japanese Influence on Western Art since 1858*, trans. Mary Whittall, *et al.* (London, 1981).

WILDE, OSCAR, *Intentions* (London, 1891).

—— *Essays and Lectures* (London, 1908).

WILHELM, J. J., *Ezra Pound in London and Paris 1908–1925* (London, 1990).

WILLIAMSON, KENNEDY, *W. E. Henley: A Memoir* (London, 1930).

WOODS, MARGARET, *Aëromancy and Other Poems* (London, 1896).

WOOLF, LEONARD, *Sowing: An Autobiography of the Years 1880–1904* (London, 1967).

WOOLF, VIRGINIA, 'Mr. Bennett and Mrs. Brown', *Collected Essays*, 4 vols. (London, 1966–67), i. 319–37.

WORDSWORTH, WILLIAM, *Poetical Works*, ed. Thomas Hutchinson, rev. Ernest de Selincourt (Oxford, 1978).

YASHIRO YUKIO, *Watashi no bijutsu henreki* (Tokyo, 1972).

—— 'Lawrence Binyon', *Bulletin of Eastern Art* (Tokyo), 7–8 (July–Aug. 1940), 19–23.

—— 'Nihon bijitsu no onjintachi: Laurence Binyon', *Bungei-shunjū* (Tokyo), 30 Sept. 1961, 63–77.

YEATS, W. B., *Autobiographies* (London, 1955).

—— *Collected Letters of W. B. Yeats*, ed. John. Kelly, 3 vols. to date (Oxford, 1986–   ).

—— 'Favourite Books of 1901: Some Readers: Mr. W. B. Yeats', *Academy*, 7 Dec. 1901, 568.

—— (ed.), *The Oxford Book of Modern Verse* (Oxford, 1936).

—— *W. B. Yeats and T. Sturge Moore: Their Correspondence 1901–1937*, ed. Ursula Bridge (London, 1953).

MANUSCRIPTS

Full details of all unpublished manuscript materials quoted in this study are given in the notes. Many come from the Binyon Archive, owned by Mrs Nicolete Gray and now deposited in the British Library as uncatalogued Loan Collection 103, which contains a great many manuscripts, including fair copies and drafts of published and unpublished poems, plays, translations, and lectures, as well as brief memoirs of LB by CMB, Cyril Bailey, and Robert Routh. In addition to a large cache of letters to LB, the archive also contains letters from LB to various correspondents and, in a few cases, such as those to Gordon Bottomley, CMB's copies of the originals. Other Binyon letters and manuscripts are either held by the libraries and museums listed in the introduction or remain in private hands. Other unpublished manuscript materials used in this study are in the library of Trinity College, Oxford, and the Central Archives and Department of Prints and Drawings at the British Museum.

Index

Italic numbers indicate monochrome plates, **bold** numbers colour plates.